Finite-State Language Processing

Language, Speech, and Communication

Finite-State Language Processing

edited by
Emmanuel Roche and Yves Schabes

A Bradford Book
The MIT Press
Cambridge, Massachusetts
London England

This book was set in Computer Modern by the editors and was printed and bound in the United States of America.

Library of Congress Cataloging-in-Publication Data

Finite-State Language Processing / edited by Emmanuel Roche and Yves Schabes.
    p.   cm. —(Language, speech, and communication)
"A Bradford book."
Includes index.
ISBN 0-262-18182-7 (hc: alk. paper)
    1. Natural language processing (Computer science). I. Roche, Emmanuel. II. Schabes, Yves. III. Series.
QA76.9.N38F56   1997
006.3ı5ı015113—dc2   96-48159
                                           CIP

Contents

Preface

The theory of finite-state automata is rich, and finite-state automata techniques are used in a wide range of domains, including switching theory, pattern matching, pattern recognition, speech processing, handwriting recognition, optical character recognition, encryption algorithm, data compression, indexing, and operating system analysis (e.g., Petri-net).

Finite-state devices, such as finite-state automata, graphs, and finite-state transducers, have been present since the emergence of computer science and are extensively used in areas as various as program compilation, hardware modeling, and database management. Although finite-state devices have been known for some time in computational linguistics, more powerful formalisms such as context-free grammars or unification grammars have typically been preferred. However, recent mathematical and algorithmic results in the field of finite-state technology have had a great impact on the representation of electronic dictionaries and on natural language processing. As a result, a new technology for language is emerging out of both industrial and academic research. This book, a discussion of fundamental finite-state algorithms, constitutes an approach from the perspective of natural language processing.

The book is organized as follows.

Chapter 1. *Emmanuel Roche and Yves Schabes.* In this introductory chapter, the basic notions of finite-state automata and finite-state transducers are described. The fundamental properties of these machines are described and illustrated with simple formal language examples as well as natural language examples. This chapter also explains the main algorithms used with finite-state automata and transducers.

Chapter 2. *David Clemenceau. Finite-State Morphology: Inflections and Derivations in a single Framework using Dictionaries and Rules.* This chapter describes how finite-state techniques can be used to encode a large scale morphological lexicon where productive derivational rules apply. The productive nature of derivational morphology is a source of complications for morphological analysis. Many words are not listed in any static morphological dictionary, no matter how big or accurate it is. In other words, the size of the lexicon is infinite. Many unknown words fall into the category of words derived from a stem and inflectional affixes. For example, the word *reanalysizable* is most likely not found in any dictionary. However, this word is part of the language in the sense that it can be used and it is easily understandable. In this chapter the author shows how finite-state transducers can be used naturally to handle this problem. In addition, Clemenceau shows that the use of a large dictionary and derivational rules lead to a homogeneous and efficient representation using finite-state transducers.

Chapter 3. *Kimmo Koskenniemi. Representations and Finite-state Components in Natural Language.* Koskenniemi describes a formal system called "two-level rules" which encodes finite-state transducers. The declarative rules hold in parallel between the phenomenon in question and its analysis. Each two-level rule is then compiled to a finite-state transducer and the set of rules are combined using the intersection operation on finite-state transducers. Koskenniemi illustrates the applicability of two-level rules to morphology and syntax.

Chapter 4. *Lauri Karttunen. The Replace Operator.* This chapter introduces a replace operator to the calculus of regular expressions and defines a set of replacement expressions that concisely encode several alternate variations of the operation. Replace expressions denote regular relations, defined in terms of other regular-expression operators. The basic case is unconditional obligatory replacement. This chapter develops several versions of conditional replacement that allow the operation to be constrained by context.

Chapter 5. *Fernando C. N. Pereira and Rebecca N. Wright. Finite-State Approximation of Phrase-Structure Grammars.* Phrase-structure grammars are effective models for important syntactic and semantic aspects of natural languages, but can be computationally too demanding for use as language models in real-time speech recognition. Therefore, finite-state models are used instead, even though they lack expressive power. To reconcile those two alternatives, the authors design an algorithm to compute finite-state approximations of context-free grammars and context-free-equivalent augmented phrase-structure grammars. The approximation is exact for certain context-free grammars generating regular languages, including all left-linear and right-linear context-free grammars. The algorithm has been used to build finite-state language models for limited-domain speech recognition tasks.

Chapter 6. *Max D. Silberztein. The Lexical Analysis of Natural Languages.* This chapter shows how finite-state techniques can be used in the lexical analysis of natural language text. The task of lexically analyzing text goes well beyond the recognition of single words. In this approach, complex words such as the compound *hard disk* are analyzed and marked in the lexical analysis process. Max Silberztein shows how simple words, complex words (such as compound words) and local syntactic rules can be encoded within the same finite-state framework. In addition, the chapter also shows how local finite-state grammars can be used in the task of disambiguating the output of the lexical analysis of text.

Chapter 7. *Emmanuel Roche and Yves Schabes. Deterministic Part-of-Speech Tagging with Finite-State Transducers.* Using the problem of part-of-speech tagging, this chapter illustrates the use of a cascade of finite-state transducers combined with composition to perform part-of-speech tagging. It· also illustrates the use of the determinization algorithm for finite-state transducers. In this chapter, a finite-state tagger inspired by Eric Brill's rule-based tagger is presented. It operates in optimal time in the sense that the time to assign tags to a sentence corresponds to the time required to deterministically follow a single path in a deterministic finite-state machine. This result is achieved by encoding the application of the rules found in the tagger as a non-deterministic finite-state transducer and then turning it into a deterministic transducer. The resulting deterministic transducer yields a part-of-speech tagger whose speed is dominated by the access time of mass storage devices. The results presented in this paper are more general than part-of-speech tagging since it is shown that, in general, transformation-based systems can be turned into subsequential finite-state transducers.

Chapter 8. *Emmanuel Roche. Parsing with Finite-State Transducers.* This chapter describes how finite-state transducers can be used for natural language parsing.

Chapter 9. *Atro Voutilainen. Designing a (Finite-State) Parsing Grammar.* The author shows how the intersection of finite-state automata provide an efficient way to implement a parser. In this approach, phrase boundaries (such as markers that specify the beginning and the end of a noun phrase) are encoded in the local rules represented with finite-state machines. This chapter discusses the design of a finite-state parsing grammar from a linguistic point of view. Attention is paid to the specification of the grammatical representation that can be viewed as the linguistic task definition of the parser, and to the design of the parsing grammar and the heuristic data-driven component. Illustrations are given from an English grammar.

Chapter 10. *Pasi Tapanainen. Applying a Finite-State Intersection Grammar.* This chapter deals with the potential quadratic explosion of the intersection algorithm for finite-state automata. Given an input sentence and a syntactic grammar encoded by a set of finite-state automata, the result of applying the grammar to the input string can be seen as the intersection of the input with all of the grammar rules. Although the final result of this intersection is small, intermediate results can explode in size. In addition, a precompilation of the grammar into one single finite-state automaton yields an automaton whose size cannot be practically managed. The author shows how different ordering schemes can be used to guarantee that the intermediate results of the intersection do not explode in size.

Chapter 11. *Maurice Gross. The Construction of Local Grammars.* Gross observes that while a systematic categorization of the objects to be studied is an important part of sciences such as biology or astronomy, such categorizations are rare to nonexistent in the field of linguistics. Gross's goal is to account for all the possible sentences within a given corpus and beyond. This chapter gives examples where the finite constraints encoded with finite-state automata can be exhaustively described in a local way, that is, without interferences from the rest of the grammar. These examples demonstrate that a cumulative approach to the construction of a grammar is indeed possible.

Chapter 12. *Mehryar Mohri. On the Use of Sequential Transducers in Natural Language Processing.* This chapter considers the use of a type of transducers that support very efficient programs: deterministic or sequential transducers. It examines several areas of computational linguistics such as morphology, phonology and speech processing. For each, the author briefly describes and discusses the time and space advantages offered by these transducers.

Chapter 13. *Jerry R. Hobbs, Douglas Appelt, John Bear, David Israel, Megumi Kameyama, Mark Stickel, and Mabry Tyson. FASTUS: A Cascaded Finite-state Transducer for Extracting Information from Natural-Language Text.* This chapter illustrates the technique of combining a cascade of finite-state transducers with composition. The authors show how such a cascade can be used to build a system for extracting information from free text in English, and potentially other languages. The finite-state automata have been built and tested using a corpus of news articles and transcripts of radio broadcasts on Latin American terrorism. The resulting system called **FASTUS** (a slightly permuted acronym for Finite-State Automaton Text Understanding System) is able to fill templates recording, among other things, the perpetrators and victims of each terrorist act, the occupations of the victims, the type of physical entity attacked or destroyed, the date, the location, and the effect on the targets. FASTUS has been very successful in practice. The system is an order of magnitude faster than any comparable system that does not take advantage of the finite-state techniques. Moreover, within a very short development time, state-of-the-art performance can be achieved. FASTUS has been shown to be very competitive with other systems in competitions organized by the Message Understanding Conference.

Chapter 14. *Éric Laporte. Rational Transductions for Phonetic Conversion and Phonology.* Phonetic conversion, and other conversion problems related to phonetics, can be performed by finite-state tools. This chapter presents a finite-state conversion system, BiPho, based on transducers and bimachines. The linguistic data used by this system are described in a readable format and actual computation is efficient. The system constitutes a spelling-to-phonetics conversion system for French.

Chapter 15. *Fernando C. N. Pereira and Michael D. Riley. Speech Recognition by Composition of Weighted Finite Automata.* This chapter presents a general framework based on weighted finite automata and weighted finite-state transducers for describing and implementing speech recognizers. The framework allows us to represent uniformly the information sources and data structures used in recognition, including context-dependent units, pronunciation dictionaries, language models and lattices. Furthermore, general but efficient algorithms can used for combining information sources in actual recognizers and for optimizing their application. In particular, a single *composition* algorithm is used both to combine in advance information sources such as language models and dictionaries and to combine acoustic observations and information sources dynamically during recognition.

Acknowledgments

The editors would like to thank several people who helped us to bring this project to fruition. We thank MERL - A Mitsubishi Electric Research Laboratory, Information Technology America, Cambridge, USA. We also thank the anonymous referees for their advice regarding revisions of this book. And finally, we thank professor Stuart Shieber and the students at Harvard University who took part to the 1996 seminar on "Engineering Approaches to Natural Language Processing" for valuable comments on previous versions of this volume.

1 Introduction

Emmanuel Roche and Yves Schabes

The theory of finite-state automata is rich, and finite-state automata techniques are used in a wide range of domains, including switching theory, pattern matching, pattern recognition, speech processing, handwriting recognition, optical character recognition, encryption algorithm, data compression, indexing, and operating system analysis (e.g., Petri-net).

Finite-state devices, such as finite-state automata, graphs, and finite-state transducers, have been present since the emergence of computer science and are extensively used in areas as various as program compilation, hardware modeling, and database management. Although finite-state devices have been known for some time in computational linguistics, more powerful formalisms such as context-free grammars or unification grammars have typically been preferred. However, recent mathematical and algorithmic results in the field of finite-state technology have had a great impact on the representation of electronic dictionaries and on natural language processing. As a result, a new technology for language is emerging out of both industrial and academic research. This book, a discussion of fundamental finite-state algorithms, constitutes an approach from the perspective of natural language processing.

In this chapter, we describe the fundamental properties of finite-state automata and finite-state transducers, and we illustrate the use of these machines through simple formal language examples as well as natural language examples. We also illustrate some of the main algorithms used in connection with finite-state automata and transducers.

1.1 Preliminaries

Finite-state automata (FSAs) and finite-state transducers (FSTs) are the two main concepts used in this book. Both kinds of machines operate on strings or, in other words, on sequences of symbols. Since the notion of string is so prevalent, in this section we define this concept as well the notations that are used throughout this book.

Strings are built out of an alphabet. An alphabet is simply a set of symbols or characters, and can be finite (as is the English alphabet) or infinite (as is the set of the real numbers). A string is a finite sequence of symbols. The set of strings built on an alphabet Σ is also called the *free monoid* Σ^*. Several notations facilitate the manipulations of strings. For example, depending on the context, either *word* or $w \cdot o \cdot r \cdot d$ denotes the following sequence:

$$(a_i)_{i=1,4} = (w, o, r, d) \tag{1.1}$$

In addition, $\cdot$ denotes the concatenation of strings defined as follows:

$$(a_i)_{i=1,n} \cdot (b_j)_{j=1,m} = (c_i)_{i=1,n+m} \tag{1.2}$$

with

$$c_i = \begin{cases} a_i & \text{if } i \leq n \\ b_{i-n} & n+1 \leq i \leq n+m \end{cases}$$

However, this notation is rarely used in practice. Instead, $wo \cdot rd$ or simply *word* denotes the concatenation of "*wo*" and "*rd*". The empty string, that is the string containing no character, is denoted by ϵ. The empty string is the neutral element for the concatenation operation. Expressed formally, for a string $w \in \Sigma^*$:

$$w \cdot \epsilon = \epsilon \cdot w = w \tag{1.3}$$

Given two strings u and v, $u \wedge v$ denotes the string that is the longest common prefix of u and v.

Another notion important for the understanding of FSAs and FSTs is the notion of sets of strings. Concatenation, union, intersection, subtraction, and complementation are operations commonly used on sets of strings.

If $L_1 \subseteq \Sigma^*$ and $L_2 \subseteq \Sigma^*$ are two sets of strings, the concatenation of L_1 and L_2 is defined as follows:

$$L_1 \cdot L_2 = \{u \cdot v | u \in L_1 \text{ and } v \in L_2\} \tag{1.4}$$

The following notations are often used, for any string $u \in \Sigma^*$ and any set $L \subseteq \Sigma^*$:

$$
\begin{aligned}
u^0 &= \epsilon & (1.5)\\
u^n &= u^{n-1} \cdot u & (1.6)\\
L^0 &= \{\epsilon\} & (1.7)\\
L^n &= L^{n-1} \cdot L & (1.8)\\
L^* &= \bigcup_{n \geq 0} L^n & (1.9)
\end{aligned}
$$

With this notation in hand, the following operations are defined for two sets of strings, L_1 and and L_2:

$$
\begin{aligned}
L_1 \cup L_2 &= \{u | u \in L_1 \text{ or } u \in L_2\} & (union) & (1.10)\\
L_1 \cap L_2 &= \{u | u \in L_1 \text{ and } u \in L_2\} & (intersection) & (1.11)\\
L_1 - L_2 &= \{u | u \in L_1 \text{ and } u \notin L_2\} & (subtraction) & (1.12)\\
\overline{L} &= \Sigma^* - L & (complementation) & (1.13)\\
L_1^{-1} \cdot L_2 &= \{w | \exists u \in L_1, u \cdot w \in L_2\} & (inverse) & (1.14)\\
L_1 \cdot L_2^{-1} &= \{w | \exists u \in L_2, w \cdot u \in L_1\} & (inverse) & (1.15)
\end{aligned}
$$

These notations are extremely useful. For instance, in order to extract the set of words to which a given prefix (e.g., "un") can apply, the following can be used:

$$
\begin{aligned}
\{un\}^{-1} \cdot \{unlikely, unacceptable, heavily\} &= \\
\{likely, acceptable\} & \qquad (1.16)
\end{aligned}
$$

In general, the identification of a string u with the singleton $\{u\}$ permits the use of the notations $u^{-1} \cdot L$ and $u^{-1} \cdot v$ instead of $\{u\}^{-1} \cdot L$ and $\{u\}^{-1} \cdot \{v\}$.

1.2 Finite-State Automata

A few fundamental theoretical properties make FSAs very flexible, powerful and efficient. FSAs can be seen as defining a class of graphs and also as defining languages.

1.2.1 Definitions

On the first interpretation, an FSA can be seen as simply an oriented graph with labels on each arc.

Definition 1 (FSA) *A finite-state automaton A is a 5-tuple*
(Σ, Q, i, F, E) *where Σ is a finite set called the* alphabet, *Q is a finite set
of* states, *$i \in Q$ is the* initial state, *$F \subseteq Q$ is the set of* final states *and
$E \subseteq Q \times (\Sigma \cup \{\epsilon\}) \times Q$ is the set of* edges.

FSAs are seen in this construct as defining a class of graphs.

We adhere to the following conventions when describing an FSA pictorially: final states are depicted by two concentric circles; ϵ represents the empty string; and unless otherwise specified, the initial state (usually labeled 0) is the leftmost state appearing in the figure.

For example, the automaton $A_{m2} = (\{0, 1\}, \{0, 1\}, 0, \{0\}, E_{m2})$ with $E_{m2} = \{(0, 0, 0), (0, 1, 1), (1, 1, 1), (1, 0, 0)\}$ is shown on the left in Figure 1.1. This automaton represents in binary form the sets of multiples of two.

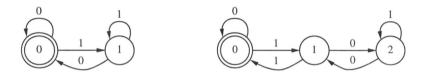

Figure 1.1: *Left*: finite-state automaton representing in binary form multiples of two. *Right*: finite-state automaton representing in binary form multiples of three.

Similarly, the automaton $A_{m3} = (\{0, 1\}, \{0, 1, 2\}, 0, \{0\}, E_{m3})$ with $E_{m3} = \{(0, 0, 0), (0, 1, 1), (1, 1, 0), (1, 0, 2), (2, 1, 2), (2, 0, 1)\}$ is shown on the right in Figure 1.1. This automaton represents in binary form the set of multiples of three.

Another traditional definition consists with replacing in Definition 1 the set of edges E with a transition function d from $Q \times (\Sigma \cup \{\epsilon\})$ to 2^Q. The equivalence of the two definitions is expressed by the following equation:

$$d(q', a) = \{q \in Q | \exists (q', a, q) \in E\}$$

Both definitions are static and relate FSAs to a specific class of graphs.

On the second interpretation, an FSA represents a set of strings over the alphabet Σ, namely the set of those strings for which there is a path from the initial state to a terminal state. Formally, this is best stated by first extending the set of edges E along the lines of the definition following:

Definition 2 ($\hat{E}$) *The extended set of edges $\hat{E} \subseteq Q \times \Sigma^* \times Q$ is the smallest set such that* *(i)* $\forall q \in Q, (q, \epsilon, q) \in \hat{E}$

(ii) $\forall w \in \Sigma^*$ *and* $\forall a \in \Sigma \cup \{\epsilon\}$, *if* $(q_1, w, q_2) \in \hat{E}$ *and* $(q_2, a, q_3) \in E$
then $(q_1, w \cdot a, q_3) \in \hat{E}$.

The transition function d can be similarly extended:

Definition 3 *(d) The extended transition function $\hat{d}$, mapping from $Q \times \Sigma^*$ onto 2^Q, is that function such that*

(i) $\forall q \in Q, \hat{d}(q, \epsilon) = \{q\}$

(ii) $\forall w \in \Sigma^*$ *and* $\forall a \in \Sigma \cup \{\epsilon\}$,

$$\hat{d}(q, w \cdot a) = \bigcup_{q_1 \in \hat{d}(q,w)} d(q_1, a)$$

Having extended the set of edges and the transition function to operate on strings, we can now relate an FSA to a language. A finite-state automaton A defines the following language $L(A)$:

$$L(A) = \{w \in \Sigma^* | \hat{d}(i, w) \cap F \neq \emptyset\} \tag{1.17}$$

A language is said to be *regular* or *recognizable* if it can be defined by an FSA.

1.2.2 Closure Properties

Much of the strength of FSAa is due to a few very important results. Kleene's theorem, one of the first and most important results about FSAs, relates the class of languages generated by FSAs to certain closure properties. This result makes the theory of finite-state automata a very versatile, descriptive framework.

Theorem 1 *(Kleene, 1956) The family of regular languages over Σ^* is equal to the smallest family of languages over Σ^* that contains the empty set, the singleton sets, and that is closed under Kleene star, concatenation, and union.*

This theorem renders FSA equivalent to syntactic descriptions. It states that regular expressions, such as those used in many computer programs, are equivalent to FSAs.

Related to Kleene's Theorem, FSAs have been shown to be closed under union, Kleene star, concatenation, intersection and complementation, thus allowing for natural and flexible descriptions.

- **Union**. The set of regular languages is closed under union: if A_1 and A_2 are two FSAs, it is possible to compute an FSA $A_1 \cup A_2$ such that $L(A_1 \cup A_2) = L(A_1) \cup L(A_2)$.

- **Concatenation**. The set of regular languages is closed under concatenation: if A_1 and A_2 are two FSA, it is possible to compute an FSA $A_1 \cdot A_2$ such that $L(A_1 \cdot A_2) = L(A_1) \cdot L(A_2)$.

- **Intersection**. The set of regular languages is closed under intersection: if $A_1 = (\Sigma, Q_1, i_1, F_1, E1)$ and $A_2 = (\Sigma, Q_2, i_2, F_2, E2)$ are two FSAs, it is possible to compute an FSA denoted $A_1 \cap A_2$ such that $L(A_1 \cap A_2) = L(A_1) \cap L(A_2)$. Such an automaton can be constructed as follows: $A_1 \cap A_2 = (\Sigma, Q_1 \times Q_2, (i_1, i_2), F_1 \times F_2, E)$ with

$$E = \bigcup_{(q_1, a, r_1) \in E_1, (q_2, a, r_2) \in E_2} \{((q_1, q_2), a, (r_1, r_2))\} \qquad (1.18)$$

- **Complementation**. The set of regular languages is closed under complementation: if A is an FSA, it is possible to compute an FSA $-A$ such that $L(-A) = \Sigma^* - L(A)$.

- **Kleene star**. The set of regular languages is closed under Kleene star: if A is an FSA, it is possible to compute an FSA A^* such that $L(A^*) = L(A)^*$.

The above closure properties of FSAs are powerful; other well-known formalisms available in language processing do not satisfy all of them. For example, although the class of context-free grammars are closed under union, concatenation, and intersection with regular languages, context-free grammars are closed under neither general intersection nor complementation. These two properties are very useful in practice, especially when FSAs are used to express sets of constraints, since they allow the FSAs to combine incrementally in a natural fashion.

1.2.3   Space and Time Efficiency

In addition to their flexibility due to their closure properties, FSAs can also be turned into canonical forms that allow for optimal time and space efficiency. These unique properties, not typically shared with other frameworks used in natural language processing (such as context-free grammars), also entail the decidability of a wide range of questions, as we will see in the next section.

In general, a given input string may lead to several paths in an FSA, $A = (\Sigma, Q, i, F, d)$, since the image of the transition function d of a given symbol a can be a set of states ($d : Q \times (\Sigma \cup \{\epsilon\}) \rightarrow 2^Q$). If the the transition function is a mapping $Q \times \Sigma$ to Q (i.e. there is no epsilon transition and there is at most one transition for a given label), the automaton is said to be *deterministic*.

Definition 4 (Deterministic FSA) *A deterministic FSA is a 5-tuple* (Σ, Q, i, F, d) *where Σ is a finite set constituting the* alphabet, *Q is a finite set of* states, *$i \in Q$ is the* initial state, *$F \subseteq Q$ is the set of* final states, *and d is the* transition function *that maps $Q \times \Sigma$ to Q.*

Thus, if the automaton is in a state $q \in Q$ and the symbol read from the input is a, then $d(q, a)$ uniquely determines the state to which the automaton passes. This property entails high run-time efficiency, since the time it takes to recognize a string is linearly proportional to its length.

Nondeterministic automata permit several possible "next states" for a given combination of a current state and input symbol. However, for any given nondeterministic automaton NFA $= (\Sigma, Q, i, F, d)$, there is an equivalent deterministic automaton DFA $= (\Sigma, Q', i, F', d')$. The states of the deterministic automaton can be constructed as all of the subsets of the set of states of the nondeterministic automaton, as follows:

$$Q' = 2^Q \tag{1.19}$$

F' is the set of states in Q' containing a final state in Q:

$$F' = \{q' \in Q' | q' \cap F \neq \emptyset\} \tag{1.20}$$

And d' is defined as follows:

$$d'(q', a) = \bigcup_{q \in q'} d(q, a) \tag{1.21}$$

The resulting FSA is deterministic in the sense that given an input symbol and a current state, a unique next state is determined.

Furthermore, a deterministic automaton can be reduced to an equivalent automaton that has a minimal number of states (Hopcroft, 1971). This result optimally minimizes the space of deterministic FSAs.

The above two results (determinization and minimization) together yield an optimal time and space representation for FSAs. In addition to such computational implications, the determinization and minimization of finite-state machines allow finite-state machines to have powerful decidability properties.

1.2.4   Decidability Properties

Given the FSAs A, A_1, and A_2, and the string w, the following properties are decidable:

$$\text{Membership: } w \stackrel{?}{\in} L(A) \tag{1.22}$$

$$\text{Emptyness: } L(A) \stackrel{?}{=} \emptyset \tag{1.23}$$

$$\text{Totality: } L(A) \stackrel{?}{=} \Sigma^* \tag{1.24}$$

$$\text{Subset: } L(A_1) \stackrel{?}{\subseteq} L(A_2) \tag{1.25}$$

$$\text{Equality: } L(A_1) \stackrel{?}{=} L(A_2) \tag{1.26}$$

This is not the case for most traditional frameworks used in natural language processing. For example, only the first two properties are decidable for context-free grammars. Such properties are very convenient when developing FSAs, since they allow the grammar writer to test the consistency of incremental versions of a grammar written within the framework.

1.2.5   A Formal Example

Consider the following examples describing multiples of two, three, and six in binary form. These formal examples have been chosen for their simplicity and clarity.

The FSA shown on the right in Figure 1.1 generates the strings 0, 11, 110, 1001, among others. This automaton generates the set of binary representations of multiples of three. As shown by Eilenberg (1974) and Perrin (1990), this can be seen by the following construction from first principles. Each state represents the remainder of the division by three with the numerical value of the substring read so far. In the automaton on the right in Figure 1.1, state 0 is associated with the remainder 0, state 1 with the remainder 1, and state 2 with the remainder 2. When constructing the transitions, it suffices to notice that if w is the string of digits read so far, the numerical value of the string wd where $d \in \{0, 1\}$ is $2 * w + d$; therefore, the remainder of the division by three of wd is d plus two times the remainder of the division by three of w (the result expressed in modulo three). The FSA for multiples of two shown on the left in Figure 1.1 can be similarly constructed. Eilenberg (1974) and Perrin (1990) generalize this construction to any multiples.

Suppose we now wish to construct the FSA representing multiples of six in binary form. We could try to build this automaton from first principles. Although this is possible, the same automaton can be built from simpler automata, since the set of multiples of 6 is the intersection of the set of multiples of three with the set of multiples of two. We have already shown the automata for multiples of two and three (see Figure 1.1). The FSA for the set of multiples of six can be constructed as the intersection of these two automata, following (1.18). The resulting FSA is shown in Figure 1.2.

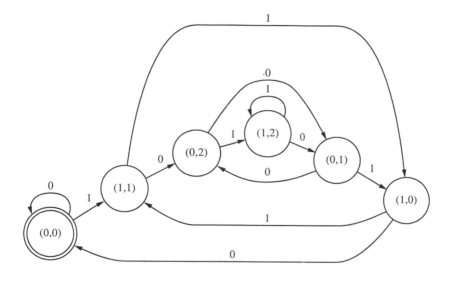

Figure 1.2: FSA for multiples of six, obtained by intersecting the FSA of multiples of two with the FSA of multiples of three.

The automaton shown in Figure 1.2 is not minimal, however, since the states $(0, 2)$ and $(1, 2)$ as well as the states $(1, 1)$ and $(0, 1)$ are equivalent. The corresponding minimal automaton is shown in Figure 1.3.

1.2.6 A Natural Language Example

In this section, we illustrate the flexibility and usefulness of the closure properties in a simple example of local syntactic constraints, that is, constraints operating on a local context. This example also illustrates the uniformity achieved by the finite-state framework. In this framework, the input string, the lexicon, and the local syntactic rules are all represented as FSAs and the application of rules corresponds to the application of operations to FSAs. These operations produce other FSAs.

The local syntactic rules we consider in the following example encode

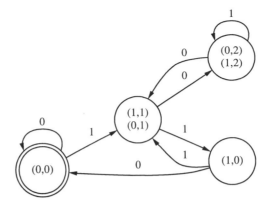

Figure 1.3: Minimal automaton corresponding to the automaton shown in Figure 1.2.

Figure 1.4: FSA encoding the morphological information for the word *that*.

constraints on the lexical ambiguity of words in a context. Suppose we wish to analyze the following sentence:

He hopes that this works

A dictionary would identify the word *He* as a pronoun, *hopes* as a noun or a verb, *that* as a pronoun, a conjunction or a determiner, *this* as a determiner or a pronoun, and *works* as a noun or a verb. Such morphological information encoded in the dictionary is represented naturally by FSAs. The FSA of Figure 1.4 is associated with the word *that* because it encodes precisely the same morphological information as does the dictionary.

Moreover, since the morphological information of each word is represented by an automaton, the morphological analysis of the input sentence can also be represented as an FSA, as shown in Figure 1.5. This encoding allows for a

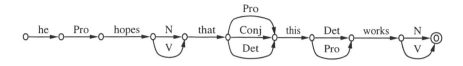

Figure 1.5: Automaton representing the morphological analysis of *He hopes that this works*.

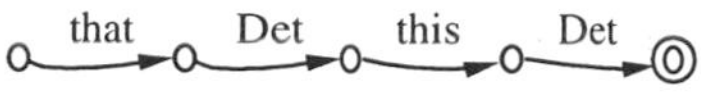

Figure 1.6: Automaton representing the negative rule C_1 that the partial analysis "*that Det this Det*" is not possible.

compact representation of morphological ambiguities.

So far, we have shown that both a dictionary and the morphological analysis of a sentence can be represented as FSAs. The disambiguating rules can also be represented as FSAs. For example, we can encode a negative rule that states that the partial analysis "*that Det this Det*" is not possible. This negative constraint can be encoded by the automaton shown in Figure 1.6. The application of a negative constraint C to a sentence S yields the sentence[1]

$$S' \;=\; S - (\Sigma^* \cdot C \cdot \Sigma^*) \tag{1.27}$$

Applying the constraint in Figure 1.6 to the sentence in Figure 1.5 yields the automaton shown in Figure 1.7. The rule in Figure 1.8 rules out the sequence "*that Det ? V*" (where ? stands for any word). The application of this rule to the FSA in Figure 1.7 results in Figure 1.9.

We have applied two negative rules, one after the other. However, the closure properties of FSAs allow us to combine the two negative constraints C_1 and C_2 into one single rule, $C_1 \cup C_2$.

$$(S - \Sigma^* \cdot C_1 \cdot \Sigma^*) - \Sigma^* \cdot C_2 \cdot \Sigma^* = S - \Sigma^* \cdot (C_1 \cup C_2) \cdot \Sigma^* \tag{1.28}$$

---

[1] The reader can easily verify that $L_1 - L_2 = L1 \cap \overline{L_2}$.

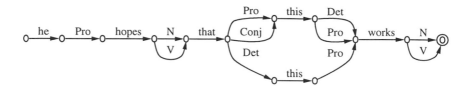

Figure 1.7: Result of the application of the negative constraint in Figure 1.6 to Figure 1.5.

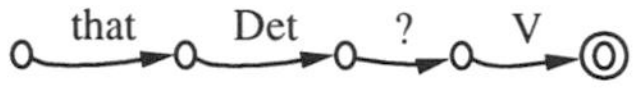

Figure 1.8: Automaton representing the negative rule C_2 that the partial analysis "*that Det ? V*" is not possible.

Using the notation $\overline{A}$ for $\Sigma^* - A$, and given the fact that $A - B = A \cap \overline{B}$ (1.28), we have:

$$(A - B) - C = A \cap \overline{B} \cap \overline{C} = A \cap \overline{B \cup C} = A - (B \cup C)$$

Therefore,

$$(S - \Sigma^* \cdot C_1 \cdot \Sigma^*) - \Sigma^* \cdot C_2 \cdot \Sigma^*$$
$$= S - (\Sigma^* \cdot C_1 \cdot \Sigma^* \cup \Sigma^* \cdot C_2 \cdot \Sigma^*)$$

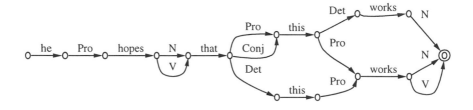

Figure 1.9: Result of the application of the negative rule in Figure 1.8 to Figure 1.7.

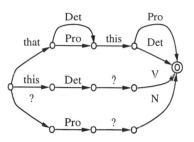

Figure 1.10: A sample grammar of negative local constraints.

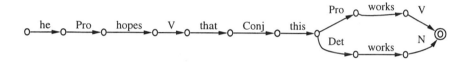

Figure 1.11: Result of the application of the negative grammar in Figure 1.10 to the input shown in Figure 1.5.

$$= S - \Sigma^* \cdot (C_1 \cup C_2) \cdot \Sigma^*$$

Negative rules can in this way be combined using the union operation to form a single rule.

Using such principles, we can derive a grammar of negative local constraints. An example of such a grammar is shown in Figure 1.10. The application of this negative grammar to the input shown in Figure 1.5 yields the automaton in Figure 1.11.

This simple example illustrates the homogeneity and flexibility of FSAs. The input string, the dictionary, the grammar, and the output of the analysis are all represented as FSAs. The elegant construction of the grammar, from a collection of negative constraints combined with the union operation over FSAs, was possible because of the closure properties of the FSAs.

In addition, the decidability properties of FSAs provide unique tests that are useful in the construction of the grammar. For example, when a new rule is proposed, the fact that the inclusion of two finite-state languages is decidable allows us to test whether the proposed rule is subsumed by another one. Similarly, we can test whether grammars are identical.

And finally, the algorithmic properties of FSAs, i.e. their determinization and their minimizability, allow us to construct compact grammars that can be applied very efficiently.

1.3   Finite-State Transducers

The concept of FSTs is the other main concept discussed in this book. FSTs can be interpreted as defining a class of graphs, a class of relations on strings, or a class of transductions on strings.

1.3.1   Definitions

On the first interpretation, an FST can be seen as an FSA, in which each arc is labeled by a pair of symbols rather than by a single symbol.

Definition 5 (FST) *A Finite-State Transducer is a 6-tuple* $(\Sigma_1, \Sigma_2, Q, i, F, E)$ *such that:*

- Σ_1 *is a finite alphabet, namely the input alphabet*

- Σ_2 *is a finite alphabet, namely the output alphabet*

- Q *is a finite set of states*

- $i \in Q$ *is the initial state*

- $F \subseteq Q$ *is the set of final states*

- $E \subseteq Q \times \Sigma_1^* \times \Sigma_2^* \times Q$ *is the set of edges*

This definition illustrates the graph interpretation of FSTs.

For example, the FST $T_{d3} = (\{0, 1\}, \{0, 1\}, \{0, 1, 2\}, E_{d3})$ where $E_{d3} = \{(0, 0, 0, 0), (0, 1, 0, 1), (1, 0, 0, 2), (1, 1, 1, 0), (2, 1, 1, 2), (2, 0, 1, 1)\}$ is shown in Figure 1.12. We will later see that this transducer functionally encodes division by three of binary numbers.

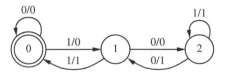

Figure 1.12: Transducer T_{d3} representing division by 3.

We will also use the notion of *path* defined as follows:

Definition 6 (path) *Given an FST*
$T = (\Sigma_1, \Sigma_2, Q, i, F, E)$, *a path of* T *is a sequence* $((p_i, a_i, b_i, q_i))_{i=1,n}$ *of edges* E *such that* $q_i = p_{i+1}$ *for* $i = 1$ *to* $n - 1$.

A successful path is a path that starts from an initial state and ends in a final state.

Definition 7 (successful path) *Given an FST* $T = (\Sigma_1, \Sigma_2, Q, i, F, E)$, *a successful path* $((p_i, a_i, b_i, q_i))_{i=1,n}$ *of* T *is a path of* T *such that* $p_1 = i$ *and* $q_n \in F$

An alternative definition consists in replacing the set of edges E by a transition function d a mapping from $Q \times \Sigma_1^*$ to 2^Q, and an emission function δ a mapping from $Q \times \Sigma_1^* \times Q$ into $2^{\Sigma_2^*}$. The two definitions give rise to the following equations:

$$d(q, a) = \{q' \in Q | \exists (q, a, b, q') \in E\} \tag{1.29}$$
$$\delta(q, a) = \{b \in \Sigma_2^* | \exists (q, a, b, q') \in E\} \tag{1.30}$$

We can associate an FSA with an FST by considering the pairs of symbols on the arcs as symbols of an FSA, as illustrated by the following definition.

Definition 8 (Underlying FSA) *If* $T = (\Sigma_1, \Sigma_2, Q, i, F, E)$ *is an FST, its underlying finite-state automaton* (Σ, Q, i, F, E') *is as follows:*

$$\Sigma = \Sigma_1 \times \Sigma_2 \tag{1.31}$$
$$(q_1, (a, b), q_2) \in E' \quad iff \quad (q_1, a, b, q_2) \in E \tag{1.32}$$

All properties of FSAs also hold on the underlying automaton of a transducer. For example, the minimization and determinization algorithms can be applied to the underlying FSA. However, as we will see, the same notions denote other concepts when FSTs are not interpreted as FSAs.

In addition to defining the underlying automaton, it is sometimes useful to consider the first (or second) component of the labels on the arcs of a given FST. This leads to the following definition:

Definition 9 (First and second projection) *The first projection and the second projection of an FST* $T = (\Sigma_1, \Sigma_2, Q, i, F, E)$ *are the FSAs* $p_1(T)$ *and* $p_2(T)$ *such that:*

$$p_1(T) = (\Sigma_1, Q, i, F, E_{p1})$$
$$s.t. \ E_{p1} = \{(q, a, q') | (q, a, b, q') \in E\} \tag{1.33}$$
$$p_2(T) = (\Sigma_2, Q, i, F, E_{p2})$$
$$s.t. \ E_{p2} = \{(q, b, q') | (q, a, b, q') \in E\} \tag{1.34}$$

Under this second interpretation illustrated in Definition 10, FSTs represent relations on strings. On this interpretation, the set of edges, the transition function, and the emission function are extended to apply to strings rather than to symbols:

Definition 10 ($\hat{E}$) *The extended set of edges $\hat{E}$, is the least subset of $Q \times \Sigma_1^* \times \Sigma_2^* \times Q$ such that*

   (i) $\forall q \in Q, (q, \epsilon, \epsilon, q) \in \hat{E}$
   (ii) $\forall w_1 \in \Sigma_1^*, \forall w_2 \in \Sigma_2^*$ *if* $(q_1, w_1, w_2, q_2) \in \hat{E}$ *and* $(q_2, a, b, q_3) \in E$
     then $(q_1, w_1 a, w_2 b, q_3) \in \hat{E}$.

This allows us to associate a relation $L(T)$ on $\Sigma_1^* \times \Sigma_2^*$ with an FST T as follows:

$$
\begin{aligned}
L(T) \quad = \quad & \{(w_1, w_2) \in \Sigma_1^* \times \Sigma_2^* | \exists (i, w_1, w_2, q) \in \hat{E} \\
& \text{with } q \in F\}
\end{aligned} \tag{1.35}
$$

For example, the transducer T_{d3} of Figure 1.12 contains the pair $(11, 01)$. Since $(0, 1, 0, 1)$ and $(1, 1, 1, 0) \in E$, $(0, 11, 01, 0)$ is in $\hat{E}$. The reader is invited to check that the relation $L(T_{d3})$ contains exactly all pairs such that the first element is a multiple of 3, and such that the second element is the quotient of the division by three of the first element.

The notion of a projection of an FST T as illustrated in Definition 9 corresponds to the following notion of a projection of $L(T)$:

Proposition 1 *If $T = (\Sigma_1, \Sigma_2, Q, i, F, E)$ is an FST, then*

$$
L(p_1(T)) \quad = \quad \{w_1 \in \Sigma_1^* | \exists w_2 \in \Sigma_2^* \text{ s.t. } (w_1, w_2) \in L(T)\} \tag{1.36}
$$
$$
L(p_2(T)) \quad = \quad \{w_2 \in \Sigma_2^* | \exists w_1 \in \Sigma_1^* \text{ s.t. } (w_1, w_2) \in L(T)\} \tag{1.37}
$$

On the third interpretation of FSTs, a transducer T can be seen as a mapping $|T|$ from the set of strings in Σ_1^* to the power set of strings in $2^{\Sigma_2^*}$:

$$
|T|(u) \quad = \quad \{v \in \Sigma_2^* | (u, v) \in L(T)\} \tag{1.38}
$$

For example, $|T_{d3}|(11) = \{01\}$. We can also write by extension of the notation $|T_{d3}|(11) = 01$ if the image is a singleton.[2] We extend this notation to apply to sets of strings:

---

[2] If there is no possibility of confusion in the context, the notations are often further extended to denote the transducer and the transduction by the same symbol. For instance, one might write $T_{d3}(11) = 01$.

$$\text{if } V \subseteq \Sigma^*, |T|(V) \quad = \quad \bigcup_{v \in V} |T|(v) \tag{1.39}$$

Definition 11 (Rational Transductions and Rational Functions) *A transduction* $\tau : \Sigma_1^* \to 2^{\Sigma_2^*}$ *is a* rational transduction *if there exists an FST T such that* $\tau = |T|$. *If, for any string u in the input set Σ_1^*, $|T|(u)$ is either the empty set or a singleton, $|T|$ is a* rational function.

1.3.2 Closure Properties

As with FSAs, FSTs are powerful because of the various closure and algorithmic properties.

Proposition 2 (Closure under Union) *If T_1 and T_2 are two FSTs, there exists an FST $T_1 \cup T_2$ such that $|T_1 \cup T_2| = |T_1| \cup |T_2|$, i.e. s.t. $\forall u \in \Sigma^*, |T_1 \cup T_2|(u) = |T_1|(u) \cup |T_2|(u)$.*

Proposition 3 (Closure under Inversion) *If $T = (\Sigma_1, \Sigma_2, Q, i, F, E)$ is an FST, there exists an FST T^{-1} such that $|T^{-1}|(u) = \{v \in \Sigma^* | u \in |T|(v)\}$. Furthermore, the transducer $(\Sigma_2, \Sigma_1, Q, i, F, E^{-1})$ s.t.*

$$(q_1, a, b, q_2) \in E^{-1} \quad iff \quad (q_1, b, a, q_2) \in E \tag{1.40}$$

is such a transducer.

Before turning our attention to the property of closure under composition, we note in the following remark that a transducer that has input or output transitions on words can be turned into a transducer that has transitions on letters.

Remark 1 (Letter Transducer) *If $T_1 = (\Sigma_1, \Sigma_2, Q, i, F, E_1)$ is a transducer such that $\epsilon \notin |T_1|(\epsilon)$ then, there is a* letter *transducer $T_2 = (\Sigma_1, \Sigma_2, Q_2, i_2, F_2, E_2)$ such that*

(i) $|T_1| = |T_2|$
(ii) $E_2 \subseteq (Q_1 \times (\Sigma_1 \cup \{\epsilon\}) \times (\Sigma_2 \cup \{\epsilon\}) \times Q_2)$
(iii) $E_2 \cap (Q_1 \times \{\epsilon\} \times \{\epsilon\} \times Q_2) = \emptyset$

Informally speaking, (ii) is achieved by breaking up each edge of T_1 into simple letter edges by adding intermediate states to T_2. (iii) is achieved by eliminating arcs labeled with (ϵ, ϵ) using the traditional epsilon removal algorithm for FSAs (i.e. by considering the transducer as an FSA for which (ϵ, ϵ) is the epsilon symbol).

We can now give a constructive statement of the property of closure under composition, with no loss of generality, by restricting the property to letter transducers.

Proposition 4 (Closure under Composition) *Given two letter FSTs $T_1 = (\Sigma_1, \Sigma_2, Q, i, F, E_1)$ and $T_2 = (\Sigma_2, \Sigma_3, Q_2, i_2, F_2, E_2)$, there exists an FST $T_1 \circ T_2$ such that for each $u \in \Sigma_1^*$, $|T_1 \circ T_2|(u) = |T_2|(|T_1|(u))$. Furthermore, the transducer $T_3 = (\Sigma_1, \Sigma_3, Q_1 \times Q_2, (i_1, i_2), F_1 \times F_2, E_3)$ s.t.*

$$
\begin{aligned}
E_3 \;=\; & \{((x_1, x_2), a, b, (y_1, y_2))| \\
& \exists c \in \Sigma_2 \cup \{\epsilon\} \; s.t. \; (x_1, a, c, y_1) \in E_1 \; and \; (x_2, c, b, y_2) \in E_2\}
\end{aligned}
$$

satisfies

$$|T_3|(u) = |T_1 \circ T_2|(u) = |T_2|(|T_1|(u)), \forall u \in \Sigma_1^*$$

However, unlike the set of FSAs, the set of rational transductions is not closed under intersection. This means that if T_1 and T_2 are two FSTs, it is possible that there exists no FST T_3 such that $|T_3|(u) = |T_1|(u) \cap |T_2|(u)$ for any $u \in \Sigma_1^*$.

For example, the transducer $T_{a_n b_m}$ shown on the left in Figure 1.13 defines the transduction $|T_{a_n b_m}|(c^n) = \{a^n b^m | m \geq 0\}$ and the transducer $T_{a_m b_n}$ shown on the right on Figure 1.13 defines the transduction $|T_{a_m b_n}|(c^n) = \{a^m b^n | m \geq 0\}$. The intersection of these relations is such that $|T_1 \cap T_2|(c^n) = |T_1|(c^n) \cap |T_2|(c^n) = \{a^n b^n | n \geq 0\}$. This relation cannot be encoded as an FST, since while the second projection of an FST is a regular language, $\{a^n b^n | \geq 0\}$ is not a regular language.

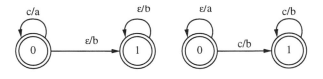

Figure 1.13: *Left.* FST $T_{a_n b_m}$. *Right.* FST $T_{a_m b_n}$.

There are cases in which the intersection of two FSTs is itself an FST. The class of ϵ-free transducers is closed under intersection and has therefore been used extensively in numerous applications, such as morphology and phonology.

Definition 12 (ϵ-**free letter transducer**) *A finite-state transducer* $T = (\Sigma_1, \Sigma_2, Q, i, F, E)$ *is an* ϵ-*free letter FST iff*

$$E \subseteq Q \times \Sigma_1 \times \Sigma_2 \times Q \tag{1.41}$$

Proposition 5 *The class of* ϵ-*free letter FSTs is closed under intersection. In addition, the intersection of two* ϵ-*free letter FSTs is obtained by intersecting their underlying FSAs.*

1.3.3 A Formal Example

To illustrate the flexibility induced by the closure properties, let us return to the example of the transducer T_{d3} in Figure 1.12. Suppose we want to build a transducer that computes division by 9. There are two ways to attack the problem. The first is to build the transducer from first principles. The second is to build the transducer T_{d3} that encodes division by three and then compose it with itself, since $T_{d9} = T_{d3} \circ T_{d3}$. This method renders the problem parallel to numerous problems of language processing for which decomposition can be used.

The transducer T_{d9}, computed by composing T_{d3} with itself, is shown in Figure 1.14.

It is also interesting that the inverse transducer of T_{d3}, that is, T_{d3}^{-1}, maps any binary number to the product of itself times three.

1.3.4 A Natural Language Example

We will now illustrate the above two techniques for FSTs on a simplified case of derivational morphology. In this example, our objective is to derive words from the prefix *co* and a lexicon of simple English words. We assume that our lexicon comprises the following three words:

> *offer*
> *design*
> *develop*

From this lexicon, we wish to derive the words *co-offer*, *codesign* and *codevelop*. For the purpose of illustration, we assume that the prefix *co* requires a hyphen when the following letter is *o*. Otherwise, the prefix *co* is concatenated with no hyphen.

The problem is stated formally in terms of relations on strings. The symbolic string $CO+ \cdot w$ represents the morphological derivation in which the prefix *co* has been applied to a given word w. The problem then consists in finding a rational function τ_{co} such that $\tau_{co}(CO+ \cdot w)$ is the correct prefixed word. In our case, the function should yield the following identities:

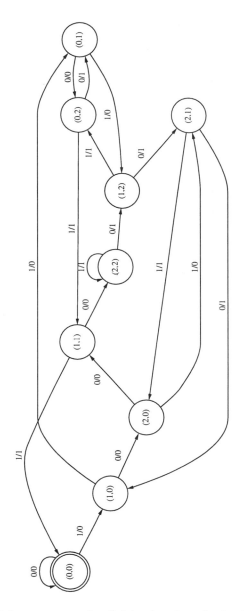

Figure 1.14: FST that computes the division by nine, obtained by composing with itself the FST for division by three found in Figure 1.12.

$$\tau_{co}(CO+\textit{offer}) \quad = \quad \textit{co-offer}$$
$$\tau_{co}(CO+\textit{design}) \quad = \quad \textit{codesign}$$
$$\tau_{co}(CO+\textit{develop}) \quad = \quad \textit{codevelop}$$

There is little interest in describing this function extensionally. Instead, we wish to construct a function that we can apply to any English word without our having to encode the English lexicon in the function itself. There are two simple methods to build an FST for the function τ_{co}. The first method illustrates that FSTs are closed under composition, and the second illustrates that ϵ-free letter transducers are closed under intersection.

1.3.4.1   Rule Composition

The rule composition approach consists in building a series of cascaded FSTs. The output of a transducer is fed to the input of the next transducer. The idea is to write a series of rules, from the most general to the most specific.

In the below example, the first transducer T_{co1} encodes the most general rule, namely the rule that concatenates the prefix *co*. It transforms the symbolic string $CO+w\cdot$ to $co\cdot w$ and acts as the identity function in all other cases. The corresponding transducer is shown in Figure 1.15. In Figure 1.15 and in the following figures, a question mark (?) on an arc transition originating at state i stands for any input symbol that does not appear as an input symbol on any other outgoing arc from i. An arc labeled ?/? on an arc transition originating at state i stands for the input-output identity for any input symbol that does not appear as an input symbol on any other outgoing arc from i.

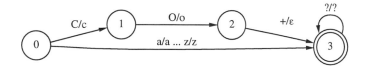

Figure 1.15: Transducer T_{co1} representing the general prefixation rule.

The second transducer T_{co2} encodes the most specific rule, namely the rule that adds a hyphen to words starting with the letter o. That is, the symbolic string $CO+o\cdot w$ is rewritten as $co\text{-}o\cdot w$. In all other cases, this rule acts as the identity function. The corresponding transducer is shown in Figure 1.16.

The transducer that represents the whole mapping of τ_{co} is obtained by composing T_{co2} with T_{co1}:

$$\tau_{co} = |T_{co2} \circ T_{co1}|$$

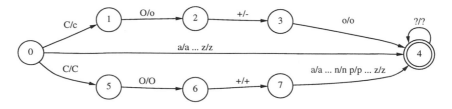

Figure 1.16: Transducer T_{co2} representing the specific prefixation of *co* to words beginning with *o*.

The final mapping (see Figure 1.17) achieves the desired effect. Given a word that does not start with the letter *o* (say, *design*), T_{co2} acts as the identity function and T_{co1} transforms the string *CO+* to *co* (and therefore maps *CO+design* to *codesign*). Expressed formally:

$$
\begin{aligned}
(T_{co2} \circ T_{co1})(\text{CO+design}) &= T_{co1}(T_{co2}(\text{CO+design})) \\
&= T_{co1}(CO\text{+}design) \\
&= codesign
\end{aligned}
$$

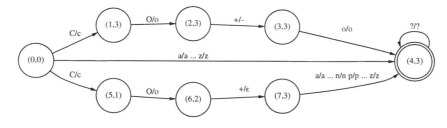

Figure 1.17: Transducer $T_{co2} \circ T_{co1}$.

On the other hand, given a word which starts with the letter *o* (say *offer*), T_{co2} transforms the string *CO+offer* to *co-offer* and T_{co1} acts as the identity function on *co-offer*:

$$
\begin{aligned}
(T_{co2} \circ T_{co1})(\text{CO+offer}) &= T_{co1}(T_{co2}(\text{CO+offer})) \\
&= T_{co1}(co\text{-}offer) \\
&= co\text{-}offer
\end{aligned}
$$

This simplified example illustrates how to write a sequence of rules from the most general to the most specific. (A similar approach was introduced originally in the field of computational phonology, in which rules describe the way an abstract phoneme is realized as a sound depending on the context. Each abstract symbol is transformed by default into a given sound, and a set of more specific rules describe how the realizations vary according to context).

1.3.4.2 Rule Intersection

The second way to build a transducer that represents the final mapping τ_{co} is to approximate iteratively with a sequence of intersections. This method can be seen as successively approximating a mapping. Each transducer constructed with this approach encodes a specific phenomenon and acts as the identity function for all other cases. By intersecting all such transducers, the method guarantees that common behavior is maximized.

We restrict ourselves to ϵ-free letter transducers, since these are closed under intersection (see Section 1.2.2). In addition, we use the number 0 as an additional symbol to make the input and output equal in length. To eliminate this symbol from the final output, we compose the result of the intersection with a transducer that erases this symbol (see Figure 1.18).

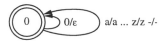

Figure 1.18: FST T_0 used to erase all occurrences of the intermediate symbol 0.

In our example of the prefixation of *co*, we start with the transducer T_1 shown in Figure 1.19, which systematically attaches the prefix *co* both with and without a hyphen and acts as the identity function in all other cases. T_1 behaves functionally as follows:

$$CO\text{+}offer \quad \overset{|T_1|}{\longrightarrow} \quad \{co0offer,\ co\text{-}offer\} \tag{1.42}$$

$$CO\text{+}design \quad \overset{|T_1|}{\longrightarrow} \quad \{co0design,\ co\text{-}design\} \tag{1.43}$$

$$w \quad \overset{|T_1|}{\longrightarrow} \quad \{w\} \tag{1.44}$$

T_1 is an approximation of the relation we wish to construct since it realizes a superset of that relation. For example, both *cooffer* and *co-offer* are associated with the symbolic string *CO+offer*. For this input, we wish to eliminate the

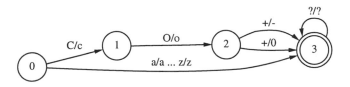

Figure 1.19: T_1

output string *cooffer*. To remedy this problem, we construct the transducer T_2 shown in Figure 1.20. T_2 attaches the prefix *co* with a hyphen only to words that begin with *o* and attaches it both with and without a hyphen otherwise. That is, T_2 acts functionally as follows:

$$CO+\textit{offer} \quad \overset{|T_2|}{\to} \quad \{\textit{co-offer}\} \tag{1.45}$$

$$CO+\textit{design} \quad \overset{|T_2|}{\to} \quad \{\textit{co0design, co-design}\} \tag{1.46}$$

$$w \quad \overset{|T_2|}{\to} \quad \{w\} \tag{1.47}$$

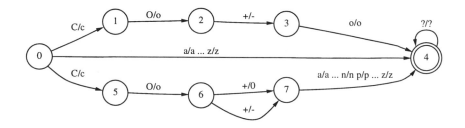

Figure 1.20: T_2

On the other hand, given the input *CO+design*, we need to eliminate the output string *co-design*. In order to do so, we construct the transducer T_3 shown in Figure 1.21. T_3 attaches the prefix *co* without a hyphen to words that do not start with an *o* and attaches it both with and without a hyphen otherwise. T_3 acts functionally as follows:

$$CO+\textit{offer} \quad \overset{|T_3|}{\to} \quad \{\textit{co0offer, co-offer}\} \tag{1.48}$$

$$CO+design \quad \overset{|T_3|}{\to} \quad \{co0design\} \tag{1.49}$$

$$w \quad \overset{|T_3|}{\to} \quad \{w\} \tag{1.50}$$

$$\tag{1.51}$$

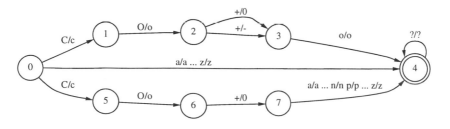

Figure 1.21: T_3

Therefore, the transducer $(T_1 \cap T_2 \cap T_3) \circ T_0$ realizes the desired mapping.[3] It attaches the prefix *co* with a hyphen to precisely those words that start with the letter *o*, and it attaches *co* without a hyphen to precisely those words that do not start with *o*.

$$CO+offer \quad \overset{|(T_1 \cap T_2 \cap T_3) \circ T_0|}{\longrightarrow} \quad \{co\text{-}offer\} \tag{1.52}$$

$$CO+design \quad \overset{|(T_1 \cap T_2 \cap T_3) \circ T_0|}{\longrightarrow} \quad \{codesign\} \tag{1.53}$$

$$w \quad \overset{|(T_1 \cap T_2 \cap T_3) \circ T_0|}{\longrightarrow} \quad \{w\} \tag{1.54}$$

1.3.5 Ambiguity

In addition to being classified by the same properties that classify FSAs (such as the properties of cyclicity and determinicity), rational transductions are often classified with respect to their ambiguity. The term *transduction* does not rule out multiple outputs; this is in contrast with the term *function*[4] which is reserved for cases of at most one output. For a transduction, there is an input word that can be mapped to finitely, and possibly infinitely, many outputs.

---

[3] It not strictly necessary to keep T_1 in this intersection since $T_1 \cap T_2 \cap T_3 = T_2 \cap T_3$, but this example illustrates the general idea of successive approximation. T_1 is here the most general approximation of the solution.

[4] The term *mapping* is sometimes also used. We avoid this terminology and use the verb "map" in a neutral manner that does not imply that the transducer in question is a function.

For example, the transducer $T_{a \to b \cdot c^*}$ in Figure 1.22 maps the input a to an infinite set of outputs corresponding to the regular expression $b \cdot c^*$. These kinds of transductions, for which an input can be mapped to an infinite number of outputs, often arise in intermediate results and are very common in practice.

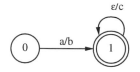

Figure 1.22: Transducer $T_{a \to b \cdot c^*}$.

The first characterization of finite-state transducers takes into account whether there is an input associated with infinitely many outputs.

Definition 13 (Simply Finitely Ambiguous) *A finite-state transducer T is simply finitely ambiguous if for any string w, the set $|T|(w)$ is finite.*

Definition 14 (Infinitely Ambiguous) *An FST T that is not simply finitely ambiguous is infinitely ambiguous.*

For instance, the transducer $T_{a^n \to (b|c)^n}$ in Figure 1.23 is simply finitely ambiguous since $dom(|T|) = a^*$ and $|\,|T|(a^n)\,| = 2^n$.

Figure 1.23: Simply finitely ambiguous transducer $T_{a^n \to (b|c)^n}$.

The second characterization illustrates those cases in which the ambiguity is bounded independently of the input string.

Definition 15 (Uniformly Ambiguous) *An FST T is uniformly finitely ambiguous if there exists a number N such that, for any input string w, $|\,|T|(w)\,| \leq N$.*

The transducer $T_{a^n \to (b|c)^n}$ in Figure 1.23 is not uniformly finitely ambiguous, while the transducer $T_{a \to b|c}$ in Figure 1.24 is.

If a transduction is uniformly finitely ambiguous then it is equivalent to a finite union of rational functions. For the sake of simplicity, we refer to such a

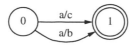

Figure 1.24: Uniformly finitely ambiguous transducer $T_{a \to (b|c)}$.

transduction as a finite union of rational functions rather than uniformly finitely ambiguous.

In summary, the various levels of ambiguity are characterized by the terms shown in Figure 1.25.

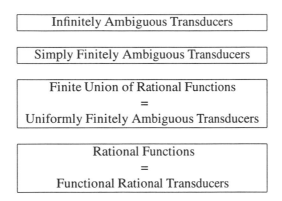

Figure 1.25: Various levels of ambiguity of rational transductions.

1.3.6 Rational Functions

We now turn our focus to rational functions. Since rational functions as well as rational transductions are represented in practice by transducers, we will first have to say how transducers that represent rational functions can be distinguished from transducers that represent non-functional transductions; this will be the main topic of this section. Later in the chapter, we will describe several operations that apply only to functional transductions, thus making such transductions important in numerous concrete situations.

First, a remark about terminology: the reader should be aware that in the literature as well as in this book, rational functions are sometimes also called *finite-state functions*, *finite-state mappings*, or *rational partial functions*.

Sometimes, it can be known a priori that a given transducer represents a function. For instance, the transducer of Section 1.3.4.1 was built by composing rules represented by transducers. Since each individual rule is functional, and since the composition of two functions is still a function, the final result, namely the composition of all rules, is still a function. However, such a line of reasoning is not always available and special methods are then required to decide whether a given transducer represents a function. Consider the method of Section 1.3.4.2: each rule is represented by a non-functional transducer, and the final system is obtained by computing the intersection of each of these transducers. Nothing in such a construction guarantees that the result is a function. On the other hand, the system is expected to compute a prefixation on words, a prefixation that is functional[5]. Hence, a program that decides whether a transducer is functional can be used as a debugging tool: if the system is not functional, whereas the correct solution to the problem demands functional analysis, then the list of intersections is probably incomplete.

Schützenberger proved the decidability of the question of whether a given transducer is functional:

Theorem 2 *(Schützenberger 1975) Given a transducer T, it is decidable whether $|T|$ is functional.*

This question of decidability can be difficult. In the case of the transducer in Figure 1.24, it is obvious that the transducer is not functional since a can clearly be mapped to either b or c. However, it is not so obvious whether the transducer in Figure 1.26 is functional. An input string such as ab can take any of three successful paths, and one needs to check that each path leads to the same output. In that case, each of the three paths leads to the output bcd. In general though, an approach based on the enumeration of all possible input strings is not feasible.

Importantly, rational functions can be represented by a certain class of transducers, namely the class of unambiguous transducers.

Definition 16 (Unambiguous transducer) *An* unambiguous transducer *is a transducer for which each input is the label of at most one successful path.*

Neither the transducer in Figure 1.24 nor the one in Figure 1.26 is unambiguous. By contrast, the transducer of Figure 1.27, representing the same transduction as Figure 1.26, is unambiguous. Obviously, any transduction represented by an unambiguous transducer is functional, and the following theorem shows that the converse is also true:

---

[5]The system handles a simplified prefixation system. In a complete prefixation the system would be expected to be a finite union of rational functions, since numerous prefixation rules are optional.

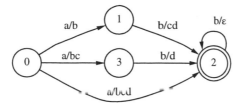

Figure 1.26: T_α: Ambiguous transducer that represents a rational function.

Theorem 3 *(Eilenberg 74) Any rational function τ can be represented by an unambiguous transducer if $\tau(\epsilon) = \emptyset$ or $\{\epsilon\}$.*

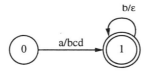

Figure 1.27: Unambiguous representation of $T_{ab^* \to bcd}$.

We will now describe an algorithm that, given any transducer that represents a function, builds an unambiguous transducer that represents the same function. The same algorithm will be used later to decide the prior question whether a transduction is functional.

Consider again the transducer T_α in Figure 1.26. This transducer is ambiguous, since the string ab is the input of three successful paths, namely

$$\text{path}_1 = (0, a, b, 1) \cdot (1, b, cd, 2)$$

$$\text{path}_2 = (0, a, bc, 3) \cdot (3, b, d, 2)$$

$$\text{path}_3 = (0, a, bcd, 2) \cdot (2, b, \epsilon, 2)$$

Before building the corresponding unambiguous transducer, we apply two simplification operations on the ambiguous transducer. The first one consists in restricting the input labels of the transition to simple letters (as opposed to ϵ and multi-letter words).

Proposition 6 (epsilon removal for transducers)

If $T = (\Sigma_1, \Sigma_2, Q, i, F, E)$ is such that $|T|(\epsilon) = \emptyset$ and such that there is no loop

$$(q_1, \epsilon, u_1, q_2) \cdot \ldots \cdot (q_n, \epsilon, a_n, q_1)$$

whose input labels are in $\{\epsilon\}$ then there exists a transducer

$$T' = (\Sigma_1, \Sigma_2, Q, i, F, E')$$

such that $|T| = |T'|$ and

$$E' \subseteq Q \times \Sigma_1 \times \Sigma_2^* \times Q$$

In other words, for a restricted class of transducers, it is possible to remove all epsilons on the inputs of the transitions. Informally speaking, epsilon removal for transducers is similar to epsilon removal for automata. Recall first that E can be assumed to be a subset of $Q \times \Sigma_1 \cup \{\epsilon\} \times \Sigma_2^* \times Q$. We then define $E_\epsilon = E \cap (Q \times \{\epsilon\} \times \Sigma_2^* \times Q)$ and the concatenation of edges by $(q_1, a, u, q_2) \cdot (q_3, b, v, q_4) = (q_1, a \cdot b, u \cdot v, q_4)$ if $q_2 = q_3$. With these definitions in hand, the set E' of edges of the new transducer T' can be defined as follows:

$$E' = \hat{E}_\epsilon \cdot (E - E_\epsilon) \cdot \hat{E}_\epsilon$$

In other words, E' is the set of edges of the original transducer extended on the left and right, with edges whose input labels are ϵ. The fact that there is no loop labeled with ϵ as input guarantees that the set $\hat{E}_\epsilon$ is finite, and that therefore E' can be built effectively. It is easy to show that $(i, u, v, q) \in \hat{E}'$ with $q \in F$ if and only if $(i, u, v, q) \in \hat{E}$, and that therefore $|T'| = |T|$.[6]

To consider a particular case, suppose T is a function such that $|T|(\epsilon) = \emptyset$. Then T can be assumed to be *epsilon-free*, that is, if E is its set of edges, then $E \subseteq Q \times \Sigma_1 \times \Sigma_2^* \times Q$.

Before building the unambiguous transducer of a given function, we need a second simplification illustrated in the following remark:

Remark 2 *If $T = (\Sigma_1, \Sigma_2, Q, i, F, E)$ is a transducer then there exists a transducer $T' = (\Sigma_1, \Sigma_2, Q', i', F', E')$ satisfying $|T| = |T'|$ such that if*

$$(i, u_1, v_1, q_1) \cdot \ldots \cdot (q_{n-1}, u_n, v_n, q)$$

and

$$(i, u_1, v_1', q_1') \cdot \ldots \cdot (q_{n-1}', u_n, v_n', q')$$

are two paths of T', then there exists some j such that $v_j \neq v_j'$.

---

[6]The case of ϵ should be handled separately.

In other words, if two paths have the same input, they have different outputs. T' is obtained from T by determinizing the underlying automaton.

Note that it is still possible that the outputs, when concatenated together, build the same word. For instance, the transducer T_α in Figure 1.26 verifies the above remark but it still has at least the following three paths:

$$\text{path}_1 = (0, a, b, 1) \cdot (1, b, cd, 2)$$

$$\text{path}_2 = (0, a, bc, 3) \cdot (3, b, d, 2)$$

$$\text{path}_3 = (0, a, bcd, 2) \cdot (2, b, \epsilon, 2)$$

for which the inputs are similar but for which the outputs, when concatenated, each lead to the word bcd.

Building an equivalent unambiguous transducer consists in selecting a particular path, for each input string of the domain. Since the transducer represents a function, each path generates the same output therefore, selecting one in particular will not modify the set of outputs for the input string. For instance, for the input string ab, the unambiguous transducer equivalent to T_α contains path_1 but not path_2 or path_3.

Definition 17 (Output decomposition)
*If $(i, a_1, u_1, q_1) \cdot \ldots \cdot (q_{n-1}, a_n, u_n, q_n)$ is a path of an FST
$T = (\Sigma_1, \Sigma_2, Q, i, F, E)$, then the output decomposition of this path is the word*

$$u_1 \cdot \odot \cdot u_2 \cdot \odot \cdot \ldots \cdot \odot \cdot u_n$$

of $(\Sigma_2 \cup \{\odot\})^*$ in which $\odot$ is a separation mark between the output labels.

Since the previous remark guarantees that if two paths have the same input, their output decompositions are different, we are now able to define an ordering on paths. Suppose that Σ_2 is ordered. We then extend the ordering to $\Sigma_2 \cup \{\odot\}$ by $\odot < a$ for $a \in \Sigma_2$. This ordering on $\Sigma_2 \cup \{\odot\}$ also defines an ordering on $(\Sigma_2 \cup \{\odot\})^*$ and on paths: $\text{path}_i < \text{path}_j$ if and only if the output decomposition of path_i is less than the output decomposition of path_j. Given such an ordering, we can select a minimal path for each input string. For instance, the three decompositions of our above example are ordered as follows: $b \odot cd < bc \odot d < bcd \odot \epsilon$, and path_1 is therefore selected. In other words, for each input string, we select the path that emits symbols later than the others.

This process of selecting the minimal path for each input string can be applied directly to a transducer by means of the algorithm in Figure 1.28.

Function **UNAMBIGUOUS**
Input: FST $T = (\Sigma_1, \Sigma_2, Q, i, F, E)$
Output: FST $T_2 = (\Sigma_1, \Sigma_2, Q_2, i_2, F_2, E_2)$

$$Q_2 = F_2 = E_2 = \emptyset; i_2 = q = 0;$$
$$C[0] = (i, \emptyset);$$
do{
$\quad Q_2 = Q_2 \cup \{q\};$
$\quad (x_1, S) = C[q];$
$\quad$ if $(x_1 \in F)$ and $S \cap F = \emptyset$ then $F_2 = F_2 \cup \{q\};$
$\quad$ foreach $(x_1, a, w, y_1) \in E$
$\quad\quad S' = \emptyset;$
$\quad\quad$ foreach $(x_1, a, w', y_1') \in E$ s.t. $w' < w$
$\quad\quad\quad S' = S' \cup \{y_1'\};$
$\quad\quad$ foreach $x_2 \in S$
$\quad\quad\quad$ foreach $(x_2, a, w', y_2') \in E$
$\quad\quad\quad\quad S' = S' \cup \{y_2\};$
$\quad\quad$ if $(S' \cap \{y_1\} = \emptyset)$
$\quad\quad\quad e = \text{addSet}(C, (y_1, S'));$
$\quad\quad\quad E_2 = E_2 \cup \{(q, a, w, e)\};$
$\quad q + +;$
}while$(q < \text{Card}(C));$
Return $T_2;$

Function **addSet**
Input: (C, x)
Output: state number e
// C is an array of elements of the same type as x.

$n = \text{Card}(C);$
if $\exists p < n$ s.t. $C[p] = x$
$\quad e = p;$
else
$\quad C[e = n + +] = x;$
Return $e;$

Figure 1.28: Algorithm for building an unambiguous transducer representing a function.

We will now illustrate this algorithm on T_α. The output, the transducer T_β in Figure 1.29, will later be pruned into the final transducer in Figure 1.30. The states of T_β are built dynamically, starting with the initial state. Each state contains a pair (x_1, S) in which x_1 refers to a state of Q (state set of the original transducer) and in which S refers to a subset of Q. x_1 indicates a position in T, S indicates the set of positions that could be followed with the same input but with a strictly smaller output (in the sense defined above). The initial state is labeled $(0, \emptyset)$ to indicate that the state being followed in T_α is 0, and that, at this point, this is the path with the smallest output. The program then builds on the transition of this initial state: the first transition, labeled a/b, corresponds to the transition $(0, a, b, 1)$ of T_α and points to a set labeled $(1, \emptyset)$. 1 indicates the arrival state 1 of $(0, a, b, 1)$; $\emptyset$ indicates that no smaller path can be followed with a as input. In contrast, the second transition $((0, \emptyset), a, bc, (3, \{1\}))$ corresponds to the transition $(0, a, bc, 3)$ of T_α, but, in that case, a strictly smaller path with the same input is also possible. $(0, a, b, 1) < (0, a, bc, 3)$, and therefore, this second transition points to a state labeled $(3, \{1\})$, in which $\{1\}$ indicates that there is a smaller path whose last state is the state 1 of T_α. In a similar way, the third transition $((0, \emptyset), a, bcd, (2, \{3, 1\}))$ corresponds to $(0, a, bcd, 2)$ in T_α, while $\{3, 1\}$ indicates that two strictly smaller paths, with an identical input, end at the states 3 and 1 of T_α.

This completes the transitions of the initial state. The transitions of the states $(1, \emptyset)$ and $(2, \emptyset)$ follow the same construction. For the state $(3, \{1\})$, however, the situation is different: the algorithm first builds the transition $((3, \{1\}), b, d, (2, \{2\}))$, but then notes that $S' \cap \{y_1\} = \{2\} \cap \{2\} = \{2\}$ is not empty. This means that from state $(0, \emptyset)$ to $(2, \{2\})$ there is a strictly smaller path with the same input (from 0 to 2) and that therefore, the current path, since it is not minimal, should be removed. Hence, the state $(3, \{1\})$ has no output transition and will be deleted during pruning. Similarly, the state $(3, \{3, 1\})$ has no output transition; it is not deleted during pruning, however, since it is a terminal state.

Note that this algorithm works for any input transducer, that is, it terminates on any input. If the transduction represented by the input transducer is functional, then the result represents the same transduction. If, on the contrary, the transduction is not functional, the resulting unambiguous transducer represents a rational function whose domain is equal to the domain of the original transducer and whose outputs are included in the outputs of the original transduction. That is, given any transducer T, if T_2 is the transducer built from T by means of the algorithm in Figure 1.28 then T_2 verifies the following: $\text{Dom}(T_2) = \text{Dom}(T)$, and for each $x \in \text{Dom}(T)$, $\|T_2|(x)\| = 1$ and $|T_2|(x) \subseteq |T|(x)$.

We have yet to discuss how to decide whether the transduction represented by a given transducer is functional. In other words, for all we have said so far,

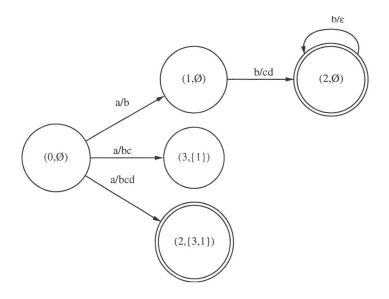

Figure 1.29: T_β: Building an unambiguous representation (before pruning).

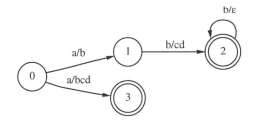

Figure 1.30: T_β: Unambiguous representation (after pruning).

we do not know whether the unambiguous transducer just built represents the same transduction or whether it is strictly included in the original one. We now turn our attention to this problem.

An algorithm that, given any transducer, decides whether the transduction is functional is given in Figure 1.32. This algorithm works in two steps. Given an input transducer T_2, the first step consists in building the unambiguous transducer T_1 by means of the algorithm in Figure 1.28. The second step consists in comparing the unambiguous transducer T_1 with the original transducer T_2. The equivalence of the two transducers is equivalent to the functionality of the original transducer. Since the unambiguous transducer is guaranteed to be functional, then, if the transducers are equivalent, the original transducer

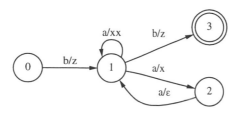

Figure 1.31: Non-functional transducer (Blattner and Head, 1977).

is also functional. If the transducers are not equivalent, then T_1 is such that $\mathrm{Dom}(T_1)=\mathrm{Dom}(T_2)$ and $|T_1|(x) \subseteq |T_2|(x)$, there is one $x \in \mathrm{Dom}(T_1)$ such that $|T_1|(x)$ is strictly included in $|T_2|(x)$, and therefore $||T_2|(x)| > 1$. Since in general it is not decidable whether two transducers are equivalent, the key is to be able to answer the question in the particular case of functional transducers.

We compare the unambiguous transducer T_1 with the original transducer T_2 by taking T_1 as a model and testing whether T_2 is compatible with T_1. To test for compatibility we build a third transducer T_3 whose states are labeled by triples $(x_1, x_2, \pm u)$ or (x_1, x_2, OUT), in which x_1 is a state of the unambiguous transducer T_1, x_2 is a state of T_2 and $\pm u$ indicates an emission delay between T_1 and T_2. More precisely, the triple (x_1, x_2, t) indicates that we follow a path $(i, \alpha, \beta, x_1) \in \hat{E}$ in T and a path $(i_2, \alpha, \beta', x_2) \in \hat{E}_2$ in T_2 such that $\beta' = \beta \cdot u$ if $t = +u$ or $\beta = \beta' \cdot u$ if $t = -u$. In addition, the last term of the triple can be equal to a special value OUT that indicates that the outputs of the paths $(i, \alpha, \beta, x_1) \in \hat{E}$ and $(i_2, \alpha, \beta', x_2) \in \hat{E}_2$ are incompatible, that is, that β is not a prefix of β' and β' is not a prefix of β. This comparison indicates that there are two cases in which the original transducer is not equivalent to the unambiguous one:

1. if both states x_1 and x_2 are final and if t is different from ϵ (this shows that a successful path from T_1 and a path from T_2 have the same input but different outputs); and

2. if there is a path $((x_1, x_2, t), \omega, \omega', (x_1, x_2, t')) \in \hat{E}_3$ with $t \neq t'$ (This shows that there is a loop that adds some delay between the outputs of T_1 and T_2, and that therefore, this delay can grow to be unbounded; this also shows that there exist two paths that have similar inputs but different outputs.)

Let us illustrate this algorithm on two simple examples.

Function **IS_FUNCTIONAL**
Input: FST $T_2 = (Q_2, i_2, F_2, E_2)$
Output: boolean result
$T_1 = (Q, i, F, E) = UNAMBIGUOUS(T_2 = (Q_2, i_2, F_2, E_2));$
   $T_3 = (\Sigma_1, \Sigma_2, Q_3, i_3, F_3, E_3);$
   $Q_3 = F_3 = E_3 = \emptyset; i_3 = q = 0;$
   $C[0] = (i_1, i_2, \epsilon);$
   result=YES;
   do{
       $Q_3 = Q_3 \cup \{q\};$
       $(x_1, x_2, u) = C[q];$
       if $(x_1 \in F$ and $x_2 \in F_2$ and $u \neq \epsilon)$ result=NO;BREAK;
       if $(u \neq$ OUT$)$
          foreach $(x_1, a, w, y_1) \in E_1$
             foreach $(x_2, a, w', y_2) \in E_2$
                if $(u > 0)$ $v_1 = w; v_2 = w' \cdot u;$
                else $v_1 = w \cdot u; v_2 = w';$
                if $(|v_1| > |v_2|)$
                    if $(v_2^{-1} \cdot v_1 \neq \emptyset)$ $v = -v_2^{-1} \cdot v_1;$
                  else $v =$ OUT;
                else if $(|v_1| \leq |v_2|)$
                    if $(v_1^{-1} \cdot v_2 \neq \emptyset)$ $v = +v_1^{-1} \cdot v_2;$
                  else $v =$ OUT;
                if $(\exists p, l$ s.t. $q \in \hat{d}_3(p, l)$
                    and s.t. $C[p] = (y_1, y_2, v')$ with $v' \neq v)$
                result=NO;BREAK;
                $e =$addSet$(C, (y_1, y_2, v));$
                $E_3 = E_3 \cup \{(q, a, w, e)\};$
       else if $(u ==$ OUT$)$
          foreach $(x_1, a, w, y_1) \in E_1$
             foreach $(x_2, a, w', y_2) \in E_2$
               $e =$addSet$(C, (y_1, y_2,$ OUT$));$
               $E_3 = E_3 \cup \{(q, a, w, e)\};$
       $q + +;$
   }while$(q <$ Card$(C));$
   Return result;

Figure 1.32: Algorithm to decide whether a transduction is functional.

First, consider the transducer $T_{a \to (b|c)}$ in Figure 1.24, which is obviously not functional. The unambiguous transducer is simply the two-state transducer $T_1 = (\Sigma_1, \Sigma_2, \{0, 1\}, 0, \{1\}, \{(0, a, b, 1)\})$. When we compare T_1 and $T_{a \to (b|c)}$, the first state of T_3 is labeled $(0, 0, \epsilon)$. From this state there is the transition

$$((0, 0, \epsilon), a, b, (1, 1, \epsilon)) \in E_3$$

but also the transition

$$((0, 0, \epsilon), a, b, (1, 1, \text{OUT})) \in E_3$$

which indicates that the outputs (b and c) are incompatible. When the program inspects the state labeled $(1, 1 \text{ OUT})$, it notes that 1 is final both in $T_{a \to (b|c)}$ and in T_1, and that therefore the two transducers are not equivalent, which in turn shows that $T_{a \to (b|c)}$ is not functional.

Consider now the second example, the transducer T_{ω_1} in Figure 1.31. This transducer is not functional since, for instance,

$$|T_{\omega_1}|(baab) = \{zxxz, zxz\}.$$

The first step builds the unambiguous transducer T_{ω_2} of Figure 1.33. The comparison of T_{ω_1} with T_{ω_2} is illustrated by the transducer T_{ω_3} in Figure 1.34. The first state built is labeled, as for the first example, $(0, 0, \epsilon)$. Since from either state 0 of T_{ω_2} or state 0 of T_{ω_1} the only possible transition is $(0, b, z, 1)$, the only transition from the initial state of T_{ω_3} is the edge $((0, 0, \epsilon), b, z, (1, 1, \epsilon))$, in which the epsilon of $(1, 1, \epsilon)$ indicates that the outputs are identical up to this point. From the state labeled $(1, 1, \epsilon)$ the situation is different: the input label a corresponds to two transitions in T_{ω_2} and to two transitions in T_{ω_1}, both labeled a/xx and a/x. This situation leads to four different transitions in the new construction T_{ω_3}. Two of them, $((1, 1, \epsilon), a, xx, (4, 1, \epsilon))$ and $((1, 1, \epsilon), a, x, (2, 2, \epsilon))$, indicate that the outputs are identical; the other two, $((1, 1, \epsilon), a, xx, (4, 2, -x))$ and $((1, 1, \epsilon), a, x, (2, 1, x))$, indicate a delay between the emissions of T_{ω_1} and the emissions of T_{ω_2}. In other words, $((1, 1, \epsilon), a, xx, (4, 2, -x))$ indicates that there is an input string leading to 4 in T_{ω_2} and to 2 in T_{ω_1} such that the emissions of T_{ω_1} have a delay of x compared to the emissions of T_{ω_2}. The other states of T_{ω_3} are built in a similar way. The program stops when the transition $((2, 1, x), a, \epsilon, (1, 1, xxx))$ is built. T_3 contains a path from $(1, 1, \epsilon)$ to $(1, 1, xxx)$, which shows that a delay is growing within this loop, and that therefore, the loops from 1 to 1 in T_{ω_2} and from 1 to 1 in T_{ω_1} generate different outputs.

Note that it is not necessary when applying this algorithm to build the set of transitions E_3; it is only necessary to build the states.

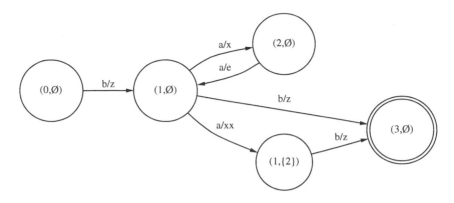

Figure 1.33: T_{ω_2}: Application of the UNAMBIGUOUS algorithm.

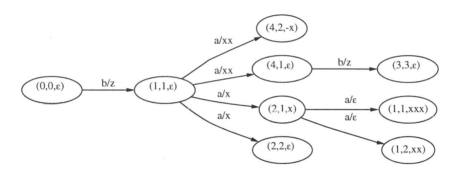

Figure 1.34: T_{ω_3} Example of the IS_FUNCTION algorithm.

Let us now reconsider the prefixation problem of section 1.3.4.2. Recall that the final transducer is built through a sequence of transducer intersections. From the point of view of the linguist who has to formulate the rules, such a system is usually fairly difficult to design, and so, rules are commonly omitted during the development stage. But because this kind of incompleteness is sometimes difficult to observe, it can stay hidden in the system for a long time and elude testing. However, if the final transduction is supposed to be functional, as is the case here, then an incompleteness result in the non-functionality of the final transduction can be detected. Suppose for instance that an incomplete system results in the transducer T_{CO} in Figure 1.35.[7] The

---

[7] To simplify the exposition, the letter a stands for any letter different from o whereas A stands for the whole alphabet. Furthermore, a/a stands for all transitions whose input is a letter othen than o and whose output is identical to the input. Similarly, A/A stands for all transitions whose

first step in deciding whether T_{CO} is a function is to build an unambiguous transducer T'_{CO} such that $\mathrm{Dom}(|T'_{CO}|) = \mathrm{Dom}(T_{CO})$, $|T'_{CO}|(x) \subseteq |T_{CO}|(x)$ for each $x \in \Sigma^*$. This transducer is built, as described earlier by means of the algorithm UNAMBIGUOUS, and its compilation is illustrated in Figure 1.36. The comparison of T'_{CO} with T_{CO} is illustrated in Figure 1.37. When the program reaches the state labeled $(3, 5,'' +'')$ and completes the transitions $(3, e, e, 4)$ of T'_{CO} and $(3, e, e, 4)$ of T_{CO}, $v_1 = +e$, $v_2 = e$; hence, $v = $ OUT, which leads to the state $(4, 4, $ OUT$)$. Since 4 is final and since the state is marked OUT, the program halts and returns the answer *NO* for "non-functional". This example illustrates how the formal decidability properties of finite-state transducers are useful in debugging situations.

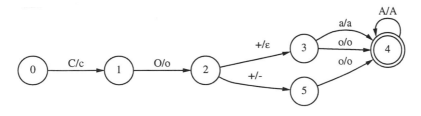

Figure 1.35: Incorrect transducer T_2 for "CO" prefixation.

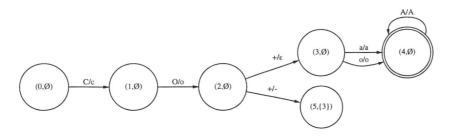

Figure 1.36: $T'_2 = $UNAMBIGUOUS$(T_2)$ representing a function.

An interesting consequence of decidability of the functionality of a transduction is that the equivalence of rational functions is decidable, although the equivalence of rational transductions is not. If f_1 and f_2 are two rational functions represented respectively by T_1 and T_2, then f_1 and f_2 are equivalent if

---

output is identical to the input.

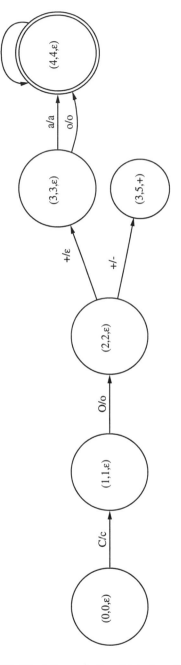

Figure 1.37: Deciding whether T_2 is functional.

and only if they have the same domain[8] and if $|T_1 \cup T_2|$ is functional[9].

1.3.7 Applying a Transducer

We now turn our attention to the application of a transducer to a given input. This fundamental operation is more complex than it first appears.

Consider the following mapping of words to their phonetic transcriptions:[10]

ought	$o_1 t$
our	*our*
oubliette	$o_2 blEet$
ouabain	$wa_1 bain$

This table can be seen as a mapping from orthographic forms to phonetic transcriptions. The transcriptions are represented by the FST shown in Figure 1.38.

One way of computing the output of a given input consists in traversing the transducer in all ways that are compatible with the current input symbol performing backtracking if necessary until a complete path is found. For instance, given T_o and the input *oubliette*, state 0 moves to to state 1 and output *o1*. From state 1, state 2 follows with the empty string ϵ as output. At this point, the next letter *b* does not match any transition from state 2, and so backtracking up to state 0 needs to be performed.

A more natural way to compute the output of a transducer for a given input, is to view the input as an FSA. On this method, the application of the transducer to the input is computed as a kind of intersection of the transducer with the automaton. This kind of intersection is similar to the previously described intersection of FSAs. It is computed between the first projection of the FST and the input FSA. In this case, though, the arcs in the resulting FSA are labeled with the corresponding output label from the FST. For simplicity, we formally define this operation for only those FSTs whose input labels are non-empty letters.

---

[8] This test is achieved by checking the equivalence of the automata representing their respective domains.

[9] The union of two transducers is defined as the union of their underlying automata. Moreover, the union of two transducers represents the union of the transductions represented by each transducer, that is $|T_1 \cup T_2| = |T_1| \cup |T_2|$.

[10] The phonetic symbols are adapted from those found in the *American Heritage Dictionary*. An *ouabain* is "a white poisonous glucoside"; an *oubliette* is "a dungeon with a trap door in the ceiling as its only means of entrance or exit" (*The American Heritage Dictionary*).

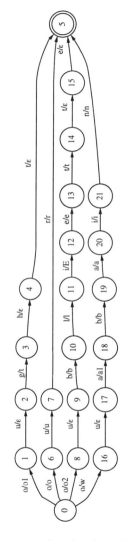

Figure 1.38: Transducer T_o representing the phonetic transcription of the words *ought*, *our*, *oubliette* and *ouabain*.

Definition 18 (Intersection of an FST and an FSA) *Given an FST*
$T_1 = (\Sigma, \Sigma_1, Q_1, i_1, F_1, E_1)$ *where* $E_1 \subseteq Q_1 \times \Sigma_1 \times \Sigma_2^* \times Q_1$, *and an FSA*
$A_2 = (\Sigma, Q_2, i_2, F_2, E_2)$, *where* $E_2 \subseteq Q_2 \times \Sigma_1 \times Q_2$, *the intersection of* T_1
with A_2 *is defined as the FSA* $A = (\Sigma, Q_1 \times Q_2, (i_1, i_2), F_1 \times F_2, E)$ *with*
$E \subseteq (Q_1 \times Q_2) \times \Sigma_2^* \times (Q_1 \times Q_2)$ *such that:*

$$E \;=\; \bigcup_{(q_1,a,b,r_1) \in E_1, (q_2,a,r_2) \in E_2} ((q_1, q_2), b, (r_1, r_2)) \tag{1.55}$$

The FSA for *oubliette* is shown in Figure 1.39. The intersection of the FST T_o in Figure 1.38 with the automaton for *oubliette* in Figure 1.39 is shown in Figure 1.40.

Once the intersection has been applied, it is necessary to prune the resulting automaton. This operation can be performed more efficiently for deterministic transducers for which at each point there is at most one transition compatible with the input. In such a case, no backtracking is necessary and the intersection consists in following a single path in the FST. Moreover, in some cases, FSTs can be turned into an equivalent deterministic transducer. An example of this is shown in Figure 1.38.

Deterministic FSTs are described in more detail in the following section.

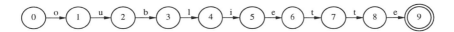

Figure 1.39: Automaton $A_{oubliette}$ representing the string *oubliette*.

1.3.8 Determinization

Transducers such as the transducer T_3 in Figure 1.12 are easy to implement, since for each state there is at most one outgoing transition whose input label corresponds to a given input symbol. Suppose, for instance, that T_3 is applied to the input string *11*. The output can be computed as follows: starting at the initial state 0 with an input label 1, i.e. using the edge $(0, 1, 0, 1)$, the first letter of the output string is 0 and the transducer moves to state 1. At this point, the remaining input string is the one letter word *1*, which can lead only to state 0 and output the letter *1*. The input string is then empty, and since the current state, i.e. 0, is final, the output string (that is, 01) is the concatenation of all the output symbols, which shows that $|T_3|(11) = 01$.

More formally, this type of transducer is called *subsequential* and is defined as follows (Schützenberger, 1977):

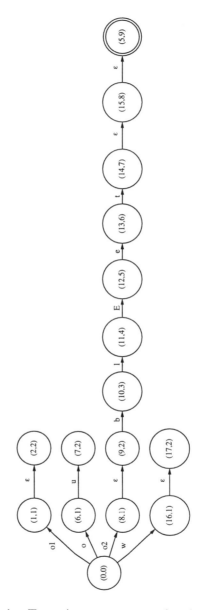

Figure 1.40: Applying T_o on $A_{oubliette}$ representing the string *oubliette*.

Definition 19 (subsequential transducer) *A subsequential transducer T is an eight-tuple*
$(\Sigma_1, \Sigma_2, Q, i, F, \otimes, *, \rho)$ *in which*

- Σ_1, Σ_2, Q, *i and F are defined as for transducers.*

- $\otimes$ *is the deterministic state transition function that maps $Q \times \Sigma_1$ to Q (written as $q \otimes a = q'$).*

- $*$ *is the deterministic emission function that maps $Q \times \Sigma_1$ to Σ_2^* (written as $q * a = w$).*

- ρ *is the final emission function that maps F to Σ^* (written as $\rho(q) = w$).*

The denomination of subsequential transducers stems from the fact that they define a subclass of FSTs[11]. If

$$T = (\Sigma_1, \Sigma_2, Q, i, F, E)$$

is a transducer such that $E \subseteq Q \times \Sigma_1 \times \Sigma_2^* \times Q$ and such that, for all $q \in Q$ and for all $x \in \Sigma_1$, there is at most one $w \in \Sigma_2^*$ and one $q' \in Q$ such that $(q, x, w, q') \in E$, then one can define the partial mapping $\otimes$ as $q \otimes a = q'$ if $\exists (q, a, w, q') \in E$, the partial mapping $*$ as $q \otimes q' = w$ if $\exists (q, a, w, q') \in E$, and the final output function as $\rho(q) = \epsilon$ for $q \in F$.

As is the case with automata and transducers, the transition and emission functions can be extended in the following way:

- $q \otimes \epsilon = q$, $q * \epsilon = \epsilon$ for $q \in Q$

- $q \otimes (w \cdot a) = (q \otimes w) \otimes a$ for $q \in Q$, $w \in \Sigma_1^*$ and $a \in \Sigma_1$

- $q * (w \cdot a) = (q * w) \cdot ((q \otimes w) * a)$ for $q \in Q$, $w \in \Sigma_1^*$ and $a \in \Sigma_1$

Once this extension is defined, a subsequential transducer

$$\tau = (\Sigma_1, \Sigma_2, Q, i, F, \otimes, *, \rho)$$

defines a partial mapping $|\tau|$ from Σ_1^* to Σ_2^* such that

- $|\tau|(w) = (i * w) \cdot \rho(i \otimes w)$ if $i \otimes w$ is defined

- $|\tau|(w) = \emptyset$ otherwise

---

[11] This is true modulo the final emission function. However, if one adds an end of input marker $ to Σ_1, the final emission function can be replaced by a simple transition whose input label is the symbol $.

Historically, the terminology for deterministic, sequential or subsequential transducers has been confusing in the sense that the same words have been often used for different notions, depending on the author and the context. The transducers we defined as subsequential are sometimes called *deterministic transducers* or *sequential transducers*. We avoid speaking of deterministic transducers since these are easily confused with transducers that, when considered as automata whose labels are the pairs of labels of transducers, are deterministic. In other words, deterministic transducers can be defined as transducers with $E \subseteq Q \times \Sigma_1 \times \Sigma_2^* \times Q$ such that, for each $q \in Q$, $a \in \Sigma_1$, and $w \in \Sigma_2^*$, there is at most one $q' \in Q$ such that $(q, a, w, q') \in Q$. On this definition, the transducer T_o in Figure 1.38 is deterministic but not subsequential. The term *sequential* refers to sequential transducers, which we will discuss only in the restricted context of bimachines (see the following section).

Definition 20 *A* sequential transducer, *also called a* generalized sequential machine *(Eilenberg, 1974), is a six-tuple* $(\Sigma_1, \Sigma_2, Q, i, \otimes, *)$ *such that,*

- Σ_1 *and* Σ_2 *are two finite alphabets*

- Q *is a finite set of states*

- $i \in Q$ *is the initial states*

- $\otimes$ *is the partial deterministic transition function mapping* $Q \times \Sigma_1$ *on* Q, *noted* $q \otimes a = q'$

- $*$ *is the partial emission function mapping* $Q \times \Sigma_1$ *on* Σ_2^*, *noted* $q * a = w$

In other words, a sequential transducer is a subsequential transducer for which all the states are final and for which $\rho(q) = \epsilon$ for all $q \in Q$. Naturally, functions that can be represented by subsequential transducers are called *subsequential functions*, and functions that can be represented by sequential transducers are called *sequential functions* (and sometimes also *left sequential functions*).

For any non-subsequential transducer, that represents a subsequential function, it is possible to build explicitly an equivalent subsequential transducer. For instance, the transducer T_o in Figure 1.38 is equivalent to the transducer τ_o in Figure 1.41m which can be constructed from T_o.

The algorithm that realizes this transformation, i.e., that, given a transducer that represents a subsequential function, builds a subsequential transducer that represents the same function, is given in Chapter 7. The prior question, however, is whether the transducer is one that represents a subsequential function. Sometimes, the answer can be known by means of a construction. For instance, if the transducer represents a functional transduction and is acyclic, then the

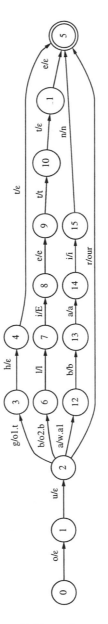

Figure 1.41: Subsequential transducer τ_o equivalent to T_o.

transduction is subsequential. Very often, however, such information is not known a priori.

We now describe two algorithms that answer this question in a systematic manner. We illustrate them with an example that also shows that simple phenomena can lead to non-subsequential rational functions. Consider the following long list of frozen expressions:

> They <u>take</u> this fact <u>into account</u>
> They should <u>keep</u> this new problem <u>under control</u>
> The flood problems <u>keep</u> the hardest-hit areas virtually
> <u>out of reach</u> to rescuers.

The problem is to mark in the text the places at which one particular expression appears. One way of doing so is to attach a numerical identifier to the verb. A sentence such as

> They should keep this new problem under control

would then be transformed into

> They should keep-1 this new problem under control

and a sentence such as

> The flood problems keep the hardest-hit areas virtually out of reach
> to rescuers

would be transformed into

> The flood problems keep-2 the hardest-hit areas virtually out of
> reach to rescuers

This method could be used as the first step of a syntactic analyzer. This kind of preprocessing would, for instance, trigger a parser specific to the frozen expression. To simplify, let us focus on the transformations just illustrated, from the sentences containing the expression *keep ... under control* to the same sentence where *keep* is transformed to *keep-1*, and from the sentence containing the expression *keep ... out of reach* to the same sentence where *keep* is transformed to *keep-2*. This simple task can be modeled by the transducer T_{keep} in Figure 1.42. We reduce the input alphabet Σ_1 to $\{a, keep, under, control, out, of, reach\}$ and the output alphabet Σ_2 to $\{a, keep-1, keep-2, under, control, out, of, reach\}$, with the convention that the symbol a represents any word other than *keep, keep-1, keep-2, under, control, out, of,* or *reach.* Given these simplifications, T_{keep} performs the following mappings:

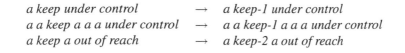

a keep under control	$\longrightarrow$	*a keep-1 under control*
a a keep a a a under control	$\longrightarrow$	*a a keep-1 a a a under control*
a keep a out of reach	$\longrightarrow$	*a keep-2 a out of reach*

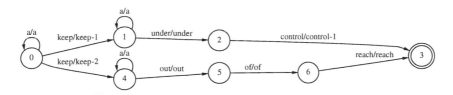

Figure 1.42: Transducer T_{keep} marking two frozen expressions.

We are now in a position to see that the transduction $|T_{keep}|$ is not subsequential, that is, there is no subsequential transducer that represents it. But first, we have to show that the transduction is functional. This is done, as described in the previous section, by first computing the unambiguous transducer in Figure 1.43. Since this transducer is equivalent to the original transducer, we know that (1) the transduction is functional, and that (2) the original transducer T_{keep} is unambiguous. We will now examine two algorithms for deciding whether a function is subsequential.

The first algorithm, given in Figure 1.45, computes the square of the unambiguous transducer while comparing the outputs. More precisely, given an unambiguous transducer $T = (\Sigma_1, \Sigma_2, Q, i, F, E)$, this algorithm builds the transducer $T_2 = (\Sigma_1, \Sigma_2, Q_2, i_2, F_2, E_2)$ on the same alphabets with $Q_2 \subseteq Q \times \Sigma_1^* \times Q \times \Sigma_1^*$ as follows: for each $w \in \Sigma_1^*$ such that $(i, w, w_1, q_1) \in \hat{E}$ and $(i, w, w_2, q_2) \in \hat{E}$, if $l = w_1 \wedge w_2$, $v_1 = l^{-1} \cdot w_1$ and $v_2 = l^{-1} \cdot w_2$ (we call v_1 and v_2 the *delayed outputs*) then there is a path $((i, \epsilon, i, \epsilon), w, l, (q_1, v_1, q_2, v_2)) \in \hat{E}_2$ such that $v_1 \wedge v_2 = \epsilon$. A state (q_1, v_1, q_2, v_2) represents the fact that there are two paths in T with the same input and with $l \cdot v_1$ and $l \cdot v_2$ as output.

To apply this algorithm, consider T_{keep} and the transducer in Figure 1.44. The transition from the initial state $(i, \epsilon, i, \epsilon)$, labeled keep/$\epsilon$, to the state $(1, \text{keep-1}, 2, \text{keep-2})$ results from the transitions $(0, \text{keep}, \text{keep-1}, 1)$ and $(0, \text{keep}, \text{keep-2}, 4)$ of T_{keep}. The longest factor common to keep-1 and keep-2 is ϵ. Since each path of $(q, w, w', q') \in \hat{E}$ of T can be combined with itself, T_2 contains the paths $((q, \epsilon, q, \epsilon), w, w', (q', \epsilon, q', \epsilon))$, as shown in Figure 1.44.

The efficacy of the algorithm lies in the fact that if there is a path $((q_1, u_1, q_2, u_2), w, w', (q_1, u_1', q_2, u_2')) \in \hat{E}_2$, then $u_1 = u_1'$ and $u_2 = u_2'$. If this is not the case then the same label w will generate an infinite number of states (q_1, u, q_2, u'). It can be proven using the following theorem and two definitions that such behavior appears if and only if the original transducer is subsequential.

Theorem 4 *A rational function is subsequential if and only if it has bounded variations.*

Definition 21 *The left distance between two strings u and v is $\| u, v \| = |u| + |v| - 2|u \wedge v|$.*

Definition 22 *A rational function has bounded variations if and only if for all $k \geq 0$, there exists $K \geq 0$ s.t. $\forall u, v \in dom(f)$, if $\| u, v \| \leq k$ then $\| f(u), f(v) \| \leq K$.*

So, for example, $|T_{keep}|$ doesn't have bounded variations since

$$\| |T_{keep}|(\text{keep} \cdot a^n \cdot \text{under control}), |T_{keep}|(\text{keep} \cdot a^n \cdot \text{out of reach}) \|$$
$$= (n + 3) + (n + 4)$$

The same property mentioned in Theorem 4 is used again in the second algorithm, represented in Figure 1.47 and illustrated with the same example of T_{keep} in Figure 1.46. This algorithm compares all the paths that share the same input, by building a transducer, called the *twinning construction* (Choffrut, 1977), whose set of states is the cartesian product of the original transducer, and whose transition labels are built in the following way: if there is a transition $(x_1, u, v_1, y_1) \in E$ and a transition (x_2, u, v_2, y_2) in the original transducer, then there is a transition $((x_1, x_2), u, (v_1, v_2), (y_1, y_2))$ in the twinning construction.

For instance, since there are two transitions, namely

$$(0, keep, \text{keep-1}, 1)$$

and

$$(0, keep, \text{keep-2}, 4)$$

in T_{keep}, one can build the transition

$$((0, 0), keep, (\text{keep-1}, \text{keep-2}), (1, 4))$$

(see the construction in Figure 1.46).

The power of the algorithms lies in the fact that if the transduction is subsequential, then the loops in the construction have a special property. It has been shown (Choffrut, 1977; Berstel, 1979) that the original transduction

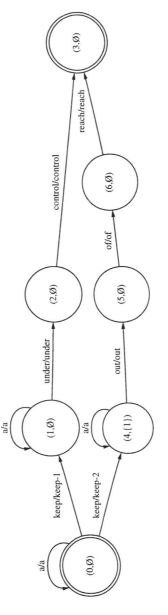

Figure 1.43: Unambiguous transducer representation of T_{keep}.

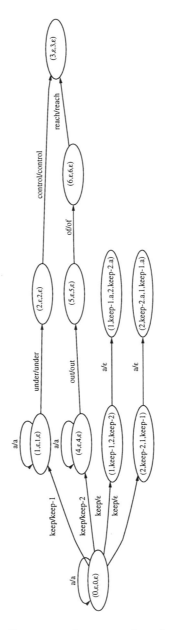

Figure 1.44: Square prefix construction to test the subsequentiality of T_{keep}.

Function **IsSubsequential**
Input: Unambiguous transducer $T = (\Sigma_1, \Sigma_2, Q, i, F, E)$
Ouput: boolean RESULT

$Q_2 = \emptyset; E_2 = \emptyset; C[0] = (0, \epsilon, 0, \epsilon)$; RESULT=YES;
do {
$\quad Q_2 = Q_2 \cup \{q\};$
$\quad (x_1, u_1, x_2, u_2) = C_1[q];$
$\quad$ foreach $(x_1, a, w, y_1) \in E$
$\quad\quad$ foreach $(x_2, a, w', y_2) \in E$
$\quad\quad v = u_1 \cdot w \wedge u_2 \cdot w';$
$\quad\quad v_1 = v^{-1} \cdot (u_1 \cdot w);$
$\quad\quad v_2 = v^{-1} \cdot (u_2 \cdot w');$
$\quad\quad e =$addSet$(C, (y_1, v_1, y_2, v_2));$
$\quad\quad E_2 = E_2 \cup \{(q, a, v, e)\};$
$\quad\quad$ if $(\exists p < q$ s.t. $(y_1, u'_1, y_2, u'_2) = C[p]$ and w s.t. $q = \hat{d}(p, w)$
$\quad\quad$ with $u'_1 \neq v_1$ or $u'_2 \neq v_2)$
$\quad\quad\quad$ RESULT=NO;BREAK;
$\quad q + +;$
}while$(q < $Card$(C));$

Figure 1.45: First Algorithm for deciding whether a function is subsequential.

is subsequential if for each loop $((q, q), u, v, (q, q)) \in \hat{E}_{twin}$, and if $\exists \alpha, \beta$ s.t. $((i, i), \alpha, \beta, (q, q)) \in \hat{E}_{twin}$, if $u, v \neq \epsilon$ there exists some $\gamma \in \Sigma_2^*$ s.t. $(\beta = \alpha \cdot \gamma$ and $\gamma \cdot v = u \cdot \gamma)$ or $(\alpha = \beta \cdot \gamma$ and $\gamma \cdot u = v \cdot \gamma)$. This condition is tested by the algorithm in Figure 1.47. In our example, the paths $((0, 0), keep, ($keep-1, keep-2$), (1, 4))$ and $((1, 4), a, (a, a), (1, 4))$ illustrates a loop that doesn't meet this condition; therefore, the transduction $|T_{keep}|$ is not subsequential.

1.3.9 Minimization

As is the case with deterministic FSAs, deterministic FSTs can achieve space efficiency by means of a minimization algorithm. We refer the reader to Chapter 12 for more details on this kind of algorithm.

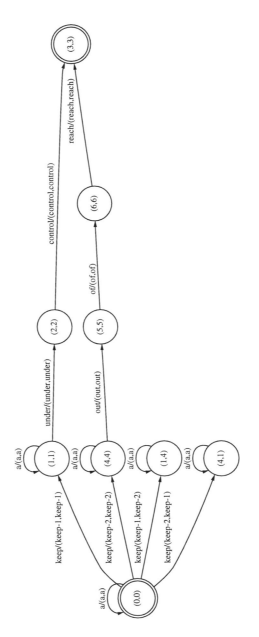

Figure 1.46: Twinning for testing the subsequentiality.

Function **TWINNING**
Input: Unambiguous transducer $T = (\Sigma_1, \Sigma_2, Q, i, F, E)$
Output: boolean RESULT

$Q_2 = \emptyset; i_2 = 0; E_2 = \emptyset; C[0] = (i, i);$
do {
$\quad Q_2 = Q_2 \cup \{q\};$
$\quad (x_1, x_2) = C[q];$
$\quad$ foreach $(x_1, a, w, y_1) \in E$
$\quad\quad$ foreach $(x_2, a, w', y_2) \in E$
$\quad\quad\quad e = \text{addSet}(C, (y_1, y_2));$
$\quad\quad\quad E_2 = E_2 \cup \{(q, (w, w'), e)\};$
$\quad q++;$
} while($q < \text{Card}(C)$);
RESULT=YES;
foreach $q \le |C|$
$\quad$ foreach loop $(q, u_1, (v_1, v_1'), q_1) \ldots (q_{n-1}, u_n, (v_n, v'n), q)$
$\quad$ s.t. $q_i \ne q$ for $i = 1, n-1$
$\quad\quad$ foreach path $(i_2, \alpha_1, (\beta_1, \beta_1'), p_1) \ldots (p_{m-1}, \alpha_m, (\beta_m, \beta_m'), q)$
$\quad\quad$ s.t. $p_i \ne q$ for $i = 1, m-1$
$\quad\quad\quad \alpha = \alpha_1 \cdot \ldots \cdot \alpha_m; \beta = \beta_1 \cdot \ldots \cdot \beta_m; \beta' = \beta_1' \cdot \ldots \cdot \beta_m';$
$\quad\quad\quad u = u_1 \cdot \ldots \cdot u_n; v = v_1 \cdot \ldots \cdot v_n; v' = v_1' \cdot \ldots \cdot v_n';$
$\quad\quad\quad$ if $v \ne \epsilon$ or $v' \ne \epsilon$
$\quad\quad\quad\quad \omega = \beta \wedge \beta';$
$\quad\quad\quad\quad$ if $\omega = \beta$
$\quad\quad\quad\quad\quad \gamma = \omega^{-1} \cdot \beta';$
$\quad\quad\quad\quad\quad$ if $\gamma \cdot v' \ne v \cdot \gamma$
$\quad\quad\quad\quad\quad\quad$ RESULT=NO;BREAK;
$\quad\quad\quad\quad$ else if $\omega = \beta$
$\quad\quad\quad\quad\quad \gamma = \omega^{-1} \cdot \beta;$
$\quad\quad\quad\quad\quad$ if $\gamma \cdot v \ne v' \cdot \gamma$
$\quad\quad\quad\quad\quad\quad$ RESULT=NO;BREAK;
$\quad\quad\quad\quad$ else
$\quad\quad\quad\quad\quad$ RESULT=NO;BREAK;
Return RESULT;

Figure 1.47: Twinning algorithm for deciding whether a function is subsequential.

1.3.10   Determinization and Factorization

We saw in the previous section that the transduction represented by the transducer T_{keep} in Figure 1.42 is not equivalent to any subsequential transducer. We will now show that it is possible to apply this transduction to any given input in a deterministic manner by using a slightly more complex device called a *Bimachine* (Schützenberger, 1961). This device was introduced in part because of the observation that a representation of a transduction by a subsequential transducer privileges one reading direction of the input string, namely that of left to right, even though in general there is no a priori reason to read from left to right.

We will now reconsider the transduction $|T_{keep}|$ and show that although it is not subsequential, it can be represented by a bimachine which is a deterministic device.

Definition 23 *A bimachine B is a 5-tuple $(\Sigma_1, \Sigma_2, A_1, A_2, \delta)$ in which*

- Σ_1 *is the input alphabet*

- Σ_2 *is the output alphabet*

- $A_1 = (\Sigma_1, Q_1, i_1, F_1, d_1)$ *is a deterministic FSA for which $F_1 = \emptyset$*

- $A_2 = (\Sigma_1, Q_2, i_2, F_2, d_2)$ *is a deterministic FSA for which $F_2 = \emptyset$*

- δ *is the emission partial mapping function from $Q_1 \times \Sigma_1 \times Q_2$ into Σ_2^**

As it can be for automata and transducers, the emission function δ can be extended to strings with $\hat{\delta}$ in the following way. $\hat{\delta}$ is the least function such that:

- $\hat{\delta}(q_1, \epsilon, q_2) = \epsilon$ for $q_1 \in Q_1$, $q_2 \in Q_2$,

- if $w \in \Sigma_1^*$, $a \in \Sigma_1$, $q_1 \in Q_1$, $q_2 \in Q_2$ then $\hat{\delta}(q_1, w \cdot a, q_2) = \hat{\delta}(q_1, w, d_2(q_2, a)) \cdot \delta(\hat{d}_1(q_1, w), a, q_2)$ (we assume that if any expression is the empty set then the result is the empty set).

Once this extension is defined, a bimachine B defines a function $|B|$ such that for any w in Σ_1^* $|B|(w) = \hat{\delta}(i_1, w, i_2)$.

We will now construct the bimachine B_{keep} equivalent to T_{keep}, i.e. such that $|B_{keep}| = |T_{keep}|$. We will then show how to compute the output of any given string; how this bimachine is equivalent to the decomposition of two special transducers; and finally, how to build such a device from any transducer representation.

The bimachine $B_{keep} = (\Sigma_1, \Sigma_2, A_{1,keep}, A_{2,keep}, \delta)$ is represented by the automata $A_{1,keep}$ of Figure 1.48 and $A_{2,keep}$ of Figure 1.49 and by the emission function δ.

$\delta(0, a, 0) = a$

$\delta(0, keep, 2) = \text{keep-1}$

$\delta(0, a, 3) = a$

$\delta(0, keep, 6) = \text{keep-2}$

$\delta(1, under, 1) = under$

$\delta(1, a, 2) = a$

$\delta(1, out, 5) = out$

$\delta(1, a, 6) = a$

$\delta(2, control, 0) = control$

$\delta(4, of, 4) = of$

$\delta(5, reach, 0) = reach$

Alternatively, the emission function δ can defined by the matrix in Figure 1.50, for which $\delta(q_1, a, q_2) = w$ if and only if there is a pair (a, w) at row q_1 and column q_2 of the matrix.

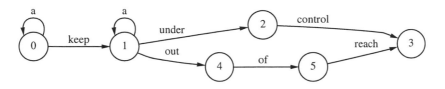

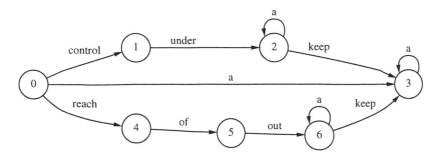

Figure 1.48: Automaton $A_{1,keep}$ of the bimachine B_{keep}.

Figure 1.49: Automaton $A_{2,keep}$ of the bimachine B_{keep}.

Let us now see how the bimachine B_{keep} computes the output of the string

$s = a\ keep\ a\ a\ under\ control$

	0	1	2	3	4	5	6
0	(a,a)		(keep,keep-1)	(a,a)			(keep,keep-2)
1		(under,under)	(a,a)			(out,out)	(a,a)
2	(control,control)						
3							
4					(of,of)		
5	(reach,reach)						

Figure 1.50: Matrix representing the emission function δ of B_{keep}.

One way to derive the output is to compute $\hat{\delta}(0, s, 0)$ from the definition of $\hat{\delta}$.

$$
\begin{aligned}
&\hat{\delta}(0, a \cdot keep \cdot a \cdot a \cdot under \cdot control, 0) \\
&\quad = \hat{\delta}(0, a \cdot keep \cdot a \cdot a \cdot under, \, d_2(0, control)) \\
&\qquad \cdot \delta(\hat{d}_1(0, a \cdot keep \cdot a \cdot a \cdot under), control, 0) \\
&\quad = \hat{\delta}(0, a \cdot keep \cdot a \cdot a \cdot under, 1) \cdot \delta(2, control, 0) \\
&\quad = \hat{\delta}(0, a \cdot keep \cdot a \cdot a \cdot under, 1) \cdot control \\
&\quad = \hat{\delta}(0, a \cdot keep \cdot a \cdot a, d_2(1, under)) \\
&\qquad \cdot \delta(\hat{d}_1(0, a \cdot keep \cdot a \cdot a), under, 1) \cdot control \\
&\quad = \hat{\delta}(0, a \cdot keep \cdot a \cdot a, 2) \cdot \delta(1, under, 1) \cdot control \\
&\quad = \hat{\delta}(0, a \cdot keep \cdot a \cdot a, 2) \cdot under \cdot control \\
&\quad = \hat{\delta}(0, a \cdot keep \cdot a, d_2(2, a)) \\
&\qquad \cdot \delta(\hat{d}_1(0, a \cdot keep \cdot a), a, 2) \cdot under \cdot control \\
&\quad = \hat{\delta}(0, a \cdot keep \cdot a, 2) \cdot \delta(1, a, 2) \cdot under \cdot control \\
&\quad = \hat{\delta}(0, a \cdot keep \cdot a, 2) \cdot a \cdot under \cdot control \\
&\quad = \hat{\delta}(0, a \cdot keep, 2) \cdot a \cdot a \cdot under \cdot control \\
&\quad = \hat{\delta}(0, a, d_2(2, keep)) \delta(\hat{d}_1(0, a), keep, 2) \cdot a \cdot a \cdot under \cdot control \\
&\quad = \hat{\delta}(0, a, 3) \delta(0, keep, 2) a \cdot a \cdot under \cdot control \\
&\quad = \hat{\delta}(0, a, 3) \cdot keep\text{-}1 \cdot a \cdot a \cdot under \cdot control \\
&\quad = a \cdot keep\text{-}1 \cdot a \cdot a \cdot under \cdot control
\end{aligned}
$$

This last line translates into:

$$
|B|(s) = \hat{\delta}(0, s, 0) = a \cdot keep\text{-}1 \cdot a \cdot a \cdot under \cdot control
$$

There is, however, a more effective process for computing the output of a given string. It works in two steps; first, automaton A_1 processes the string while retaining the sequence of states visited; then, A_2 processes the input string backward. The current state of A_2 together with information about the states stored from the first pass make it possible to arrive at the correct output symbol in the matrix representing δ.

Let us illustrate this method on the same input string, namely

$s = $ "a keep a a under control"

Given this input, the only path through A_1 is the sequence of states 0011123. We then read the input string backward through A_2. The first symbol is therefore *control*, while the current state of A_2 is the initial state 0. Since the state q_1 of A_1 stored during the first pass is 2, we go to row 2, column 0 of the matrix with the string *control* as input. The matrix gives us as output the symbol *control*. Taken as input, the symbol *control* moves us to state 1 of A_2 and, at this point, the current symbol is *under* while the state of A_1 is 1. We then find row 1, column 1 of the matrix with the word *under* as input and find as output the symbol *under*. The next two symbols, namely *a* and *a*, are processed the same way, and they both produce the letter *a* as output. The next input symbol is *keep*, whilte the current state of A_2 is 2 and the corresponding state of A_1 is 0; findind row 0, column 1 in the matrix with *keep* as input shows that the output symbol is, without ambiguities, *keep-1*. The last input symbol *a* is processed in the same way to produce the output *a*. Finally, each output is concatenated into a string, which we reverse, to produce the final output string, namely

a keep-1 a a under control.

which is the expected result.

The process just illustrated is equivalent to applying two subsequential transducers successively. If we consider the same example, the first pass is equivalent to applying the subsequential transducer $\tau_{left,keep}$ found in Figure 1.51. This transducer is simply the automaton A_1 with output labels. For each transition of the automaton starting from state q and labeled with the word w, the corresponding transition in the transducer has w as input label and (w, q) as output label. Therefore, applying the transducer $\tau_{left,keep}$ consists in marking each label of the input string with the state reached in the automaton. For instance, the output of *a keep a a under control* is the sequence *(a,0) (keep,0) (a,1) (a,1) (under,1) (control,2)*.

Similarly, performing the second pass of the bimachine is equivalent to applying a second transducer, $\tau_{right,keep}$ found in Figure 1.52, to the reversed output of the previous transducer. Hence, the sequence (control,2) (under,1) (a,1) (a,1) (keep,0) (a,0) is processed through $\tau_{right,keep}$ to produce the output *control under a a keep-1 a*, which is also reversed in the final bimachine output to become *a keep-1 a a under control.*

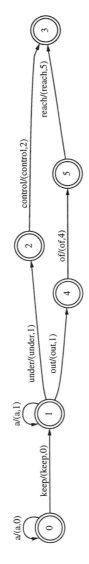

Figure 1.51: Sequential transducer $\tau_{left,keep}$ equivalent to the first pass of the bimachine B_{keep}.

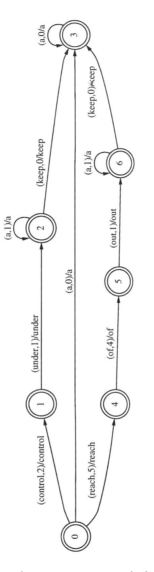

Figure 1.52: Sequential transducer $\tau_{right,keep}$ equivalent to the second pass of the bimachine B_{keep}.

The algorithm of Figure 1.53 gives us an explicit process for transforming a bimachine into a right sequential transducer and a left sequential transducer.

Function **BiTransform**
Input: $B = (A_1, A_2, \delta)$
      in which $A_1 = (\Sigma_1, Q_1, i_1, F_1, d_1)$, $A_2 = (\Sigma_1, Q_2, i_2, F_2, d_2)$
Output: $T_1 = (\Sigma_1, (\Sigma_1 \times Q_1), Q_1, i_1, \otimes_1, *_1)$
          $T_2 = ((\Sigma_1 \times Q_1), \Sigma_2, Q_2, i_2, \otimes_2, *_2)$,

    foreach $q_1 \in Q_1$ and $a \in \Sigma_1$ s.t. $d_1(q_1, a) \neq \emptyset$
        $q_1 \otimes_1 q = q_2$;
        $q_1 *_1 a = (q_1, a)$;
    foreach $a \in \Sigma_1$, $q_1 \in Q_1$, $q_2 \in Q_2$ s.t. $\delta(q_1, a, q_2) \neq \emptyset$
        $q_2 \otimes_2 (a, q_1) = d_2(q_2, a)$
        $q_2 *_2 (a, q_1) = \delta(q_1, a, q_2)$
    Return T_1, T_2;

Figure 1.53: Transforming a Bimachine into a left and right sequential transducer.

So far, we have shown how to process an input string through a bimachine and how to transform a bimachine into two transducers. The obvious and remaining question is: how did we build the bimachine in the first place? We now assume that we have a transduction represented by a transducer, and that we would like to represent it as a bimachine. We have just shown that a bimachine is equivalent to the composition of two sequential machines. This implies in particular that any transduction represented by a bimachine is functional; therefore, before we can build a bimachine from the transducer we must determine whether the transduction is functional. This condition moreover is sufficient, i.e., if the transduction is functional we can build a bimachine that represents it. We determine the functionality of the transduction, as described in section 1.3.6, by building an unambiguous transducer. Taking T_{keep} as example, this leads to the construction of the function in Figure 1.43 which in this case is equivalent to the initial transducer. The resulting unambiguous transducer has with be compared to the initial one to decide whether the transduction is functional; this is achieved by means of the algorithm in Figure 1.32 (Section 1.3.6). Once this is done, the unambiguous transducer can be transformed into a bimachine through the algorithm of Figure 1.54. This algorithm is very simple. If A is the automaton representing the domain of T obtained by removing the output labels, then A_1 is the determinization of A from left to right and A_2 is the determinization of A from right to left. The emission function is defined such that if (q_1, a, w, q') is a transition of T such that q_1 is in a subset S_1 of A_1 and q_2 is in a subset S_2 of A_2, then $\delta(S_1, a, S_2) = w$.

1.4 Bibliographical Notes

The theoretical aspects of FSAs and FSTs have been extensively studied and documented by, among many others, Eilenberg (1974), (1976), Berstel (1979), Perrin (1990), Salomaa and Soittola (1978) and Salomaa (1973).

Perrin (1990) includes a discussion on arithmetic automata and transducers, relied on heavily in this introduction.

Roche (1992) provides more details on the use of negative constraints grammar.

The discussion in Section 1.3.4 was inspired by the work of Karttunen, Kaplan, and Zaenen (1992) and Kaplan and Kay (1994).

The main result of Section 1.3.5 is due to Schützenberger (1976). The proof that functions can be represented by unambiguous transducers is due to Eilenberg (1974). We have taken here an algorithmic approach that builds on the already constructive proof of Eilenberg. The first proof of the decidability of the functionality of transducers can be found in Schützenberger (1976). Blattner and Head (1977) also give a proof of the same property, and conclude that it is difficult to find a more effective proof, such as the one available for the decidability of sequentiality. We have here developed an algorithmic view, providing an algorithm that is practical in non-trivial cases.

The determinization of FSTs is described by Mohri (1994b) and in Chapter 7 of this book. The minimization of FSTs is described by Reutenauer (1991) and Mohri (1994a).

The notion of bimachine is attributable to Schützenberger (1961). A proof of the decidability of the sequentiality of FSTs is found in Choffrut (1977).

References

Berstel, Jean. 1979. *Transductions and Context-Free Languages*. Teubner, Stuttgart.

Blattner, Merra and Tom Head. 1977. Single-valued a-transducers. *Journal of Computer and System Sciences*, 15:310–327.

Choffrut, Christian. 1977. Une caractérisation des fonctions séquentielles et des fonctions sous-séquentielles en tant que relations rationnelles. *Theoretical Computer Science*, 5:325–338.

Eilenberg, Samuel. 1974. *Automata, languages, and machines, Volume A.* Academic Press, New York.

Eilenberg, Samuel. 1976. *Automata, languages, and machines, Volume B.* Academic Press, New York.

Hopcroft, John E. 1971. An $n \log n$ algorithm for minimizing the states in a finite automaton. In Z. Kohavi, editor, *The Theory of Machines and Computations.* Academic Press, pages 189–196.

Kaplan, Ronald M. and Martin Kay. 1994. Regular models of phonological rule systems. *Computational Linguistics*, 20(3):331–378.

Karttunen, Lauri, Ronald M. Kaplan, and Annie Zaenen. 1992. Two-level morphology with composition. In *Proceedings of the 14th International Conference on Computational Linguistics (COLING'92).*

Kleene, Stephen C. 1956. Representation of events in nerve nets and finite automata. In *C.E. Shannon and J.McCarthy, editors, Automata Studies.* Princeton University Press.

Mohri, Mehryar. 1994a. Minimisation of sequential transducers. In *Lecture Notes in Computer Science, Proceedings of the Conference on Computational Pattern Matching 1994.* Springer-Verlag.

Mohri, Mehryar. 1994b. On some applications of finite-state automata theory to natural language processing.

Perrin, Dominique. 1990. Finite automata. *Handbook of Theoretical Computer Science*, pages 2–56.

Reutenauer, Christophe. 1991. Subsequential functions: characterizations, minimization, examples. In *Proceedings of Internantional Meeting of Young Computer Scientists, Lecture Notes in Computer Science.*

Roche, Emmanuel. 1992. Text disambiguation by finite-state automata: an algorithm and experiments on corpora. In *COLING-92. Proceedings of the Conference, Nantes.*

Salomaa, Arto and Matti Soittola. 1978. *Automata-Theoretic Aspects of Formal Power Series.* Springer-Verlag, Texts and Monographs in Computer Science.

Salomaa, A. 1973. *Formal Languages.* Academic Press, New York, NY.

Schützenberger, Marcel Paul. 1961. A remark on finite transducers. *Information and Control*, 4:185–187.

Schŭtzenberger, Marcel Paul. 1976. Sur les relations rationnelles entre monoïdes libres. *Theoretical Computer Science*, 3:243–259.

Schŭtzenberger, Marcel Paul. 1977. Sur une variante des fonctions sequentielles. *Theoretical Computer Science*, 4:47–57.

Function **BuildBiMachine**
Input: $T = (\Sigma_1, \Sigma_2, Q, i, F, E)$ with T unambiguous
Output: $B = (A_1 = (\Sigma_1, Q_{A_1}, i_{A_1}, F_{A_1}, d_{A_1})$
            $A_2 = (\Sigma_2, Q_{A_2}, i_{A_2}, F_{A_2}, d_{A_2}), \delta)$

Step 1. Compute A_1:
$Q_{A_1} = \emptyset; q = 0; i_{A_1} = 0; F_{A_1} = \emptyset; C_1[0] = \{i\};$
do {
    $Q_{A_1} = Q_{A_1} \cup \{q\};$
    $S = C_1[q];$
    foreach $a \in \Sigma_1$ s.t. $\exists q' \in S$ and $(q', a, w, q'') \in E$
        $S' = \emptyset;$
        foreach $(q', a, w, q'') \in E$ s.t. $q' \in S$, $w \in \Sigma_2^*$ and $q'' \in Q$
            $S' = S' \cup \{q''\};$
        $e = $addSet$(C_1, S');$
        $d_{A_1}(q, a) = e;$
    $q + +;$
}while$(q < $Card$(C));$
Step 2. Compute A_2:
$Q_{A_2} = \emptyset; q = 0; i_{A_2} = 0; F_{A_2} = \emptyset; C_2[0] = \{i\};$
do {
    $Q_{A_2} = Q_{A_2} \cup \{q\};$
    $S = C_2[q];$
    foreach $a \in \Sigma_1$ s.t. $\exists q' \in S$ and $(q'', a, w, q') \in E$
        $S' = \emptyset;$
        foreach $(q'', a, w, q') \in E$ s.t. $q' \in S$, $w \in \Sigma_2^*$ and $q'' \in Q$
            $S' = S' \cup \{q''\};$
        $e = $addSet$(C_2, S');$
        $d_{A_2}(q, a) = e;$
    $q + +;$
}while$(q < $Card$(C));$
Step 3. Compute δ:
foreach $q_1 \in Q_{A_1}, q_2 \in Q_{A_2}, a \in \Sigma_1$
    $\delta(q_1, a, q_2) = \emptyset;$
foreach $q_1 \in Q_{A_1}, q_2 \in Q_{A_2}, a \in \Sigma_1$
    if $\exists q \in C_1[q_1], q' \in C_2[q_2]$ and $(q, a, w, q') \in E$
        $\delta(q_1, a, q_2) = w;$
Return B

Figure 1.54: Algorithm for building a bimachine from an unambiguous representation.

2 Finite-State Morphology: Inflections and Derivations in a Single Framework Using Dictionaries and Rules

David Clemenceau

2.1 Introduction

Dictionary completeness is a fundamental issue when analyzing large corpora. When a word encountered in a text cannot be found in an electronic lexicon, the analysis of the sentence is highly compromised. We present in this paper a morpho-syntactic framework aiming at the enhancement of electronic dictionaries by providing the recognition and the analysis of derivatives in texts.

It has been shown by (Courtois and Laporte, 1991) that, when a simple word appearing in a text is not found in the dictionary of simple inflected words DICOF[1], it is often a derived word. The reason for that phenomenon is that derived forms of simple words are often missing in dictionaries. If one looks in DICOS for the derived forms of the verb *activer* (*to activate*), it appears that *activable, activabilité, suractivation* and *suractivable* have not been entered. This situation reflects the content of paper dictionaries: they do not mention words derived according to general and productive derivation rules. But in an electronic dictionary these holes are a great handicap for text analysis, since derivatives occur frequently in texts, especially in newspapers and technical texts; an example is:

---

[1]DICOF is an electronic dictionary of inflected forms made at the LADL. It contains about 700,000 entries and is automatically generated from DICOS, the dictionary of simple forms, which contains about 80,000 entries in their canonical form. (Courtois, 1990)

> *La* **décontextualisation** *est* **injustifiable** *du point de vue géopolitique.*[2]

In traditional derivational morphology such phenomena are treated at word level by means of word-formation rules, either morphological as in (Koskenniemi, 1983) or morphological and semantic as in (Corbin, 1984). As we will see, this approach does not account for many restrictions and interpretations. In contrast, we propose an approach aiming at a fine description of the derivational paradigm of the 12,000 entries of the LADL lexicon-grammar of French verbs[3] (Clemenceau, 1992b; Clemenceau, 1992c). In order to describe these paradigms, we used syntactic definitions of derivational operators, based on Harrisian transformations as in:

(1) *Le verrouillage active l'alarme.* (N_0 V N_1)

The locking mechanism activates the alarm.

(2) *L'alarme active le verrouillage.* (N_1 V N_0)

The alarm activates the locking mechanism.

(3) *Le verrouillage et l'alarme s'entre-activent.* (N_0 et N_1 s'entre-V)

The locking mechanism and the alarm interactivate.

Using this syntactic approach, we defined a tree-based representation of derivational paradigms. Besides a significant enrichment of the dictionary of simple forms DICOS, this study led to the design of a new dictionary of simple forms, that we will call SDICOS for Structured DICOS, which contains syntactic links between the words deriving from the same entry of the lexicon. A new version of the dictionary of inflected forms, DICOF, was generated from DICOS, enriched with these derivatives, and compiled into a finite-state transducer. Moreover, SDICOS was also compiled into a transducer. We thus present an efficient tool that first, recognizes derivatives in texts, and then, provides syntactic information for these derivatives by giving the syntactic transformations that link them to their root verb described in the lexicon-grammar.

However, the complete syntactic description of 12,000 verbs has complex implications for the morphological processes. Taking fully advantage of this

---

[2] *"Decontextualization is unjustifiable from a geopolitical point of view."* Edgar Morin, Le Monde, 91/01/16.

[3] The lexicon-grammar of verbs can be seen as a matrix of 12,000 rows (the verb entries) and 300 columns (the syntactic properties). For each entry a "+" or a "-" in each column indicates whether it satisfies the associated syntactic property. Moreover, a sub-categorization of entries into tables, according to their main construction, has been designed (Gross, 1968; Gross, 1975; Boons, Guillet, and Leclère, 1976a; Boons, Guillet, and Leclère, 1976b)).

information will take some time[4]. Moreover, the description of the derivational behavior of nouns and adjectives must also be done. Thus, we designed a morphological analyzer, called MORPHO, which is a finite-state transducer merging DICOF and a two-level system (Koskenniemi, 1983; Koskenniemi, 1984) for new derivatives recognition.

At the end of this paper, we present a single framework, made of MORPHO and SDICOS, which recognizes derivatives in texts and provides full syntactic information when dealing with SDICOS entries, and partial otherwise.

2.2 Towards a Structured Dictionary

2.2.1 Syntactic approach to derivational morphology

The possibilities of derivation of a given word are closely linked with its syntactic properties. The verb *coller*, for example, has different meanings, which enter, among others, the three different constructions:

(4) *Max colle l'affiche (au+sur le) mur.*

Max sticks the poster on the wall.

(5) *Max colle Marie.*

Max clings to Marie.

(6) *Ce résultat colle avec mes prévisions.*

This result fits my prediction.

but the prefix *dé-* can be applied to the first use of the verb only:

(7) *Max décolle l'affiche du mur.*

Max unsticks the poster from the wall.

(8) **Max décolle Marie.*

*Max unclings Marie.

(9) **Ce résultat décolle de mes prévisions.*

*This result unfits my prediction.

These three different uses of the verb *coller* correspond to three separate entries in the lexicon-grammar of verbs. Because of the fine separation of verb uses that has been made in the lexicon-grammar, and since the syntactic

---

[4]At the present time, we have tested our method of describing derivational paradigms on the entries of four tables of the lexicon-grammar only.

properties of a verb select its derivational possibilities, we were led to study the derivational behavior of each entry of the lexicon-grammar of verbs.

Another argument for the use of the lexicon-grammar as the basis of our study is the correlation between the membership of a table and the derivational properties of a verb. Table 38LD, for instance, to which *coller* (4) belongs, and whose definition is the construction: N_0 V N_1 Loc N_2, where *Loc* is a preposition of place and N_2 a locative phrase interpreted as the **destination** of the process, contains many verbs that accept the prefix *dé-*, other tables do not contain any verb accepting it.

The use of the lexicon-grammar also allowed us to observe regularities in the syntactic and semantic modifications brought by the application of a derivational process to a verb. In the case of table 38LD, for example, the prefix *dé-* always generates verbs which belong to table 38LS, also defined by N_0 V N_1 Loc N_2, but where the locative N_2 is interpreted as the **source** of the process:

> (10) *Max charge les colis sur le camion.*
>
> *Max loads the parcels onto the truck.*
>
> (11) *Max décharge les colis du camion.*
>
> *Max unloads the parcels from the truck.*
>
> (12) *Max a programmé ce numéro dans son spectacle.*
>
> *Max programmed this act in his show.*
>
> (13) *Max a déprogrammé ce numéro de son spectacle.*
>
> *Max unprogrammed this act from his show.*

The scope of this study is the regular and productive derivational phenomena. Thus, we kept only the derivatives which satisfy the following two criteria:

- forms that result from a productive derivational process;

- forms that are understandable in the general language.

The first criterion led us to set aside words built with scientific affixes like *iono-, médullo-,* . . . [5]. The second one led us to reject words such as *surcollage* whose construction follows productive rules but which can be only linked to a technical use of the base form, here the oenological use of *coller*[6].

---

[5] The prefix *iono-* is based on the noun *ion* (*ion*) that can be found in derivatives like *ionosphère* (*ionosphere*) which is a very ionized part of the *atmosphere*. As for *medullo-*, it comes from the noun *moelle* (*marrow*, or the technical term *medulla*), and is mainly used in medical terms.

[6] We then deal with a separate entry, corresponding to a technical use of the verb coller: adding a substance to a wine in order to extract the floating particles.

Defining derivational operators (i.e. affixes) by their spelling presents two kinds of drawbacks:

- one could separate a unique derivational operator into several affixes, according to morphonological variants, as in the case of the prefix *dé-* which is written *dés-* before a vowel;

- one could merge two syntactically different affixes because they share the same spelling. The prefix *co-*, for instance, corresponds to two constructions by symmetries that are syntactically different:

    – symmetry of subjects:

    > (14) *L'acide active la réaction.* (N_0 V N_1)
    > *The acid activates the reaction.*
    > (15) *L'acide coactive la réaction avec le catalyseur.* (N_0 $co-$ V N_1 *avec* N_0')
    > *The acid coactivates the reaction with the catalyst.*
    > (16) *L'acide et le catalyseur coactivent la réaction.* (N_0 *et* N_0' $co-$ V N_1)
    > *The acid and the catalyst coactivate the reaction.*

    – symmetry of objects:

    > (17) *Max a activé l'alarme.* (N_0 V N_1)
    > *Max activated the alarm.*
    > (18) Max a coactivé l'alarme avec le verrouillage.
    > (N_0 co-V N_1 avec N_1')
    > *Max coactivated the alarm with the locking mechanism.*
    > (19) *Max a coactivé l'alarme et le verrouillage.*
    > (N_0 co-V N_1 et N_1')
    > *Max coactivated the alarm and the locking mechanism.*

Since *coactiver* has two sets of syntactic and derivational properties, we had to distinguish two verbs. This representation was reached by defining syntactic derivational operators using a transformational approach that establishes a relationship among a set (usually a pair) of sentences. We distinguished four kinds of relationship:

- Harrisian transformations as in the case of the two operators corresponding to the prefix *co-*;

- transformations involving support verbs as in the example of nominalization below (Giry-Schneider, 1978):

(20) *Max a collé l'affiche (au+sur le) mur.* $(N_0 \ V \ N_1 \ \text{Loc} \ N_2)$

Max stuck the poster on the wall.

(21) *Max a fait le collage de l'affiche (au+sur le) mur.* $(N_0 \ V_{sup}$
$V - n \ \text{de} \ N_1 \ \text{Loc} \ N_2)$

Max did the sticking of the poster on the wall.

- substitutions of an adverbial phrase by a prefix as in:

  (22) *Le Japon moderne est trop américanisé.*

  Modern Japan is too much americanized.

  (23) *Le Japon moderne est suraméricanisé.*

  Modern Japan is overamericanized.

- semantic relations as for the prefix *dé-* which expresses the symmetric process of the one expressed by the base verb:

  (24) *Max a activé l'alarme.*

  Max made the alarm active.

  (25) *Max a désactivé l'alarme.*

  Max made the alarm inactive.

We give in Table 2.1 the prefixal operators that we studied. As for suffixal operators, we took into account nominalizations and verbal adjectives.

In order to encode the derivational paradigm of each verb, we followed an approach similar to the one that has been used in the process of building the lexicon-grammar of verbs: transformational at first, defining the set of transformations relevant to each table, which can be seen as a maximal derivational paradigm; and then, lexicalist, encoding the restrictions attached to each entry of the lexicon-grammar, since two different entries have never the same set of properties.

2.2.2   A tree representation of derivational paradigms

The representation of derivational paradigms by tree structures is a widely shared technique, but it raises various problems. A first question deals with the nature of the links used in the tree structure. Two possibilities arise: linking complex derivatives, i.e. words containing several prefixes and/or suffixes, through a unique path to their base word, or else using links that correspond to a single derivational operator. We have chosen the second possibility which seems more relevant from a linguistic point of view. For a derivative such as *décollable* in:

	OPERATOR	**EXAMPLE**
C	*co-* (symmetry of subjects)	*IBM et MICROSOFT ont codéveloppé OS/2.* *IBM and Microsoft have codeveloped OS/2.*
O	*co-* (symmetry of objects)	*L'alarme et le verrouillage sont toujours coactivés.* *The alarm and the locking mechanism are always coactivated.*
E	*entre-*	*Max et Luc s'entraident.* *Max and Luc help each other.*
A	*auto-*	*Ce moteur s'autorégule.* *This engine is self-regulating.*
S	*sur-*	*Le catalyseur suractive la réaction.* *The catalyst (over + super) activates the reaction.*
s	*sous-*	*Max a sous-activé le réacteur.* *Max underactivated the reactor.*
R	*re-*	*Max a recollé l'affiche sur le mur.* *Max restuck the poster on the wall.*
I	*in-*	*L'alarme est restée inactivée.* *The alarm staid unactivated.*
D	*dés-*	*Max a décollé l'affiche du mur.* *Max unstuck the poster from the wall.*

Table 2.1: Prefixal operators

(26) *Cette affiche est décollable.*

This poster is unstickable. (= can be unstuck)

the "global link" representation would have proposed the base sentence:

(27) *Max colle cette affiche (au+sur le) mur.*

Max sticks this poster on the wall.

even though the transformational relationship between (26) and (27) is not clear. On the contrary, the representation we chose links *décollable* to the verb *décoller* through the productive derivational transformation V-able that can be expressed by the sentences below (Leeman, 1988):

N_0 *V* N_1 *Loc* N_2
N_1 *ÊTRE Vpp Loc* N_2 *par* N_0
N_1 *POUVOIR ÊTRE Vpp Loc* N_2 (ϵ + *par* N_0)
N_1 *ÊTRE V-able Loc* N_2 (ϵ + *par* N_0)

(28) *Max décolle cette affiche du mur.*

Max unsticks this poster from the wall.

(29) *Cette affiche est décollée du mur par Max.*

This poster is unstuck from the wall by Max.

(30) *Cette affiche peut être décollée du mur (ϵ + par Max).*

This poster can be unstuck from the wall (ϵ + by Max).

(31) *Cette affiche est décollable du mur (ϵ + par Max).*

This poster is unstickable from the wall (ϵ + by Max).

As a consequence of this choice, each branch of our derivational trees corresponds to a unique derivational operator[7], as can be seen in the figure below which shows the first three levels of the derivational tree of the verb *coller* in sentence (4). As for the leaves, they contain either a word or a regular expression when orthographic variants exist.

This choice of the "relative link" representation implies splitting up complex derivational processes into sequences of single operators. Derivational processes corresponding to prefixes only, or suffixes only, are easily analyzable in an intuitive way, but the situation is not so clear for derivatives containing a prefix and a suffix. We found four possibilities in these cases, whether none, one or both of the two derivatives corresponding to the addition of the prefix only and the suffix only exist. A derivative like *incollable* (*unstickable*) is easily linkable with the verb *coller*, through the adjective *collable*, since the verb *incoller* does not exist:

(32) *Cette affiche est collable.*

This poster is stickable.

(33) **Max a incollé l'affiche.*

*Max unstuck the poster. (= did not stick).

On the other hand, parasynthetic derivatives, like *invincible* , cannot be decomposed because none of the partially derived words exist:

(34) **Cette armée est vincible.*

This army is defeatable.

(35) **Nous avons invaincu cette armée.*

*We undefeated this army.

---

[7] As a result of our syntactic definition of derivational operators, a word like *strangulation* is linked by the single operator V-n to the verb *étrangler* (*to strangle*) even though this derivational process involves both a prefixal and a suffixal morphological modification.

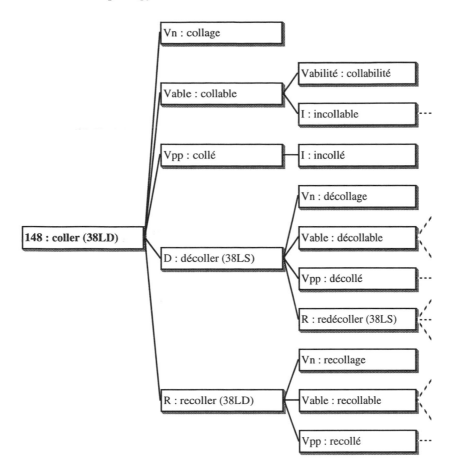

Figure 2.1: The first three levels of the derivational tree of *coller* (38LD)

In such cases, we had to define branches that are the combination of two derivational operators, here V-able and the prefixal operator *I*.

When the word with the prefix only and the word with the suffix only both exist, two possibilities arise:

- one of the links is not relevant from a linguistic point of view: *décollable*, for instance, could derive from the verb *décoller* or from the adjective collable, but since the prefix *dé-* only applies to verbs the second possibility is not relevant.

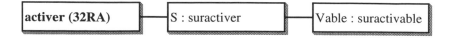

Figure 2.2: The derivational tree of *suractivable*

- both links are relevant. These derivatives are sometimes slightly ambiguous. The word *suractivable*, for instance, can be considered as ambiguous on the basis of the two possible analyses:

(36) *Ce réacteur peut être suractivé.*

This reactor can be superactivated.

(37) *Ce réacteur est très facilement activable.*

This reactor is very easily activatable. (or activable?)

For other words, like *suractivé*, the presence of two analyses do not correspond to any semantic ambiguity. In all cases, we have chosen to put the prefixes in factor, which corresponds for suractivable to the analysis of (36) which can be represented by the tree of Figure 2.2.

2.2.3 Building the derivational trees

The building process of our derivational trees can be split up in two stages: first, we generated automatically a tree for each entry of a given table of the lexicon-grammar, and then we encoded the various restrictions corresponding to each entry specificities[8]. The generation process is based on two types of data:

- derivational tree, called maximum tree, which corresponds to all the derivational phenomena that can be observed for a given table;

- table where we recorded the nominalizations of each entry, since this kind of derivation is unpredictable on both syntactic and morphological points of view. For instance, the verb *blanchir* of table 32RA accepts two nominalizations depending on the kind of complement it takes:

(38) *Cette usine blanchit du sucre.*

This factory refines sugar.

(39) *Max blanchit le mur.*

---

[8]We present here a brief description of these operations, for a more detailed description see (Clemenceau, 1993).

Max whitewashes the wall.

(38) [Vn] = (40) *Cette usine fait le blanchissage du sucre.*

This factory makes the refining of sugar.

(39) [Vn] = (41) *Max fait le blanchiment du mur.*

Max makes the whitewashing of the wall.

The generation stage consists in building for each entry of the lexicon-grammar table the surface forms of the derivatives that appear in the maximum tree of the table. For nominalizations, it uses the tables where we recorded the nominalizations of each entry, whereas for the other derivational operators it uses a set of morphological rules expressed in the two-level formalism described in (Koskenniemi, 1983)[9].

Once these trees were built, we had to encode manually the several restrictions that appeared either at the syntactic, morphological or even pragmatic level as in:

(42) *Max a renversé du vin sur son pantalon.*

Max spilled some wine on his trousers.

(42) [D] = (43) **Max a dérenversé du vin de son pantalon.*

*Max unspilled some wine from his trousers.

2.2.4 Recognition and generation of derived forms with finite-state transducers

2.2.4.1 Introduction

We describe in this chapter the modifications that our study of the derivational behavior of lexicon-grammar entries brought to LADL dictionaries. This study led to an enhancement of LADL dictionaries on two points:

- An enrichment of both DICOS and DICOF, since the description of 5% of the lexicon-grammar led to the doubling of the size of these dictionaries;

- A lexicon structuration that enhances the morphological stage of the syntactic analysis of texts.

In order to describe these morphological tools which provide inflectional and derivational analyses as shown in Figure 2.3, we first present the DICOF transducer and the modifications brought by our study to this transducer, and then, SDICOS which is the transducer that provides the information of our derivational trees when a derivative is encountered in a text.

---

[9]This morphological tool is quite similar, though simpler, to the two-level tool described at the end of this article.

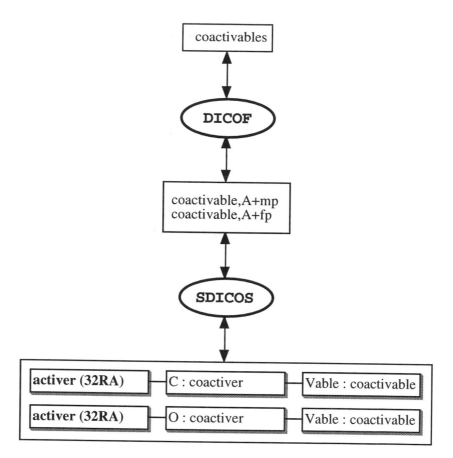

Figure 2.3: The analysis of an inflected derivative.

2.2.4.2   The DICOF transducer

The DICOF transducer establishes the relationship between an inflected word, i.e. a DICOF entry, and its canonical form, i.e. a DICOS entry. Therefore, it can be seen as the implementation of a lexicon containing couples made of an inflected word and its lexical form, i.e. its canonical form followed by its category and its inflection code (Roche, 1993), as in the examples below:

inculperont	$\longleftrightarrow$	*inculper,V+F3p*
aimeront	$\longleftrightarrow$	*aimer,V+F3p*
chevaux	$\longleftrightarrow$	*cheval,N+mp*
carnavals	$\longleftrightarrow$	*carnaval,N+mp*
pommes	$\longleftrightarrow$	*pomme,N+fp*
pommes	$\longleftrightarrow$	*pommer,V+P2s*
pommes	$\longleftrightarrow$	*pommer,V+S2s*

This transducer, a sample of which is given in Figure 2.4 [10], can generate or recognize the 700,000 entries of DICOF. It takes 948 Ko in memory and analyzes 1,100 words per second[11].

Our description of the derivational paradigms of lexicon-grammar entries led to the doubling of both dictionaries DICOS and DICOF. The comparison presented in the table below between the DICOF transducer before and after this derivational study shows that its size is almost unchanged (7% increase) and that the speed of the look-up procedure is the same. The reason of these good results can be found in the association of the two following phenomena:

- the DICOF transducer is small and effective because it takes into account the regularities of DICOF entries;

- the new entries of DICOF that are generated by our study led to an increase of these regularities.

	NUMBER OF ENTRIES	SIZE (Ko)	SPEED (words/second)
DICOF TRANSDUCER	612,848	948	1,100
NEW DICOF TRANSDUCER	1,301,976	1,014	1,100

2.2.4.3 SDICOS, the structured DICOS transducer

Our tree structuring of derivational paradigms brings a first level of lexicon structuration: one can look for all the derived words of a given entry of the lexicon-grammar. But this formalism is not convenient for text analysis since a derivative found in a text can hardly be linked with the root of its derivational tree. In fact, we need a formalism that, given a derivative, allows us to retrieve the tree(s) that contain it and provides the explicit link between this word and

---

[10]Terminal states are represented by black dots.

[11]These figures were observed on a NeXT computer.

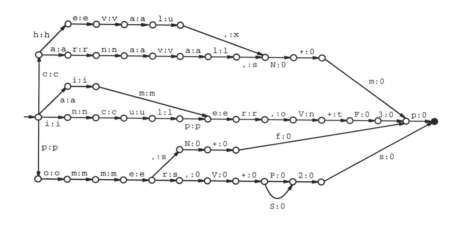

Figure 2.4: A sample of the DICOF transducer

the root of each of these trees (i.e. the path that links the derivative to the root of the tree through other derivatives). To fulfill this requirement, we built a transducer called SDICOS that associates surface forms, i.e. canonical forms of derivatives along with their category, and lexical forms that provide all the information contained in our derivational trees. Thus, the two derivatives *coactivable* and *incoactivable* are encoded with the following associations:

$$
\begin{array}{lcl}
\textit{C1+activer+Vable.32RA/5} & \longleftrightarrow & \textit{coactivable,A} \\
\textit{I3+C1+activer+Vable.32RA/5} & \longleftrightarrow & \textit{incoactivable,A} \\
\textit{O1+activer+Vable.32RA/5} & \longleftrightarrow & \textit{coactivable,A} \\
\textit{I3+O1+activer+Vable.32RA/5} & \longleftrightarrow & \textit{incoactivable,A}
\end{array}
$$

where the indexation of the derivational operators involved leads, with the help

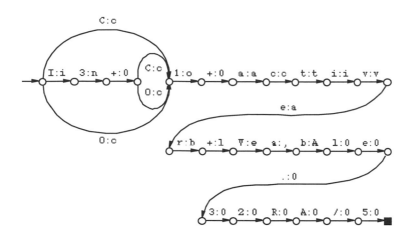

Figure 2.5: SDICOS, the Structured DICOS transducer

of a post-processing stage, to the four trees, corresponding to *coactivable* and *incoactivable*.

In order to build SDICOS, we tested several encodings of these associations and we noticed that an increase in terms of compressing performance led to a decrease of the look-up procedure speed. We chose an average solution which corresponds to the following encoding:

$$I3+C1+32RA.activer/5+Vable \quad \longleftrightarrow \quad inco0000000activable,A$$

where *0* is the null symbol.

This encoding which corresponds to the transducer of Figure 2.5 led to a representation of the 99,460 derivatives that our study already covers which takes 97 Ko in memory and analyzes, or generates, 519 words per second, post-processing included.

2.3 MORPHO: a Morphological Analyzer Based on a Dictionary and a Two-Level System

2.3.1 Aims

The framework made of the DICOF and SDICOS transducers provides the recognition (resp. generation) of derivatives along with a rich syntactic analysis. However, building the derivational paradigm of the 12,000 verb entries of the lexicon-grammar will take some time. Moreover, the description of the derivational behavior of nouns and adjectives must also be done. Concrete nouns, for example, are frequently used for derivatives generation, as in *débureautisation* (?*desofficization* or ?*decomputerization*) that we encountered in a corpus analysis experiment described in (Clemenceau, 1992a), or in:

> *On se gausse de son positivisme forcené (. . .) et de sa* **feuilletonisation** *du news.*[12]

In order to design a tool that tags the words of a text, avoiding, as much as possible, "lexical holes" that jeopardize the full analysis of texts, we decided to build a finite-state transducer that will contain the dictionary of inflected forms, DICOF, along with a rule-based heuristic system for unknown derivatives recognition. This tool recognizes, and generates, three kinds of words:

- DICOF entries as *inculperont* (the third person of plural in the future indicative tense of *to charge*) or *inculpables* (the plural form of the adjective *chargeable*) in the same way as the DICOF transducer that we just described does;

- derivatives that are not DICOF entries, but which are made of a DICOF entry with one or more prefixes as *coïnculperont* or *co-inculperont*, and *coïnculpables* or *co-inculpables*[13];

- derivatives that are not DICOF entries, made of a DICOS entry with one or more derivational suffixes (and eventually prefixes). The inflectional behavior of such words cannot be processed by DICOF and should be dealt with by the heuristic part of our tool.

Moreover, this tool should comply to the two following criteria in order to supply reliable analyses of inflected words:

- DICOF entries and derivatives made of a DICOF entry with one or more prefixes, i.e. the first two categories recognized by our tool, should not be affected by the heuristic processing of inflections, since their inflectional behavior is actually recorded in DICOF and, furthermore, the rule-based system that we designed handles only the inflectional behavior of words ending with one of the derivational suffixes that we took into account[14];

---

[12]"*Its frenzied positivism (. . .) and its serialization of news are derided.*" Frédéric Filloux, *Libération*, 92/09/26.

[13]These words do not appear in usual French dictionaries, however the adjective *coïnculpé* which means *co-defendant* does appear.

[14]It was shown in (Clemenceau, 1993) that describing the inflectional behavior of all DICOS entries by means of rules would lead to the DICOF transducer in a much more complex way than the description made at LADL, especially with regards to updates.

- a clear distinction should be done between the analyses resulting of the DICOF transducer look-up procedure and those produced by the heuristic part of our tool. This distinction is achieved by the use of two different symbols for morphemes concatenation: the symbol + for DICOS entries inflections, and the symbol $\star$ for all the concatenations that are recognized by our rule-based system. Thus, our tool should supply the following analyses for the three kinds of words that it handles:

(44)   *inculperont* $\longleftrightarrow$ *inculper,V+F3p*

(45)   *coïnculperont* $\longleftrightarrow$ *co_$\star$inculper,V+F3p*

(46)   *coïnculpabilités* $\longleftrightarrow$ *co_$\star$inculpable,A$\star$ité,N$\star$.f$\star$s.p*

where the third analysis, which is a full heuristic one, means that the derivative *coïnculpabilités* is the plural form of the feminine noun *coïnculpabilité* which derived from the adjective entry of DICOS *inculpable* with the prefix *co-* and the suffix *-ité*.

2.3.2   The two-level system

2.3.2.1   Two-level morphology

In his 1983 thesis, Kimmo Koskenniemi proposed a declarative system of constraints for describing morphological phenomena (Koskenniemi, 1983). These constraints are called two-level rules. The main difference between two-level rules and rewrite rules, introduced in the 1960s by (Chomsky and Halle, 1968), is their static nature. For instance, the following rewrite-rule:

$$a \rightarrow b \;/\; c_-$$

means that the underlying symbol a is rewritten as the surface symbol b in the environment following c. There are two important consequences of the dynamic nature of this type of rule. First, after underlying a is written as surface b, a is no longer available for any other rules. Second, rewrite rules can only apply in one direction, from underlying representation to surface representation. They cannot be reversed to go from surface to underlying representation. On the contrary, the corresponding two-level rule:

$$a : b \Leftarrow c : c_-$$

expresses the relationship between the underlying (lexical) a and the surface b as a static correspondence. Rather than rewriting a as b, this two-level rule states that a lexical *a* corresponds to a surface *b* in the environment following *c:c*, which is also a lexical-to-surface correspondence. This rule does not change *a* into *b*, so *a* is still available to other rules[15].

There are two consequences of the static nature of two-level rules:

- in a two-level system, rules are not ordered. Each rule can be compiled into a finite-state transducer and at each step of the recognition (resp. generation) process, all the rules are applied in parallel. An equivalence between an underlying symbol and a surface symbol will be allowed if it is recognized by all the rules, i.e. by all the transducers of the rule set.

- two-level rules can be applied for both recognition and generation of surface forms.

We present in the following chapters the method we applied in order to design a transducer based on the two-level model for unknown derivatives recognition.

2.3.2.2   The prefixes automaton

This automaton, called PREF(A)[16], contains about 100 prefixes. A sample of it is given in Figure 2.6.

This figure raises two remarks:

- we took into account two kinds of hyphens, an optional one, represented by the symbol _ like in *dé_*, *co_* and *sur_*, and an obligatory one represented by - like in *sous-*;

- this automaton recognizes concatenations of two or more prefixes.

With this automaton, we built the automaton PREF(A) • DICOS(A) which is the concatenation of PREF(A) with the automaton that recognizes all the words which begin with a DICOS entry. A sample of this automaton that recognizes all the sequences of the following type:

$$(\epsilon + (\text{Pref}*)^*) \; DICOS\_entry \; A^*$$

where *A* represents the system alphabet and the symbol * "one or more", is given in Figure 2.7.

---

[15]This opposition between dynamic and static rules can be linked with the opposition in computer science between procedural and declarative programming.

[16]The notation (A) will be used in order to characterize automata versus transducers.

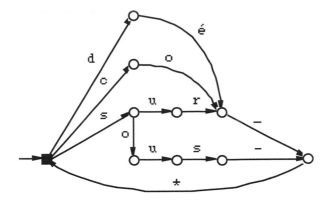

Figure 2.6: A sample of PREF(A)

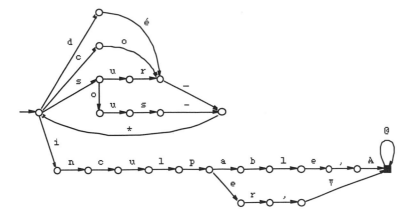

Figure 2.7: A sample of PREF(A) • DICOS(A)

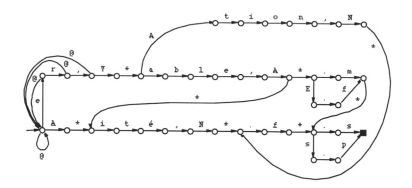

Figure 2.8: A sample of SUF(A)

2.3.2.3 The suffixes automaton

This automaton, a sample of which is given in Figure 2.8, complies with two fundamental criteria:

- derivational suffixes apply to specific syntactic categories and produce derivatives with an other category. The suffix *-ité*, for instance, applies only to adjective entries of DICOS, and produces a noun. That can be seen in Figure 2.8 where the string *⋆ité* follows the symbol *A* which is the adjective mark, like in *inculpable,A*, and is followed by the string *,N* which is the noun mark, like in *inculpabilité,N*;

- inflectional suffixes do not apply to plain DICOS entries but only to words made of a DICOS entry with a derivational suffix. The feminine suffix, for instance, which is represented by the string *.f*, can apply to adjective entry, i.e. ending with *A*, only if this entry contains a derivational suffix like *able,A*.

We made the intersection of SUF(A) with the automaton of Figure 2.7 in order to design the automaton of Figure 2.9 that recognizes the sequences of the following type:

$(\epsilon + (\text{Pref}\star)^*)$ DICOS_entry $(\star\text{derivational\_Suffix})^*$ $\star$inflectional_Suffix

This expression corresponds to lexical forms such as:

co_⋆inculpable,A⋆ité,N⋆.f⋆s.p

which are exactly the lexical forms of the words we want our two-level system to recognize in texts.

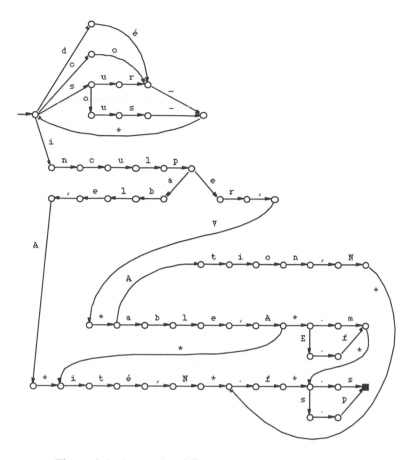

Figure 2.9: A sample of (PREF(A) • DICOS(A)) ∩ SUF(A)

2.3.2.4 The final transducer

The automaton of Figure 2.9 represents the lexicon of our two-level tool, i.e. the set of valid lexical forms. The relationship between these lexical forms and their corresponding surface forms has still to be established by means of two-level rules. The set of derivational affixes we took into account led to a 69 morphological rules set that covers most of the derivational phenomena we could observed (Guilbert, 1971; Clemenceau, 1993).

In order to apply these rules to the lexicon of our system, we had first to compile them into a unique transducer with the two-level rules compiler described in (Clemenceau, 1993) and (Roche, 1993). The intersection of this transducer, RULES, and the lexicon transducer[17] led to a unique transducer a sample of which is given in Figure 2.10. This transducer is the heuristic part of our morphological analyzer, it recognizes, and generates, derivatives corresponding to the third kind of words our analyzer should take into account, i.e. derivatives that are not DICOF entries, made of a DICOS entry with one or more derivational suffixes and eventually prefixes. This tool provides analyses such as:

$$(46) \; coïnculpabilités \longleftrightarrow co\_{\star}inculpable,A{\star}ité,N{\star}.f{\star}s.p$$

This transducer provides in fact four analyses corresponding to this derivative. First, it takes into account the following orthographic variant:

$$(46') \; co\text{-}inculpabilités \longleftrightarrow co\_{\star}inculpable,A{\star}ité,N{\star}.f{\star}s.p$$

The other analysis, which is a double one because of that orthographic variant, corresponds to a deeper morphological analysis, i.e. an analysis where the verb inculper, which is a DICOS entry, is taken as the root word of the derivative:

$$(47) \; co(ï+\text{-}i)nculpabilités \longleftrightarrow co\_{\star}inculper,V{\star}able,A{\star}ité,N{\star}.f{\star}s.p$$

2.3.3   Merging the two-level system with the DICOF transducer

The transducer of Figure 2.5 takes into account the following lexical forms only:

$$(\epsilon + (Pref{\star})^{*}) \; DICOS\_entry \; ({\star}derivational\_Suffix)^{*} \; {\star}inflectional\_Suffix$$

Thus, it cannot produce the analyses (44) and (45) that our morphological analyzer should produce, i.e. the analyses of the surface forms *inculperont* and *coïnculperont*. Analysis (44) is already produced by the DICOF transducer:

$$(44) \; inculperont \longleftrightarrow inculper,V+F3p$$

Therefore, the DICOF transducer has to be modified in order to produce (45), and then merged with the transducer of Figure 2.10. The transducer that produces DICOF analyses as well as (45) can be formally defined by the following expression:

---

[17]The lexicon transducer is the result of the application of the operator TRANS to the lexicon automaton of Figure 2.9. This operator modifies an automaton into a transducer where each word recognized by the automaton is associated to any string.

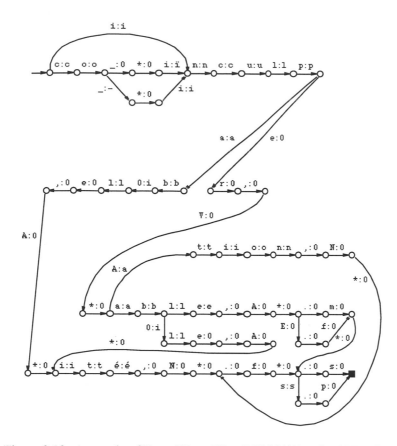

Figure 2.10: A sample of Trans((PREF(A) • DICOS(A)) ∩ SUF(A)) ∩ RULES

$$\{(\text{TRANS}(\text{PREF}(A) \bullet \text{DICOF}(A)) \cap \text{RULES})$$
$$\text{o}$$
$$(\text{ID}(\text{PREF}(A)) \bullet \text{DICOF})\}$$

where the meaning of the symbols is the following:

- TRANS: the operator that transforms an automaton into a transducer where each word of the automaton is associated to any string;

- PREF(A): the prefix automaton of Figure 2.6;

- •: the concatenation of automata;

- DICOF(A): the automaton that recognizes all the entries of DICOF;

- ∩: the intersection of transducers;

- RULES: the transducer that represents our 69 morphological rules;

- O: the composition of transducers as functions;

- ID: the operator that transforms an automaton into a transducer where each word of the automaton is associated to itself;

- DICOF: the transducer of DICOF.

The first line of this expression corresponds to a transducer that provides the following analysis:

(45a) *coïnculperont* ⟷ *co_*inculperont*

As for the second line, it provides:

(45b) *co_*inculperont* ⟷ *co_*inculper,V+F3p*

Therefore, the composition of these two transducers produces (45):

(45) *coïnculperont* ⟷ *co_*inculper,V+F3p*

The final transducer, called MORPHO, complies with the criteria that we defined for our morphological analyzer. This transducer, a sample of which is given in Figure 2.11, can be formally defined by the following expression:

$$MORPHO = \{TRANS((PREF(A) \bullet DICOS(A)) \cap SUF(A)) \cap RULES\}$$
$$\cup$$
$$\{(TRANS(PREF(A) \bullet DICOF(A)) \cap RULES)$$
$$O$$
$$(ID(PREF(A)) \bullet DICOF)\}$$

which represents the union of the final two-level transducer of Figure 2.10 with the DICOF transducer modified in order to produce (45).

2.3.4   Results

MORPHO, which contains 123,000 states and 258,000 transitions, takes 1.4 Mo of RAM and analyzes 1,100 words per second. These figures can be compared to the corresponding ones for the DICOF transducer which takes 950 Ko of RAM and runs at the same speed than MORPHO. This morphological analyzer showed a good recognition rate of derivatives in a corpus analysis experiment made on a corpus of 1,300,000 words (Clemenceau, 1992a; Clemenceau,

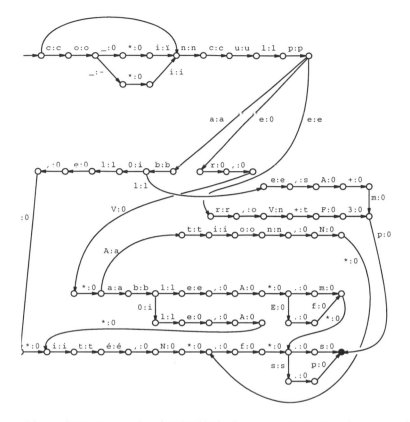

Figure 2.11: A sample of MORPHO, the morphological analyzer transducer

1993). Moreover, the framework made of MORPHO, structured DICOS and the lexicon-grammar of French verbs provides a reliable and evolutive tool for morpho-syntactic analyses that we describe in the next chapter.

2.4 A Single Framework for Inflections and Derivations Recognition and Generation

The system that we describe here is made of MORPHO, our morphological analyzer, and SDICOS, the transducer of Structured DICOS. It provides morpho-syntactic information that can be used in conjunction with the lexicon-grammar of verbs in order to provide the syntactic analysis of a sentence.

When analyzing a derivative with this framework, three kinds of situations can occur as shown in Figure 2.12:

- DICOF entries like *coactivables* whose canonical form is a Structured DICOS entry can be fully analyzed and the sentence can then be linked to a lexicon-grammar entry by means of syntactic transformations;

- DICOF entries like *coïnculpés* whose canonical form is not yet a Structured DICOS entry can be partially analyzed: the category and inflection code of the word are provided by DICOF and the morphemes based analysis provided by MORPHO provides partial syntactic information;

- words that are not DICOF entries like *débureautisations* correspond to morphemes based analyses only and these analyses provide two kinds of information: first, the category and inflection code of the word, second, a basis for a partial syntactic analysis.

2.4.1   Structured DICOS entries

When analyzing a sentence, the framework made of our morphological analyzer and Structured DICOS provides morpho-syntactic information that can be usefully used by a syntactic analyzer. For instance, in a sentence like:

(48) *La réaction est coactivable par l'acide et le catalyseur.*

The reaction is coactivatable by the acid and the catalyst. (or *coactivable* ?)

The system provides two kinds of information as shown in Figure 2.12: first, MORPHO provides the inflection code and the category of *coactivable*, and then SDICOS provides two morpho-syntactic analyses based on the entry *to activate* of table 32RA of the lexicon-grammar of verbs. The main construction of 32RA entries is:

(49) $N_0 \ V \ N_1$

Moreover, it is recorded in table 32RA that *to activate* can appear in the following structure:

(50) N_1 *POUVOIR ÊTRE Vpp by* N_0

N_1 *can be Vpp by* N_0

Because the three derivational operators *C, O* and *Vable* correspond to syntactic transformations, a syntactic analyzer as the one described in (Roche, 1993) can compare sentence (48) to the two following structures corresponding to the alternative between *C* and *O*:

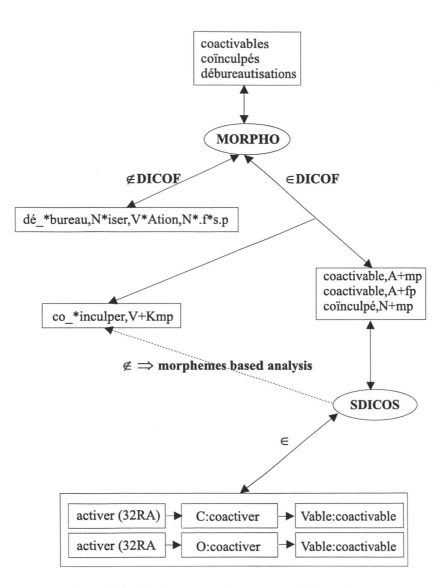

Figure 2.12: The three kinds of morpho-syntactic analyses

(51) N_1 *POUVOIR ÊTRE Vpp par N_0 et N_0'*

(51) [C] =(52) N_1 *pouvoir être co-Vpp par N_0 et N_0'*

(52) *[Vable]* = (53) N_1 *être co-Vable par N_0 et N_0'*

N_1 *be co-able by N_0 and N_0'*

(54) N_1 *et N_1' POUVOIR ÊTRE Vpp par N_0*

(54) [O] = (55) N_1 *et N_1' POUVOIR co-Vpp par N_0*

(55) [Vable] = (56) N_1 *et N_1' ÊTRE co-Vable par N_0*

N1 and N1' BE co-Vable by N0

Such a syntactic analyzer would associate the underlying structure (53) to sentence (48) since the comparison between structure (56) and sentence (48) would fail.

This morpho-syntactic framework can also be used for generation of texts. For instance, if the generation system had to build a sentence based on structure (54) with:

N_0	:=	*la télécommande (the remote control)*
N_1	:=	*l'alarme (the alarm)*
N_1'	:=	*le verrouillage (the locking mechanism)*

Structured DICOS would indicate that structures (55) and (56) are correct and provide the surface canonical form of the derivative: *coactivable,A*. Then MORPHO would associate the surface inflected form *coactivables* to the lexical form *coactivable,A+mp* in order for the generation system to build the following sentence:

(57) L'alarme et le verrouillage sont coactivables par la télécommande.

The alarm and the locking mechanism are coactivatable by the remote control.

2.4.2   Other derivatives

Derivatives which are not yet Structured DICOS entries are either DICOF entries like *coïnculpé* or not, like *débureautisations*. In the first case, MORPHO provides two kinds of analyses: DICOF analyses

(*coïnculpé,N+mp*)

with the category and the inflection codes of the derivative and morphemes based analyses

(*co_⋆inculper,V+Kmp*)

whereas in the second case MORPHO provides only morphemes based analyses

(dé_⋆bureau,N⋆iser,V⋆Ation,N⋆.f⋆s.p)

In both cases, these morphemes based analyses contain partial syntactic information.

First, it should be noticed that morphemes based analyses do not establish a relationship between a derivative and a lexicon-grammar entry. Thus, the verb *démonter* in:

(58) *Max a démonté son train électrique.*

Max dismantled his electric train.

will be associated to the following lexical form: *dé_⋆monter, V+Kms*, without distinction between the three following lexicon-grammar entries:

(59) *Max a monté son train électrique.*

Max assembled his electric train.

(60) *Max a monté l'escalier.*

Max went upstairs.

(61) *Max est monté au premier étage.*

Max went upstairs to the first floor.

whereas the prefix *dé* cannot be applied to entries (60) and (61).

Nevertheless, morphemes based analyses provide partial syntactic information. For instance, the derivative *coïnculpés* in the sentence:

(62) *Luc et Max ont été coïnculpés dans cette affaire.*

Luc and Max were co-defendants in this case.

will be associated to the following lexical form: *co_⋆inculper, V+Kmp* which corresponds to two syntactic analyses using our derivational operators: *C+inculper* and *O+inculper*. Since the automaton describing all the correct structures that can enter the lexicon-grammar entry *inculper* contains the following structures (Roche, 1993):

(63) N_0 V N_1

(63) [Passive] = (64) N_1 *ÊTRE Vpp* (ϵ + *par N_0*)

the verb *coïnculper* can enter the following structures:

(64) [C] = (65) N_1 *ÊTRE Vpp* (ϵ + *par N_0 et N_0'*)

(64) [O] = (66) N_1 *et N_1' ÊTRE Vpp* (ϵ + *par N_0*)

where structure (66) provides the underlying structure of sentence (62).

2.5   Conclusion

The opposition between lexical methods based on electronic dictionaries and heuristic methods using rules systems has been present for years in the computational linguistics domain. Lexical methods have been criticized because they lead to dictionaries whose size was said to be too big for natural language processing. On the other hand, heuristic methods that are based on the regularity of natural language phenomena do not account for many restrictions and interpretations at the morphological and syntactic levels. Morphology, and especially lexical creativity, is a field where this opposition has been very active. A few years ago, it seemed unrealistic to use DICOF with its 700,000 entries on a micro-computer. However, (Revuz, 1991) and (Roche, 1993) showed that, with the help of the finite-state automata theory, such a dictionary could be compiled into very efficient computational tools that can be used on microcomputers because of their reasonable size. However, heuristic methods could seem more appropriate in order to deal with lexical creativity because these phenomena are quite regular, and, moreover, because adding all the possible derivatives to a dictionary like DICOF seemed unrealistic and would lead to a dictionary too large to be used.

We wanted to show in this study that lexical creativity phenomena should be dealt with by mixing these two different approaches. Heuristic methods using morphological rules, and especially the two-level method, could appear more appropriate to account for derivational phenomena which are very regular, but we showed that they cannot provide the same level of description than DICOF and, moreover, that they do not account for many syntactic restrictions that occur in derivational phenomena. On the other hand, the systematic description of the derivational paradigm of each French word that could seemed unrealistic appeared to be feasible and, moreover, it did not lead to unusable dictionaries since doubling the size of DICOF by adding new derivatives led only to a 7% increase of the DICOF transducer without any change in the speed of the look-up procedure. However, such an approach takes time and may not account for some new derivatives appearing in texts. That is the reason why we developed a two-level tool in order to recognize derivatives that are not yet recorded in Structured DICOS. Nevertheless, the analyses provided by this tool are both less rich and less reliable than the information recorded in DICOF and Structured DICOS.

References

Boons, J.P., A. Guillet, and C. Leclère. 1976a. *La structure des phrases simples en français: (constructions non complétives) I-Les verbes intransitifs.*

Droz, Genève.

Boons, J.P., A. Guillet, and C. Leclère. 1976b. La structure des phrases simples en français: Classes de constructions transitives. Technical Report 6, LADL, Université Paris VII.

Chomsky, N. and M. Halle. 1968. *The sound pattern of English.* Harper and Row, New York.

Clemenceau, D. 1992a. Dictionary completeness and corpus analysis. In *Proceedings of COMPLEX'92*, pages 91–100, Budapest, Hungaria.

Clemenceau, D. 1992b. Enrichissement et structuration de dictionnaires électroniques. Langue Française. *Larousse, Paris*, 96:6–19.

Clemenceau, D. 1992c. Towards a structured dictionary. Technical Report 31, LADL, Université Paris VII.

Clemenceau, D. 1993. *Structuration du lexique et reconnaissance de mots dérivés.* Ph.D. thesis, Université Paris VII.

Thèse de doctorat.

Corbin, D. 1984. Méthodes en morphologie dérivationnelle. *Cahiers de lexicologie*, 44:3–17.

Courtois, B. and E. Laporte. 1991. Une expérience de dépouillement de textes: les mots non reconnus. Technical report, Autogen, Genelex projet.

Courtois, B. 1990. Un système de dictionnaires électroniques pour les mots simples du français. *Langue Française*, 87.

Giry-Schneider, J. 1978. *Les nominalisations en français. L'opérateur faire dans le lexique.* Droz, Genève.

Gross, M. 1968. *Grammaire transformationnelle du français, syntaxe du verbe.* Larousse, Paris.

Gross, M. 1975. *Méthodes en syntaxe, régime des constructions complétives.* Hermann, Paris.

Guilbert, L. 1971. Fondements lexicologiques du dictionnaire. De la formation des unités lexicales. *GLLF, t. I*, pages IX–LXXX1.

Koskenniemi, K. 1983. Two-level morphology: a general computational model for word-form recognition and production. Technical Report Publication 11, University of Helsinki, Department of General Linguistics, Helsinki.

Koskenniemi, K. 1984. A general computational model for word-form recognition and production. In *COLING'84*, pages 178–181.

Leeman, D. 1988. Échantillons des adjonctions au DELAS d'adjectifs en able. Rapport du programme de recherches coordonnées 'informatique linguistique'. Technical report, Université Paris X, Nanterre.

Revuz, D. 1991. *Dictionnaires et lexiques. Méthodes et algorithmes.* Ph.D. thesis, Université Paris VII.

Thèse de doctorat.

Roche, E. 1993. *Analyse syntaxique transformationnelle du français par transducteurs et lexique-grammaire.* Ph.D. thesis, Université Paris VII. *Thèse de doctorat.*

3 Representations and Finite-State Components in Natural Language

Kimmo Koskenniemi

There has been no consensus over the question how complex natural languages actually are, and with what kinds of mathematical devices they ought to be described. The following discussion deals with certain phenomena in phonology, lexicon and syntax in terms of finite-state machines, and representations.

Finite-state machines are abstract mathematical devices, in fact they are as simple as devices can be. Their complexity is easy to assess: more states and transitions are needed to describe more complex phenomena. Small finite-state machines correspond to intuitively simple formal languages. Finite-state machines operate in a straightforward manner. Therefore, most finite-state machines have efficient computer implementations. At least, as compared to Turing machines and any of the general rewriting systems, finite-state machines appear to be predictable and well-understood.

3.1 A Framework

The phenomena in this chapter are studied within a framework of a few *representations* and *relations* between the representations. Sometimes these restrictions refer to only one representation, and we prefer to call them *constraints*. Some representations of a natural language description can be directly observed, such as the written forms of word-forms or sentences. Others are invented by the scholars to serve as building blocks of a theory to describe or to explain linguistic phenomena.

3.1.1   Conceptual simplicity

Representations are most useful if we wish to *understand* parts of the natural
language systems. We appear to be fairly poor in our capacity of understanding
or mastering dynamic processes. As a consequence of this, it is very difficult to
write correct computer programs, and even more difficult to prove that a given
program is error-free. We are somewhat better off with static representations,
constraints and relations, provided that there are not too many representations,
and that the relations are not too complex.

Traditional rewriting rules in phonology constitute an example where individual relations are simple, but we have many distinct representations: the
intermediate stages of the rewriting process. Another example of several representations is found in the transformational syntactic theories. Between the
deep structure and the surface structure in the early transformational theories,
there was a host of intermediate representations. The output of one rule was
the input for another, and each rule related two successive representations.

Other things being equal, we ought to prefer theories with fewer representations. In principle, they should be easier to master, or simpler in the sense of
Occam's razor. To be fair, the complexity of the relations also counts, and a
theory with few representations but complicated relations might be deemed as
less elegant.

On the other hand, reducing intermediate representations might add to
the complexity of the relation between the extreme representations. Thus,
the choice of representations and relations depend on each other. Indeed, the
choice of appropriate representations turns out to be extremely crucial, as noted
by Atro Voutilainen elsewhere in this volume.

3.1.2   Decomposing a relation

Complex relations are difficult to understand, and to express unless we can
partition them to smaller components. The two examples, two-level morphology and finite-state syntax which are discussed in the following, express all
facts of the relation as independent rules. Each rule operates directly on the
ultimate representations where no intermediate representations ever exist. One
can consider each rule as a requirement which must hold irrespective of any
other rules. In this way, the grammar or rule set is, in effect, a conjunction of all
elementary rules, as opposed to a composition of rules applied in a sequence.

3.1.3   Bidirectionality

Constraints pertaining to a single representation are useful for expressing regularities in language, e.g. phonotactic or morphotactic structures of word-forms.

Relations between distinct representations let us speak about parsing and generation. If we suppose that we have the description of the relation, and one of the representations, the task is called either *parsing* or *generation* depending on which representation is missing.

We might produce two parallel representations for a large set of linguistic units (words or sentences) by manual or semiautomatic coding before we have formulated the relation. In this case, we are at the starting point of a *discovery procedure*.

3.1.4 Grammar writer's view

Descriptions of phonological, morphological or syntactic structures are often presented as if the rules would be the first and primary things written by the grammarian. The linguist could, and maybe should, proceed in an other order, by first establishing the relevant representations and then proceed with designing the rules. The establishment of representations can be done in a very concrete way, by setting up a grammar definition corpus where relevant examples (words or sentences) are given the appropriate corresponding representations (cf. Atro Voutilainen, in this volume).

This method of first fixing the representations in a concrete way, leaves the field open for competing rule sets and even different rule formalisms to account for the relation. In fact, the writing of the rules is then a kind of implementation task. This would be a analogous to implementing a program according to a formal specification of the task that the program is expected to accomplish. This empirical view could further motivate us to devote more consideration to representations.

3.2   Two-Level Morphology

In order to make the above discussion more concrete, we study an example: the two-level morphology (or phonology). This model is for morphological analysis and generation. It is a general, language-independent framework which has been implemented for a host of different languages (Finnish, English, Russian, Swedish, German, Swahili, Danish, Basque, Estonian, etc.). It proposes two representations and one relation:

- The *surface representation* of a word-form. If we wish to study the language in linguistic terms, the surface representation would be the phonemic form of the word, i.e. a sequence of phonemes. In practical situations we often choose the written form instead, because written text is readily available in sufficient amounts.

- The *morphophonemic representation* or the lexical representation of a word-form. Whereas the stems and affixes of the surface form tend to have alternating shapes, the morphophonemic representation is often invariant or constant. Alternating phonemes, thus, correspond to morphophonemes in this representation.

- The *rule component* which consists of two-level rules. Rules are finite-state transducers which directly relate the two representations to each other. Each rule is a very permissive relation between the representations so that it only cares about one detail. The full relation holds if and only if all single rule relations hold simultaneously.

This is depicted schematically in figure 3.1.

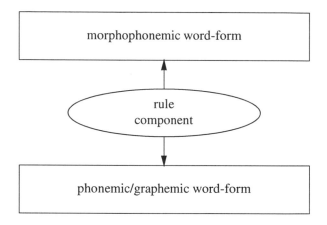

Figure 3.1: Two-level morphology

3.2.1   A simple two-level example

An example will help us to understand the concepts. English is not particularly good in this respect because on the one hand, there is so little inflection and hardly any (morpho)phonological alternations, and on the other, the English orthography is so far from the phonemic representation of words. Our first example deals with English nouns ending in **y**, e.g. **sky**. As we know, in the plural forms, we have a **i** instead of the **y**, e.g. **skies** (this orthographic convention is not manifested in the pronunciation).

We can assume that there is an underlying form for the stem **sky** and the plural ending **-es**, and that in the combination, the **y** is realized as **i**:

```
s   k   y   -   e   s
s   k   i   0   e   s
```

Here the morpheme boundary - always corresponds to zero on the surface. We define the upper string to be the morphophonemic representation and the lower string to be the surface representation. In addition to these representations, we need to account for their relation. By default, each segment (i.e. phoneme, letter, morphophoneme) corresponds to itself, e.g. **s:s**, or the boundary to zero, i.e. **-:0**. The discrepancy to be described, is **y:i** which should be allowed when followed by the plural ending. The plural ending can best be recognized on the lexical representation, because a sequence **yes** would be quite acceptable in a written word-form.

There are two things to be said about the correspondence:

- Not just any **y** may correspond to an **i**, the plural ending gives a *permission* to this correspondence.

- In this particular position, the **y** must correspond to an **i**, there is *no other choice*. Especially the **y** may not correspond to itself.

Effectively, this is an "if and only if" condition which is expressed using a double arrow rule:

```
y:i <=> _ -: e: s: ;
```

3.2.2 Further two-level examples

Let us consider some further examples from Finnish which is a language with agglutination and a number of morphophonological alternations. Word-forms are built by suffixing the stems with various endings, and several clearly identifiable endings may follow in a succession. Because of this agglutination, one can produce thousands of distinct word-forms from each noun, adjective or verb stem. Because of morphophonological alternations, some of the stems and endings have slightly different shapes in different combinations.

The stem of a Finnish word **kauppa** 'a shop' has some such variations. These alternations appear to be regular, and they occur according to the inflectional endings attached to it: **kaupa ssa** 'in a shop' (inessive singular), and **kaupo i ssa** 'in shops' (inessive plural). The surface representations are here obvious because the writing system is (almost) phonemic. There is more freedom in choosing the morphophonemic representation. One straightforward policy is to choose the representation blindly according to the alternations occurring on the surface. The base form of 'shop' would have the morphophonemic (the upper) and the surface (the lower) representations:

```
k   a   u   p   p/0  a/o
k   a   u   p   p    a
```

Here we have chosen to use **p/0** to represent a morphophoneme which abbreviates either **p** or nothing **0** (zero) on the surface level. This is an example of a more general alternation called *consonant gradation* which affects the stops (**k**, **p** and **t**) in Finnish. The forms where the stop is intact is called *strong* forms, and those where a stop has been deleted, voiced or assimilated are *weak* forms. In the above example, **a/o** denotes a morphophoneme which corresponds to either **a** or **o** (letter "o") on surface.

The inessive singular form of **kauppa** 'in a shop' would be:

```
k   a   u   p   p/0  a/o  s   s   ä/a
k   a   u   p   0    a    s   s   a
```

Here we have the weak grade, i.e. **p/0** disappears from the surface form. The ending **s s ä/a** contains another morphophoneme **ä/a** which agrees in front/back harmony with the stem. This is called the *vowel harmony* of Finnish.

Finally, the inessive plural form corresponds to:

```
k   a   u   p   p/0  a/o  i/j  s   s   ä/a
k   a   u   p   0    o    i    s   s   a
```

Here we have, again the weak form of the stop. The stem final **a/o** is now **o** on the surface. This kind of stem final vowel alternations are common in Finnish. The suffixal **i/j** triggers the mutated form of the vowel, and is itself subject to a variation: it is realized as a semivowel **j** when it is between vowels in the surface, and as **i** elsewhere.

3.2.3   Interpreting the representations

This approach of defining the lexical representations is mechanical, and it corresponds to the IA (item and arrangement) type of grammatical description. This style leaves no independent status to the lexical representation. It is, thus, just an abbreviation of what is observed in the alternating surface forms. The lexical level loses here most of its relevance and status. This might be a disappointment, but at least we could be satisfied with the fact that we can understand this kind of a lexical representation fairly thoroughly.

The above choice of lexical representations is, of course, not the only possibility. Quite often, the lexical representations are chosen to be phonologically motivated, i.e. sequences of phonemes which are identical to phonemes which occur in surface forms. This would correspond to the IP (item and process) style of describing language.

3.2.4 Two-level rules

One merit of the IA style approach is that the deduction of individual rules in that framework is nearly mechanical. We have to look at each morphophoneme (e.g. **p/0** or **a/o**) and find out the conditions when each of the realizations is permitted. It appears that **p/0** is realized as **0** before a closed syllable and elsewhere as **p**. In a simplified form, the two-level rule might be:

```
p/0:0 <=> _ Vowel: (:i) Cons: [Cons: | #:] ;
```

Here the double arrow means that the morphophoneme may correspond to zero only if it occurs in the context given by the rule, and that in the given context the morphophoneme may correspond to nothing else but the zero. The rule assumes that the set of vowels has been defined as **Vowel** and consonants as **Cons**. The number sign indicates the end of the word-form. Round parentheses indicate optionality whereas the square brackets are used for grouping. A vertical bar means "or".

The other morphophonological alternation in the example was **a/o**. Here we propose a rule which permits the realization **o** exactly when a plural **i/j** follows:

```
a/o <=> _ i/j: ;
```

In fact, the proper establishment of the rules would require more examples than given above. One alternative realization for each morphophoneme will be selected as the default realization. The default is the one which has the least consistent contexts where it occurs. Those with some explicit contextual criterion, are taken care of by rules, one for each non-default realization.

In all versions of the two-level morphology, the rules are independent and parallel. No intermediate results between the underlying lexical representation and the surface representation exist, neither in the process of recognition, nor in the generation, and not even as auxiliary concepts in the theoretical apparatus defining the model. This restriction is significant and implies certain simplicity in the model as compared to less restricted rewriting systems. The difference pertains to the conceptual simplicity rather than computational complexity, because some distinct models may be reduced to an identical implementation through massive application of the finite-state calculus.

3.2.5 Finite-state implementation of two-level rules

The two-level model can be implemented in terms of finite-state calculus, but in principle, the model can be implemented in other ways as well. The finite-state implementation uses finite-state transducers for the rules. The transducers which are used here, are special cases, where no true epsilons exist. Deletions of characters, and insertions (epenthesis) use a true character zero **0** instead. Such transducers are equivalent to finite-state automata, and have all the algebraic properties in common. Thus, the rule-automaton for the second rule would be (in tabular form):

	a/o:a	a/o:o	i/j:	other
final 1	2	3	1	1
final 2	2	3	fail	1
3	fail	fail	1	fail

The rows correspond to states, state 1 is the initial state, and all states, except state 3, are final states. Column labels indicate for which pairs that column is used. "Other" denotes any other pair, not mentioned in the table. Pair **i/j:** refers to any pair where the lexical character is the morphophoneme **i/j**.

The full two-level system could be described as having two additional components. A so called "deleting transducer" deletes the zero characters from the representations which the rules use for the surface forms. This deletion produces the actual surface forms which do not have any zero characters in them. The other component introduces arbitrary zero characters on the lexical representations of the rules, in case rules need to insert some characters which do not exist in the lexicon.

The rules can be transformed into finite-state transducers either by hand (Koskenniemi, 1983; Antworth, 1990) or using a special rule compiler which automates the process (Koskenniemi, 1986; Kinnunen, 1986; Karttunen, Koskenniemi, and Kaplan, 1987; Karttunen and Beesley, 1992).

3.2.6   Complexity of the two-level model

Already the first implementations of the two-level analyzer were fairly unproblematic. There is a slight overhead of using many automata instead of one, but still, recognition speeds in the range of 400 – 1000 word-forms per second could easily be reached with full scale lexicons. Each rule was stored separately, and the run-time engine operated them in parallel. Thus, individual morphophonological rules were present in the implementation as separate components. This feature gave the possibility of claiming certain naturalness to this type of implementation.

The first complexity encountered was the difficulty in producing the intersection of the rule-automata. A single automaton would be equivalent to the set of parallel automata, but faster in execution. During the 1980's, the intersection for complex sets of rules proved to be prohibitively large and difficult to compute with machines then available.

The difficulty to produce the intersection can, most likely, be explained by the fact that many of the rules turn out to be independent of each other.

E.g. in Finnish morphophonology, vowel harmony is entirely independent of consonant gradation, and these could overlap with vowel doubling or detection of two identical vowels. In such circumstances the size of the intersection automaton often is almost equal to the product of the sizes of the component automata. In this way, the size grows very rapidly when more automata are included. Consider the following automaton which implements the Finnish vowel harmony (partially):

	any other	a o u	ä/a:a	ä/a:ä
final 1	1	2	fail	1
final 2	2	2	2	fail

The following 12 state rule-automaton implements (roughly) the Finnish consonant gradation for **p**:

	other	vowel	cons	p	p/0:p	p/0:0	#:0
final 1	1	2	1	1	1	fail	1
final 2	1	2	1	11	12	3	1
3	fail	4	fail	fail	fail	fail	fail
4	fail	fail	5	6	6	fail	fail
5	fail	fail	1	1	1	fail	1
6	fail	fail	1	1	7	3	1
final 7	1	8	1	1	1	fail	1
final 8	1	2	10	10	9	3	1
final 9	1	8	fail	fail	fail	fail	fail
final 10	1	2	fail	fail	fail	fail	fail
final 11	1	2	1	1	7	3	1
final 12	1	8	1	1	7	3	1

If these two automata are intersected, the result has 24 states. The number of states in the result is, thus, the product of the sizes of the two original automata. The vowel harmony automaton has to keep track of the harmony value, and the only way an automaton can remember is by being in a distinct state. The gradation automaton keeps track of the quality of the following syllable with the same means. These two criteria being independent of each other, the result is bound to multiply in size.

Another kind of possible source of complexity was pointed out by Ed Barton, Bob Berwick and Eric Ristad (1987). Their line of reasoning was based on the reduction of arbitrary satisfaction problems into corresponding two-level rules. Using the two-level engine, they were able to solve the satisfaction problem. The satisfaction problem is known to require an exponential number of steps to execute in the worst case. The two-level engine was bound require the same. Barton et al. implied that this was not only a theoretical phenomenon, but also a real one examplified by vowel harmony rules.

Most morphophonological alternations are strictly local in nature. The context which affects the alternation consists of one or a few neighboring phonemes or morphphonemes. Harmony-like phenomena exist in some families of languages, most notably in Altaic languages. The exponential behavior was suggested to occur according to the number of independent harmonies (or similar phenomena) in a language. After several years of occasional searching, we have found languages with two clear harmonies (Turkish), and some ones with possibly three harmonies (Kashmir, Brahuviki). When recognizing word-forms with the two-level engine, the harmonies do not cause nondeterminism. When generating word-forms, there will be nondeterminism if and only if the harmony is regressive (spreads from later to earlier morphemes). Thus, this kind of exponential behavior in natural languages seems to occur only with exponent 0, or in some worst cases, with 2 (or possibly 3). This is, of course, not exponential behavior, but a factor 1 (or 2) in the so called *grammar constant*. Normally, exponential behavior refers to processing time requirements which grow exponentially according to the length of the input string. Here is no such effect. The grammar constant refers to a constant factor which affects the parsing speed according to the number of rules in the grammar (Koskenniemi and Church, 1988).

3.3   Finite-State Syntactic Grammar

This section discusses an extension of the above principles to surface syntactic analysis. Similar observations about the choice of representations and independence of rules are made on this domain. First, we however relate the finite-state oriented version to a predecessor.

3.3.1   (Sequential) constraint grammar

Karlsson (1990) proposed a surface-syntactic parsing framework which consisted of a sequential scheme of the parsing process and a rule formalism with a parsing program. This framework is commonly known as "Constraint Grammar" (CG). Lauri Karttunen proposed later a term "Sequential Constraint Grammar" (SCG) for this approach. The steps relevant to the surface-syntactic phase were:

- Context sensitive morphological disambiguation of word-forms. The ambiguities remaining after the morphological analysis are resolved, where possible, according to the surrounding context whithin the sentence.

- Establishment of intrasentential clause boundaries so that the syntactic rules may distinguish contexts within a subclause from those extending beyond the current clause.

- Assignment of syntactic functions to individual words. A tag in each word-form indicates whether a word is a premodifier, a head of a subject, etc.

There are two kinds of sequential processes in this framework: (1) the sequence of the above steps which are both described and executed in that order, and (2) the way in which the individual rule sets are executed. The latter kind of sequentiality was not really intended to be relevant and the grammar writers were not encouraged to rely on any particular order of the rules. The parser implementations, indeed, process the rules within each packet in significantly different orders, but we will not go into any details of it. Furthermore, the rule formalism of SCG is not relying on any kind of standard finite-state machinery or regular expressions.

3.3.2 Parallel constraint grammar

The finite-state syntax proposed in Koskenniemi (1990) is based on almost identical syntactic representation as Fred Karlsson's constraint grammar. This framework was later given a name "Finite-State Intersection Grammar" (FSIG) by Jussi Piitulainen, and a name "Parallel Constraint Grammar" (PSG) by Lauri Karttunen (we will use the latter term here). Each word in a sentence analyzed in the PSG framework is associated with a syntactic tag which identifies its syntactic role as is the case in the SCG. An apparent difference in the representations of SCG and PSG is that the the latter commits to a more accurate identification of the clause structure of the sentence by explicitly marking a restricted form of center embedding. The tag representation in both frameworks is very close to the traditional syntactic representation which has been used for centuries.

The sequential CG views the sentence as a sequence word cohorts, where each word has a bunch of readings. The basic task of the grammar rules is to delete extraneous readings in the cohorts. In contrast to this, the parallel framework defines the rules in terms of single *complete* readings. The PCG rules discard readings of the whole sentence on the basis of local flaws in them. The set of one (or a few) sentence readings which passes all rules is, then, the parse of the sentence. The following could be one of the PCG parses for the sentence "time flies like an arrow":

```
@@ time N NOM SG @SUBJ @ fly V PRES SG3 @MAINV @ like PREP
@ADVL @ an DET ART SG @DN> @ arrow N NOM SG @<P @@
```

In a more readable form (with some white space added) this string of 29 tokens would be:

```
@@
    time    N NOM SG        @SUBJ
@
    fly     V PRES SG3      @MAINV
@
    like    PREP            @ADVL
@
    an      DET ART SG      @DN>
@
    arrow   N NOM SG        @<P
@@
```

This is a correct sentence reading, and it is a string of tokens of various types:

- Boundary symbols: @ @ delimiting sentences, @ between words. There are three further boundaries available: @ / between clauses, @ < starting and @ > terminating a center embedding.

- Base forms: "time", "fly", ..

- Morphosyntactic and syntactic features: "N", "V", ... for par of speech, "NOM", ... for case etc., and finally the syntactic tags which all start with "@".

3.3.3   One or two levels?

The first published version of the present type of finite-state syntax was based on an single-level version of the machinery used in two-level phonological rules (although the very first pilot experiments were made using the existing morphological two-level machinery a few years earlier). A two-level version would be very much like the generating mode in the morphological model, see figure 3.2.

The correct syntactic tags would be (epenthetically) created at the end of each word-form. The one-level variation is essentially equivalent to the two-level setup in but possibly somewhat simpler.

In the single-level approach, it is assumed that the morphologically analyzed sentence is first enriched with all possible alternative tags for all various syntactic roles of each word, and all possible types of boundaries between each two words. In principle, one could visualize this setup by feeding each possible augmented sentence to the rule component as in figure 3.3.

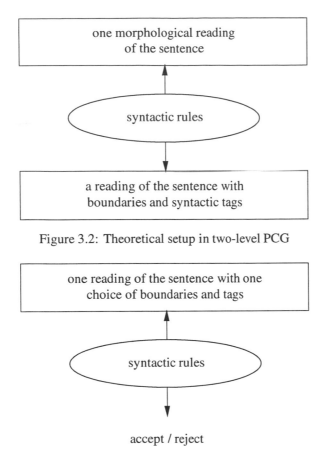

Figure 3.2: Theoretical setup in two-level PCG

Figure 3.3: Theoretical setup in one-level PCG

The morphologically analyzed sentence is, in practice, represented as a finite-state automaton which corresponds to all possible readings of the sentence. All combinations provided by the morphological analysis are included, even if they are obviously incorrect in a wider context.

3.3.4 Sequentiality and the representations

Let us study the differences in these two frameworks, SCG and PSG.

In the sequential CG the grammar writer faces at least four representations (see also figure 3.4):

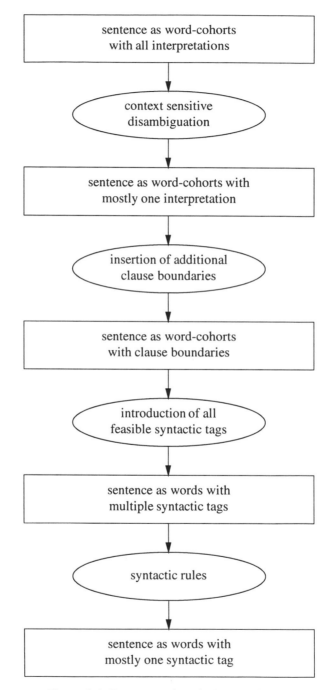

Figure 3.4: Representations in Sequential CG

1. The output from the morphological analysis, i.e. bunches of readings (cohorts) for each word-form, and these grouped to strings corresponding to a full sentence. This is the input to morphological disambiguation phase. The output of the disambiguation is of similar shape, but has (in most cases) less readings in each cohort.

2. The output of the clause boundary stage would be like the previous but augmented with some tags indicating the location of some additional clause boundaries.

3. The sentence enriched with possible syntactic tags which have been inserted to words where they formally could exist (in CG terminology, this is called mapping). The syntactic phase then deletes many of the alternative syntactic tags according to contextual criteria. Again, the input and the output to this stage is identical in format, but it simply contains fewer syntactic tags.

The existence of several representations is an obvious, even if slight burden. From the grammar writers point of view there are further problems. The disambiguation would be logical to describe, if one could refer to clause boundaries and syntactic functions. The clause boundaries would be easier to locate, if you could have unique interpretations of the word-forms, and the syntactic functions available. Not to mention that syntactic functions are easier to describe, if the words are unique and the clause boundaries properly located.

In the sequential framework with distinct representations for each phase, this is a bit hard to handle. The representations in SCG make one obvious implementation very straightforward, namely the Unix pipeline where each representation is either standard input or standard output of some phase. This is very concrete, efficient and simple, but such an implementation excludes the kinds of constraints which were sketched above. Earlier phases could not depend on the decisions made at a later stage.

On the other hand, the parallel setup is here better off. Theoretically, the rules refer to distinct full readings of the sentence. A reading might be discarded on any of the above mentioned reasons:

- It might contain an inappropriate reading of some word, i.e. morphological disambiguation might invalidate the reading.

- A clause boundary might fail to exist where expected, or exist where it conflicts with some rules.

- A syntactic tag might occur without its proper context.

There is conceptually no problem in the rule formalism to exercise all of the mixed conditions mentioned at the beginning of this section. There is just one representation where all constraints can be explicitly checked because all markings for syntactic roles and clause boundaries are visible. Thus, the grammar-writer can freely refer to all kinds of contextual information, no matter for which purpose a rule is written. Thus, if the implementation can manage with the computation in reasonable time and space limits, we have a fair solution to the surface syntactic parsing problem.

3.3.5   Implementations

The syntactic analysis provides, in principle, a subset of all possible readings of the sentence where the resulting readings satisfy all the constraints imposed by the rules. The rules of the finite-state syntax are compiled into finite-state automata. There are many ways in which the compilation of the rules and the run-time parsing could be accomplished (as experimented by Pasi Tapanainen, cf. Koskenniemi & al., 1988 , and Tapanainen in this volume).

The implementational problems arise because rules often delete possible readings of a sentence in an inefficient manner. Where one would wish single arcs of the sentence automaton to be deleted, rules actually delete even more readings, but in a fragmentary way. Finite-state networks turn out to be complicated in this respect. An automaton which represents fewer strings (or readings) can often be much larger than one which represents more strings.

Several approaches are being explored in order to establish a robust and efficient parsing algorithm for PCG grammars. It is too early to speculate which method will prove to be best.

3.4   Experiences

There has been some discussion, especially by Noam Chomsky in 1960s and by Gerald Gazdar later on, whether the syntax of e.g. English could be (reasonably) described with context-free grammars or not. Eva Ejerhed and Ken Church went a bit further in their attempts to use regular grammars in the early 1980s (Ejerhed and Church, 1983). These approaches used formalisms directly from the Chomsky hierarchy as the reference scale for complexity.

The two-level morphology and the finite-state PCG syntax should not be confused with that approach which expressed the syntactic rules as rewriting rules. Two-level system and the finite-state PCG have relations or constraints which are built out of finite-state components. These systems as a whole (or otherwise) are not rewriting systems (or they are rather untypical ones, if so interpreted). They combine a set of rules (or rule-automata) as intersections, or as conjunctive constraints, all of which must be simultaneously satisfied (as regular grammars they would have prohibitively many rules).

These two systems are, however, monotonic to a great extent. Each rule has to be satisfied separately, the order in which the rules are applied does not affect the theoretical outcome of the analysis. (Execution times might vary, and some orders might be harder to process, even prohibitively difficult.) Monotonicity means two kinds of things: (a) theoretical clarity and elegance, and (b) the obligation to write only rules which are true (you cannot correct a mistake at a later stage).

Individual details and facts about morphophonological alternations, and surface-syntactic distributional constraints seem to be expressible using two-level rules and those of the finite-state syntax. Whether these formalisms arc the most adequate for their tasks is a matter of taste.

Along with the two-level morphology, came some claims about the inherent simplicity of finite-state solutions. These were followed by claims about certain inherent complexities in the behavior of such finite-state systems. The morphology and the lexicon can be handled with finite-state methods in several efficient ways. No inherent complexities have been observed in that area.

As the Finite-state PCG was first proposed, there was little experience about the potential complexity of describing syntactic phenomena with finite-state machinery. The syntactic ones turned abut to be much more problematic:

- Certain types of rules were difficult to compile into finite-state automata because the resulting machine becomes so large.

- The run-time parsing is sometimes either slow or demands lots of memory or both.

References

Antworth, Evan. 1990. *PC-KIMMO: A Two-level Processor for Morphological Analysis*. Summer Institute of Linguistics, Texas.

Barton, Edward, Robert Berwick, and Eric Ristad. 1987. *Computational Complexity and Natural Language*. The MIT Press.

Ejerhed, Eva and Kenneth Church. 1983. Finite-state parsing. In Fred Karlsson, editor, *Papers from the Seventh Scandinavian Conference of Linguistics*. Department of General Linguistics, University of Helsinki, Publications, Number 9–10, pages 410–432.

Karlsson, Fred. 1990. Constraint grammar as a framework for parsing running text. In *Papers presented for the 13th International Conference on Computational Linguistics, COLING-90, Helsinki, Vol. 3*, pages 168–173.

Karttunen, Lauri and Kenneth Beesley. 1992. Two-level rule compiler. Technical Report ISTL-92-2, Xerox, Palo Alto Research Center, California.

Karttunen, Lauri, Kimmo Koskenniemi, and Ronald Kaplan. 1987. A compiler for two-level phonological rules. In *Tools for Morphological Analysis*. Center for the Study of Language and Information, Stanford University, California, pages 1–61.

Kinnunen, Maarit. 1986. Morfologisten sääntöjen kääntäminen äärellisiksi automaateiksi: Translating morphological rules to finite-state automata. Master's thesis, University of Helsinki, Department of Computer Science.

Koskenniemi, Kimmo and Kenneth W. Church. 1988. Two-level morphology and finnish. In *Proceedings of the 12th International Conference on Computational Linguistics, COLING-88, Budapest*, pages 335—339.

Koskenniemi, Kimmo, Pasi Tapanainen, and Atro Voutilainen. 1992. Compiling and using finite-state syntactic rules. In *Proceedings of the 14th International Conference on Computational Linguistics, COLING-92, Nantes, Vol. 1*, pages 156–162.

Koskenniemi, Kimmo. 1983. *Two-level Morphology: A General Computational Model for Word-Form Recognition and Production*. Publications, No. 11. University of Helsinki, Department of General Linguistics.

Koskenniemi, Kimmo. 1986. Compilation of automata from morphological two-level rules. In Fred Karlsson, editor, *Papers from the Fifth Scandinavian Conference on Computational Linguistics, Helsinki, December 11–12, 1985*. University of Helsinki, Department of General Linguistics, Publications, No. 15, Helsinki, pages 143–149.

Koskenniemi, Kimmo. 1990. Finite-state parsing and disambiguation. In *Papers presented for the 13th International Conference on Computational Linguistics, COLING-90, Helsinki, Vol. 2*, pages 229–323.

4 The Replace Operator

Lauri Karttunen

This paper introduces to the calculus of regular expressions a replace operator and defines a set of replacement expressions that concisely encode several alternate variations of the operation. Replace expressions denote regular relations, defined in terms of other regular-expression operators. The basic case is unconditional obligatory replacement. We develop several versions of conditional replacement that allow the operation to be constrained by context. The replacement operation is now included in the Xerox finite-state calculus.

4.1 Introduction

Linguistic descriptions in phonology, morphology, and syntax typically make use of an operation that replaces some symbol or sequence of symbols by another sequence or symbol. We consider here the replacement operation in the context of finite-state grammars. This includes many frameworks for phonological, morphological and syntactic description. Kaplan and Kay (1981, 1994) demonstrate that classical phonological rewrite rules can be implemented as finite-state transducers. The two-level model of Koskenniemi (1983) presents another finite-state formalism for constraining symbol-by-symbol replacements in morphology. The constraint grammar of Karlsson et al. (1994) has its own replacement formalism designed for morphological and syntactic disambiguation. It employs constraint rules that delete given morphological or syntactic tags in specified contexts. Finite-state syntax, proposed by Koskenniemi (1990), Koskenniemi, Tapanainen, and Voutilainen (1992), and Voutilainen (1994), accomplishes the same task by adapting the two-level formalism to express syntactic constraints. Brill (1992) improves the result of statistical part-of-speech disambiguation by rules that replace some initially assigned tags by new tags in appropriate contexts. Each of these frameworks has its own rule formalism for replacement operations.

Our purpose in this paper is twofold. One is to define replacement in a more general way than is done in some of these formalisms, explicitly allowing replacement to be constrained by input and output contexts, as in two-level rules, but without the restriction of only single-symbol replacements. The second objective is to define replacement within a general calculus of regular expressions so that replacements can be conveniently combined with other kinds of operations, such as composition and union, to form complex expressions. We have already incorporated the new expressions into the Xerox implementation of the finite-state calculus. Thus we can construct transducers directly from replacement expressions as part of the general calculus without invoking any special rule compiler.

We start with a standard kind of regular-expression language and add to it two new operators, $\rightarrow$ and $(\rightarrow)$. These new operators can be used to describe regular relations which relate the strings of one regular language to the strings of another regular language that contain the specified replacement. The replacement may be unconditional or it may be restricted by left and right contexts. The $\rightarrow$ operator makes the replacement obligatory, $(\rightarrow)$ makes the replacement optional. For the sake of completeness, we also define the inverse operators, $\leftarrow$ and $(\leftarrow)$, and the corresponding bidirectional variants, $\leftrightarrow$ and $(\leftrightarrow)$. Several new types of regular expressions have been defined for these operators, and they are described below.

The replacement operators are close relatives of the rewrite-operator defined in Kaplan and Kay 1994, but they are not identical to it. We discuss their relationship in a section at the end of the paper where we also point out the differences between our replacement expressions and two-level rules (Koskenniemi 1993).

4.1.1   Simple regular expressions

The replacement operators are defined by means of regular expressions. Some of the operators we use to define them are specific to Xerox implementations of the finite-state calculus, but equivalent formulations could easily be found in other notations.

The table below describes the types of expressions and special symbols that are used to define the replacement operators.

(A) option (union of A with the empty string)

~A complement (negation)

\A term complement (all single symbols in the complement of A)

$A contains (all strings containing at least one A)

A* Kleene star

A+ Kleene plus

A/B ignore (A possibly interspersed with strings from B)

A B concatenation

A | B union

A & B intersection

A - B relative complement (minus)

A . × . B crossproduct (Cartesian product)

A . ∘ . B composition

Square brackets, [ ] , are used for grouping expressions. Thus [A] is equivalent to A while (A) is not. The order in the above table corresponds to the precedence of the operations. The prefix operators (∼, \ , and $) bind more tightly than the postfix operators (* , +, and /), which in turn rank above concatenation. Union, intersection, and relative complement are considered weaker than concatenation but stronger than crossproduct and composition. Our new replacement operator has the same rank as crossproduct. Operators sharing the same precedence are interpreted left-to-right. Taking advantage of all these conventions, the fully bracketed expression

$$[[[\sim[a]]^* \ [[b]/x]] \ | \ c] \ . \times . \ d; \tag{4.1}$$

can be rewritten more concisely as

$$\sim a^* \ b/x \ | \ c \ . \times . \ d; \tag{4.2}$$

Note that expressions that contain the crossproduct (. × .) or the composition (. ∘ .) operator describe regular relations rather than regular languages. A regular relation is a mapping from one regular language to another one. Regular languages correspond to simple finite-state automata; regular relations are modeled by finite-state transducers.

In the relation A . × . B, we call the first member, A, the upper language and the second member, B, the lower language. This choice of words is motivated by the linguistic tradition of writing the result of a rule application underneath the original form. In a cascade of compositions, R1 . ∘ . R2, ..., . ∘ . Rn, which models a linguistic derivation by rewrite-rules, the upper side of the first relation, R1, contains the "underlying lexical form," while the lower side of the last relation, Rn, contains the resulting "surface form."

We also have operators that extract one side of a regular relation: R.1 describes the upper-side language of the relation R; the language on the lower side is R.2.

Some of the operations listed above are defined only for simple regular languages (intersection, complement, relative complement, crossproduct); others apply to both languages and relations (concatenation, union, option, Kleene star and plus). See Kaplan and Kay 1994 for discussion.

To make the notation less cumbersome, we systematically ignore the distinction between the language A and the identity relation that maps every string of A into itself. Correspondingly, a simple automaton may be thought of as representing a language or as a transducer for its identity relation. For the sake of convenience, we also equate a language consisting of a single string with the string itself. Thus the expression abc may denote, depending on the context, (i) the string abc, (ii) the language consisting of the string abc, and (iii) the identity relation on that language.

We recognize two kinds of symbols: simple symbols (a, b, c, etc.) and symbol pairs (a:b, y:z, etc.). The symbol pair a:b can be thought of as the crossproduct of a and b, the minimal relation consisting of a (the upper symbol) and b (the lower symbol). Because we regard the identity relation on A as equivalent to A, we can, and usually do, write a:a as just a. There are two special symbols

0   epsilon (the empty string).

?   any symbol in the known alphabet and its extensions.

A third special symbol, #, is introduced in section 4.3.4.2. The escape character, %, allows letters that have a special meaning in the calculus to be used as ordinary symbols. Thus %& denotes a literal ampersand as opposed to &, the intersection operator; %0 is the ordinary zero symbol.

The following simple expressions appear frequently in our formulas:

[ ]   the empty-string language. The corresponding minimal automaton, the epsilon fsm, consists of a single final start state without any transitions.

~$ [ ]   the null set. The corresponding minimal automaton, the null fsm, consists of a single nonfinal start state without any transitions.

?*   the universal ("sigma-star") language: all possible strings of any length including the empty string. Alternately, we may view it as the universal identity relation. The corresponding minimal automaton consists of a single final start state with a single looping transition labeled ?. It has no other symbols in its alphabet. The negation, ~[?*], describes the null set, thus ?* and $ [ ] are equivalent expressions.

4.2 Unconditional Replacement

To the regular-expression language described above, we add the new replacement operator. The unconditional replacement of UPPER by LOWER is written

$$\text{UPPER} \rightarrow \text{LOWER} \tag{4.3}$$

Here UPPER and LOWER are any regular expressions that describe simple regular languages. We define this replacement expression as

$$[\text{NO\_UPPER } [\text{UPPER} . \times . \text{ LOWER}]]^* \text{ NO\_UPPER}; \tag{4.4}$$

where NO_UPPER abbreviates ~$[UPPER - [ ]]. The definition describes a regular relation whose members contain any number (including zero) of iterations of [UPPER . × . LOWER], possibly alternating with strings not containing UPPER that are mapped to themselves. Note that if UPPER does not contain the empty string, ~$[UPPER] and ~$[UPPER - [ ]] are equivalent. But if UPPER contains the empty string, ~$[UPPER] is null whereas ~$[UPPER - [ ]] at least contains the empty string. We need the latter language in our definition to get the intended meaning for UPPER → LOWER.

4.2.1 Examples

We illustrate the meaning of the replacement operator with a few simple examples. The regular expression

$$\text{a b } | \text{ c} \rightarrow \text{x}; \qquad (\text{same as } [[\text{a b}] | \text{c}] \rightarrow \text{x}) \tag{4.5}$$

describes a relation consisting of an infinite set of pairs such as

```
a   b   a   c   a
    x   a   x   a
```

where all occurrences of ab and c are mapped into x interspersed with unchanging pairings. It also includes all possible pairs like

```
x   a   x   a
x   a   x   a
```

that do not contain either ab or c anywhere.

Figure 4.1 shows the state diagram of a transducer that encodes this relation. The transducer consists of states and arcs that indicate a transition from state to state over a given pair of symbols. For convenience we represent identity pairs by a single symbol; for example, we write a:a as a. The symbol ? represents the identity pairs of symbols that are not explicitly present in the network. In this case, ? stands for any identity pair other than a:a, b:b, c:c, and x:x. Transitions that differ only with respect to the label are collapsed into a single multiply labelled arc. The state labeled 0 is the start state. Final states are distinguished by a double circle.

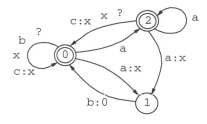

Figure 4.1: a b | c → x

Every pair of strings in the relation corresponds to a path from the initial 0 state of the transducer to a final state. The abaca to xaxa path is 0-1-0-2-0-2, where the 2-0 transition is over a c:x arc. When applied in the inverse direction to an x, the transducer produces three results, namely ab, c, and x, where the last alternative represents an unchanged x in the upper-side language. The corresponding paths through the network are 0-1-0, 0-0 (over c:x), and 0-0 (over x).

The replace operator → is like the crossproduct operator . × . in that it constructs a relation out of two regular languages. Consequently, it can be combined with other relations in composition, union, concatenation and other operations that are defined for regular relations.

Replacement expressions such as [a b | c → x] may be thought of as denoting string replacement rules. The application of such a rule to a string can be modeled quite directly in the following way:

(i) construe the input string as an identity relation;

(ii) compose it with the upper side of the replacement relation;

(iii) extract the lower-side language from the composite relation.

More generally, we may apply replacement rules to any regular set, such as a lexicon, thus rewriting in a single operation a possibly infinite set of strings. The development of lexical transducers (Karttunen, Kaplan, and Zaenen 1992, Karttunen 1994) is based on this insight.

In (ii), the upper side of the replacement relation is matched against the input. We generally refer to the upper side of → relations as the input side because they are generally intended to be applied in that direction. However, all relations are inherently bidirectional; from a formal point of view, there is no privileged input side. We discuss the effect of composing a string with the lower side of a replacement relation in section 4.2.3.

It is important to keep in mind that the result of (ii) is not an output string but a relation that links the input to the output. To get the output, we need another auxiliary operation that extracts the lower-side language, which may contain any number of output strings. We have such an operator in our regular-expression language, namely .2. Thus we can easily write single regular expressions that capture the conventional notion of "applying a rule." For example, consider the application of the relation [a b → x] to the string baab. In this case, the expression is [b a a b . ∘ . a b → x].2, more perspicuously written as

$$[\text{b a a b.} \circ \text{. a b} \rightarrow \text{x}].2; \tag{4.6}$$

which simultaneously (i) constructs the input language, (ii) composes it with replacement relation, and (iii) extracts the lower-side language of relation. Here the result of (ii) is the simple input/output relation:

```
b   a   a   b
b   a   x
```

We use this graphical way of illustrating the effect of replacement relations throughout the paper, but we avoid the term "rule" in order not to be confused by other possible interpretations of this term. On the other hand, we often fail to distinguish carefully between regular expressions, the corresponding automata, and the relations they express, treating them as interchangeable for the sake of convenience.

In case a given input string matches the replacement relation in two ways, two outputs are produced. For example,

$$\text{a b | b c} \rightarrow \text{x;} \tag{4.7}$$

maps abc to both ax and xc:

```
a   b   c          a   b   c
a   x              x   c
```

Because the two targets of the replacement operation overlap here, only one of them can be replaced at one time. Thus we get two outputs in such cases. The corresponding transducer paths in Figure 4.2 are 0-1-3-0 and 0-2-0-0, where the last 0-0 transition is over a c arc.

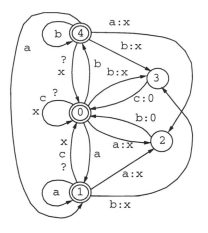

Figure 4.2: a b | b c → x

If this ambiguity is not desirable for some purpose, we may write two replacement expressions and combine them in a way that indicates which replacement should be preferred if a choice has to be made. For example, if the ab match should have precedence, we can write

$$a\ b\ \to\ x.\circ.\ b\ c\ \to\ x; \tag{4.8}$$

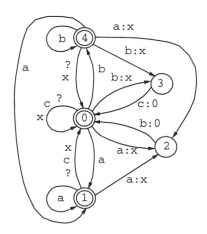

Figure 4.3: a b → x . ∘ . b c → x

This composite relation produces the same output as the previous one except for strings like abc where it unambiguously makes only the first replacement, giving xc as the output. The abc to xc path in Figure 4.3 is 0-2-0-0. Because the b:x arc leading from state 1 to state 3 is missing, the transducer does not map abc into ax.

This is an easy case because there is no overlap between UPPER and LOWER. Otherwise we would have to assign precedence in a more complicated way, introducing intermediate auxiliary symbols, as we do in section 4.2.3 for another purpose.

4.2.2 Special cases

Let us illustrate the meaning of the replacement operator by considering what our definition implies in a few special cases.

If UPPER is the empty set, as in

$$[\ ] \quad \rightarrow \ \texttt{a} \ | \ \texttt{b}; \qquad\qquad (4.9)$$

the expression compiles to a transducer that freely inserts as and bs in the input string. In order to have this result, we carefully defined NO_UPPER as ~$[UPPER - [ ]] rather than as simply ~$UPPER in the definition of → in (4.9). In the latter case NO_UPPER would denote the null set here because ~$[[ ]] is null. Consequently, (4.9) as a whole would denote something quite different from what we intend, namely, the null relation.

If UPPER describes the null set, as in,

$$\sim\$ \ [\ ] \quad \rightarrow \ \texttt{a} \ | \ \texttt{b}; \qquad\qquad (4.10)$$

the LOWER part is irrelevant because there is no replacement. This expression is a description of the universal identity relation, where every string maps to itself.

If LOWER describes the empty set, replacement becomes deletion. For example,

$$\texttt{a} \ | \ \texttt{b} \ \rightarrow \ [\ ] \ ; \qquad\qquad (4.11)$$

removes all as and bs from the input.

All the replacement expressions discussed so far have one property in common: the language on the upper side of the relation is the universal language. That is an important property since it means that every string, including all the ones where no replacement takes place, have a counterpart on the lower side. The corresponding transducer never fails on any input in this direction. However, in one situation that is not the case. If LOWER describes the null set, as in

$$\texttt{a} \ | \ \texttt{b} \ \rightarrow \ \sim\$ \ [\ ] \ ; \qquad\qquad (4.12)$$

all strings containing UPPER, here a or b, are excluded from the upper-side language. Everything else is mapped to itself. An equivalent expression is ~$[a | b].

4.2.3   Inverse and bidirectional replacement

When two relations are composed with one another, the result generally depends on which relation is ordered first in the composition. The same is true for the application of a relation to a string. So far we have looked only at cases where the input is ordered first and composed with the upper side of a replacement relation. In that direction, the → relation is privative: it replaces every instance of UPPER by LOWER. For example,

```
        a b                 a b
        .o.      yields
    a b  → x                  x
```

where no ab on the upper side survives to the lower side. But the → relation is not privative in the inverse direction. If the relation and the output string of the above application are composed in the opposite order, we get two results:

```
    a b  → x            a b      x
        .o.      yields         ,
         x                 x     x
```

The latter case represents an x in the upper language of [a b → x] that is mapped to itself.

These examples are useful here because they help us to illustrate the meaning of ← , the inverse replacement operator.

```
    UPPER  ←  LOWER                                    (4.13)
```

is defined as the inverse of the relation LOWER → UPPER. The difference between → and ← can be seen by comparing the above two examples with the corresponding applications of [a b ← x].

```
    a b  → x            a b      a b
        .o.      yields         ,
    a b  ← x            a b       x
```

Two results are produced because ab in the upper language may correspond to either ab or x in the lower language of [a b ← x].

```
a  b  ←  x              a  b
  .o.      yields
    x                      x
```

The inverse replacement, a b ← x, is privative in the upward direction: no xs on the lower side of [a b ← x] survive to the upper side.

The bidirectional replacement relation,

UPPER ↔ LOWER   (4.14)

can be defined as a composition of the corresponding ← and → expressions. The most straightforward definition would be

```
UPPER  →  LOWER
        .o.
UPPER  ←  LOWER ;
```

However, this simple composition of → and ← expressions does not have the intended meaning. It fails to connect UPPER and LOWER because of a mismatch in the middle layer of the composition.

To get the desired result, we introduce in the definition of ↔ an arbitrary auxiliary symbol, @. The purpose of @ is to serve as a pivot that links the upper UPPER and the lower LOWER in the intended way:

```
UPPER  →  %@
        .o.
%@  ←  LOWER ;
```

Because the linking @ is eliminated in the composition, in the resulting relation UPPER in the upper language always corresponds to LOWER in the lower language, and vice versa.

To complete the definition, we need only to eliminate any trace of @s from the upper and the lower side of the relation. A simple way to accomplish the task is to compose both sides with the relation ~$[%@] that eliminates all strings containing @ and maps everything else to itself.

Thus

UPPER ↔ LOWER   (4.15)

is defined as

```
~$[%@]
  .o.
UPPER  →  %@
  .o.
%@  ←  LOWER
  .o.
~$[%@] ;
```

The bidirectional relation is privative in both directions. For example, [a b ↔ x] maps all instances of ab into x, and vice versa. Because the replacement is obligatory, in this case there are no xs in the upper-side language of the relation and no ab sequences on the lower side. Nevertheless, there are cases in which the lower side of an UPPER ↔ LOWER relation contains instances of UPPER, even though the relation is privative. They may arise as a result of the replacement. For example, consider the relation

$$ab \leftrightarrow b; \tag{4.16}$$

applied to the string aab:

```
    a a b              a a b
     .o.      yields
    a b  ↔ b             a b
```

In this case we have an ab on the lower side but it does not correspond to an ab on the upper side.

The auxiliary symbol in the definition of ↔ is a preview of the method we use extensively in Section 4.3 to define conditional replacement.

4.2.4   Optional replacement

An optional version of unconditional replacement is derived simply by replacing NO_UPPER in (4.4) with ?* , the sigma-star language.

$$\text{UPPER} \ (\rightarrow) \ \text{LOWER} \tag{4.17}$$

is defined as

$$[?^* \ [\text{UPPER} \ . \times . \ \text{LOWER}]]^* \ ?^* \ ; \tag{4.18}$$

Because any instance of UPPER matches ?* , as well as UPPER it may be retained as such or replaced by LOWER. An alternate, equivalent definition of optional replacement is [$[UPPER → LOWER]]* , that is, the relation containing any number (including zero) of obligatory replacements

The optional version of ← is defined analogously.

4.3   Conditional Replacement

We now extend the notion of simple replacement by allowing the operation to be constrained by a left and a right context. A conditional replacement expression has four components: UPPER, LOWER, LEFT, and RIGHT. They must all be regular expressions that describe a simple language, not a relation. In other words, they may not contain any symbol pairs, the crossproduct (. × .) or the composition (. ∘ .) operators, and, of course, not the replacement operator → itself, unless these expressions are wrapped inside some operator, such as .1 and .2, that extracts a simple language from a relation. We write the replacement part UPPER → LOWER, as before, and the context part as LEFT ‿ RIGHT, where the underscore indicates where the replacement takes place.

In addition, we need a separator between the replacement and the context part. Traditionally, replacement rules are written

$$\text{UPPER} \rightarrow \text{LOWER/LEFT \_ RIGHT.} \qquad (4.19)$$

However, that notation is not suitable for us. One trivial reason is that / in our regular-expression calculus is the "ignore" operator. A more serious issue is that there are several ways in which a context may be used to constrain the replacement. We recognize four modes of applying the constraints; thus we have to distinguish them in our notation. For this reason we use four alternate separators, ‖ , // , \\ and \/ , which gives rise to four types of conditional replacement expressions:

1. Upward-oriented:

$$\text{UPPER} \rightarrow \text{LOWER \| LEFT \_ RIGHT;} \qquad (4.20)$$

2. Right-oriented:

$$\text{UPPER} \rightarrow \text{LOWER // LEFT \_ RIGHT;} \qquad (4.21)$$

3. Left-oriented:

$$\text{UPPER} \rightarrow \text{LOWER \\ LEFT \_ RIGHT;} \qquad (4.22)$$

4. Downward-oriented:

$$\text{UPPER} \rightarrow \text{LOWER \/ LEFT \_ RIGHT;} \qquad (4.23)$$

All four kinds of replacement expressions describe a relation that maps UPPER to LOWER between LEFT and RIGHT leaving everything else unchanged. The difference is in the interpretation of "between LEFT and RIGHT." We must distinguish whether we are talking about the upper context, the lower context, or some combination of the two. We provide four interpretations, soon to be made precise, but one can imagine others. We start with the upward-oriented (‖) version because it is the most straightforward way of using a context to constrain a replacement and is, therefore, the easiest to understand.

Except for the context separator, the syntax of all four versions of replacement expressions is the same. Later on we will also allow for multiple contexts, with a separating comma: LEFT1 _ RIGHT1, LEFT2 _ RIGHT2, ... , LEFTn _ RIGHTn. This extension of the formalism has not yet been implemented.

The LEFT and RIGHT parts are optional. Thus

$$
\begin{array}{l}
\text{UPPER} \;\rightarrow\; \text{LOWER} \;\|\; \text{LEFT} \;\_\; ;\\
\text{UPPER} \;\rightarrow\; \text{LOWER} \;\|\; \_\; \text{RIGHT} \; ;\\
\text{UPPER} \;\rightarrow\; \text{LOWER} \;\|\; \_\; ;
\end{array}
$$

are also well-formed regular expressions. The compiler supplies the empty-string language for a missing context. Thus the last of the three expressions above is equivalent to

$$
\text{UPPER} \;\rightarrow\; \text{LOWER} \;\|\; [\;] \;\_\; [\;] \; ; \tag{4.24}
$$

The conditional versions of inverse, $\leftarrow$, and biconditional, $\leftrightarrow$, replacement are just as their unconditional counterparts except for the constraints imposed by the context.

4.3.1   Definition of conditional replacement

4.3.1.1   Overview: divide and conquer

We define UPPER $\rightarrow$ LOWER $\|$ LEFT _ RIGHT and the other versions of conditional replacement in terms of expressions that are already in our regular-expression language, including the unconditional version just defined. Our general intention is to make the conditional replacement behave exactly like unconditional replacement except that the operation does not take place unless the specified context is present.

This may seem a simple matter but it is not, as Kaplan and Kay 1994 show. There are several sources of complexity. One is that the part that is being replaced may at the same time serve as the context of another adjacent replacement. Another complication is the fact we just stated: there are several ways to constrain a replacement by a context. In many cases the effect is the same regardless of how the contextual constraints are applied, in other cases the outcomes are strikingly different.

We solve the problem by using a technique that was originally invented for the implementation of phonological rewrite rules (Kaplan and Kay 1981, 1994) and later adapted for two-level rules (Kaplan, Karttunen, Koskenniemi 1987, Karttunen and Beesley 1992). The strategy is first to decompose the complex relation into a set of relatively simple components, define the components independently of one another, and then define the whole operation as a composition of these auxiliary relations.

We define the conditional replacement relation as the composition of several intermediate relations. There are six of them, to be defined shortly:

(1) InsertBrackets

(2) ConstrainBrackets

(3) LeftContext

(4) RightContext

(5) Replace

(6) RemoveBrackets

Relations (1), (5), and (6) involve the unconditional replacement operator defined in the previous section.

The composition of these relations in the order given defines the upward-oriented (||) replacement. When an input string is composed with the upper side of the relation, it replaces UPPER by LOWER when UPPER is between LEFT and RIGHT in the input context, leaving the string otherwise unchanged. We will define the other variants of the replacement expression shortly.

Two auxiliary bracket symbols, $<$ and $>$, are introduced in (1) and (6). The distribution of the auxiliary brackets is controlled by (2), (3), and (4). (2) constrains them with respect to each other, (3) and (4) with respect to left and right contexts. The left bracket, $<$, indicates the end of a complete left context. The right bracket, $>$, marks the beginning of a complete right context. The replacement expression (5) includes the auxiliary brackets on both sides of the relation. The final result of the composition does not contain any brackets. (1) removes them from the upper side, (6) from the lower side.

4.3.1.2 Basic definition

The full specification of the six component relations is given below. Note that in our regular-expression language, we have to prefix our auxiliary context markers with the escape symbol % to distinguish them from other uses of $<$ and $>$ in the Xerox finite-state calculus.

We define the component relations in the following way. Note that UPPER, LOWER, LEFT, and RIGHT are placeholders for regular expressions of any complexity. In each case we give a regular expression that precisely defines the component, followed by an English sentence describing the same language or relation.

(1) InsertBrackets

$$[\ ] \quad \leftarrow \ \% < \quad |\ \% > \quad ; \qquad\qquad (4.25)$$

The relation that eliminates from the upper-side language all context markers that appear on the lower side.

Alternatively one may think of the relation as a transducer that freely inserts brackets mapping in the other direction. It is the inverse of the relation in clause (6) of the definition. For the technical reason just explained we have to write our brackets as $\% <$ and $\% >$ in the regular expression.

(2) ConstrainBrackets

$$\sim\$[\% < \quad \% > \ ]; \qquad\qquad (4.26)$$

The language consisting of strings that do not contain $< \ >$ anywhere.

Note that the strings on the lower side of (1) are interspersed with unconstrained bursts of $<$ s and $>$ s. In particular, if two brackets occur next to each other, they may come in either order, $< \ >$ or $> \ <$. For reasons that will soon become evident, we only want to allow the second possibility. The composition of (1) and (2) invokes this constraint.

(3) LeftContext

$$\sim[\ \sim[...\mathbf{LEFT}][\ < \ ...]]\ \&\ \sim[[...\mathbf{LEFT}]\ \sim[\ < \ ...]]; \qquad (4.27)$$

The language in which any instance of $<$ is immediately preceded by LEFT, and every LEFT is immediately followed by $<$, ignoring irrelevant brackets.

Here [...LEFT] is an abbreviation for

$$[[?^* \ LEFT/[\% < \ |\ \% >]] - [?^* \ \% <]]$$

that is, any string ending in LEFT, ignoring all brackets except for a final $<$. Similarly, [$\% < ...$] stands for [$\% < /\% > \ ?^*$], any string beginning with $<$, ignoring the other bracket.

(4) RightContext

$$\sim[[... >] \sim[\text{RIGHT}...]\& \sim[\sim[... >][\text{RIGHT}...]; \qquad (4.28)$$

The language in which any instance of $>$ is immediately followed by RIGHT, and any RIGHT is immediately preceded by $>$, ignoring irrelevant brackets.

Here $[... >]$ abbreviates $[?^* \% > /\% <]$, and RIGHT... stands for $[\text{RIGHT}/[\% < | \% >] - [\% > ?^*]]$, that is, any string beginning with RIGHT, ignoring all brackets except for an initial $> ..$

(5) Replace

$$\% < UPPER/[\% < | \% >]\% >$$
$$\rightarrow \quad \% < LOWER/[\% < | \% >]\% > ; \qquad (4.29)$$

The unconditional replacement of $< \text{UPPER} >$ by $< \text{LOWER} >$, ignoring irrelevant brackets.

Here UPPER' is an abbreviation for UPPER/$[\% < | \% >]$. We could eliminate the brackets because here they serve no further purpose. But for other versions of the rule, one or both of the brackets must be kept, so we may just as well always preserve them in the replacement.

This replacement clause is intended only for nonempty UPPERs. It is useful to have another replacement formula for epenthesis rules. We will discuss this case later in Section 4.3.4.3.

The inverse and bidirectional versions of conditional replacement are defined with the corresponding operator, $\leftarrow$ or $\leftrightarrow$, respectively, in step (5). See section 4.2.3 for discussion.

(6) RemoveBrackets

$$\% < | \% > \quad \rightarrow \quad [ ] ; \qquad (4.30)$$

The relation that maps the strings of the upper language to the same strings without any context markers.

The upper-side brackets are eliminated by the inverse replacement defined in (1).

The complete definition of our first version of conditional replacement is the composition of these six relations:

```
UPPER  → LOWER  ‖ LEFT  _  RIGHT ;
```

```
              InsertBrackets
                   . ∘ .
              ConstrainBrackets
                   . ∘ .
               LeftContext
                   . ∘ .
               RightContext
                   . ∘ .
                 Replace
                   . ∘ .
              RemoveBrackets ;
```
(4.31)

The composition with the left- and right-context constraints prior to the replacement means that any instance of UPPER that is subject to replacement is surrounded by the proper context on the upper side. Within this region, replacement operates just as it does in the unconditional case. The relative order of the two context constraints could be reversed without an effect.

4.3.1.3 Left-, right-, and downward-oriented replacement

We may choose to delay the application of one or the other context constraint so that the constraint is checked on the lower side of the replacement relation. So far we have used only one out of four logical possibilities. Three other versions of conditional replacement can be defined by varying the order of the three middle relations in the composition. In the right-oriented version (//), the left context is checked on the lower side of replacement:

```
UPPER  → LOWER  // LEFT  _  RIGHT ;
```

```
                   . . .
               RightContext
                   . ∘ .
                 Replace
                   . ∘ .
                LeftContext
                   . . .
```
(4.32)

The left-oriented version applies the constraints in the opposite order:

$$\begin{array}{c} \text{UPPER} \quad \rightarrow \text{ LOWER} \quad \backslash\backslash \text{ LEFT} \quad \_\quad \text{RIGHT} ; \\ \cdots \\ \text{LeftContext} \\ .\circ. \\ \text{Replace} \\ .\circ. \\ \text{RightContext} \\ \cdots \end{array} \tag{4.33}$$

The first three versions roughly correspond to the three alternative interpretations of phonological rewrite rules discussed in Kaplan and Kay 1994. The upward-oriented version corresponds to simultaneous rule application; the right- and left-oriented versions can model rightward or leftward iterating processes, such as vowel harmony and assimilation.

The fourth logical possibility is that the replacement operation is constrained by the lower context.

$$\begin{array}{c} \text{UPPER} \quad \rightarrow \text{ LOWER} \quad \backslash/ \text{ LEFT} \quad \_\quad \text{RIGHT} ; \\ \\ \cdots \\ \text{Replace} \\ .\circ. \\ \text{LeftContext} \\ .\circ. \\ \text{RightContext} \\ \cdots \end{array} \tag{4.34}$$

When the component relations are composed together in this manner, UPPER gets mapped to LOWER just in case it ends up between LEFT and RIGHT in the output string. As in the upward-oriented case, the relative order of the two context constraints with respect to each other is irrelevant.

4.3.2 Examples

Let us illustrate the consequences of these definitions with a few examples. Consider the upward-oriented replacement relation:

$$\text{a b} \rightarrow \text{x} \parallel \text{c(d)} \_ \text{e} \mid \text{f}; \tag{4.35}$$

The infinite set of strings in this relation includes pairs like

$$\begin{array}{ccc} \text{c d a b e} & , & \text{c a b f} & , & \text{c d x e} \\ \text{c d x e} & & \text{c x f} & & \text{c d x e} \end{array} \tag{4.36}$$

Consequently, the transducer compiled from the rule maps cdabe to cdxe. In the reverse direction, it maps cdxe to both cdxe and cdabe because in this case the x on the lower side could correspond to an x or to an ab on the upper side. As we mentioned already in connection with the unconditional version of the operation, we can write expressions such as

$$
\begin{array}{l}
\texttt{[c d a b e} \\
\quad\quad\texttt{.o.} \\
\texttt{a b } \rightarrow \texttt{ x } \| \texttt{ c (d) \_ e } | \texttt{ f] .2 ;}
\end{array}
\tag{4.37}
$$

which simultaneously defines the replacement, applies it to cdabe and extracts the result. Here, as before, .2 denotes the operation that yields the lower-side language of a relation.

In order to understand the logic of the replacement constraints, it is useful to consider a concrete example in two stages. Let us first compose our sample word, not with the replacement expression itself, but with the initial four components in its definition:

$$
\begin{array}{c}
\texttt{c d a b e} \\
\texttt{.o.} \\
\texttt{InsertBrackets} \\
\texttt{.o.} \\
\texttt{ConstrainBrackets} \\
\texttt{.o.} \\
\texttt{LeftContext} \\
\texttt{.o.} \\
\texttt{RightContext ;}
\end{array}
\tag{4.38}
$$

This composition defines a very simple relation consisting of the pair

$$
\begin{array}{ccccccccc}
\texttt{c} & & \texttt{d} & & \texttt{a} & \texttt{b} & & \texttt{e} \\
\texttt{c} & \texttt{<} & \texttt{d} & \texttt{<} & \texttt{a} & \texttt{b} & \texttt{>} & \texttt{e}
\end{array}
\tag{4.39}
$$

Two left brackets on the lower side mark the two places in the word that satisfy the left context of the rule. The single $>$ indicates the beginning of a right context. Because the replacement target is between two context brackets, ab is replaced by x when we continue the composition with the remaining two component expressions:

$$
\begin{array}{c}
\texttt{c < d < a b > e} \\
\texttt{.o.} \\
\texttt{Replace} \\
\texttt{.o.} \\
\texttt{RemoveBrackets ;}
\end{array}
\tag{4.40}
$$

Because the context markers are removed by the final composition, the result is the simple relation

$$
\begin{array}{ccccc}
c & d & a & b & e \\
c & d & x & e & .
\end{array}
\qquad (4.41)
$$

The transducer compiled from [a b → x || c (d) e | f] of course does not contain any context markers. It transduces cdabe to cdxe in one single step without any intermediate levels. The auxiliary context markers are only used internally by the regular-expression compiler to hardwire the context constraints into the labels and state transitions of the network.

As already mentioned, one of the complications of conditional replacement is that the target of the replacement may simultaneously serve as a part of the context of an adjacent replacement. In such cases, it may happen that the four ways of invoking the context constraints lead to different results. Let us first consider four versions of the same replacement expression, starting with the upward-oriented version

$$
a \, b \;\rightarrow\; x \; \| \; a \, b \; \_ \; a \; ; \qquad (4.42)
$$

applied to the string ababab. The resulting relation is

$$
\begin{array}{cccccc}
a & b & a & b & a & b & a \\
a & b & x & & x & & a
\end{array}
\qquad (4.43)
$$

It is easy to see why this is so. The phantom intermediate bracketed result in this case is $>$ ab $>$ $<$ ab $>$ $<$ ab $>$ $<$ a with two marked application sites. Because the replacement is obligatory, both occurrences of ab are replaced by x.

This example gives us an opportunity to point out the effect of the ConstrainBrackets, (2), that prohibits $<$ $>$ sequences. In the case at hand, the end of the left context meets the beginning of the right context in three places where ab is followed by an a. Without this constraint on the context markers, $>$ ab $<$ ab $<$ $>$ ab $>$ $<$ a would also be a valid intermediate result. Here the middle part $<$ ab $<$ $>$ ab $>$ matches the upper side of the replacement relation in two ways: (i) $<$ ab $<$ $>$ (ignoring the intervening $<$) and (ii) $<$ $>$ ab $>$ (ignoring the intervening $>$). In the first case, when $<$ ab $<$ $>$ is replaced by x, the following ab $>$ remains unchanged because of the missing context bracket; in the second case the preceding $<$ ab survives for the same reason. In other words, without ConstrainBrackets the replacement would sometimes be optional.

A transducer for the a b → x || a b _ a relation is shown in Figure 4.4.

The path through the network that maps ababab to abxxa is 0-1-2-5-7-5-6-3.

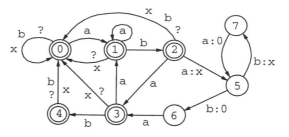

Figure 4.4: a b → x ‖ a b _ a

4.3.3   Right-, left- and downward-oriented replacement

Let us now consider the remaining three variants of our replacement expression, first the right-oriented version.

$$a \quad b \quad \rightarrow \quad x \quad // \quad a \quad b \quad \_ \quad a; \tag{4.44}$$

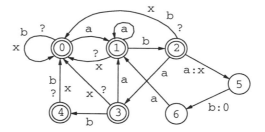

Figure 4.5: a b → x // a b _ a

As can be seen in Figure 4.5, applying this to abababa we now get a different result:

[60]

$$
\begin{array}{llll}
a b & a b & a b a \\
a b & x & a b a
\end{array}
\tag{4.45}
$$

following the path 0-1-2-5-6-1-2-3.

Why? It is because the right-oriented version is defined so that the Left-Context constraint pertains to the lower side of the replace relation. If we postulate the intermediate bracketing for abxaba we see that it meets the constraint: > ab < x > ab > < a. But the corresponding representation for abxxa, $>$ ab $<$ x $>$ $<$ x $>$ a, is not in the LeftContext language because the left bracket in x $>$ $<$ x is not preceded by ab. Consequently, this replacement result is eliminated in the composition with LeftContext.

The left-oriented version of the rule shows the opposite behavior because it constrains the left context on the upper side of the replacement relation and the RightContext constraint applies to the lower side.

$$a \; b \;\; \rightarrow \; x \;\; \backslash\backslash \; a \; b \; \_ \; a \; ; \tag{4.46}$$

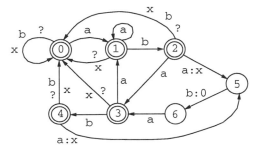

Figure 4.6: a b $\rightarrow$ x $\backslash\backslash$ a b $\_$ a

As shown in Figure 4.6, with ababada composed on the upper side, it yields

$$\begin{array}{ccccccc} a & b & a & b & a & b & a \\ a & b & a & b & x & & a \end{array} \tag{4.47}$$

by the path 0-1-2-3-4-5-6-3. The first two occurrences of ab remain unchanged because neither one has the proper context on the lower side to be replaced by x.

Finally, the downward-oriented fourth version (Figure 4.7):

$$a \; b \;\; \rightarrow \; x \;\; \backslash/ \; a \; b \; \_ \; a \; ; \tag{4.48}$$

This time, surprisingly, we get two outputs from the same input:

$$\begin{array}{lcl} \begin{array}{ccccccc} a & b & a & b & a & b & a \\ a & b & x & a & b & a \end{array} & , & \begin{array}{ccccccc} a & b & a & b & a & b & a \\ a & b & a & b & x & & a \end{array} \end{array}$$

Path

$$0 - 1 - 2 - 5 - 6 - 1 - 2 - 3$$

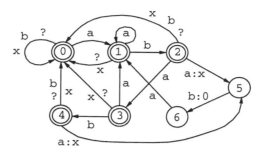

Figure 4.7: a b → x \/ a b _ a

yields abxaba, path

$$0 - 1 - 2 - 3 - 4 - 5 - 6 - 1$$

gives us ababxa.

It is easy to see that if the constraint for the replacement pertains to the lower side, then in this case it can be satisfied in two ways.

If LOWER overlaps with the left or the right context, different versions of the replacement rule often have interestingly different effects. Consider the upward- and right-oriented replacements when LOWER and LEFT are the same:

$$a \ \rightarrow \ b \ \| \ b \ \_ \ \text{vs.} \ a \ \rightarrow \ b \ // \ b \ \_ \qquad (4.49)$$

They make different replacements for inputs like baa:

$$
\begin{array}{ccc}
\text{b a a} & & \text{b a a} \\
.\text{o.} & \text{yields} & \\
a \ \rightarrow \ b \ \| \ b \ \_ \ ; & & \text{b b a}
\end{array}
$$

(4.50)

$$
\begin{array}{ccc}
\text{b a a} & & \text{b a a} \\
.\text{o.} & \text{yields} & \\
a \ \rightarrow \ b \ // \ b \ \_ \ ; & & \text{b b b}
\end{array}
$$

The upward-oriented version does not replace the second a because that a does not have a b on its left on the upper side. The right-oriented version replaces both as they both have a b on the left side in the output. Once the leftmost a in a string of as is replaced by a b, all the adjacent as to the right of it follow suite. For example, baaaaa is replaced by bbbbbb. This is why we call this version "right-oriented." The \\ and \/ versions of the rule give the same result here as || and //, respectively.

Now consider the opposite case where LOWER and RIGHT are the same:

$$a \rightarrow b \; || \; \_ \; b \; \text{vs.} \; a \rightarrow b \; \backslash\backslash \; \_ \; b \qquad (4.51)$$

Here the left-oriented version iterates to the left for inputs like aab:

```
        a a b                a a b
        .o.        yields
    a   , b  || _ b ;        a b b
```
$$(4.52)$$
```
        a a b                a a b
        .o.        yields
    a  → b  \\ _ b ;         b b b
```

In the upward-oriented case, the first a remains unchanged because it is not next to an upper-side b. The left-oriented version makes the change because there is an adjacent b on the lower side. In this case, the right-oriented and upward-oriented replacements are equivalent; the downward-oriented version gives the same result as the left-oriented replacement.

If there is no overlap between UPPER, LOWER and the adjacent contexts, then all four versions of the replacement rule give exactly the same result.

4.3.4 Special cases

Let us consider some special cases that help us to clarify the semantics of the $\rightarrow$ operator.

If LOWER contains at least the empty string, the language on the upper side of the replacement relation is always the sigma-star language, which contains all strings of any length, including the empty string. This holds for all replacement expressions, conditional or unconditional. The language of the lower side of the relation, on the other hand, is usually more constrained when the replacement is obligatory because it excludes the strings where UPPER remains unchanged in the replacement context.

4.3.4.1 Null components

As we noted before, we can also write replacement rules where LOWER describes the null set, as in

$$a \; b \rightarrow \; \sim\$ \; [\;] \quad || \; x \; \_ \; y \; ; \qquad (4.53)$$

This yields a simple relation that maps everything to itself but it excludes all strings that contain xaby. Thus replacement by the null set amounts to a prohibition. A simpler equivalent regular expression is $\sim\$[x \; a \; b \; y]$.

In any rule where UPPER describes a null set, such as

$$\sim\$\ [\ ] \quad \rightarrow \quad a \quad \| \quad x \quad \_ \quad y \quad ; \qquad (4.54)$$

the other components are irrelevant because the expression as a whole just compiles to the sigma-star language, including the case where LOWER describes the null set. The same goes for expressions where one or both contexts are null, as in

$$a \quad \rightarrow \quad x \quad \| \quad \sim\$\ [\ ] \quad \_ \quad b \quad ; \qquad (4.55)$$

These results follow directly from the definition of conditional replacement without any extra stipulation.

4.3.4.2 Boundary symbol

The context part of a replacement expression is implicitly extended to indefinitely far to the left and to the right beyond what is explicitly specified. Thus

$$\texttt{LEFT\_RIGHT} \qquad (4.56)$$

actually means

$$\texttt{?* LEFT \_ RIGHT ?*} \qquad (4.57)$$

Although this is a useful convention, sometimes it is desirable to refer to the beginning or to the end of a string to constrain a replacement.

A special boundary symbol, #, indicates the beginning of a string when in the left context and the end of the string in the right context. For example,

$$a \quad \rightarrow \quad x \quad \| \quad \# \quad | \quad b \quad \_ \quad ; \qquad (4.58)$$

replaces a by x in the beginning of a string and after a b. As the example shows, # is syntactically like any other regular-expression symbol, but the compiler gives the boundary symbol its intended interpretation and removes it from the alphabet of the network.

The special interpretation of # can be canceled by prefixing it with the escape character %.

4.3.4.3 Epsilon replacements

As we mentioned earlier, in connection with unconditional replacement expressions, if UPPER designates the empty-string language, the result is the identity relation regardless of what LOWER is. The definition of the Replace relation given above (5), would make this true for the conditional replacement as well.

But we choose to have a more useful result for the conditional case by using another Replace relation when UPPER is empty. If we in that case substitute

$$\% > \quad \% < \quad \rightarrow \% < \quad \text{LOWER}\% > \tag{4.59}$$

rather than

$$\% < \quad \text{UPPER}/[\% < \quad | \% >]\% >$$
$$\rightarrow \qquad\qquad\qquad \text{c} \tag{4.60}$$
$$\% < \quad \text{LOWER} \% > \quad ,$$

then the final relation that emerges from the composition is more interesting. It inserts one occurrence of LOWER in all places that meet the context constraints. Thus

$$[\ ] \quad \rightarrow \text{LOWER} \ || \quad \_ \ ; \tag{4.61}$$

does not have the same meaning anymore as

$$[\ ] \quad \rightarrow \text{LOWER}; \tag{4.62}$$

For example,

$$\begin{array}{ccc} \text{a b} & & \text{a b} \\ .\text{o}. & \text{yields} & \\ [\ ] \rightarrow \text{x} & & \text{x}^* \ \text{a} \ \text{x}^* \ \text{b} \ \text{x}^* \end{array} \tag{4.63}$$

because the $[\ ] \rightarrow$ x relation freely introduces xs everywhere in the output string. The lower-side language here is [a b]/x. In contrast,

$$\begin{array}{ccc} \text{a b} & & \text{a b} \\ .\text{o}. & \text{yields} & \\ [\ ] \rightarrow \text{x} \ || \ \_ & & \text{x a x b x} \end{array} \tag{4.64}$$

because an empty context condition is always satisfied but only one copy of x is inserted at each site. Similarly,

$$[\ ] \quad \rightarrow \text{x} \ | \ \text{y} \ || \ \text{a} \ \_ \ \text{b}; \tag{4.65}$$

yields a relation that inserts an x or a y between every a and b. Thus

$$\begin{array}{c} \text{a b a b a} \\ .\text{o}. \\ [\ ] \rightarrow \text{x} \ | \ \text{y} \ || \ \text{a} \_ \text{b} \end{array} \tag{4.66}$$

yields an output relation with four pairs:

```
a    b    a    b    a    ,    a    b    a    b    a
a  x b  a  x b  a    a  x b  a  y b  a
```

```
a    b    a    b    a    ,    a    b    a    b    a
a  y b  a  x b  a    a  y b  a  y b  a
```

This treatment of epsilon rules brings up an important issue of interpretation. Our definition of conditional replacement associates each application with a pair of context brackets. Because there is only one pair of $>$ $<$ brackets available at any application site, our rule allows only single replacements. This is why in the previous example we get just one x or y at each insertion site rather than an infinite sequence of xs and ys.

It can be argued that the latter result would be more consistent from a general point of view, but we feel that it would be much less practical. If the infinite regression of insertions is needed, it can easily be obtained by using a Kleene star in LOWER:

$$[\ ] \quad \rightarrow \ [x \mid y] + \ \| \ a \ \_ \ b; \qquad\qquad (4.67)$$

4.4   Comparisons

4.4.1   Phonological rewrite rules

Our definition of replacement is in its technical aspects very closely related to the way phonological rewrite-rules are defined in Kaplan and Kay 1994, but there are important differences. The initial motivation in their original 1981 presentation was to model a left-to-right deterministic process of rule application. In the course of exploring the issues, Kaplan and Kay developed a more abstract notion of rewrite rules that allowed the constraints on the operation to refer to both input and output strings. They invented the technique of encoding the context conditions with the help of auxiliary markers. We used the same method in the two-level rule compiler (Karttunen, Kaplan, and Koskenniemi 1987). Although the final 1994 version of the Kaplan and Kay paper lays out a sophisticated general framework, which we exploit here, it remains focused on the initial target of modeling a deterministic procedural application of rewrite rules.

The definition of replacement that we give in this paper has a very different starting point. The basic case for us is unconditional obligatory replacement, which we define in a purely relational way without any consideration of how replacement might be applied. The $\rightarrow$ operator is like any other operator in the calculus of regular expressions in that it is defined in terms of other expressions. By starting with obligatory replacement, we can easily also define an optional version of the operator. For Kaplan and Kay, the primary notion is optional rewriting. It is quite cumbersome for them to provide an obligatory version.

Although people may agree, in the case of simple phonological rewrite rules, what the outcome of a deterministic rewrite operation should be, it is not clear that this is the case for replacement expressions that involve arbitrary regular languages. For that reason, we prefer to define the replacement operator in relational terms without relying on an uncertain intuition about a procedure that plays no role in current phonological theories.

In spite of the very different motivation, both systems give the same result in a great number of cases. But sometimes they diverge, in particular with respect to right- and left-oriented replacement, which Kaplan and Kay especially focused on. It appears that in the upward-oriented case there is no difference except that Kaplan and Kay's formulation incorporates a directionality constraint. The application sites are to be selected either from left-to-right or from right-to-left without overlaps. This makes a difference in cases such as (4.7) where we allow two outcomes but Kaplan and Kay *a priori* choose one or the other.

4.4.2　Two-level rules

Our definition of replacement also has a close connection to two-level rules. A two-level rule always specifies whether a context element belongs to the input (= lexical) or the output (= surface) context of the rule. The two-level model also shares our pure relational view of replacement as it is not concerned about the application procedure.

In one respect the two-level model is more expressive than our extended regular-expression calculus. In the two-level formalism it is possible to refer to both the lexical and the surface context on the same side, as in

$$a : x \ < \ = \ > \quad :a \ b: \ \_ \ ; \tag{4.68}$$

This rule says that the a:x correspondence is obligatory and allowed if and only if a:x is next to a surface a (regardless of what is on the lexical side) followed by a lexical b (not considering what became of it on the surface side). Our definition does not allow this case because each context constraint applies either before or after the replacement but not both.

This feature of the two-level formalism comes from the fact that all symbols are treated as atomic in the two-level regular-expression calculus. The move from "feasible pairs" to real fst pairs happens only after the rules have been compiled to simple automata. Because 0s in the two-level calculus are not epsilons but ordinary symbols, the rule writer must carefully keep in mind all possible deletion and insertion sites so that pairs with one-sided zeros, such as x:0 and 0:y, are included in all relevant contexts. Because two-level rules (in the $<\,=$ direction) are limited to single-symbol correspondences, it is very cumbersome to express multisegment replacements.

The present formalism can be extended to constrain replacements with respect to upper and lower contexts on the same side of the replacement site. One solution is to allow for several context specifications with alternate orientation. For example,

$$\text{a} \rightarrow \text{x} \ // \ \text{a} \ (?) \ \_ \ \| \ \text{b} \ \_ \ ; \qquad\qquad (4.69)$$

would have a similar effect as the two-level rule above. It constrains the replacement with a double condition on the left of the replacement, requiring an a on the lower side, possibly followed by some unspecified symbol, and a b on the upper side.

4.5 Conclusion

The goal of this paper has been to introduce to the calculus of regular expressions a replace operator, $\rightarrow$, with a set of associated replacement expressions that concisely encode alternate variations of the operation.

We defined unconditional and conditional replacement, taking the unconditional obligatory replacement as the basic case. We provide a simple declarative definition for it, easily expressed in terms of the other regular-expression operators, and extend it to the conditional case providing four ways to constrain replacement by a context.

These definitions have already been implemented. The figures in this paper correspond exactly to the output of the regular-expression compiler in the Xerox finite-state calculus.

Acknowledgments

This work is based on many years of productive collaboration with Ronald M. Kaplan and Martin Kay. I am particularly indebted to Kaplan for writing a very helpful critique, even though he strongly prefers the approach of Kaplan and Kay 1994. Special thanks are also due to Kenneth R. Beesley for help on the definitions of the replace operators and for expert editorial advice. I am grateful to Jean-Pierre Chanod, Makoto Kanazawa, André Kempe, Pasi Tapanainen, and Annie Zaenen for helping to correct many technical and rhetorical weaknesses of the initial draft.

References

Brill, Eric (1992). A simple rule-based part of speech tagger. In Proceedings of the Third Conference on Applied Natural Language Processing, ACL, Trento, Italy.

Kaplan, Ronald M., and Kay, Martin (1981). Phonological Rules and Finite-State Transducers. Paper presented at the Annual Meeting of the Linguistic Society of America. New York.

Kaplan, Ronald M. and Kay, Martin (1994). Regular Models of Phonological Rule Systems. Computational Linguistics. 20:3 331-378. 1994.

Karlsson, Fred, Voutilainen, Atro, Heikkilä, Juha, and Anttila, Arto (1994) Constraint Grammar: a Language-Independent System for Parsing Unrestricted Text. Mouton de Gruyter, Berlin, 1994.

Karttunen, Lauri, Kaplan, Ronald M., Zaenen, Annie (1992). Two-Level Morphology with Composition. In the Proceedings of Coling-92. Nantes, France.

Karttunen, Lauri, Koskenniemi, Kimmo, and Kaplan, Ronald M. (1987) A Compiler for Two-Level Phonological Rules. In Report No. CSLI-87-108. Center for the Study of Language and Information. Stanford University.

Karttunen, Lauri and Beesley, Kenneth R. (1992). Two-Level Rule Compiler. Technical Report. ISTL-92-2. Xerox Palo Alto Research Center.

Karttunen, Lauri (1994). Constructing Lexical Transducers. In the Proceedings of Coling-94. Kyoto, Japan.

Koskenniemi, Kimmo (1983). Two-Level Morphology: A General Computational Model for Word-Form Recognition and Production. Department of General Linguistics. University of Helsinki.

Koskenniemi, Kimmo (1990). Finite-State Parsing and Disambiguation. In the Proceedings of Coling-90. Helsinki, Finland.

Koskenniemi, Kimmo, Tapanainen, Pasi, and Voutilainen, Atro (1992). Compiling and using finite-state syntactic rules. In the Proceedings of Coling-92. Nantes, France.

Voutilainen, Atro (1994) Three Studies of Grammar-Based Surface Parsing of Unrestricted English Text. The University of Helsinki. 1994.

5 Finite-State Approximation of Phrase-Structure Grammars

Fernando C. N. Pereira and Rebecca N. Wright

Phrase-structure grammars are effective models for important syntactic and semantic aspects of natural languages, but can be computationally too demanding for use as language models in real-time speech recognition. Therefore, finite-state models are used instead, even though they lack expressive power. To reconcile those two alternatives, we designed an algorithm to compute finite-state approximations of context-free grammars and context-free-equivalent augmented phrase-structure grammars. The approximation is exact for certain context-free grammars generating regular languages, including all left-linear and right-linear context-free grammars. The algorithm has been used to build finite-state language models for limited-domain speech recognition tasks.

5.1 Motivation

Grammars for spoken language systems are subject to the conflicting requirements of language modeling for recognition and of language analysis for sentence interpretation. For efficiency reasons, most current recognition systems rely on finite-state language models. These models, however, are inadequate for language interpretation, since they cannot express the relevant syntactic and semantic regularities. Augmented phrase structure grammar (APSG) formalisms, such as unification grammars (Shieber, 1985a), can express many of those regularities, but they are computationally less suitable for language modeling because of the inherent cost of computing state transitions in APSG parsers.

The above conflict can be alleviated by using separate grammars for language modeling and language interpretation. Ideally, the recognition grammar should not reject sentences acceptable by the interpretation grammar and as far as possible it should enforce the constraints built into the interpretation grammar. However, if the two grammars are built independently, those goals are difficult to maintain. For that reason, we have developed a method for approximating APSGs with finite-state acceptors (FSAs). Since such an approximation is intended to serve as language model for a speech-recognition front-end to the real parser, we require it to be *sound* in the sense that the approximation accepts all strings in the language defined by the APSG. Without qualification, the term "approximation" will always mean here "sound approximation."

If no further requirements were placed on the closeness of the approximation, the trivial algorithm that assigns to any APSG over the alphabet Σ the regular language Σ^* would do, but of course this language model is useless. One possible criterion for "goodness" of approximation arises from the observation that many interesting phrase-structure grammars have substantial parts that accept regular languages. That does not mean that grammar rules are in the standard forms for defining regular languages (left-linear or right-linear), because syntactic and semantic considerations often require that strings in a regular set be assigned structural descriptions not definable by left- or right-linear rules. An ideal criterion would thus be that if a grammar generates a regular language, the approximation algorithm yields an acceptor for that regular language. In other words, one would like the algorithm to be *exact* for all APSGs yielding regular languages. However, we will see later that no such general algorithm is possible, that is, any approximation algorithm will be inexact for some APSGs yielding regular languages. Nevertheless, we will show that our method is exact for left-linear and right-linear grammars, and for certain useful combinations thereof.

5.2   The Approximation Method

Our approximation method applies to any context-free grammar (CFG), or any constraint-based grammar (Shieber, 1985a; Carpenter, 1992) that can be fully expanded into a context-free grammar.[1] The resulting FSA accepts all the sentences accepted by the input grammar, and possibly some non-sentences as well.

The implementation takes as input unification grammars of a restricted form ensuring that each feature ranges over a finite set. Clearly, such grammars can only generate context-free languages, since an equivalent CFG can be obtained by instantiating features in rules in all possible ways.

---

[1]Unification grammars not in this class must first be weakened using techniques such as Shieber's restrictor (Shieber, 1985b).

5.2.1 The basic algorithm

The heart of our approximation method is an algorithm to convert the LR(0) *characteristic machine* $\mathcal{M}(G)$ (Aho and Ullman, 1977; Backhouse, 1979) of a CFG G into an FSA for a superset of the language $L(G)$ defined by G. The characteristic machine for a CFG G is an FSA for the *viable prefixes* of G, which are just the possible stacks built by the standard shift-reduce recognizer for G when recognizing strings in $L(G)$.

This is not the place to review the characteristic machine construction in detail. However, to explain the approximation algorithm we will need to recall the main aspects of the construction. The states of $\mathcal{M}(G)$ are sets of *dotted rules* $A \rightarrow \alpha \cdot \beta$ where $A \rightarrow \alpha\beta$ is some rule of G. $\mathcal{M}(G)$ is the determinization by the standard subset construction (Aho and Ullman, 1977) of the FSA defined as follows:

- The initial state is the dotted rule $S' \rightarrow \cdot S$ where S is the start symbol of G and S' is a new auxiliary start symbol.

- The final state is $S' \rightarrow S\cdot$.

- The other states are all the possible dotted rules of G.

- There is a transition labeled X, where X is a terminal or nonterminal symbol, from $A \rightarrow \alpha \cdot X\beta$ to $A \rightarrow \alpha X \cdot \beta$.

- There is an ϵ-transition from $A \rightarrow \alpha \cdot B\beta$ to $B \rightarrow \cdot\gamma$, where B is a nonterminal symbol and $B \rightarrow \gamma$ is a rule in G.

$\mathcal{M}(G)$ can be seen as the finite-state control for a nondeterministic shift-reduce pushdown recognizer $\mathcal{R}(G)$ for G. A state transition labeled by a terminal symbol x from state s to state s' licenses a *shift* move, pushing onto the stack of the recognizer the pair $\langle s, x \rangle$. Arrival at a state containing a *completed dotted rule* $A \rightarrow \alpha\cdot$ licenses a *reduction* move. This pops from the stack $|\alpha|$ elements, checking that the symbols in the pairs match the corresponding elements of α, takes the transition labeled by A from the state s in the last pair popped, and pushes $\langle s, A \rangle$ onto the stack. (Full definitions of those concepts are given in Section 5.3.)

The basic ingredient of our approximation algorithm is the *flattening* of a shift-reduce recognizer for a grammar G into an FSA by eliminating the stack and turning reduce moves into ϵ-transitions. It will be seen below that flattening $\mathcal{R}(G)$ directly leads to poor approximations in many interesting cases. Instead, $\mathcal{M}(G)$ must first be *unfolded* into a larger machine whose states carry information about the possible shift-reduce stacks of $\mathcal{R}(G)$. The quality of the approximation is crucially influenced by how much stack information

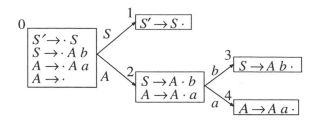

Figure 5.1: Characteristic Machine for G_1

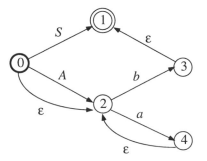

Figure 5.2: Flattened Canonical Acceptor for $L(G_1)$

is encoded in the states of the unfolded machine: too little leads to coarse approximations, while too much leads to redundant automata needing very expensive optimization.

The algorithm is best understood with a simple example. Consider the left-linear grammar G_1

$$S \to Ab$$
$$A \to Aa \mid \epsilon \quad .$$

$\mathcal{M}(G_1)$ is shown on Figure 5.1. Unfolding is not required for this simple example, so the approximating FSA is obtained from $\mathcal{M}(G_1)$ by the flattening method outlined above. The reducing states in $\mathcal{M}(G_1)$, those containing completed dotted rules, are states 0, 3 and 4. For instance, the reduction at state 3 would lead to a $\mathcal{R}(G_1)$ transition on nonterminal S to state 1, from the state that activated the rule being reduced. Thus the corresponding ϵ-transition goes from state 3 to state 1. Adding all the transitions that arise in this way we obtain the FSA in Figure 5.2. From this point on, the arcs labeled with nonterminals can be deleted, and after simplification we obtain the deterministic finite automaton (DFA) in Figure 5.3, which is the minimal DFA for $L(G_1)$.

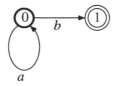

Figure 5.3: Minimal Acceptor for $L(G_1)$

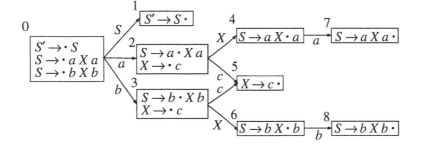

Figure 5.4: Minimal Acceptor for $L(G_2)$

If flattening were always applied to the LR(0) characteristic machine as in the example above, even simple grammars defining regular languages might be inexactly approximated by the algorithm. The reason for this is that in general the reduction at a given reducing state in the characteristic machine transfers to different states depending on stack contents. In other words, the reducing state might be reached by different routes which use the result of the reduction in different ways. The following grammar G_2

$$S \rightarrow aXa \mid bXb$$
$$X \rightarrow c$$

accepts just the two strings aca and bcb, and has the characteristic machine $\mathcal{M}(G_2)$ shown in Figure 5.4. However, the corresponding flattened acceptor shown in Figure 5.5 also accepts acb and bca, because the ϵ-transitions leaving state 5 do not distinguish between the different ways of reaching that state

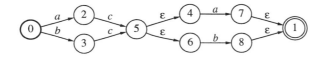

Figure 5.5: Flattened Acceptor for $L(G_2)$

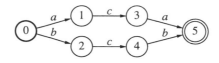

Figure 5.6: Exact Acceptor for $L(G_2)$

encoded in the stack of $\mathcal{R}(G_2)$.

Our solution for the problem just described is to unfold each state of the characteristic machine into a set of states corresponding to different stacks at that state, and flattening the corresponding recognizer rather than the original one. Figure 5.6 shows the resulting acceptor for $L(G_2)$, now exact, after determinization and minimization.

In general the set of possible stacks at a state is infinite. Therefore, it is necessary to do the unfolding not with respect to stacks, but with respect to a finite partition of the set of stacks possible at the state, induced by an appropriate equivalence relation. The relation we use currently makes two stacks equivalent if they can be made identical by *collapsing loops*, that is, removing in a canonical way portions of stack pushed between two arrivals at the same state in the finite-state control of the shift-reduce recognizer, as described more formally and the end of section 5.3.1. The purpose of collapsing a loop is to "forget" a stack segment that may be arbitrarily repeated.[2] Each equivalence class is uniquely defined by the shortest stack in the class, and the classes can be constructed without having to consider all the (infinitely) many possible stacks.

5.2.2   Grammar decomposition

Finite-state approximations computed by the basic algorithm may be extremely large, and their determinization, which is required by minimization (Aho, Hopcroft, and Ullman, 1976), can be computationally infeasible. These problems can be alleviated by first decomposing the grammar to be approximated into *subgrammars* and approximating the subgrammars separately before combining the results.

Each subgrammar in the decomposition of a grammar G corresponds to a set of nonterminals that are involved, directly or indirectly, in each other's definition, together with their defining rules. More precisely, we define a directed graph conn(G) whose nodes are G's nonterminal symbols, and which has an arc from X to Y whenever Y appears in the right-hand side of one of

---

[2]Since possible stacks can be shown to form a regular language, loop collapsing has a direct connection to the pumping lemma for regular languages.

G's rules and X in the left-hand side. Each strongly connected component of this graph (Aho, Hopcroft, and Ullman, 1976) corresponds to a set of mutually recursive nonterminals.

Each nonterminal X of G is in exactly one strongly connected component $\text{comp}(X)$ of $\text{conn}(G)$. Let $\text{prod}(X)$ be the set of G rules with left-hand sides in $\text{comp}(X)$, and $\text{rhs}(X)$ be the set of right-hand side nonterminals of $\text{comp}(X)$. Then the *defining subgrammar* $\text{def}(X)$ of X is the grammar with start symbol X, nonterminal symbols $\text{comp}(X)$, terminal symbols $\Sigma \cup (\text{rhs}(X) - \text{comp}(X))$ and rules $\text{prod}(X)$. In other words, the nonterminal symbols not in $\text{comp}(X)$ are treated as *pseudoterminal* symbols in $\text{def}(X)$.

Each grammar $\text{def}(X)$ can be approximated with our basic algorithm, yielding an FSA $\text{aut}(X)$. To see how to merge together each of these subgrammar approximations to yield an approximation for the whole of G, we observe first that the notion of strongly connected component allows us to take each $\text{aut}(X)$ as a node in a directed acyclic graph with an arc from $\text{aut}(X)$ to $\text{aut}(X')$ whenever X' is a pseudoterminal of $\text{def}(X)$. We can then replace each occurrence of a pseudoterminal X' by its definition. More precisely, each transition labeled by a pseudoterminal X' from some state s to state s' in $\text{aut}(X)$ is replaced by ϵ-transitions from s to the initial state of a separate copy of $\text{aut}(X')$ and ϵ-transitions from the final states of the copy of $\text{aut}(X')$ to s'. This process is then recursively applied to each of the newly created instances of $\text{aut}(X')$ for each pseudoterminal in $\text{def}(X)$. Since the subautomata dependency graph is acyclic, the replacement process must terminate.

5.3 Formal Properties

We will show now that the basic approximation algorithm described informally in the previous section is sound for arbitrary CFGs and is exact for left-linear and right-linear CFGs. From those results, it will be easy to see that the extended algorithm based on decomposing the input grammar into strongly connected components is also sound, and is exact for CFGs in which every strongly connected component is either left linear or right linear.

In what follows, G is a fixed CFG with terminal vocabulary Σ, nonterminal vocabulary N and start symbol S, and $V = \Sigma \cup N$.

5.3.1 Soundness

Let $\mathcal{M}$ be the characteristic machine for G, with state set Q, start state s_0, final states F, and transition function $\delta : S \times V \to S$. As usual, transition functions such as δ are extended from input symbols to input strings by defining $\delta(s, \epsilon) = s$ and $\delta(s, \alpha\beta) = \delta(\delta(s, \alpha), \beta)$. The shift-reduce recognizer $\mathcal{R}$

associated to $\mathcal{M}$ has the same states, start state and final states as $\mathcal{M}$. Its *configurations* are triples $\langle s, \sigma, w \rangle$ of a state, a stack and an input string. The stack is a sequence of pairs $\langle s, X \rangle$ of a state and a symbol. The transitions of the shift-reduce recognizer are given as follows:

Shift: $\langle s, \sigma, xw \rangle \vdash \langle s', \sigma \langle s, x \rangle, w \rangle$ if $\delta(s, x) = s'$

Reduce: $\langle s, \sigma\tau, w \rangle \vdash \langle \delta(s', A), \sigma \langle s', A \rangle, w \rangle$ if either (1) $A \rightarrow \cdot$ is a completed dotted rule in s, $s' = s$ and τ is empty, or (2) $A \rightarrow X_1 \ldots X_n \cdot$ is a completed dotted rule in s, $\tau = \langle s_1, X_1 \rangle \cdots \langle s_n, X_n \rangle$ and $s' = s_1$.

The *initial* configurations of $\mathcal{R}$ are $\langle s_0, \epsilon, w \rangle$ for some input string w, and the *final* configurations are $\langle s, \langle s_0, S \rangle, \epsilon \rangle$ for some state $s \in F$. A *derivation* of a string w is a sequence of configurations $c_0, \ldots, c_m$ such that $c_0 = \langle s_0, \epsilon, w \rangle$, c_m is final, and $c_{i-1} \vdash c_i$ for $1 \leq i \leq n$.

Let s be a state. We define the set Stacks(s) to contain every sequence $\langle q_0, X_0 \rangle \ldots \langle q_k, X_k \rangle$ such that $q_0 = s_0$ and $q_i = \delta(q_{i-1}, X_{i-1}), 1 \leq i \leq k$ and $s = \delta(q_k, X_k)$. In addition, Stacks(s_0) contains the empty sequence ϵ. By construction, it is clear that if $\langle s, \sigma, w \rangle$ is reachable from an initial configuration in $\mathcal{R}$, then $\sigma \in$ Stacks(s).

A *stack congruence* on $\mathcal{R}$ is a family of equivalence relations $\equiv_s$ on Stacks(s) for each state $s \in \mathcal{S}$ such that if $\sigma \equiv_s \sigma'$ and $\delta(s, X) = s'$ then $\sigma \langle s, X \rangle \equiv_{s'} \sigma \langle s, X \rangle$. A stack congruence $\equiv$ partitions each set Stacks(s) into equivalence classes $[\sigma]_s$ of the stacks in Stacks(s) equivalent to σ under $\equiv_s$.

Each stack congruence $\equiv$ on $\mathcal{R}$ induces a corresponding *unfolded recognizer* $\mathcal{R}_\equiv$. The states of the unfolded recognizer are pairs $\langle s, [\sigma]_s \rangle$, notated more concisely as $[\sigma]^s$, of a state and stack equivalence class at that state. The initial state is $[\epsilon]^{s_0}$, and the final states are all $[\sigma]^s$ with $s \in F$ and $\sigma \in$ Stacks(s). The transition function $\delta_\equiv$ of the unfolded recognizer is defined by

$$\delta_\equiv([\sigma]^s, X) = [\sigma \langle s, X \rangle]^{\delta(s, X)} \quad .$$

That this is well-defined follows immediately from the definition of stack congruence.

The definitions of dotted rules in states, configurations, shift and reduce transitions given above carry over immediately to unfolded recognizers. Also, the characteristic recognizer can also be seen as an unfolded recognizer for the trivial coarsest congruence.

Unfolding a characteristic recognizer does not change the language accepted:

Proposition 7 *Let G be a CFG, $\mathcal{R}$ its characteristic recognizer with transition function δ, and $\equiv$ a stack congruence on $\mathcal{R}$. Then $\mathcal{R}_\equiv$ and $\mathcal{R}$ are equivalent.*

Proof: We show first that any string w accepted by $\mathcal{R}_{\equiv}$ is accepted by $\mathcal{R}$. Let d be configuration of $\mathcal{R}_{\equiv}$. By construction, $d = \langle [\rho]^s, \sigma, u \rangle$, with $\sigma = \langle \langle q_0, e_0 \rangle, X_0 \rangle \cdots \langle \langle q_k, e_k \rangle, X_k \rangle$ for appropriate stack equivalence classes e_i. We define $\hat{d} = \langle s, \hat{\sigma}, u \rangle$, with $\hat{\sigma} = \langle q_0, X_0 \rangle \cdots \langle q_k, X_k \rangle$. If $d_0, \ldots, d_m$ is a derivation of w in $\mathcal{R}_{\equiv}$, it is easy to verify that $\hat{d}_0, \ldots, \hat{d}_m$ is a derivation of w in $\mathcal{R}$.

Conversely, let $w \in L(G)$, and let $c_0, \ldots, c_m$ be a derivation of w in $\mathcal{R}$, with $c_i = \langle s_i, \sigma_i, u_i \rangle$. We define $\bar{c}_i = \langle [\sigma_i]^{s_i}, \bar{\sigma}_i, u_i \rangle$, where $\bar{\epsilon} = \epsilon$ and $\overline{\sigma \langle s, X \rangle} = \bar{\sigma} \langle [\sigma]^s, X \rangle$.

If $c_{i-1} \vdash c_i$ is a shift move, then $u_{i-1} = x u_i$ and $\delta(s_{i-1}, x) = s_i$. Therefore,

$$
\begin{aligned}
\delta_{\equiv}([\sigma_{i-1}]^{s_{i-1}}, x) &= [\sigma_{i-1}\langle s_{i-1}, x \rangle]^{\delta(s_{i-1}, x)} \\
&= [\sigma_i]^{s_i} \quad .
\end{aligned}
$$

Furthermore,

$$
\bar{\sigma}_i = \overline{\sigma_{i-1}\langle s_{i-1}, x \rangle} = \bar{\sigma}_{i-1}\langle [\sigma_{i-1}]^{s_{i-1}}, x \rangle \quad .
$$

Thus we have

$$
\begin{aligned}
\bar{c}_{i-1} &= \langle [\sigma_{i-1}]^{s_{i-1}}, \bar{\sigma}_{i-1}, x u_i \rangle \\
\bar{c}_i &= \langle [\sigma_i]^{s_i}, \bar{\sigma}_{i-1}\langle [\sigma_{i-1}]^{s_{i-1}}, x \rangle, u_i \rangle
\end{aligned}
$$

with $\delta_{\equiv}([\sigma_{i-1}]^{s_{i-1}}, x) = [\sigma_i]^{s_i}$. Thus, by definition of shift move, $\bar{c}_{i-1} \vdash \bar{c}_i$ in $\mathcal{R}_{\equiv}$.

Assume now that $c_{i-1} \vdash c_i$ is a reduce move in $\mathcal{R}$. Then $u_i = u_{i-1}$ and we have a state s in $\mathcal{R}$, a symbol $A \in N$, a stack σ and a sequence τ of state-symbol pairs such that

$$
\begin{aligned}
s_i &= \delta(s, A) \\
\sigma_{i-1} &= \sigma\tau \\
\sigma_i &= \sigma\langle s, A \rangle
\end{aligned}
$$

and either

(a) $A \rightarrow \cdot$ is in s_{i-1}, $s = s_{i-1}$ and $\tau = \epsilon$, or

(b) $A \rightarrow X_1 \cdots X_n \cdot$ is in s_{i-1}, $\tau = \langle q_1, X_1 \rangle \cdots \langle q_n, X_n \rangle$ and $s = q_1$.

Let $\bar{s} = [\sigma]^s$. Then

$$
\begin{aligned}
\delta_{\equiv}(\bar{s}, A) &= [\sigma\langle s, A \rangle]^{\delta(s, A)} \\
&= [\sigma_i]^{s_i}
\end{aligned}
$$

We now define a pair sequence $\bar{\tau}$ to play the same role in $\mathcal{R}_{\equiv}$ as τ does in $\mathcal{R}$. In case (a) above, $\bar{\tau} = \epsilon$. Otherwise, let $\tau_1 = \epsilon$ and $\tau_i = \tau_{i-1}\langle q_{i-1}, X_{i-1}\rangle$ for $2 \le i \le n$, and define $\bar{\tau}$ by

$$\bar{\tau} = \langle [\sigma]^{q_1}, X_1\rangle \cdots \langle [\sigma\tau_i]^{q_i}, X_i\rangle \cdots \langle [\sigma\tau_n]^{q_n}, X_n\rangle$$

Then

$$
\begin{aligned}
\bar{\sigma}_{i-1} &= \overline{\sigma\tau} \\
&= \overline{\sigma\langle q_1, X_1\rangle \cdots \langle q_{n-1}, X_{n-1}\rangle}\langle [\sigma\tau_n]^{q_n}, X_n\rangle \\
&= \overline{\sigma\langle q_1, X_1\rangle \cdots \langle q_{i-1}, X_{i-1}\rangle}\langle [\sigma\tau_i]^{q_i}, X_i\rangle \cdots \langle [\sigma\tau_n]^{q_n}, X_n\rangle \\
&= \bar{\sigma}\bar{\tau} \\
\bar{\sigma}_i &= \overline{\sigma\langle s, A\rangle} \\
&= \bar{\sigma}\langle [\sigma]^s, A\rangle \\
&= \bar{\sigma}\langle \bar{s}, A\rangle \qquad .
\end{aligned}
$$

Thus

$$
\begin{aligned}
\bar{c}_i &= \langle \delta_{\equiv}(\bar{s}, A), \bar{\sigma}\langle \bar{s}, A\rangle, u_i\rangle \\
\bar{c}_{i-1} &= \langle [\sigma_{i-1}]^{s_{i-1}}, \bar{\sigma}\bar{\tau}, u_{i-1}\rangle
\end{aligned}
$$

which by construction of $\bar{\tau}$ immediately entails that $\bar{c}_{i-1} \vdash \bar{c}_i$ is a reduce move in $\mathcal{R}_{\equiv}$. $\qquad \square$

For any unfolded state p, let $\text{Pop}(p)$ be the set of states reachable from p by a reduce transition. More precisely, $\text{Pop}(p)$ contains any state p' such that there is a completed dotted rule $A \rightarrow \alpha\cdot$ in p and a state p'' containing $A \rightarrow \cdot\alpha$ such that $\delta_{\equiv}(p'', \alpha) = p$ and $\delta_{\equiv}(p'', A) = p'$. Then the *flattening* $\mathcal{F}_{\equiv}$ of $\mathcal{R}_{\equiv}$ is an NFA with the same state set, start state and final states as $\mathcal{R}_{\equiv}$ and nondeterministic transition function $\phi_{\equiv}$ defined as follows:

- If $\delta_{\equiv}(p, x) = p'$ for some $x \in \Sigma$, then $p' \in \phi_{\equiv}(p, x)$

- If $p' \in \text{Pop}(p)$ then $p' \in \phi_{\equiv}(p, \epsilon)$.

Let $c_0, \ldots, c_m$ be a derivation of string w in $\mathcal{R}$, and put $c_i = \langle q_i, \sigma_i, w_i\rangle$, and $p_i = [\sigma_i]^{p_i}$. By construction, if $c_{i-1} \vdash c_i$ is a shift move on x ($w_{i-1} = xw_i$), then $\delta_{\equiv}(p_{i-1}, x) = p_i$, and thus $p_i \in \phi_{\equiv}(p_{i-1}, x)$. Alternatively, assume the transition is a reduce move associated to the completed dotted rule $A \rightarrow \alpha\cdot$. We consider first the case $\alpha \ne \epsilon$. Put $\alpha = X_1 \ldots X_n$. By definition of reduce move, there is a sequence of states $r_1, \ldots, r_n$ and a stack σ such that $\sigma_{i-1} = \sigma\langle r_1, X_1\rangle \ldots \langle r_n, X_n\rangle$, $\sigma_i = \sigma\langle r_1, A\rangle$, r_1 contains $A \rightarrow \cdot\alpha$, $\delta(r_1, A) = q_i$, and $\delta(r_j, X_j) = r_{j+1}$ for $1 \le j < n$. By definition of stack congruence, we will then have

$$\delta_{\equiv}([\sigma\tau_j]^{r_j}, X_j) = [\sigma\tau_{j+1}]^{r_{j+1}}$$

where $\tau_1 = \epsilon$ and $\tau_j = \langle r_1, X_1 \rangle \ldots \langle r_{j-1}, X_{j-1} \rangle$ for $j > 1$. Furthermore, again by definition of stack congruence we have $\delta_\equiv([\sigma]^{r_1}, A) = p_i$. Therefore, $p_i \in \text{Pop}(p_{i-1})$ and thus $p_i \in \phi_\equiv(p_{i-1}, \epsilon)$. A similar but simpler argument allows us to reach the same conclusion for the case $\alpha = \epsilon$. Finally, the definition of final state for $\mathcal{R}_\equiv$ and $\mathcal{F}_\equiv$ makes p_m a final state. Therefore the sequence $p_0, \ldots, p_m$ is an accepting path for w in $\mathcal{F}_\equiv$. We have thus proved

Proposition 8 *For any CFG G and stack congruence $\equiv$ on the canonical* LR(0) *shift-reduce recognizer $\mathcal{R}(G)$ of G, $L(G) \subseteq L(\mathcal{F}_\equiv(G))$, where $\mathcal{F}_\equiv(G)$ is the flattening of $\mathcal{R}(G)_\equiv$.*

To complete the proof of soundness for the basic algorithm, we must show that the stack collapsing equivalence described informally earlier is indeed a stack congruence. A stack τ is a *loop* if $\tau = \langle s_1, X_1 \rangle \ldots \langle s_k, X_k \rangle$ and $\delta(s_k, X_k) = s_1$. A stack τ is a *minimal* loop if no prefix of τ is a loop. A stack that contains a loop is *collapsible*. A collapsible stack σ *immediately collapses* to a stack σ' if $\sigma = \rho \tau \upsilon$, $\sigma' = \rho \upsilon$, τ is a minimal loop and there is no other decomposition $\sigma = \rho' \tau' \upsilon'$ such that ρ' is a proper prefix of ρ and τ' is a loop. By these definitions, a collapsible stack σ immediately collapses to a unique stack $C(\sigma)$. A stack σ *collapses* to σ' if $\sigma' = C^n(\sigma)$. Two stacks are equivalent if they can be collapsed to the same uncollapsible stack. This equivalence relation is closed under suffixing, therefore it is a stack congruence. Each equivalence class has a canonical representative, the unique uncollapsible stack in it, and clearly there are finitely many uncollapsible stacks.

We compute the possible uncollapsible stacks associated with states as follows. To start with, the empty stack is associated with the initial state. Inductively, if stack σ has been associated with state s and $\delta(s, X) = s'$, we associate $\sigma' = \sigma \langle s, X \rangle$ with s' unless σ' is already associated with s' or s' occurs in σ, in which case a suffix of σ' would be a loop and σ' thus collapsible. Since there are finitely many uncollapsible stacks, the above computation is must terminate.

When the grammar G is first decomposed into strongly connected components $\text{def}(X)$, each approximated by $\text{aut}(X)$, the soundness of the overall construction follows easily by induction on the partial order of strongly connected components and by the soundness of the approximation of $\text{def}(X)$ by $\text{aut}(X)$, which guarantees that each G sentential form over $\Sigma \cup (\text{rhs}(X) - \text{comp}(X))$ accepted by $\text{def}(X)$ is accepted by $\text{aut}(X)$.

5.3.2 Exactness

While it is difficult to decide what should be meant by a "good" approximation, we observed earlier that a desirable feature of an approximation algorithm is that it be exact for a wide class of CFGs generating regular languages. We show in this section that our algorithm is exact for both left-linear and right-linear CFGs, and as a consequence for CFGs that can be decomposed into independent left and right linear components. On the other hand, a theorem of Ullian's (Ullian, 1967) shows that there can be no partial algorithm mapping CFGs to FSAs that terminates on every CFG yielding a regular language L with an FSA accepting exactly L.

The proofs that follow rely on the following basic definitions and facts about the LR(0) construction. Each LR(0) state s is the *closure* of a set of a certain set of dotted rules, its *core*. The closure $[R]$ of a set R of dotted rules is the smallest set of dotted rules containing R that contains $B \rightarrow \cdot\gamma$ whenever it contains $A \rightarrow \alpha \cdot B\beta$ and $B \rightarrow \gamma$ is in G. The core of the initial state s_0 contains just the dotted rule $S' \rightarrow \cdot S$. For any other state s, there is a state s' and a symbol X such that s is the closure of the set core consisting of all dotted rules $A \rightarrow \alpha X \cdot \beta$ where $A \rightarrow \alpha \cdot X\beta$ belongs to s'.

5.3.2.1   Left-linear grammars

A CFG G is left-linear if each rule in G is of the form $A \rightarrow B\beta$ or $A \rightarrow \beta$, where $A, B \in N$ and $\beta \in \Sigma^*$.

Proposition 9 *Let G be a left-linear CFG, and let $\mathcal{F}$ be the FSA derived from G by the basic approximation algorithm. Then $L(G) = L(\mathcal{F})$.*

Proof: By Proposition 8, $L(G) \subseteq L(\mathcal{F})$. Thus we need only show $L(\mathcal{F}) \subseteq L(G)$.

Since $\mathcal{M}(G)$ is deterministic, for each $\alpha \in V^*$ there is at most one state s in $\mathcal{M}(G)$ reachable from s_0 by a path labeled with α. If s exists, we define $\bar{\alpha} = s$. Conversely, each state s can be identified with a string $\hat{s} \in V^*$ such that every dotted rule in s is of the form $A \rightarrow \hat{s} \cdot \alpha$ for some $A \in N$ and $\alpha \in V^*$. Clearly, this is true for $s_0 = [S' \rightarrow \cdot S]$, with $\hat{s}_0 = \epsilon$. The core $\dot{s}$ of any other state s will by construction contain only dotted rules of the form $A \rightarrow \alpha \cdot \beta$ with $\alpha \neq \epsilon$. Since G is left linear, β must be a terminal string, thus $s = \dot{s}$. Therefore every dotted rule $A \rightarrow \alpha \cdot \beta$ in s results from dotted rule $A \rightarrow \cdot\alpha\beta$ in s_0 by a unique transition path labeled by α (since $\mathcal{M}(G)$ is deterministic). This means that if $A \rightarrow \alpha \cdot \beta$ and $A' \rightarrow \alpha' \cdot \beta'$ are in s, it must be the case that $\alpha = \alpha'$.

To go from the characteristic machine $\mathcal{M}(G)$ to the FSA $\mathcal{F}$, the algorithm first unfolds $\mathcal{M}(G)$ using the stack congruence relation, and then flattens the unfolded machine by replacing reduce moves with ϵ-transitions. However, the above argument shows that the only stack possible at a state s is the one corresponding to the transitions given by $\hat{s}$, and thus there is a single stack congruence state at each state. Therefore, $\mathcal{M}(G)$ will only be flattened, not unfolded. Hence the transition function ϕ for the resulting flattened automaton $\mathcal{F}$ is defined as follows, where $\alpha \in N\Sigma^* \cup \Sigma^*, a \in \Sigma$, and $A \in N$:

(a) $\phi(\bar{\alpha}, a) = \{\overline{\alpha a}\}$

(b) $\phi(\bar{\alpha}, \epsilon) = \{\bar{A} \mid A \to \alpha \in G\}$

The start state of $\mathcal{F}$ is $\bar{\epsilon}$. The only final state is $\bar{S}$.

We will establish the connection between $\mathcal{F}$ derivations and G derivations. We claim that if there is a path from $\bar{\alpha}$ to $\bar{S}$ labeled by w then either there is a rule $A \to \alpha$ such that $w = xy$ and $S \stackrel{*}{\Rightarrow} Ay \Rightarrow \alpha xy$, or $\alpha = S$ and $w = \epsilon$. The claim is proved by induction on $|w|$.

For the base case, suppose $|w| = 0$ and there is a path from $\bar{\alpha}$ to $\bar{S}$ labeled by w. Then $w = \epsilon$, and either $\alpha = S$, or there is a path of ϵ-transitions from $\bar{\alpha}$ to $\bar{S}$. In the latter case, $S \stackrel{*}{\Rightarrow} A \Rightarrow \epsilon$ for some $A \in N$ and rule $A \to \epsilon$, and thus the claim holds.

Now, assume that the claim is true for all $|w| < k$, and suppose there is a path from $\bar{\alpha}$ to $\bar{S}$ labeled w', for some $|w'| = k$. Then $w' = aw$ for some terminal a and $|w| < k$, and there is a path from $\overline{\alpha a}$ to $\bar{S}$ labeled by w. By the induction hypothesis, $S \stackrel{*}{\Rightarrow} Ay \Rightarrow \alpha a x'y$, where $A \to \alpha a x'$ is a rule and $x'y = w$ (since $\alpha a \neq S$). Letting $x = ax'$, we have the desired result.

If $w \in L(\mathcal{F})$, then there is a path from $\bar{\epsilon}$ to $\bar{S}$ labeled by w. Thus, by the claim just proved, $S \stackrel{*}{\Rightarrow} Ay \Rightarrow xy$, where $A \to x$ is a rule and $w = xy$ (since $\epsilon \neq S$). Therefore, $S \stackrel{*}{\Rightarrow} w$, so $w \in L(G)$, as desired. □

5.3.2.2 Right-linear grammars

A CFG G is right linear if each rule in G is of the form $A \to \beta B$ or $A \to \beta$, where $A, B \in N$ and $\beta \in \Sigma^*$.

Proposition 10 *Let G be a right-linear CFG and $\mathcal{F}$ be the FSA derived from G by the basic approximation algorithm. Then $L(G) = L(\mathcal{F})$.*

Proof: As before, we need only show $L(\mathcal{F}) \subseteq L(G)$.

Let $\mathcal{R}$ be the shift-reduce recognizer for G. The key fact to notice is that, because G is right-linear, no shift transition may follow a reduce transition. Therefore, no terminal transition in $\mathcal{F}$ may follow an ϵ-transition, and after any ϵ-transition, there is a sequence of ϵ-transitions leading to the final state $[S' \to S\cdot]$. Hence $\mathcal{F}$ has the following kinds of states: the start state, the final state, states with terminal transitions entering and leaving them (we call these *reading* states), states with ϵ-transitions entering and leaving them (*prefinal* states), and states with terminal transitions entering them and ϵ-transitions leaving them (*crossover* states). Any accepting path through $\mathcal{F}$ will consist of a sequence of a start state, reading states, a crossover state, prefinal states, and a final state. The exception to this is a path accepting the empty string, which has a start state, possibly some prefinal states, and a final state.

The above argument also shows that unfolding does not change the set of strings accepted by $\mathcal{F}$, because any reduction in $\mathcal{R}_{\equiv}$ (or ϵ-transition in $\mathcal{F}$), is guaranteed to be part of a path of reductions (ϵ-transitions) leading to a final state of $\mathcal{R}_{\equiv}$ ($\mathcal{F}$).

Suppose now that $w = w_1 \dots w_n$ is accepted by $\mathcal{F}$. Then there is a path from the start state s_0 through reading states $s_1, \dots, s_{n-1}$, to crossover state s_n, followed by ϵ-transitions to the final state. We claim that if there there is a path from s_i to s_n labeled $w_{i+1} \dots w_n$, then there is a dotted rule $A \rightarrow x \cdot yB$ in s_i such $B \overset{*}{\Rightarrow} z$ and $yz = w_{i+1} \dots w_n$, where $A \in N, B \in N \cup \Sigma^*, y, z \in \Sigma^*$, and one of the following holds:

(a) x is a nonempty suffix of $w_1 \dots w_i$,

(b) $x = \epsilon, A'' \overset{*}{\Rightarrow} A, A' \rightarrow x' \cdot A''$ is a dotted rule in s_i, and x' is a nonempty suffix of $w_1 \dots w_i$, or

(c) $x = \epsilon, s_i = s_0$, and $S \overset{*}{\Rightarrow} A$.

We prove the claim by induction on $n - i$. For the base case, suppose there is an empty path from s_n to s_n. Because s_n is the crossover state, there must be some dotted rule $A \rightarrow x \cdot$ in s_n. Letting $y = z = B = \epsilon$, we get that $A \rightarrow x \cdot yB$ is a dotted rule of s_n and $B = z$. The dotted rule $A \rightarrow x \cdot yB$ must have either been added to s_n by closure or by shifts. If it arose from a shift, x must be a nonempty suffix of $w_1 \dots w_n$. If the dotted rule arose by closure, $x = \epsilon$, and there is some dotted rule $A' \rightarrow x' \cdot A''$ such that $A'' \overset{*}{\Rightarrow} A$ and x' is a nonempty suffix of $w_1 \dots w_n$.

Now suppose that the claim holds for paths from s_i to s_n, and look at a path labeled $w_i \dots w_n$ from s_{i-1} to s_n. By the induction hypothesis, $A \rightarrow x \cdot yB$ is a dotted rule of s_i, where $B \overset{*}{\Rightarrow} z, uz = w_{i+1} \dots w_n$, and (since $s_i \neq s_0$), either x is a nonempty suffix of $w_1 \dots w_i$ or $x = \epsilon, A' \rightarrow x' \cdot A''$ is a dotted rule of $s_i, A'' \overset{*}{\Rightarrow} A$, and x' is a nonempty suffix of $w_1 \dots w_i$.

In the former case, when x is a nonempty suffix of $w_1 \dots w_i$, then $x = w_j \dots w_i$ for some $1 \leq j < i$. Then $A \rightarrow w_j \dots w_i \cdot yB$ is a dotted rule of s_i, and thus $A \rightarrow w_j \dots w_{i-1} \cdot w_i yB$ is a dotted rule of s_{i-1}. If $j \leq i-1$, then $w_j \dots w_{i-1}$ is a nonempty suffix of $w_1 \dots w_{i-1}$, and we are done. Otherwise, $w_j \dots w_{i-1} = \epsilon$, and so $A \rightarrow \cdot w_i yB$ is a dotted rule of s_{i-1}. Let $y' = w_i y$. Then $A \rightarrow \cdot y' B$ is a dotted rule of s_{i-1}, which must have been added by closure. Hence there are nonterminals A' and A'' such that $A'' \overset{*}{\Rightarrow} A$ and $A' \rightarrow x' \cdot A''$ is a dotted rule of s_{i-1}, where x' is a nonempty suffix of $w_1 \dots w_{i-1}$.

Symbol	Category	Features
s	sentence	n (number), p (person)
np	noun phrase	n, p, c (case)
vp	verb phrase	n, p, t (verb type)
args	verb arguments	t
det	determiner	n
n	noun	n
pron	pronoun	n, p, c
v	verb	n, p, t

Table 5.1: Categories of Example Grammar

In the latter case, there must be a dotted rule $A' \to w_j \ldots w_{i-1} \cdot w_i A''$ in s_{i-1}. The rest of the conditions are exactly as in the previous case.

Thus, if $w = w_1 \ldots w_n$ is accepted by $\mathcal{F}$, then there is a path from s_0 to s_n labeled by $w_1 \ldots w_n$. Hence, by the claim just proved, $A \to x \cdot yB$ is a dotted rule of s_n, and $B \stackrel{*}{\Rightarrow} z$, where $yz = w_1 \ldots w_n = w$. Because the s_i in the claim is s_0, and all the dotted rules of s_i can have nothing before the dot, and x must be the empty string. Therefore, the only possible case is case 3. Thus, $S \stackrel{*}{\Rightarrow} A \to yz = w$, and hence $w \in L(G)$. The proof that the empty string is accepted by $\mathcal{F}$ only if it is in $L(G)$ is similar to the proof of the claim. □

5.3.3 Decompositions

If each $\text{def}(X)$ in the strongly-connected component decomposition of G is left-linear or right-linear, it is easy to see that G accepts a regular language, and that the overall approximation derived by decomposition is exact. Since some components may be left-linear and others right-linear, the overall class we can approximate exactly goes beyond purely left-linear or purely right-linear grammars.

5.4 Implementation and Example

The example in the appendix is an APSG for a small fragment of English, written in the notation accepted by our grammar compiler. The categories and features used in the grammar are described in Tables 5.1 and 5.2 (categories without features are omitted). The example grammar accepts sentences such as

```
i give a cake to tom
```

Feature	Values
n (number)	s (singular), p (plural)
p (person)	1 (first), 2 (second), 3 (third)
c (case)	s (subject), o (nonsubject)
t (verb type)	i (intransitive), t (transitive), d (ditransitive)

Table 5.2: Features of Example Grammar

```
tom sleeps
i eat every nice cake
```

but rejects ill-formed inputs such as

```
i sleeps
i eats a cake
i give
tom eat
```

It is easy to see that the each strongly-connected component of the example is either left-linear or right linear, and therefore our algorithm will produce an equivalent FSA. Grammar compilation is organized as follows:

1. Instantiate input APSG to yield an equivalent CFG.

2. Decompose the CFG into strongly-connected components.

3. For each subgrammar def(X) in the decomposition:

   (a) approximate def(X) by aut(X);

   (b) determinize and minimize aut(X);

4. Recombine the aut(X) into a single FSA using the partial order of grammar components.

5. Determinize and minimize the recombined FSA.

For small examples such as the present one, steps 2, 3 and 4 can be replaced by a single approximation step for the whole CFG. In the current implementation, instantiation of the APSG into an equivalent CFG is written in Prolog, and the other compilation steps are written in C, for space and time efficiency in dealing with potentially large grammars and automata.

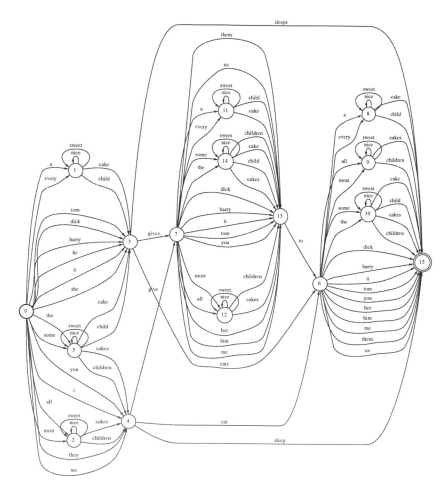

Figure 5.7: Approximation for Example Grammar

For the example grammar, the equivalent CFG has 78 nonterminals and 157 rules, the unfolded and flattened FSA 2615 states and 4096 transitions, and the determinized and minimized final DFA shown in Figure 5.7 has 16 states and 97 transitions. The runtime for the whole process is 1.78 seconds on a Sun SparcStation 20.

Substantially larger grammars, with thousands of instantiated rules, have been developed for a speech-to-speech translation project (Roe et al., 1992). Compilation times vary widely, but very long compilations appear to be caused by a combinatorial explosion in the unfolding of right recursions that will be discussed further in the next section.

5.5   Informal Analysis

In addition to the cases of left-linear and right-linear grammars and decompositions into those cases discussed in Section 5.3, our algorithm is exact in a variety of interesting cases, including the examples of Church and Patil (Church and Patil, 1982), which illustrate how typical attachment ambiguities arise as structural ambiguities on regular string sets.

The algorithm is also exact for some self-embedding grammars[3] of regular languages, such as

$$S \rightarrow aS \mid Sb \mid c$$

defining the regular language $a^* c b^*$.

A more interesting example is the following simplified grammar for the structure of English noun phrases:

NP → Det Nom | PN
Det → Art | NP 's
Nom → N | Nom PP | Adj Nom
PP → P NP

The symbols Art, Adj, N, PN and P correspond to the parts of speech article, adjective, noun, proper noun and preposition, and the nonterminals Det, NP, Nom and PP to determiner phrases, noun phrases, nominal phrases and prepositional phrases, respectively. From this grammar, the algorithm derives the exact DFA in Figure 5.8. This example is typical of the kinds of grammars with systematic attachment ambiguities discussed by Church and Patil (Church and Patil, 1982). A string of parts-of-speech such as

Art N P Art N P Art N

is ambiguous according to the grammar (only some constituents shown for simplicity):

Art [$_{Nom}$N [$_{PP}$P[$_{NP}$Art [$_{Nom}$ N [$_{PP}$P [$_{NP}$Art N]]]]]]
Art [$_{Nom}$[$_{Nom}$N [$_{PP}$P [$_{NP}$Art N]]] [$_{PP}$P [$_{NP}$Art N]]]

However, if multiplicity of analyses are ignored, the string set accepted by the grammar is regular and the approximation algorithm obtains the correct DFA.

---

[3] A grammar is self-embedding if and only if licenses the derivation $X \stackrel{*}{\Rightarrow} \alpha X \beta$ for nonempty α and β. A language is regular if and only if it can be described by some non-self-embedding grammar.

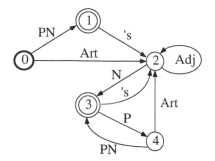

Figure 5.8: Acceptor for Noun Phrases

However, we have no characterization of the class of CFGs for which this kind of exact approximation is possible.

As an example of inexact approximation, consider the self-embedding CFG

$$S \rightarrow aSb \mid \epsilon$$

for the nonregular language $a^n b^n, n \geq 0$. This grammar is mapped by the algorithm into an FSA accepting $\epsilon \mid a^+ b^+$. The effect of the algorithm is thus to "forget" the pairing between a's and b's mediated by the stack of the grammar's characteristic recognizer.

Our algorithm has very poor worst-case performance. First, the expansion of an APSG into a CFG, not described here, can lead to an exponential blow-up in the number of nonterminals and rules. Second, the subset calculation implicit in the LR(0) construction can make the number of states in the characteristic machine exponential on the number of CF rules. Finally, unfolding can yield another exponential blow-up in the number of states.

However, in the practical examples we have considered, the first and the last problems appear to be the most serious.

The rule instantiation problem may be alleviated by avoiding full instantiation of unification grammar rules with respect to "don't care" features, that is, features that are not constrained by the rule.

The unfolding problem is particularly serious in grammars with subgrammars of the form

$$S \rightarrow X_1 S \mid \cdots \mid X_n S \mid Y \qquad . \qquad (5.1)$$

It is easy to see that the number of unfolded states in the subgrammar is exponential in n. This kind of situation often arises indirectly in the expansion of an APSG when some features in the right-hand side of a rule are unconstrained and thus lead to many different instantiated rules. However, from the proof of

Proposition 10 it follows immediately that unfolding is unnecessary for right-linear grammars. Therefore, if we use our grammar decomposition method first and test individual components for right-linearity, unnecessary unfolding can be avoided. Alternatively, the problem can be circumvented by left factoring (5.1) as follows:

$$S \rightarrow ZS \mid Y$$
$$Z \rightarrow X_1 \mid \cdots \mid X_n$$

5.6   Related Work and Conclusions

Our work can be seen as an algorithmic realization of suggestions of Church and Patil (Church, 1980; Church and Patil, 1982) on algebraic simplifications of CFGs of regular languages. Other work on finite-state approximations of phrase structure grammars has typically relied on arbitrary depth cutoffs in rule application. While this may be reasonable for psycholinguistic modeling of performance restrictions on center embedding (Pulman, 1986), it does not seem appropriate for speech recognition where the approximating FSA is intended to work as a filter and not reject inputs acceptable by the given grammar. For instance, depth cutoffs in the method described by Black (Black, 1989) lead to approximating FSAs whose language is neither a subset nor a superset of the language of the given phrase-structure grammar. In contrast, our method will produce an exact FSA for many interesting grammars generating regular languages, such as those arising from systematic attachment ambiguities (Church and Patil, 1982). It is important to note, however, that even when the result FSA accepts the same language, the original grammar is still necessary because interpretation algorithms are generally expressed in terms of phrase structures described by that grammar, not in terms of the states of the FSA.

Several extensions of the present work may be worth investigating.

As is well known, speech recognition accuracy can often be improved by taking into account the probabilities of different sentences. If such probabilities are encoded as rule probabilities in the initial grammar, we would need a method for transferring them to the approximating FSA. Alternatively, transition probabilities for the approximating FSA could be estimated directly from a training corpus, either by simple counting in the case of a DFA or by an appropriate version of the Baum-Welch procedure for general probabilistic FSAs (Rabiner, 1989).

Alternative pushdown acceptors and stack congruences may be considered with different size-accuracy tradeoffs. Furthermore, instead of expanding the APSG first into a CFG and only then approximating, one might start with a pushdown acceptor for the APSG class under consideration (Lang, 1988), and approximate it directly using a generalized notion of stack congruence that takes into account the instantiation of stack items. This approach might well reduce the explosion in grammar size induced by the initial conversion of APSGs to CFGs, and also make the method applicable to APSGs with unbounded feature sets, such as general constraint-based grammars.

We do not have any useful quantitative measure of approximation quality. Formal-language theoretic notions such as the rational index of a language (Boasson, Courcelle, and Nivat, 1981) capture a notion of language complexity but it is not clear how it relates to the intuition that an approximation is "worse" than another if it strictly contains it. In a probabilistic setting, a language can be identified with a probability density function over strings. Then the Kullback-Leibler divergence (Cover and Thomas, 1991) between the approximation and the original language might be a useful measure of approximation quality.

Finally, constructions based on finite-state transducers may lead to a whole new class of approximations. For instance, CFGs may be decomposed into the composition of a simple fixed CFG with given approximation and a complex, varying finite-state transducer that needs no approximation.

Appendix—APSG formalism and example

Nonterminal symbols (syntactic categories) may have features that specify variants of the category (eg. singular or plural noun phrases, intransitive or transitive verbs). A category *cat* with feature constraints is written

$$cat\#\, [c_1, \ldots, c_m]\;.$$

Feature constraints for feature f have one of the forms

$$f \;=\; v \tag{5.2}$$

$$f \;=\; c \tag{5.3}$$

$$f \;=\; (c_1, \ldots, c_n) \tag{5.4}$$

where v is a variable name (which must be capitalized) and $c, c_1, \ldots, c_n$ are feature values.

All occurrences of a variable v in a rule stand for the same unspecified value. A constraint with form (5.2) specifies a feature as having that value. A constraint of form (5.3) specifies an actual value for a feature, and a constraint of form (5.4) specifies that a feature may have any value from the specified set of values. The symbol "!" appearing as the value of a feature in the right-hand side of a rule indicates that that feature must have the same value as the feature of the same name of the category in the left-hand side of the rule. This notation, as well as variables, can be used to enforce feature agreement between categories in a rule, for instance, number agreement between subject and verb.

It is convenient to declare the features and possible values of categories with category declarations appearing before the grammar rules. Category declarations have the form

$$\text{cat } cat\#[\quad f_1 \quad = \quad (v_{11}, \dots, v_{1k_1}),$$
$$\dots,$$
$$f_m \quad = \quad (v_{m1}, \dots, v_{mk_m}) \quad].$$

giving all the possible values of all the features for the category.

The declaration

    start *cat*.

declares *cat* as the start symbol of the grammar.

In the grammar rules, the symbol "`'`" prefixes terminal symbols, commas are used for sequencing and "`|`" for alternation.

```
start s.

cat s#[n=(s,p),p=(1,2,3)].
cat np#[n=(s,p),p=(1,2,3),c=(s,o)].
cat vp#[n=(s,p),p=(1,2,3),type=(i,t,d)].
cat args#[type=(i,t,d)].

cat det#[n=(s,p)].
cat n#[n=(s,p)].
cat pron#[n=(s,p),p=(1,2,3),c=(s,o)].
cat v#[n=(s,p),p=(1,2,3),type=(i,t,d)].

s => np#[n=!,p=!,c=s], vp#[n=!,p=!].

np#[p=3] => det#[n=!], adjs, n#[n=!].
np#[n=s,p=3] => pn.
np => pron#[n=!, p=!, c=!].

pron#[n=s,p=1,c=s] => 'i.
pron#[p=2] => 'you.
pron#[n=s,p=3,c=s] => 'he | 'she.
pron#[n=s,p=3] => 'it.
pron#[n=p,p=1,c=s] => 'we.
pron#[n=p,p=3,c=s] => 'they.
pron#[n=s,p=1,c=o] => 'me.
pron#[n=s,p=3,c=o] => 'him | 'her.
pron#[n=p,p=1,c=o] => 'us.
pron#[n=p,p=3,c=o] => 'them.
```

```
vp => v#[n=!,p=!,type=!], args#[type=!].

adjs => [].
adjs => adj, adjs.

args#[type=i] => [].
args#[type=t] => np#[c=o].
args#[type=d] => np#[c=o], 'to, np#[c=o].

pn => 'tom | 'dick | 'harry.

det => 'some| 'the.
det#[n=s] => 'every | 'a.
det#[n=p] => 'all | 'most.

n#[n=s] => 'child | 'cake.
n#[n=p] => 'children | 'cakes.

adj => 'nice | 'sweet.

v#[n=s,p=3,type=i] => 'sleeps.
v#[n=p,type=i] => 'sleep.
v#[n=s,p=(1,2),type=i] => 'sleep.

v#[n=s,p=3,type=t] => 'eats.
v#[n=p,type=t] => 'eat.
v#[n=s,p=(1,2),type=t] => 'eat.

v#[n=s,p=3,type=d] => 'gives.
v#[n=p,type=d] => 'give.
v#[n=s,p=(1,2),type=d] => 'give.
```

Acknowledgments

We thank Mark Liberman for suggesting that we look into finite-state approximations, Richard Sproat, David Roe and Pedro Moreno trying out several prototypes supplying test grammars, and Mehryar Mohri, Edmund Grimley-Evans and the editors of this volume for corrections and other useful suggestions. This paper is a revised and extended version of the 1991 ACL meeting paper with the same title (Pereira and Wright, 1991).

References

Aho, Alfred V. and Jeffrey D. Ullman. 1977. *Principles of Compiler Design.* Addison-Wesley, Reading, Massachusetts.

Aho, Alfred V., John E. Hopcroft, and Jeffrey D. Ullman. 1976. *The Design and Analysis of Computer Algorithms.* Addison-Wesley, Reading, Massachusetts.

Backhouse, Roland C. 1979. *Syntax of Programming Languages—Theory and Practice.* Series in Computer Science. Prentice-Hall, Englewood Cliffs, New Jersey.

Black, Alan W. 1989. Finite-State machines from feature grammars. In Masaru Tomita, editor, *International Workshop on Parsing Technologies*, pages 277–285, Pittsburgh, Pennsylvania. Carnegie Mellon University.

Boasson, Luc, Bruno Courcelle, and Maurice Nivat. 1981. The rational index: a complexity measure for languages. *SIAM Journal of Computing*, 10(2):284–296.

Carpenter, Bob. 1992. *The Logic of Typed Feature Structures.* Number 32 in Cambridge Tracts in Theoretical Computer Science. Cambridge University Press, Cambridge, England.

Church, Kenneth W. and Ramesh Patil. 1982. Coping with syntactic ambiguity or how to put the block in the box on the table. *Computational Linguistics*, 8(3–4):139–149.

Church, Kenneth W. 1980. On memory limitations in natural language processing. Master's thesis, M.I.T.
Published as Report MIT/LCS/TR-245.

Cover, Thomas M. and Joy A. Thomas. 1991. *Elements of Information Theory.* Wiley-Interscience, New York, New York.

Lang, Bernard. 1988. Complete evaluation of Horn clauses: an automata theoretic approach. Rapport de Recherche 913, INRIA, Rocquencourt, France, November.

Pereira, Fernando C. N. and Rebecca N. Wright. 1991. Finite-state approximation of phrase-structure grammars. In *29th Annual Meeting of the Association for Computational Linguistics*, pages 246–255, Berkeley, California. University of California at Berkeley, Association for Computational Linguistics, Morristown, New Jersey.

Pulman, Steven G. 1986. Grammars, parsers, and memory limitations. *Language and Cognitive Processes*, 1(3):197–225.

Rabiner, Lawrence R. 1989. A tutorial on hidden markov models and selected applications in speech recognition. *Proceedings of the IEEE*, 77(2):257–286.

Roe, David B., Pedro J. Moreno, Richard W. Sproat, Fernando C. N. Pereira, Michael D. Riley, and Alejandro Macarrón. 1992. A spoken language translator for restricted-domain context-free languages. *Speech Communication*, 11:311–319.

Shieber, Stuart M. 1985a. *An Introduction to Unification-Based Approaches to Grammar*. Number 4 in CSLI Lecture Notes. Center for the Study of Language and Information, Stanford, California.

Distributed by Chicago University Press.

Shieber, Stuart M. 1985b. Using restriction to extend parsing algorithms for complex-feature-based formalisms. In *23rd Annual Meeting of the Association for Computational Linguistics*, pages 145–152, Chicago, Illinois. Association for Computational Linguistics, Morristown, New Jersey.

Ullian, Joseph S. 1967. Partial algorithm problems for context free languages. *Information and Control*, 11:90–101.

6 The Lexical Analysis of Natural Languages

Max D. Silberztein

6.1 The Lexical Analysis of Programming Languages and of Natural Languages

The lexical analysis of programs in the compilation process consists in segmenting the program text in lexical units and in associating with each unit a syntactic function such as 'name of a variable', 'operator', 'numerical constant', etc. For example, given the following text:

while (when == 23.7) who++;

the lexical analyser associates the character string "while" with its syntactic function, "when" and "who" with names of variables, "==" and "++" with operators and "23.7" with a numerical constant. The lexical analysis of programming languages has been intensively studied by computer scientists; an important result is the fact that all the operations necessary for the identification of the lexical units of programming langauges can be carried out by finite-state machines. As a result, powerful tools for lexical analysis, such as for instance LEX (cf. [Lesk 1975]) have been built.

The lexical analysis of texts in natural language shows many similarities to the lexical analysis of programs. Here as well, the goal is to identify the minimal units of analysis that are to constitute the starting point for syntactic analysis. For example, the lexical analyser has to segment the following text:

All of a sudden, Luc ate all the french fries

into the lexical units "all of a sudden" (adverb), "Luc" (firstname), "to eat" (verb), "all" (predeterminer), "the" (determiner), "french fry" (noun). Of course, there are many important differences between the lexical analysis of programming languages and the lexical analysis of natural languages:

- the size of the *standard* vocabulary (cf. [Garrigues 1993] concerning the notions of *basic* and *standard* vocabulary) of a natural language is in no way comparable to the vocabularies used by programming languages (dozens of key-words usually); it is therefore imperative to construct and maintain a system of dictionaries;

- words in texts are usually inflected, which requires morphological analysis in order to associate the occurrences in texts with entries in dictionaries; the ratio between the number of inflected forms and the number of entries in the dictionary can vary tremendously (it is 2 in the case of English, 10 in the case of French);

- words in natural language texts can be ambiguous at various levels such as spelling, inflection, morphology, syntax and semantics. For instance, the string "RELEVE" in French can correspond to the two forms *relevé* and *relève*. The form *relevé* can be lemmatized in three ways:

> *masculine singular adjective* relevé
> *masculine singular noun* relevé
> *past participle of the verb* relever

The form *relève* can be lemmatized in two ways:

> *féminine singular noun* relève
> *present indicative or subjunctive in first or third person singular,*
> *or second person singular imperative form of the verb* relever.

Each of these five dictionary entries is syntactically and semantically ambiguous; for instance, the verb *relever* corresponds to at least three syntactic structures:

> N_0 *relever* N_1 =: *John relève la chaise (John picks up the chair)*
> *Que P relever de* N_1 =: *Qu'il agisse ainsi relève de la police*
>   *(His acting in this manner is relevant for the police)*
> N_0 *relever que P* =: *John relève que Paul s'est trompé*
>   *(John remarks that Paul made a mistake)*

According to context, the noun *relevé* can mean *account, listing, plotting, reading, summary*, etc. In the general case, it is not possible to eliminate all ambiguities during lexical analysis; the lexical analyser must therefore represent these ambiguities and make them available to the syntactic analyser.

- There exists a systematic formal ambiguity between compound words and sequences of the same simple words; again these ambiguities cannot be resolved in general during lexical analysis. For instance, the sequence *red tape* can represent either a *red ribbon* or *bureaucraty*. It is not possible to treat this ambiguity at the level of lexical analysis and quite often, a semantic –or even pragmatic– analysis will be necessary. These ambiguities have to be represented formally and the parsing process has to start from them. The result produced by the lexical analyser cannot be linear as in the case of traditional taggers, hence it will have to be represented by an directed acyclic graph (DAG). For instance, when the lexical analyser comes to treat the sequence "red tape", it must produce the DAG shown in Figure 6.1 as a result[1]:

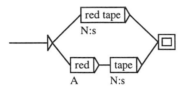

Figure 6.1: DAG for "red tape".

In Figure 6.1, "N:s" stands for **Noun singular**; "A" stands for **Adjective**. Notice that this DAG can be seen as a finite-state transducer, where the input text units are associated with produced linguistic information.

- Other issues, such as orthographic variation, the use of proper names, of acroynms and abbreviations, the resolution of elisions and contractions, the use of numbers in texts, the recognition of ends of sentences, etc. all fit very simply into the framework of the theory of finite-state machines and can be treated with finite-state transducers (cf. [Silberztein 1989],

---

[1]We use the INTEX graph editor to edit Finite-State Automata and Transducers. The representation differs from the traditional one:

- we represent transition labels in nodes, where inputs are written in the nodes and outputs are written below;

- states are let implicit (they could be drawn at the left of each node);

- each graph has exactly one initial node (the arrow in the left) and one terminal node (the double square);

- epsilon transitions are represented by arrows.

These graphs are compiled to finite-state automata and transducers, and then applied to texts. For a short description of **INTEX**, see [Silberztein 1994a].

[Silberztein 1993]); it remains, however, that the large number of phenomena to be described as well as the interaction between the different levels of analysis make lexical analysis of natural languages a highly complex undertaking.

When we speak about the *identification* of the units of a language by way of lexical analysis, we understand two things:

- on the one hand, the segmentation of the text in elementary units; the main difficulty being the definition of what these units are; for example, in sentence (1), the first occurrence of "all" is a constituent of the frozen adverb "all of a sudden", whereas the second is a unit in its own right (determiner);

- on the other hand, the association of these units with the information (syntactic, semantic, etc.) necessary for the further stages of analysis; this annotation (often referred as "tagging") will in general be accomplished on the basis of dictionary consultation.

Therefore, the *identification* of a unit does not necessarily imply that the unit *is* in fact present in the text, nor that it is completely unambiguous; it means only that it *may* be present in the text: it is up to the analysers that apply later to determine if yes or no the unit is in fact present.

Of course, the goal of lexical analysis is to pass on as few non-relevant hypotheses as possible to the analysers that follow up and thus to eliminate as many ambiguities as possible (one speaks of *minimal noise* here). But the main priority is to pass on an analysis which contains all the hypotheses that could turn out to be correct (one speaks of *zero silence* here).

6.2   The Units of Analysis

It is important to notice that once the lexical analyser considers that a sequence is a linguistic unit, the analysers that apply later no longer have access to the parts of the sequence. For example, if the lexical analyser identifies the sequence "suddenly" as an adverb, the syntactic analyser will not be able to take "sudden" or "-ly" into consideration; similarly, if the lexical analyser treats the sequence "all of a sudden" as an adverb, the constituents "all" or "sudden" are no longer available to the syntactic analyser.

In this framework, analysers cannot return to the earlier stages of analysis in order to reanalyze a lexical unit, or even to consult the dictionary again. The association of the occurrences of lexical items in the text to linguistic units in the dictionary is the function of the sole lexical analysis.

From a formal point of view, the lexical analyser must recognize two kinds of units in texts: the *simple words* and the *compound words*[2].

6.2.1 Simple words

Simple words are the lexical units that are continuous sequences of letters from a formal point of view. Here, for instance is the set of 82 letters that make up the French alphabet:

a b c d e f g h i j k l m n o p q r s t u v w x y z
A B C D E F G H I J K L M N O P Q R S T U V W X Y Z
à â ä ç é è ê ë î ï ô ö ù û ü
À Â Ä Ç É È Ê Ë Î Ï Ô Ö Ù Û ü

Some of these letters (e.g. *ö*) appear only in words with foreign origin (e.g. the "French" verb *gödéliser* comes from the proper name *Gödel*). Sequences of characters that are not in the set of letters are separators. For instance, the strings "table" and "mangerions" are simple words whereas "as a matter of fact" or "aujourd'hui" are not (the blank and the apostrophe are separators).

6.2.2 Compound words

Compound words are lexical units that are made up from two or more simple words (and therefore contain at least one separator). For instance, the sequences "hard disk", "take the bull by the horns" and "take ... into account" are compound words. Observe that the last verbal compound is not connex: it can take an arbitrary number of words between *take* and *account*.

The distinction between simple and compound words is thus purely orthographic; for instance, "deltaplane" (*hang glider*) is a simple word, whereas its orthographic variants "delta-plane" and "delta plane" are compound words. The most natural way to combine the variants of this type is to represent them in a finite-state transducer, as shown in Figure 6.2:

The transducer in Figure 6.2 is used in the following manner: every time the lexical analyser **identifies** one of these variants it **produces** the lexical unit *deltaplane.N:ms* (Noun, masculine singular), hence performing a "generalized" lemmatization. Subsequently, the analyzer will not even know which variant was present in the text.

---

[2]The delimitation we will give is rather natural for English, Spanish, French, Italian and Portuguese but less so for some Germanic languages (German, Dutch for instance). The problem with Germanic languages is not fundamentally different, since we have lexical units that are sequences of letters (e.g. Haus) and discontinuous lexical units (e.g. *aufmachen* in: *Er macht die Tür auf*); lexical units traditionally considered as compound words not containing a separator (e.g. *Schreibmaschine*) are taken to be simple words on the present view.

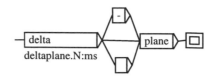

Figure 6.2: Transducer for "delta place".

6.3   The Representation of Simple Words

6.3.1   The DELAS and DELAF dictionaries

The set of simple words is specified in the dictionary DELAS of every language. For instance, the French DELAS contains more than 90,000 entries in normalized form, in general, the masculine singular for the nouns and adjectives and the infinitive for the verbs (cf. [Courtois 1990]). Each entry is classified according to its part of speech and is thus associated in an unambiguous way to a code from the set of 13 members:

A, ADV, CONJ, DET, INT, N, PREF, PREP, PRO, V, XINC

A stands for Adjective, *ADV* for Adverb, *CONJ* = Conjunction, *DET* = Determiner, *INT* = Interjection, *N* = Noun, *PREF* = Prefix, *PREP* = Preposition, *PRO* = Pronoun, *V* = Verb; *XINC* is used to represent simple words that do not occur autonomously, i.e. strings that are always constituents of compound words. For instance, the simple word "aujourd", which never occurs anywhere except in the compound "aujourd'hui", is coded XINC. In French, nouns, adjectives and verbs have inflected forms:

- nouns and adjectives can appear in the feminine and/or in the plural;

- verbs are conjugated.

In order to describe the inflection paradigms, we use finite-state transducers that represent the set of suffixes which must be appended to each entry in the DELAS to derive the corresponding inflected form. The transducer then produces the grammatical information corresponding to each generated form. Consider for example the transducer NA32 shown in Figure 6.3 of French nouns and adjectives that inflect in the same manner as *cousin* or *ami* (adjectives and nouns inflect in identical ways in French):

The symbol ⟨*E*⟩ represents the empty word. If one adds "es" to the string "cousin", one obtains the string "cousines" together with the produced

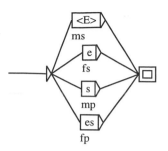

Figure 6.3: Transducer NA32.

information "fp" (feminine plural). A program that traverses the transducer reads the following DELAS entry:

ami, N32

and automatically generates the list below:

ami, ami . N32 : ms
amie, ami . N32 : fs
amis, ami . N32 : mp
amies, ami . N32 : fp

Figure 6.4 shows an excerpt of the transducer V3 of verbs of the first conjugation group examplified by the paradigm of aimer,

The character "#" is used to delete the last character, much like the "delete" key. For instance, the third path of the preceding graph must be interpreted in the following way: if one deletes the last two letters of the DELAS entry (e.g. *aimer*) and if one adds the string "ons", one obtains a form (e.g. *aimons*) with the associated information "P1p" (indicative present, first person plural). As for nouns and adjectives, starting from the following DELAS entry:

aimer, V3

the complete transducer traversal program automatically produces the 39 forms of the verb *aimer* shown in Figure 6.5.

In Figure 6.5, *W* stands for infinitive, *G* for present participle, *K* for past participle, *P* for indicative present, etc. For the complete list and the meanings of the various codes of the DELAF dictionary, see [Courtois 1990]. For French, 80 transducers are required for the representation of nouns and adjectives, and

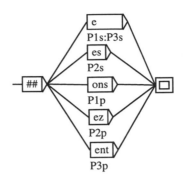

Figure 6.4: Transducer V3.

aimer,.V3:W
aimé,aimer.V3:Kms
aimés,aimer.V3:Kmp
aime,aimer.V3:P1s:P3s:S1s:S3s:Y2s
aimons,aimer.V3:P1p:Y1p
aiment,aimer.V3:P3p:S3p
aimait,aimer.V3:I3s
aimiez,aimer.V3:I2p:S2p
aimai,aimer.V3:J1s
aima,aimer.V3:J3s
aimâtes,aimer.V3:J2p
aimerai,aimer.V3:F1s
aimera,aimer.V3:F3s
aimerez,aimer.V3:F2p
aimasse,aimer.V3:T1s
aimât,aimer.V3:T3s
aimassiez,aimer.V3:T2p
aimerais,aimer.V3:C1s:C2s
aimerions,aimer.V3:C1p
aimeraient,aimer.V3:C3p

aimant,aimer.V3:G
aimée,aimer.V3:Kfs
aimées,aimer.V3:Kfp
aimes,aimer.V3:P2s:S2s
aimez,aimer.V3:P2p:Y2p
aimais,aimer.V3:I1s:I2s
aimions,aimer.V3:I1p:S1p
aimaient,aimer.V3:I3p
aimas,aimer.V3:J2s
aimâmes,aimer.V3:J1p
aimèrent,aimer.V3:J3p
aimeras,aimer.V3:F2s
aimerons,aimer.V3:F1p
aimeront,aimer.V3:F3p
aimasses,aimer.V3:T2s
aimassions,aimer.V3:T1p
aimassent,aimer.V3:T3p
aimerait,aimer.V3:C3s
aimeriez,aimer.V3:C2p

Figure 6.5: Forms of the verb aimer.

98 transducers for the verbs. The English dictionary DELAS contains 129 transducers for the inflection of nouns and 103 for the inflection of verbs.

The next step consists in traversing all the paths of the transducers associated with each entry of the DELAS dictionary; in this way one constructs automatically all the inflected forms of the language. A sorted version of this list will put together all the ambiguities. For example, the two independent entries of the French DELAS:

> *ration, N21*
> *rater, V3*

give rise both to the form *rations*:

> *rations, ration . N21:fp (feminine plural of the noun* ration*)*
> *rations, rater . V3:I1p (past tense first person plural of the verb* rater*)*

Putting together these entries, we obtain the dictionary entry:

> *rations,ration.N21:fp,rater.V3:I1p*

The list of all the forms of a language constitute the DELAF dictionary. For instance, the French DELAF contains approximately 800,000 entries. This dictionary is itself represented by a finite-state transducer that assigns to each occurrence of a text the corresponding information (cf. [Revuz 1991], [Roche 1993]). In other words, the lemmatization and morphological analysis of a text turns out to be nothing but the application of the transducer of the DELAF to the text.

Along the lines of the DELAS and the DELAF model, one also constructs dictionaries for first names, toponyms, acronyms, abbreviations, etc. adapted to various types of texts and various types of applications (cf. [Silberztein 1993]).

6.3.2 Representation of simple words by finite-state transducers

The basic idea developped until now is that the simple forms of a language are finite in number and that they must therefore be enumerated and appropriately described: it is the role of the DELAS dictionary to provide this description. But there are simple words (i.e. sequences of letters) that should not or that cannot be enumerated in extension in a dictionary. For example, let us consider simple words of the form *americanization*. The problem is that if we consider them to be simple words, i.e. non-analyzable units of the language, then we have to put them into a list which will include the following 18 forms:

> *America, american,*

americanize, americanizable, americanizability, americanization, reamericanize, reamericanization, reamericanizability, reamericanizable,
deamericanize, deamericanization, deamericanizability, deamericanizable,
redeamericanize, redeamericanization, redeamericanizability, redeamericanizable

Such a collection would amount to treating these entries as being independent; a more serious problem is that these successive derivations are themselves productive: for example, along the lines of the preceding model, we can construct *africanization, anglicization, europeanization, regermanization, desovietization,* etc. Here a list in the form of a dictionary would not be natural, since we prefer to assign linguistic categories, like *Verb, Noun, Adjective* to the morphemes *-ize, -ization, -izable* instead of repeating this information for each word. We use finite-state transducers that will on the one hand recognize all derived forms and assign the corresponding linguistic information to them on the other hand. For example, Figure 6.6 shows the transducer representing the derivational family of the noun *France* in French.

For a discussion on the syntactic operations and the restrictions involved in the derivations represented in the graph, see [M. Gross 1989]. The morphosyntactic codes produced by the transducer are attached to the morphemes and not to the words themselves as it would be the case in the dictionary. For example, the suffix *-er* is "responsible" for the production of the code V3 (verb of the first group conjugated like *aimer*); the suffix *-ilité* produces the code N21 (feminine noun taking an *s* in the plural), etc. These codes are exactly the same as those we find in the DELAS, which allows us to treat the inflection of simple words recognized by transducers in the same way as that of the entries of the dictionaries.

Finite-State transducers are also used to describe roman numerals and cardinal numbers:

XVIII, MCMXCV, XVIIIème

These objects are formally sequences of letters, but it is hardly possible to enumerate them in the form of a list; on the other hand, it is very easy to specify the corresponding transducer. We can also use finite transducers to relate and normalize orthographic variants of the same word, or synonymic variants of the same term. For example, Figure 6.7 shows the eleven orthographic variants of the French spelling of the word *kosher*.

These variants are all assigned the more current French form "casher" (A80 means invariable adjective), and we can therefore bring all the forms together in an index, or normalize their orthography in texts.

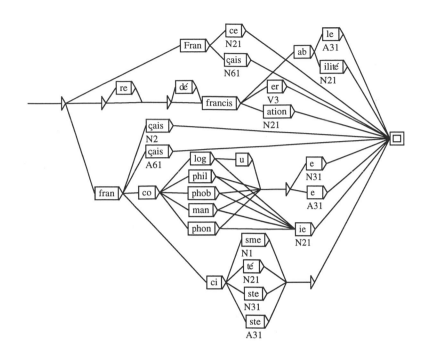

Figure 6.6: The derivational family of the noun *France*.

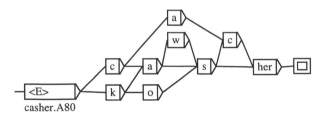

Figure 6.7: Orthographic variants of *casher*.

6.3.3 Syntactic and semantic information

The lexicon-grammar of a language describes the syntactic and semantic properties of the units of the language. For example, the description of the verbs contains for every verb the types of its complements, the prepositions that introduces these complements, the possibilities of pronominalizing the complements, of putting the verb in the passive, of nominalizing the verb, of constucting an adjective with the suffix *-able*, etc. The words as well as their properties constitute the lexicon-grammar which takes the form of a table or a binary matrix. The entries appear on the lines of the table and the columns indicate the properties that are taken into account; a "+" sign at the intersection of line and a column means that the word has the corresponding property, a "-" means that it does not. On the basis of the set of described properties, one defines the notion of ambiguity: if a particular orthographic form corresponds to several sets of properties, then it gives rise to several entries in the lexicon-grammar. For instance, in the lexicon-grammar of French, there are 8 entries for the orthographic form *voler*:

Table	Example
2	*Luc vole aider Paul*
	(Luc hurries to help Paul)
6	*Luc n'a pas volé sa claque*
	(Luc deserved the slap)
10	*Luc a volé dans ce livre que E=mc²*
	(Luc has taken from this book that $E=mc^2$)
32R3	*Luc a volé son titre de professeur*
	(Luc is not up to par as a professor)
35L	*L'avion a volé jusqu'à Gap*
	(The plane has flown to Gap)
35R	*La porte a volé en morceaux*
	(The door broke into pieces)
36DT	*Luc vole une chaise à Paul*
	(Luc steals a chair from Paul)
37E	*Luc vole Paul de 100F*
	(Luc cheats Paul out of 100F)

The name of the table that appears in the first column corresponds to a syntactic structure[3]; for instance, the table 36DT contains dative verbs that appear in the construction $N_0 \, V \, N_1 \, \text{à} \, N_2$.

The dictionaries DELAS-DELAF contain the index of the lexicon-grammars; as a result, the look-up effected by the lexical analyser provides a large amount of information, usually in an ambiguous form. For instance, an occurrence of the form *vole* gives rise to the following result:

---

[3]For more information about the organisation of French verbs in the classes of the French lexicon-grammar, see [Leclère 1990]. For French, there are also tables describing the syntactic properties of nouns, adjectives, adverbs, determiners, conjunctions and frozen expressions. For an overview of the work related to lexicon-grammars of several languages, see the bibliography of the LADL by [Leclère, Subirats 1991].

vole	*N21:fs*
voler	*V3U;i;2:P1s:P3s:S1s:S3s:Y2s*
voler	*V3;t;6:P1s:P3s:S1s:S3s:Y2s*
voler	*V3;t;10:P1s:P3s:S1s:S3s:Y2s*
voler	*V3;t;32R3:P1s:P3s:S1s:S3s:Y2s*
voler	*V3U;i;35L:P1s:P3s:S1s:S3s:Y2s*
voler	*V3U;i;35R:P1s:P3s:S1s:S3s:Y2s*
voler	*V3;t;36DT:P1s:P3s:S1s:S3s:Y2s*
voler	*V3;t;37E:P1s:P3s:S1s:S3s:Y2s*

"t" stands for transitive; "i" for intransitive; "P1s" for present indicative of the first person singular, etc. As we can see, one obtains a result that is 49 times ambiguous... Some of these ambiguities can often be removed by inspecting the context of the occurrence (see below), but most of the lexical hypotheses that the lexical analyser returns require a much finer analysis for their confirmation or for their rejection.

6.3.4   Automatic identification of the simple words in texts

There are several problems that need to be solved when we associate occurrences of sequences of letters in a text with entries in the dictionaries (and the tags of the grammars). Here are some:

- Letters in words occurring in texts do not always correspond to the ones in dictionary entries. For instance, capital letters will generally have to be rewritten in lowercase. In French, they are not always accentuated in texts; the missing accents have therefore to be reintroduced during the traversal of the transducer: for instance, the letter "E" has to match the five tags "e", "é", "è", "ê" et "ë" in the transducer of the dictionary. In German, the strings "ss", "ae", "oe" and "ue" in texts must match the tags "ß", "ä", "ö" and "ü" in the transducer of the dictionary.

- The apostrophe is used for several purposes: in compound words (e.g. *aujourd'hui*, *prud'homme*); in elisions (e.g. *j'aide*, *l'arbre*), in the English possessive form; to represent foreign letters, as a quotation mark, in angular units (e.g. 10°35'), etc. In French, the only words which can be elided are:

  > *ce, de, entre, grand, je, jusque, la, le, lorsque, me, ne presque, puisque, que, quelque, se, si, te, tu*

Most of these words are not ambiguous when elided; for instance, the token *quoiqu'* can only be an occurrence of *quoique*. But some of them, very frequent in texts, are ambiguous; for instance *l'* can represent the pronouns or the determiners *la* or *le, s'* can represent the conjunction *si* or the pronoun *se*, etc. In some cases, a simple exploration of the context of the elided words will allow the lexical parser to remove the ambiguities (see below).

- The hyphen is also used in several ways: it appears in compounds (e.g. *Jean-François*), after certain prefixes (e.g. *électro-métallique*), in compound numbers (e.g. *trente-trois*), between verbs and postponed pronouns (e.g. *dit-il*), as parentheses, for stylistic purposes, in mathematical formulas, etc. Usually, the occurrence of a hyphen can be used to remove ambiguities: most compounds can be disambiguated when they contain an hyphen; in the same manner, the two following sentences are not ambiguous, thanks to the hyphen:

  Donne-le tout à l'heure (give it in a moment)
  Donne le tout à l'heure (give the whole on time)

- Contracted words, such as *du = de le, can't = cannot*, etc. have to be rewritten during the lexical analysis; some of the rewritings yield ambiguous results that cannot be solved before a complete syntactic analysis of the sentence. Here too, in the general case, the representation of the output of a lexical parser will be a directed acyclic graph (DAG); for instance, the token *des* in French will have to be represented by the DAG shown in Figure 6.8.

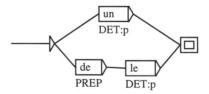

Figure 6.8: DAG for the token *des*.

(*des* is either the plural of the determiner *un*, or the contraction of the preposition *de* and the plural of the determiner *le*);

- there are other problems, like abbreviations (e.g. *Mr*) and symbols (e.g. %) which have to be replaced by the underlying word, numerals which have to be represented, sentence delimiters which must be identified, prefixes which can be added in front of most verbs, in a productive way:

auto, bi, co, de, dé, dis, dys, en, in, mé, re, ré, sub, sur, etc.

Each of these phenomena will be handled by means of finite-state transducers (cf. [Silberztein 1989], [Clemenceau 1992], [Silberztein 1993]).

6.4 Representation of Compound Words

6.4.1 The DELAC dictionary

Compound words are lexical units made up of several simple words. Even if the problem of the distinction between *simple words* and *compound words* is rather straightforward, there is the problem of making the distinction between sequences of simple words and lexicalized compound words as these are indistinguishable from a formal point of view. From the point of view of the automatic analysis of natural languages, the distinction can be expressed in the following rule:

> *if all morphological, syntactic and semantic properties of a sequence of words can be calculated from the parts of the sequence, then the sequence is analysable and there is no reason to treat it as lexicalized; if on the other hand, at least one of these properties cannot be predicted, then this property has to be attached to the entire sequence, which amounts to treating it as lexicalized.*

This definition obviously depends on the properties taken into account for the description of the language; for an overview of the properties taken into account at the LADL, cf. [Gross 1975]. The definition of compound words has led us to consider as compound words a large number of nominal structures that are not traditionally classified as compounds as such (see [Silberztein 1994b] for a discussion of the distinction between compound nouns and free noun phrases). Given our view on compounds, we estimate that there are several times more compound forms than simple forms in the language across all categories.

The LADL has undertaken to construct an electronic dictionary of compound words, called DELAC. At the moment, the French DELAC contains about 130,000 entries, of which more than 120,000 are compound nouns, 8,000 are compound adverbs and about 400 are conjunctions. The compound nouns (which can be inflected) are classified according to their morpho-syntactic structure (Noun Adjective, Noun *de* Noun, Noun Noun, etc.); the inflectional properties of each entry are indicated according to the same principle as in the DELAS dictionary. For example, here are three entries of the DELAC:

> *cousin (32) germain (32), NA; Hum : ms + +*
> *moyen-âge, AN : ms - -*
> *pomme(21) de terre, NDN; Conc : fs - +*

The first entry, *cousin germain* (*first-degree cousin*) is a compound noun of structure *Noun Adjective* (NA), it represents a human (Hum), masculine singular (ms). Each entry is assigned two symbols specifying the possibility (+) or impossibility (-) of gender and number inflection, respectively. When an entry can be inflected, the constituents that are concerned by the inflection are given the tag of the suffix transducer (the same transducer that is used in the DELAS). For example, to inflect the compound noun *cousin germain*, both constituents *cousin* and *germain* are inflected using the transducer 32; to inflect the noun *pomme de terre*, only the constituent *pomme* is inflected using the transducer 21. It is possible to inflect compound nouns in a similar way as the inflection of simple words, that is, by a mere application of the finite-state transducers that correspond to each inflectional code.

The agreement constraints between constituents can also be taken into account by the application of four finite-state transducers: one for the inflection from masculine singular to masculine plural (MSMP), one for the inflection from masculine singular to feminine singular (MSFS), one for the inflection from masculine singular to feminine plural (MSFP), and one for the inflection from feminine singular to feminine plural (FSFP). For instance, in order to get the feminine plural form of masculine singular nouns of the DELAC, one applies the following substitutions to the DELAC file (here presented in a *sed* format):

> s/:ms/:fp/g
> s/(31)/s/g
> s/(32)/es/g
> s/(33)/es/g
>
> ...

These substitutions are performed by the MSFP finite-state transducer. For a detailled description of the inflection of compounds nouns, see [Silberztein 1993]. Once all of the inflected compound forms are generated from the DELAC and their ambiguous entries put together, we get the dictionary of all the inflected compounds, the DELACF, of the form:

> *cousin germain, . NA; Hum : ms*
> *cousine germaine, cousin germain . NA; Hum : fs*

cousines germaines, cousin germain . NA; Hum : fp
cousins germains, cousin germain . NA; Hum : mp
moyen-âge, . AN : ms
pomme de terre, . NDN; Conc : fs
pommes de terre, pomme de terre . NDN; Conc : fp

The French DELACF dictionary contains about 180,000 entries; it is also implemented in the form of a finite-state transducer, which makes it possible to reduce the problem of recognizing and lemmatizing compound forms to a simple application of the transducer of the DELACF to a text.

6.4.2   Representation of compound words by finite-state transducers

As in the case of simple words, there are objects that are formally speaking compound words, but which cannot be listed in a natural way in a dictionary. For example, the numerical determiners, such as:

one, two, ...   ninety million three hundred thousand four hundred twenty-one ...

cannot be listed, but they are represented in a very natural manner by a finite transducer. By way of example, Figures 6.9, 6.10 and 6.11 illustrate the graphs that are used to represent the numerical determiners in French.

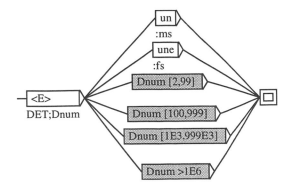

Figure 6.9: Transducer for numerical determiners.

The transducer shown in Figure 6.9 assigns for example to the simple word *un* the information "DET;Dnum:ms" (masculine singular determiner). The label "Dnum [2,99]" refers to the graph shown in Figure 6.10.

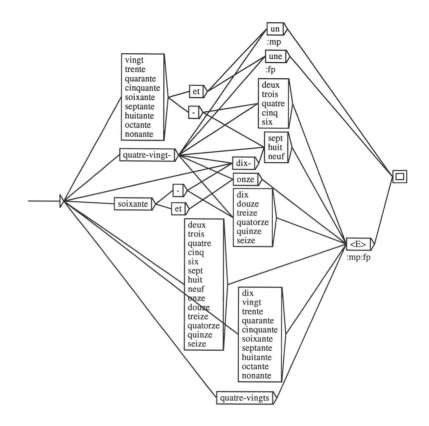

Figure 6.10: Transducer Dnum[2,99].

The label "Dnum [100,999]" refers to the graph shown in Figure 6.11.

The minimal deterministic transducer constructed from the complete series of 9 graphs contains less than 100 states (the labels being simple words or separators).

Here too, one can relate the variants of the same term by representing them in one transducer. See [Gross, same volume] for examples of transducers that represent compound words and expressions.

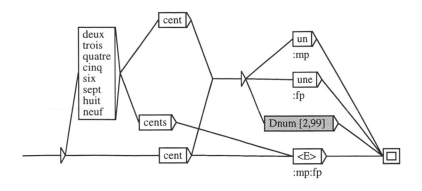

Figure 6.11: Transducer Dnum[100,999].

6.5 Representation of the Results of the Analysis, Elimination of Ambiguities by Local Grammars

We have seen that the units of the language can be described by dictionaries and graphs; in fact, both of these objects are represented internally by finite-state transducers. The lexical analysis of a text is thus performed by applying the union of all the finite-state transducers to it.

As we pointed out, the result of identifying the simple and compound words (from dictionaries or grammars) yields a significant number of ambiguities. For example, given the simple text:

> *Il vole une pomme de terre cuite (He steals a cooked potato / a clay apple)*

the lexical parser automatically builds the upper DAG in Figure 6.13 (we have not represented the semantic ambiguities). This DAG represents two entries for the word *voler* (Noun or Verb), the compound noun *pomme de terre*, the ambiguous compound noun *terre cuite* (*pottery*, or *fired clay*), two entries for the word *terre* (Noun or Verb), four entries for the word *cuite*, etc. Some of these ambiguities cannot be solved before a semantic, or even a pragmatic analysis is done: for instance, there is no way a low-level parser can decide between the two meanings: *he steals a cooked potato*, or *he steals a clay apple*.

However, by checking the context of some grammatical words (e.g. *de*, *il*, *être*, etc.), we can very often remove many ambiguities. For instance, the word *vole*, which follows the pronoun *il*, can only be a verb conjugated in the third person singular (because it follows the pronoun il); *de* can only be a preposition (because it is not followed by a plural noun or adjective), thus *terre* cannot be a verb (verbs that follow the preposition *de* are in the infinitive), etc.

All these constraints can be easily described by means of finite-state transducers. Transducers *recognize* word sequences, and *produce* synchronized strings of constraints. For example, Figure 6.12 shows the transducer that describes the right context of the pronoun *il*.

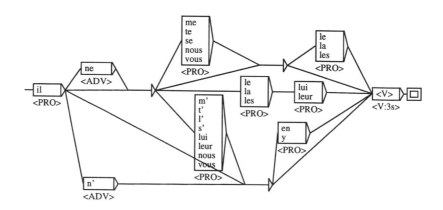

Figure 6.12: Transducer for the right context of the pronoun *il*.

This transducer is used in the following manner: every time it matches a sequence in a text, it produces a series of constraints which are then applied to each individual lexical unit of the sequence. For instance, if the lexical parser parses the *sequence "...il le leur donne..."* (*He gives it to them*), it will produce the following sequence of constraints:

Input sequence	Output sequence of constraints
il le leur donne	<PRO> <PRO> <PRO> <V:3s>

The words *il*, *le* and *leur* cannot be anything but pronouns (<PRO>); the word *donne* cannot be anything but a verb in the third person singular (<V:3s>). Usually, these transducers are built so that most sequences identified are completely disambiguated; in other words, the transducer produces only one resulting sequence of constraints for any recognized input.

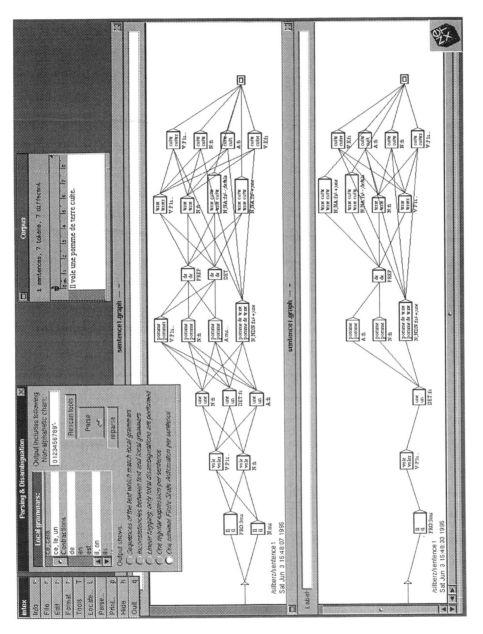

Figure 6.13: Ambiguities of Il vole une pomme de terre cuite.

Longest match

If more than one path in the transducer matches the input, there may be multiple and different resulting sequences of constraints. For instance, when the transducer in Figure 6.14 is applied to the text "*...Donne-le-leur...*" (*Give it to them*), (<V:Y> stands for verb in the imperative) it produces two sequences of constraints:

	Input sequences	Output constraints
1	donne-le	<V:Y> <PRO>
2	donne-le-leur	<V:Y> <PRO> <PRO>

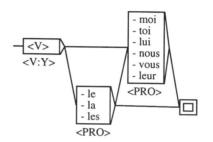

Figure 6.14: Transducer for ⟨V⟩-*LE-LUI*.

Only the longest match 2 must be taken into account, because we want the lexical parser to remove as many ambiguities as possible.

Incomplete disambiguation

If more than one sequence of constraints of the same length are produced during the application of the transducer, disambiguation may remain incomplete. For instance, consider the transducer in Figure 6.15.

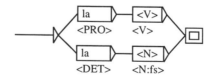

Figure 6.15: Transducer for the disambiguation of *la*.

This transducer says that when the word *la* is followed by a verb, it is a pronoun; when followed by a noun, it is a determiner (and the noun is necessarily a feminine singular noun). Now consider the DAG representing the text "... *la donne...*" (*give it*, or *the hand* in the vocabulary of card playings) shown in Figure 6.16.

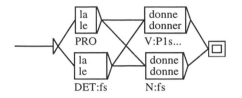

Figure 6.16: DAG for *la donne*.

The word *donne* can be either the feminine noun *donne*, or the verb *donner*. When applying the transducer of Figure 6.15 on the DAG of Figure 6.16, we push the four intermediate results shown in Figure 6.17 on a stack.

	Input sequences	Paths	Output
1	<la,le.PRO> <donne,donner.V>	la <V>	<PRO> <V>
2	<la,le.PRO> <donne,donne.N:fs>	la <N>	<DET> <N:fs>
3	<la,le.DET:fs> <donne,donner.V>	la <V>	<PRO> <V>
4	<la,le.DET:fs> <donne,donne.N:fs>	la <N>	<DET> <N:fs>

Figure 6.17: Intermediate results on the stack.

After having applied the output constraints on the input sequences, we delete the two incompatible results 2 and 3; the remaining sequences 1 and 4 are then represented by the DAG shown in Figure 6.18.

Given the DAG shown on top of Figure 6.13, we have applied the union of a series of transducers to remove ambiguities; the resulting output is shown below the first DAG. For French, we have developed a series of 30 *perfect* transducers, that is, transducers that may never remove correct lexical hypothesis, in any text. Each transducer describes the local context of one or more grammatical words, such as *a*, *de*, *est*, *mon*, *par*, etc. We think that the number of perfect transducers that could be easily designed on the same principle is much bigger (several hundred).

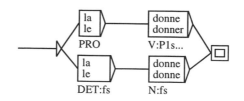

Figure 6.18: Output DAG for *le donne*.

The union of the 30 transducers give a minimal deterministic transducer of 200 states. When applied on a text, already one third of the transitions are typically removed; note that most of the remaining ambiguities concern compound words (there is a systematic ambiguity with sequences of simple words), or syntactico-semantic ambiguities which cannot be removed at this step of analysis.

The resulting DAG is meant to be the input of some subsequent analyser, in general a syntactic parser.

6.6   Tagging Programs and Lexical Analysis

A priori one could say that the many taggers that have become available – whether they are statistics or rule-based – are similar to lexical analysers: in both cases, the size of the texts treated is usually significant; many million words need to be tagged, in other words, assigned linguistic information. In reality however, lexical analysers do not have much in common with taggers; here are at least three reasons for this view:

- Taggers provide only low level information

  Most taggers simply assign parts of speech to each word in the text; this is well-known to be more than insufficient for practically all kinds of syntactic analysis. For example, it is of utmost importance to know the argument structure of verbs. In order to correctly analyse the two sentences:

  John slept two hours.
  Paul needs two hours.

one needs to know that the verb to *sleep* is intransitive (and consequently that *two hours* is a circumstantial complement) and that *to need* is transitive (thus *two hours* is the direct object complement). Moreover, one needs to know the prepositions that introduce the obligatory arguments of a verb in order to be able to distinguish the circumstantial complements, the type of the arguments of verbs (concrete noun, human, phrastic, collective, etc.), their degree of liberty (deletion, pronominalisation, infinitivisation of phrastic complements, etc.). It is therefore necessary to classify nouns in order to associate noun phrases to verbs and to detect eventual metonymies. In addition, one has to distinguish between at least two kinds of adverbs, the modifiers of adjectives and the complements of verbs:

> *John eats fast.* * *John eats very.*
> *John is very rich.* * *John is fast rich.*

There are also sentential adverbs that can occur in various positions inside a sentence:

> *Evidently, John eats fast. John evidently eats fast.*
> *John eats evidently fast. John eats fast, evidently.*

Adjectives for instance have to be classified according to whether they are used as epithets or attributes:

> *John described the actual event. *The event is actual.*
> **The alone boy is gone. The boy is alone.*

Precise syntactic analyses are impossible without such a basic classification of all the parts of speech; such a classification is both simple and reproducible. The electronic dictionaries and the lexicon-grammars built in the RELEX[4] network of laboratories are an inventory of linguistic information of this kind; the languages described so far are English, French, German, Greek, Italian, Serbo-Croatian, Spanish and Portuguese. In addition to the size and the precision of the descriptions attained up to now, a specific feature of this entreprise is that the lexical and syntactic descriptions were conceived to be *reproducible* and *exhaustive*. In this

---

[4] This network includes several research centers in Linguistics and in Computational Linguistics in France (University of Paris 7, Prof. M. Gross; University of Paris 13, Prof. G. Gross), in Germany (University of Münich, Prof. F. Günthner; University of Saarbrücken, Prof. F. Caroli), in Greece (University of Thessaloniki, Prof. A. Simeonides-Anastassiadis), in Italy (University of Salerno, Prof. A. Elia; University of Potenza, Prof. M. Conenna), in Portugal (University of Lisbon, Prof. E. Marques-Ranchodd), in Serbia (University of Belgrad, Prof. D. Vitas) and in Spain (University of Girona, Prof. L. Masso-Pellat).

sense, the underlying methodology of these efforts follows the presentation in [Gross 1975]. The requirement of reproducibility, which is at the heart of this project, has indeed enabled a community of about 100 researchers to accumulate compatible observations about natural language during the last thirty years. Technically, the descriptions consist of two levels:

- on the one hand, the elementary units of the language have to be enumerated and described in the form of *electronic dictionaries*;
- on the other hand, the way these units can be combined to form phrases and sentences has to be formalized; the description of syntactic constraints is implemented in the form of *lexicon-grammars*.

On the basis of look-up in these dictionaries, the information is passed on by the lexical analyser to the syntactic and semantic parsers.

- Taggers do not yield reliable output

  The results of standard statistics-based taggers typically involve 5% errors in the best of cases (the tagger has to be trained on a manually tagged text that is sufficiently similar). Clearly, it suffices that a single word is incorrectly tagged in a sentence for the syntactic analyser to fail. The number of sentences correctly tagged becomes in general too small.

  On the contrary, a lexical analyser should be able to treat an arbitrary text in a purely mechanical fashion (no manual pretagging, no manual post-correction) and it should provide all the necessary information to the syntactic analysers. This requirement entails that an incorrect elimination of ambiguites that will result in the rejection of a needed lexical hypothesis is inadmissible, as it will give rise to failure during the syntactic or semantic analysis. On the other hand, the fact that not all ambiguities are removed is much less serious a drawback: it is precisely one of the functions of syntactic and semantic analysis to eliminate the remaining lexical ambiguities.

  Whereas it is the primary goal of taggers to provide a non-ambiguous result (at the expense of incorrect annotations), the goal of a lexical analyser is to provide all the pertinent information (at the expense of results where the ambiguities are not completely removed).

- Taggers do not take compound words into account

  We estimate that the number of compound words is several times larger than the number of simple words in the general vocabulary of a language; and compounds are indeed very frequent in texts. For example, in ordinary texts (e.g. the whole text of the newspaper *Le Monde*, 1993), more than one third of the occurrences of words are constituents of compound words. In fact, it is quite hopeless to begin analyzing such texts without taking compounds into consideration, since by definition a compound word is a sequence of simple words that must not be analyzed! When one parses sentences that contains some compounds, such as the following:

All of a sudden, Luc ate all the french fries

We want a lexical parser to produce the following output:

All of a sudden	Adverb
Luc	Proper name
eat	Verb, preterit
all	predeterminer
the	determiner
French fry	Noun, plural

and not:

All	Pronoun
of	Preposition
a	Determiner
sudden	Noun
...	...

The extremely high frequency of compounds in texts renders the results of traditional taggers useless; on the other hand, a lexical analyser must identify them to prevent the syntactic analyser from taking off in the wrong direction too often.

6.7 Conclusion

The automatic linguistic analysis of texts requires basic information about the atomic units of the language. These linguistic (syntactic, semantic) units can be classified as simple words and compounds. The aim of the lexical analysis of texts is to identify the occurrences of these units in texts, in order to provide the next analyser (usually the syntactic parser) with all the linguistic information that may be relevant for the analysis. Many well-known problems appear during this basic step; what we have shown here is that they can all be handled by dictionaries or by finite-state transducers. It should be clear that the number of dictionaries and transducers to be built, their size and the formulation of their interactions is by no mean trivial.

The fact that dictionaries are efficiently represented by finite-state transducers indicates that the lexical parsing of texts could be performed by one large finite-state transducer that would be a composition of all the dictionaries and elementary transducers described above. Therefore, traditional discussions on how to handle lexical and morphological phenomena, either by grammatical means or by dictionaries, would tend to be much less relevant.

Finite-state transducers can also be used in more general cases in order to describe local syntactic constraints, thus disambiguating some strings. Therefore, it is natural to make the lexical parser perform some of the tasks traditionally done by syntactic parsers. The frontier between lexical analysis and syntactic analysis could then be redefined in terms of what can or cannot be described with finite state machines.

References

Clemenceau David 1992. *Problèmes de couverture lexicale.* In "Productivité et créativité lexicale". Langue française. Larousse: Paris.

Courtois Blandine 1990. *Le dictionnaire électronique des mots simples.* In "Les dictionnaires électroniques". Langue française n° 87. Larousse: Paris.

Garrigues Mylène 1992. *Dictionnaires hiérarchiques du français.* In Langue française n° 96. Larousse: Paris.

Gross Maurice 1975. *Méthodes en syntaxe.* Hermann: Paris.

Gross Maurice 1989. *The use of finite automata in the lexical representation of natural language.* In "Electronic Dictionaries and Automata in Computational Linguistics". LITP spring school on Theoretical Computer Science. Springer Verlag: Berlin-Heidelberg.

Leclère Christian 1990. *Organisation du lexique-grammaire des verbes français.* In "Les dictionnaires électroniques". Langue française n° 87, Courtois, Silberztein eds. Larousse: Paris.

Leclère Christian, Subirats Carlos 1991. *A bibliography of studies on lexicon-grammar.* Lingvisticae Investigationes, XV:2, John Benjamins: Amsterdam / Philadelphia.

Lesk M. E. 1975. Lex, *A Lexical Analyzer Generator.* Computing Science Technical Report n° 39. Bell Laboratories: Murray Hill, New Jersey.

Revuz Dominique 1991. *Dictionnaires et lexiques, méthodes et algorithmes.* Thèse de doctorat en informatique, Université Paris 7 : Paris.

Roche Emmanuel 1993. *Analyse syntaxique transformationnelle du fran-çais par transducteurs et lexique-grammaire.* Thèse de doctorat en informatique, Université Paris 7: Paris.

Silberztein Max 1989. *The Lexical analysis of French.* In "Electronic Dictionaries and Automata in Computational Linguistics". LITP spring school on Theoretical Computer Science. Springer Verlag: Berlin-Heidelberg.

Silberztein Max 1993. *Dictionnaires électroniques et analyse automatique de textes: le système INTEX.* Masson: Paris.

Silberztein Max 1994a. *INTEX: a corpus processing system.* In COLING proceedings. COLING: Kyoto.

Silberztein Max 1994b. *Les groupes nominaux productifs et les noms composés lexicalisés.* In Lingvisticae Investigationes, XVII:2, John Benjamins: Amsterdam / Philadelphia.

7 Deterministic Part-of-Speech Tagging with Finite-State Transducers

Emmanuel Roche and Yves Schabes

Stochastic approaches to natural language processing have often been preferred to rule-based approaches because of their robustness and their automatic training capabilities. This was the case for part-of-speech tagging until Brill showed how state-of-the-art part-of-speech tagging can be achieved with a rule-based tagger by inferring rules from a training corpus. However, current implementations of the rule-based tagger run more slowly than previous approaches. In this paper, we present a finite-state tagger inspired by the rule-based tagger which operates in optimal time in the sense that the time to assign tags to a sentence corresponds to the time required to follow a single path in a deterministic finite-state machine. This result is achieved by encoding the application of the rules found in the tagger as a non-deterministic finite-state transducer and then turning it into a deterministic transducer. The resulting deterministic transducer yields a part-of-speech tagger whose speed is dominated by the access time of mass storage devices. We then generalize the techniques to the class of transformation-based systems.

7.1 Introduction

Finite-state devices have important applications to many areas of computer science, including pattern matching, databases and compiler technology. Although their linguistic adequacy to natural language processing has been questioned in the past (Chomsky, 1964), there has recently been a dramatic renewal of interest in the application of finite-state devices to several aspects of natural language processing. This renewal of interest is due to the speed and the compactness of finite-state representations. This efficiency is explained by two properties: finite-state devices can be made deterministic, and they can be turned into a minimal form. Such representations have been successfully applied to different aspects of natural language processing, such as morphological analysis and generation (Karttunen, Kaplan, and Zaenen, 1992; Clemenceau, 1993), parsing (Roche, 1993; Tapanainen and Voutilainen, 1993), phonology (Laporte, 1993; Kaplan and Kay, 1994) and speech recognition (Pereira, Riley, and Sproat, 1994). Although finite-state machines have been used for part-of-speech tagging (Tapanainen and Voutilainen, 1993; Silberztein, 1993), none of these approaches has the same flexibility as stochastic techniques. Unlike stochastic approaches to part-of-speech tagging (Church, 1988; Kupiec, 1992; Cutting et al., 1992; Merialdo, 1990; DeRose, 1988; Weischedel et al., 1993), up to now the knowledge found in finite-state taggers has been handcrafted and cannot be automatically acquired.

Recently, brill-tagger, described a rule-based tagger which performs as well as taggers based upon probabilistic models and which overcomes the limitations common in rule-based approaches to language processing: it is robust and the rules are automatically acquired. In addition, the tagger requires drastically less space than stochastic taggers. However, current implementations of Brill's tagger are considerably slower than the ones based on probabilistic models since it may require RCn elementary steps to tag an input of n words with R rules requiring at most C tokens of context.

Although the speed of current part-of-speech taggers is acceptable for interactive systems where a sentence at a time is being processed, it is not adequate for applications where large bodies of text need to be tagged, such as in information retrieval, indexing applications and grammar checking systems. Furthermore, the space required for part-of-speech taggers is also an issue in commercial personal computer applications such as grammar checking systems. In addition, part-of-speech taggers are often being coupled with a syntactic analysis module. Usually these two modules are written in different frameworks, making it very difficult to integrate interactions between the two modules.

In this paper, we design a tagger that requires n steps to tag a sentence of length n, independent of the number of rules and the length of the context they require. The tagger is represented by a finite-state transducer, a framework which can also be the basis for syntactic analysis. This finite-state tagger will also be found useful combined with other language components since it can be naturally extended by composing it with finite-state transducers which could encode other aspects of natural language syntax.

Relying on algorithms and formal characterization described in later sections, we explain how each rule in Brill's tagger can be viewed as a non-deterministic finite-state transducer. We also show how the application of all rules in Brill's tagger is achieved by composing each of these non-deterministic transducers and why non-determinism arises in this transducer. We then prove the correctness of the general algorithm for determinizing (whenever possible) finite-state transducers and we successfully apply this algorithm to the previously obtained non-deterministic transducer. The resulting deterministic transducer yields a part-of-speech tagger which operates in optimal time in the sense that the time to assign tags to a sentence corresponds to the time required to follow a single path in this deterministic finite-state machine. We also show how the lexicon used by the tagger can be optimally encoded using a finite-state machine.

The techniques used for the construction of the finite-state tagger are then formalized and mathematically proven correct. We introduce a proof of soundness and completeness with a worst case complexity analysis for an algorithm for determinizing finite-state transducers.

We conclude by proving how the method can be applied to the class of transformation-based error-driven systems.

7.2 Overview of Brill's Tagger

Brill's tagger is comprised of three parts, each of which is inferred from a training corpus: a lexical tagger, an unknown word tagger and a contextual tagger. For purposes of exposition, we will postpone the discussion of the unknown word tagger and focus mainly on the contextual rule tagger, which is the core of the tagger.

The lexical tagger initially tags each word with its most likely tag, estimated by examining a large tagged corpus, without regard to context. For example, assuming that vbn is the most likely tag for the word "killed" and vbd for "shot", the lexical tagger might assign the following part-of-speech tags:[1]

(1)   Chapman/np killed/vbn John/np Lennon/np
(2)   John/np Lennon/np was/$bedz$ shot/vbd by/by Chapman/np
(3)   He/pps witnessed/vbd Lennon/np killed/vbn by/by
       Chapman/np

Since the lexical tagger does not use any contextual information, many words can be tagged incorrectly. For example, in (1), the word "killed" is erroneously tagged as a verb in past participle form, and in (2), "shot" is incorrectly tagged as a verb in past tense.

---

[1] The notation for part-of-speech tags is adapted from the one used in the Brown Corpus (Francis and Kučera, 1982): pps stands for third singular nominative pronoun, vbd for verb in past tense, np for proper noun, vbn for verb in past participle form, by for the word "by", at for determiner, nn for singular noun and $bedz$ for the word "was".

Given the initial tagging obtained by the lexical tagger, the contextual tagger applies a sequence of rules in order and attempts to remedy the errors made by the initial tagging. For example, the rules in Figure 7.1 might be found in a contextual tagger.

1. *vbn vbd* PREVTAG *np*
2. *vbd vbn* NEXTTAG *by*

Figure 7.1: Sample rules

The first rule says to change tag *vbn* to *vbd* if the previous tag is *np*. The second rule says to change *vbd* to tag *vbn* if the next tag is *by*. Once the first rule is applied, the tag for "killed" in (1) and (3) is changed from *vbn* to *vbd* and the following tagged sentences are obtained:

(4)   Chapman/*np* killed/*vbd* John/*np* Lennon/*np*
(5)   John/*np* Lennon/*np* was/*bedz* shot/*vbd* by/*by*
        Chapman/*np*
(6)   He/*pps* witnessed/*vbd* Lennon/*np* killed/*vbd* by/*by*
        Chapman/*np*

And once the second rule is applied, the tag for "shot" in (5) is changed from *vbd* to *vbn*, resulting in (8) and the tag for "killed" in (6) is changed back from *vbd* to *vbn*, resulting in (9):

(7)   Chapman/*np* killed/*vbd* John/*np* Lennon/*np*
(8)   John/*np* Lennon/*np* was/*bedz* shot/*vbn* by/*by*
        Chapman/*np*
(9)   He/*pps* witnessed/*vbd* Lennon/*np* killed/*vbn* by/*by*
        Chapman/*np*

It is relevant to our following discussion to note that the application of the NEXTTAG rule must look ahead one token in the sentence before it can be applied and that the application of two rules may perform a series of operations resulting in no net change. As we will see in the next section, these two aspects are the source of local non-determinism in Brill's tagger.

The sequence of contextual rules is automatically inferred from a training corpus. A list of tagging errors (with their counts) is compiled by comparing the output of the lexical tagger to the correct part-of-speech assignment. Then, for each error, it is determined which instantiation of a set of rule templates results in the greatest error reduction. Then the set of new errors caused by applying

A B PREVTAG C	A to B if previous tag is C
A B PREV1OR2OR3TAG C	A to B if previous 1/2/3 tag is C
A B PREV1OR2TAG C	A to B if previous one or two tag is C
A B NEXT1OR2TAG C	A to B if next one or two tag is C
A B NEXTTAG C	A to B if next tag is C
A B SURROUNDTAG C D	A to B if surrounding tags are C and D
A B NEXTBIGRAM C D	A to B if next bigram tag is C D
A B PREVBIGRAM C D	A to B if previous bigram tag is C D

Figure 7.2: Contextual Rule Templates

the rule is computed and the process is repeated until the error reduction drops below a given threshold.

After training on the Brown Corpus, using the set of contextual rule templates shown in Figure 7.2, 280 contextual rules are obtained. The resulting rule-based tagger performs as well as the state-of-the-art taggers based upon probabilistic models. It also overcomes the limitations common in rule-based approaches to language processing: it is robust, and the rules are automatically acquired. In addition, the tagger requires drastically less space than stochastic taggers. However, as we will see in the next section, Brill's tagger is inherently slow.

7.3   Complexity of Brill's Tagger

Once the lexical assignment is performed, in Brill's algorithm, each contextual rule acquired during the training phase is applied to each sentence to be tagged. For each individual rule, the algorithm scans the input from left to right while attempting to match the rule.

This simple algorithm is computationally inefficient for two reasons. The first reason for inefficiency is the fact that an individual rule is matched at each token of the input, regardless of the fact that some of the current tokens may have been previously examined when matching the same rule at a previous position. The algorithm treats each rule as a template of tags and slides it along the input, one word at a time. Consider, for example, the rule *A B PREVBIGRAM C C* that changes tag A to tag B if the previous two tags are C.

When applied to the input $CDCCA$, the pattern CCA is matched three times, as shown in Figure 7.3. At each step no record of previous partial matches or mismatches is remembered. In this example, C is compared with the second input token D during the first and second steps, and therefore, the

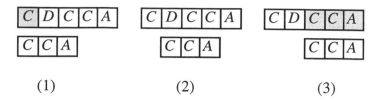

$$(1) \qquad\qquad (2) \qquad\qquad (3)$$

Figure 7.3: Partial matches of *A B PREVBIGRAM C C* on the input *C D C C A*.

second step could have been skipped by remembering the comparisons from the first step. This method is similar to a naive pattern matching algorithm.

The second reason for inefficiency is the potential interaction between rules. For example, when the rules in Figure 7.1 are applied to sentence (3), the first rule results in a change (6) which is undone by the second rule as shown in (9). The algorithm may therefore perform unnecessary computation.

In summary, Brill's algorithm for implementing the contextual tagger may require RCn elementary steps to tag an input of n words with R contextual rules requiring at most C tokens of context.

7.4   Construction of the Finite-State Tagger

We show how the function represented by each contextual rule can be represented as a non-deterministic finite-state transducer and how the sequential application of each contextual rule also corresponds to a non-deterministic finite-state transducer being the result of the composition of each individual transducer. We will then turn the non-deterministic transducer into a deterministic transducer. The resulting part-of-speech tagger operates in linear time independent of the number of rules and the length of the context. The new tagger operates in optimal time in the sense that the time to assign tags to a sentence corresponds to the time required to follow a single path in the resulting deterministic finite-state machine.

Our work relies on two central notions: the notion of a finite-state transducer and the notion of a subsequential transducer. Informally speaking, a finite-state transducer is a finite-state automaton whose transitions are labeled by pairs of symbols. The first symbol is the input and the second is the output. Applying a finite-state transducer to an input consists of following a path according to the input symbols while storing the output symbols, the result being the sequence of output symbols stored. Section 7.8.1 formally defines the notion of transducer.

Finite-state transducers can be composed, intersected, merged with the union operation and sometimes determinized. Basically, one can manipulate finite-state transducers as easily as finite-state automata. However, whereas every finite-state automaton is equivalent to some deterministic finite-state automaton, there are finite-state transducers that are not equivalent to any deterministic finite-state transducer. Transductions that can be computed by some deterministic finite-state transducer are called *subsequential functions*. We will see that the final step of the compilation of our tagger consists of transforming a finite-state transducer into an equivalent subsequential transducer.

We will use the following notation when pictorially describing a finite-state transducer: final states are depicted with two concentric circles; ϵ represents the empty string; on a transition from state i to state j, a/b indicates a transition on input symbol a and output symbol(s) b;[2] a question mark (?) on an arc transition (for example labeled $?/b$) originating at state i stands for any input symbol that does not appear as an input symbol on any other outgoing arc from i. In this document, each depicted finite-state transducer will be assumed to have a single initial state, namely the leftmost state appearing in the figures (usually labeled 0).

We are now ready to construct the tagger. Given a set of rules, the tagger is constructed in four steps.

The first step consists of turning each contextual rule found in Brill's tagger into a finite-state transducer. Following the example discussed in Section 7.2, the functionality of the rule *vbn vbd PREVTAG np* is represented by the transducer shown in Figure 7.4 on the left.

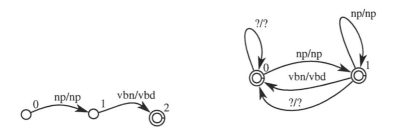

Figure 7.4: *Left:* transducer T_1 representing the contextual rule *vbn vbd PREVTAG np*. *Right:* local extension $LocExt(T_1)$ of T_1

---

[2]When multiple output symbols are emitted, a comma symbolizes the concatenation of the output symbols.

Each of the contextual rules is defined locally; that is, the transformation it describes must be applied at each position of the input sequence. For instance, the rule *A B PREV1OR2TAG C*, that changes *A* into *B* if the previous tag or the one before is *C*, must be applied twice on *C A A* (resulting in the output *C B B*). As we have seen in the previous section, this method is not efficient.

The second step consists of turning the transducers produced by the preceding step into transducers that operate globally on the input in one pass. This transformation is performed for each transducer associated with each rule. Given a function f_1 that transforms, say, a into b (i.e. $f_1(a) = b$), we want to extend it to a function f_2 such that $f_2(w) = w'$ where w' is the word built from the word w where each occurrence of a has been replaced by b. We say that f_2 is the *local extension*[3] of f_1 and we write $f_2 = LocExt(f_1)$. Section 7.8.2 formally defines this notion and gives an algorithm for computing the local extension.

Referring to the example of Section 7.2, the local extension of the transducer for the rule

   vbn vbd PREVTAG np

is shown to the right of Figure 7.4. Similarly, the transducer for the contextual rule

   vbd vbn NEXTTAG by

and its local extension are shown in Figure 7.5 and Figure 7.6.

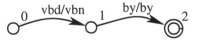

Figure 7.5: Transducer T_2 representing *vbd vbn NEXTTAG by*.

The transducers obtained in the previous step still need to be applied one after the other. The third step combines all transducers into one single transducer. This corresponds to the formal operation of composition defined on transducers. The formalization of this notion and an algorithm for computing the composed transducer are well-known and are described originally by Elgot and Mezei (1965).

Returning to our running example of Section 7.2, the transducer obtained by composing the local extension of T_2 (Figure 7.6) with the local extension of T_1 (right in Figure 7.4) is shown in Figure 7.7.

---

[3] This notion was introduced by Roche (1993).

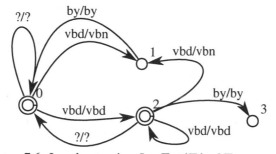

Figure 7.6: Local extension $LocExt(T_2)$ of T_2

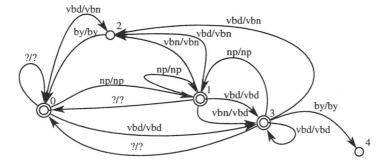

Figure 7.7: Composition $T_3 = LocExt(T_1) \circ LocExt(T_2)$

The fourth and final step consists of transforming the finite-state transducer obtained in the previous step into an equivalent subsequential (deterministic) transducer. The transducer obtained in the previous step may contain some non-determinism. The fourth step tries to turn it into a deterministic machine. This determinization is not always possible for any given finite-state transducer. For example, the transducer shown in Figure 7.8 is not equivalent to any subsequential transducer. Intuitively speaking, such a transducer has to look ahead an unbounded distance in order to correctly generate the output. This intuition will be formalized in Section 7.9.2.

However, as proven in Section 7.10, the rules inferred in Brill's tagger can always be turned into a deterministic machine. Section 7.9.1 describes an algorithm for determinizing finite-state transducers. This algorithm will not terminate when applied to transducers representing non-subsequential functions.

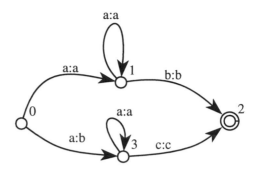

Figure 7.8: Example of a transducer not equivalent to any subsequential transducer.

In our running example, the transducer in Figure 7.7 has some non-deterministic paths. For example, from state 0 on input symbol *vbd*, two possible emissions are possible: *vbn* (from 0 to 2) and *vbd* (from 0 to 3). This non-determinism is due to the rule *vbd vbd NEXTTAG by*, since this rule has to read the second symbol before it can know which symbol must be emitted. The deterministic version of the transducer T_3 is shown in Figure 7.9. Whenever non-determinism arises in T_3, the deterministic machine emits the empty symbol ϵ, and postpones the emission of the output symbol. For example, from the start state 0, the empty string is emitted on input *vbd*, while the current state is set to 2. If the following word is *by*, the two token string *vbn by* is emitted (from 2 to 0), otherwise *vbd* is emitted (depending on the input from 2 to 2 or from 2 to 0).

Using an appropriate implementation for finite-state transducers (see Section 7.11), the resulting part-of-speech tagger operates in linear time, independent of the number of rules and the length of the context. The new tagger therefore operates in optimal time.

We have shown how the contextual rules can be implemented very efficiently. We now turn our attention to lexical assignment, the step that precedes the application of the contextual transducer. This step can also be made very efficient.

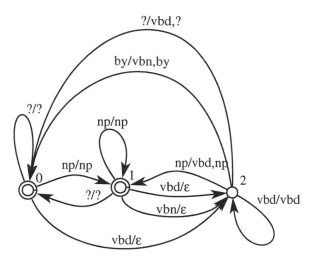

Figure 7.9: Subsequential form for T_3

7.5 Lexical Tagger

The first step of the tagging process consists of looking up each word in a dictionary. Since the dictionary is the largest part of the tagger in terms of space, a compact representation is crucial. Moreover, the lookup process has to be very fast too, otherwise the improvement in speed of the contextual manipulations would be of little practical interest.

To achieve high speed for this procedure, the dictionary is represented by a deterministic finite-state automaton with both low access time and small storage space. Suppose one wants to encode the sample dictionary of Figure 7.10. The algorithm, as described in (Revuz, 1991), consists of first building a tree whose branches are labeled by letters and whose leaves are labeled by a list of tags (such as *nn vb*) , and then minimizing it into a directed acyclic graph (DAG). The result of applying this procedure to the sample dictionary of Figure 7.10 is the DAG of Figure 7.11. When a dictionary is represented as a DAG, looking up a word in it consists simply of following one path in the DAG. The complexity of the lookup procedure depends only on the length of the word; in particular, it is independent of the size of the dictionary.

The lexicon used in our system encodes 54, 000 words. The corresponding

ads   *nns*
bag   *nn vb*
bagged   *vbn vbd*
bayed   *vbn vbd*
bids   *nns*

Figure 7.10: Sample Dictionary

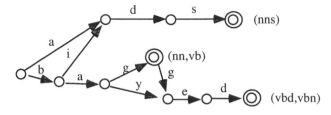

Figure 7.11: DAG representation of the dictionary found in Figure 7.10.

DAG takes 360 Kbytes of space and it provides an access time of 12, 000 words per second.[4]

7.6   Tagging Unknown Words

The rule-based system described by Brill (1992) contains a module that operates after all the known words — that is, words listed in the dictionary — have been tagged with their most frequent tag, and before the set of contextual rules are applied. This module guesses a tag for a word according to its suffix (e.g. a word with an "ing" suffix is likely to be a verb), its prefix (e.g. a word starting with an uppercase character is likely to be a proper noun) and other relevant properties.

This module basically follows the same techniques as the ones used to implement the lexicon. Due to the similarity of the methods used, we do not provide further details about this module.

---

[4]The size of the dictionary in ASCII form is 742KB.

7.7 Empirical Evaluation

The tagger we constructed has an accuracy identical[5] to Brill's tagger or the one of statistical-based methods, however it runs at a much higher speed. The tagger runs nearly ten times faster than the fastest of the other systems. Moreover, the finite-state tagger inherits from the rule-based system its compactness compared to a stochastic tagger. In fact, whereas stochastic taggers have to store word-tag, bigram and trigram probabilities, the rule-based tagger and therefore the finite-state one only have to encode a small number of rules (between 200 and 300).

We empirically compared our tagger with Eric Brill's implementation of his tagger, and with our implementation of a trigram tagger adapted from the work of Church (1988) that we previously implemented for another purpose. We ran the three programs on large files and piped their output into a file. In the times reported, we included the time spent reading the input and writing the output. Figure 7.12 summarizes the results. All taggers were trained on a portion of the Brown corpus. The experiments were run on an HP720 with 32Mbytes of memory. In order to conduct a fair comparison, the dictionary lookup part of the stochastic tagger has also been implemented using the techniques described in Section 7.5. All three taggers have approximately the same precision (95% of the tags are correct)[6]. By design, the finite-state tagger produces the same output as the rule-based tagger. The rule-based tagger — and the finite-state tagger — do not always produce the exact same tagging as the stochastic tagger (they don't make the same errors); however, no significant difference in performance between the systems was detected.[7]

	Stochastic Tagger	Rule-Based Tagger	Finite-State Tagger
Speed	1,200 w/s	500 w/s	10,800 w/s
Space	2,158KB	379KB	815KB

Figure 7.12: Overall performance comparison.

Independently, Cutting et al. (1992) quote a performance of 800 words per second for their part-of-speech tagger based on hidden Markov models.

The space required by the finite-state tagger (815KB) is decomposed as follows: 363KB for the dictionary, 440KB for the subsequential transducer and 12KB for the module for unknown words.

---

[5]Our current implementation is functionally equivalent to the tagger as described by Brill (1992). However, the tagger could be extended to include recent improvements described in more recent papers (Brill, 1994).

[6]For evaluation purposes, we randomly selected 90% of the Brown corpus for training purposes and 10% for testing. We used the Brown corpus set of part-of-speech tags.

[7]An extended discussion of the precision of the rule-based tagger can be found in (Brill, 1992).

The speed of our system is decomposed in Figure 7.13.[8]

	dictionary lookup	unknown words	contextual
Speed	12,800 w/s	16,600 w/s	125,100 w/s
Percent of the time	85%	6.5%	8.5%

Figure 7.13: Speed of the different parts of the program

Our system reaches a performance level in speed for which other very low level factors (such as storage access) may dominate the computation. At such speeds, the time spent reading the input file, breaking the file into sentences, and sentences into words, and writing the result into a file is no longer negligible.

7.8 Finite-State Transducers

The methods used in the construction of the finite-state tagger described in the previous sections were described informally. In the following section, the notions of finite-state transducers and the notion of local extension are defined. We also provide an algorithm for computing the local extension of a finite-state transducer. Issues related to the determinization of finite-state transducers are discussed in the section following this one.

7.8.1 Definition of finite-state transducers

A *finite-State transducer* T is a 5-tuple (Σ, Q, i, F, E) where: Σ is a finite alphabet; Q is the set of states or vertices; $i \in Q$ is the initial state; $F \subseteq Q$ is the set of final states; $E \subseteq Q \times \Sigma \cup \{\epsilon\} \times \Sigma^* \times Q$ is the set of edges or transitions.

For instance, Figure 7.14 is the graphical representation of the transducer:

$$T_1 = (\{a, b, c, d, e\}, \{0, 1, 2, 3\}, 0, \{3\}, \{(0, a, b, 1), (0, a, c, 2),$$
$$(1, d, d, 3), (2, e, e, 3)\}).$$

A finite-state transducer T also defines a function on words in the following way: the extended set of edges $\hat{E}$, the transitive closure of E, is defined by the following recursive relation:

---

[8] In Figure 7.13, the dictionary lookup includes reading the file, splitting it into sentences, looking up each word in the dictionary and writing the final result to a file. The dictionary lookup and the tagging of unknown words take roughly the same amount of time, but since the second procedure only applies on unknown words (around 10% in our experiments) the percentage of time it takes is much smaller.

- if $e \in E$ then $e \in \hat{E}$

- if $(q, a, b, q'), (q', a', b', q'') \in \hat{E}$ then $(q, aa', bb', q'') \in \hat{E}$.

Then the *function* f from Σ^* to Σ^* defined by $f(w) = w'$ iff $\exists q \in F$ such that $(i, w, w', q) \in \hat{E}$ is the function defined by T. One says that T represents f and writes $f = |T|$. The functions on words that are represented by finite-state transducers are called *rational functions*. If, for some input w, more than one output is allowed (e.g. $f(w) = \{w_1, w_2, \cdots\}$) then f is called a *rational transduction*.

In the example of Figure 7.14, T_1 is defined by $|T_1|(ad) = bd$ and $|T_1|(ae) = ce$.

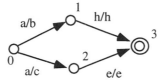

Figure 7.14: T_1: Example of Finite-State Transducer

Given a finite-state transducer $T = (\Sigma, Q, i, F, E)$, the following additional notions are useful: its state *transition function* d that maps $Q \times \Sigma \cup \{\epsilon\}$ into 2^Q defined by $d(q, ag) = \{q' \in Q | \exists w' \in \Sigma^* \text{ and } (q, a, w', q') \in E\}$; and its *emission function* δ that maps $Q \times \Sigma \cup \{\epsilon\} \times Q$ into 2^{Σ^*} defined by $\delta(q, a, q') = \{w' \in \Sigma^* | (q, a, w,', q') \in E\}$.

A finite-state transducer could be seen as a finite-state automaton, each of whose label is a pair. In this respect, T_1 would be deterministic; however, since transducers are generally used to compute a function, a more relevant definition of determinism consists of saying that both the transition function d and the emission function δ lead to sets containing at most one element, that is, $|d(q, a)| \leq 1$ and $|\delta(q, a, q')| \leq 1$. With this notion, if a finite-state transducer is deterministic, one can apply the function to a given word by deterministically following a single path in the transducer. Deterministic transducers are called *subsequential transducers* (Schützenberger, 1977)[9]. Given a deterministic transducer, we can define the partial functions $q \otimes a = q'$ iff $d(q, a) = \{q'\}$ and $q * a = w'$ iff $\exists q' \in Q$ such that $q \otimes a = q'$ and $\delta(q, a, q') = \{w'\}$. This leads to the definition of *subsequential transducers*: a subsequential transducer T' is a 7-tuple $(\Sigma, Q, i, F, \otimes, *, \rho)$ where: Σ, Q, i, F are defined as above; $\otimes$ is the deterministic state transition function that maps $Q \times \Sigma$ on Q, one writes

---

[9] A *sequential transducer* is a deterministic transducer for which all states are final. Sequential transducers are also called *generalized sequential machines* (Eilenberg, 1974).

$q \otimes a = q'$; $*$ is the deterministic emission function that maps $Q \times \Sigma$ on Σ^*, one writes $q * a = w'$; and the final emission function ρ maps F on Σ^*, one writes $\rho(q) = w$.

For instance, T_1 is not deterministic because $d(1, a) = \{a, b\}$, but it is equivalent to T_2 represented Figure 7.15 in the sense that they represent the same function, i.e $|T_1| = |T_2|$. T_2 is defined by

$$T_2 = (\{a, b, c, h, e\}, \{0, 1, 2\}, 0, \{2\}, \otimes, *, \rho)$$

where $0 \otimes a = 1, 0 * a = \epsilon, 1 \otimes h = 2, 1 * h = bh, 1 \otimes e = 2, 1 * e = ce$ and where $\rho(2) = \epsilon$.

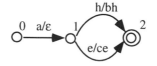

Figure 7.15: Subsequential Transducer T_2

7.8.2   Local extension

In this section, we will see how a function which needs to be applied at all input positions can be transformed into a global function that needs to be applied once on the input. For instance, consider T_3 of Figure 7.16. It represents the function $f_3 = |T_3|$ such that $f_3(ab) = bc$ and $f_3(bca) = dca$. We want to build the function that, given a word w, each time w contains ab (i.e. ab is a factor of the word) (resp. bca), this factor is transformed into its image bc (resp. dca). Suppose for instance that the input word is $w = aabcab$, as shown on Figure 7.17, and that the factors that are in $dom(f_3)$[10] can be found according to two different factorizations: i.e. $w_1 = a \cdot w_2 \cdot c \cdot w_2$[11] where $w_2 = ab$ and $w_1 = aa \cdot w_3 \cdot b$ where $w_3 = bca$. The *local extension* of f_3 will be the function that takes each possible factorization and transforms each factor according to f_3, i.e. $f_3(w_2) = bc$ and $f_3(w_3) = dca$, and leaves the other parts unchanged; here this leads to two outputs: $abccbc$ according to the first factorization, and $aadcab$ according to the second factorization.

The notion of local extension is formalized through the following definition.

---

[10]$dom(f)$ denotes the *domain* of f, that is, the set of words that have at least one output through f.

[11]If $w_1, w_2 \in \Sigma^*$, $w_1 \cdot w_2$ denotes the concatenation of w_1 and w_2. It can also be written $w_1 w_2$.

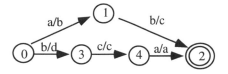

Figure 7.16: T_3: a finite-state transducer to be extended

a   a   b   c   a   b

a	a	b	c	a	b
	b	c		b	c

a	a	b	c	a	b
		d	c	a	

Figure 7.17: *Top:* input *Middle*: first factorization *Bottom*: second factorization

Definition 24 *If f is a rational transduction from Σ^* to Σ^*, the* local extension *$F = LocExt(f)$ is the rational transduction from Σ^* on Σ^* defined in the following way: if $u = a_1 b_1 a_2 b_2 \cdots a_n b_n a_{n+1} \in \Sigma^*$ then $v = a_1 b_1' a_2 b_2' \cdots a_n b_n' a_{n+1} \in F(u)$ if $a_i \in \Sigma^* - (\Sigma^* \cdot dom(f) \cdot \Sigma^*)$, $b_i \in dom(f)$ and $b_i' \in f(b_i)$.*[12]

Intuitively, if $F = LocExt(f)$ and $w \in \Sigma^*$, each factor of w in $dom(f)$ is transformed into its image by f and the remaining part of w is left unchanged. If f is represented by a finite-state transducer T and $LocExt(f)$ is represented by a finite-state transducer T', one writes $T' = LocExt(T)$.

It could also be seen that if γ_T is the identity function on $\Sigma^* - (\Sigma^* \cdot dom(T) \cdot \Sigma^*)$, then $LocExt(T) = \gamma_T \cdot (T \cdot \gamma_T)^*$.[13] Figure 7.21 gives an algorithm that computes the local extension directly.

The idea is that an input word is processed non-deterministically from left to right. Suppose for instance that we have the initial transducer T_4 of Figure 7.18 and that we want to build its local extension T_5 of Figure 7.19. When the input is read, if a current input letter cannot be transformed at the first state of T_4 (the letter c for instance), it is left unchanged: this is expressed by the looping transition on the initial state 0 of T_5 labeled $?/?$.[14] On the other

---

[12] The dot '·' stands for the concatenation operation on strings.

[13] In this last formula, the concatenation · stands for the concatenation of the graph of the function, that is for the concatenation of the transducers viewed as automata whose labels are of the form a/b.

[14] As explained before, a transition labeled by the symbol ? stands for all the transitions labeled with a letter that doesn't appear on any outgoing arc from this state. A transition labeled $?/?$ stands

hand, if the input symbol, say a, can be processed at the initial state of T_4, one doesn't know yet whether a will be the beginning of a word that can be transformed (e.g. ab) or whether it will be followed by a sequence which makes it impossible to apply the transformation (e.g. ac). Hence one has to entertain two possibilities, namely (1) we are processing the input according to T_4 and the transitions should be a/b, or (2) we are within the identity and the transition should be a/a. This leads to two kind of states: the transduction states (marked *transduction* in the algorithm) and the identity states (marked *identity* in the algorithm). It can be seen in Figure 7.19 that this leads to a transducer that has a copy of the initial transducer and an additional part that processes the identity while making sure it could not have been transformed. In other words, the algorithm consists of building a copy of the original transducer and at the same time the identity function that operates on $\Sigma^* - \Sigma^* \cdot dom(T) \cdot \Sigma^*$.

Let us now see how the algorithm of Figure 7.21 applies step by step to the transducer T_4 of Figure 7.18, producing the transducer T_5 of Figure 7.19.

In Figure 7.21, $C'[0] = (\{i\}, identity)$ of line 1 states that the state 0 of the transducer to be built is of type *identity* and refers to the initial state $i = 0$ of T_4. q represents the current state and n the current number of states. In the loop $do\{\cdots\}while(q < n)$, one builds the transitions of each state one after the other: if the transition points to a state not already built, a new state is added, thus incrementing n. The program stops when all states have been inspected and when no additional state is created. The number of iterations is bounded by $2^{\|T\|*2}$, where $\|T\| = |Q|$ is the number of states of the original transducer[15]. Line 3 says that the current state within the loop will be q and that this state refers to the set of states S and is marked by the type *type*. In our example, at the first occurrence of this line, S is instantiated to $\{0\}$ and $type = identity$. Line 5 adds the current identity state to the set of final states and a transition to the initial state for all letters that do not appear on any outgoing arc from this state. Lines 6 to 11 build the transitions from and to the identity states, keeping track of where this leads in the original transducer. For instance, a is a label that verifies the conditions of line 6. Thus a transition a/a is to be added to the *identity* state 2 which refers to 1 (because of the transition a/b of T_4) and to $i = 0$ (because it is possible to start the transduction T_4 from any place of the identity). Line 7 checks that this state doesn't already exist and adds it if necessary. $e = n + +$ means that the arrival state for this transition, i.e. $d(q, w)$, will be the last added state and that the number of states being built has to be incremented. Line 11 actually builds the transition between 0 and $e = 2$ labeled a/a. Line 12 through 17 describe the fact that it is possible to start a transduction from any *identity* state. Here one transition is added to

---

for all the diagonal pairs (a, a) s.t. a is not an input symbol on any outgoing arc from this state.

[15]In fact, $Q' \subset 2^{Q \times \{transduction, identity\}}$. Thus, $q \leq 2^{2|Q|}$.

one new state, i.e. a/b to 3. The next state to be considered is 2 and it is built like state 0 except that the symbol b should block the current output. In fact, the state 1 means that we already read a with a as output, thus if one reads b, this means that ab is at the current point, and since ab should be transformed into bc, the current identity transformation (that is $a \rightarrow a$) should be blocked: this is expressed by the transition b/b that leads to state 1 (this state is a "trash" state; that is, it has no outgoing transition and it is not final).

The following state is 3, which is marked as being of type *transduction*, which means that lines 19 through 27 should be applied. This consists simply of copying the transitions of the original transducer. If the original state was final, as for $4 = (\{2\}, transduction)$, an ϵ/ϵ transition to the original state is added (to get the behavior of T^+).

The transducer $T_6 = LocExt(T_3)$ of Figure 7.20 gives a more complete (and slightly more complex) example of applying this algorithm.

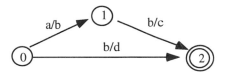

Figure 7.18: Sample Transducer T_4

7.9 Determinization

The basic idea behind the determinization algorithm comes from Mehryar Mohri[16]. In this section, after giving a formalization of the algorithm, we introduce a proof of soundness and completeness with its worst case complexity analysis.

7.9.1 Determinization algorithm

In the following, for $w_1, w_2 \in \Sigma^*$, $w_1 \wedge w_2$ denotes the longest common prefix of w_1 and w_2.

The finite-state transducers we use in our system have the property that they can be made deterministic; that is, there exists a subsequential transducer that represents the same function[17]. If $T = (\Sigma, Q, i, F, E)$ is such a finite-state

---

[16]Mohri (1994b) also gives a formalization of the algorithm.

[17]As opposed to automata, a large class of finite-state transducers, don't have any deterministic representation; they can't be determinized.

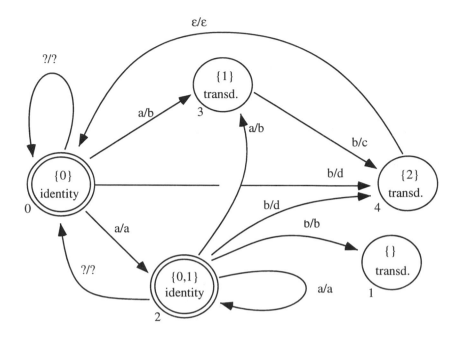

Figure 7.19: Local Extension T_5 of T_4: $T_5 = LocExt(T_4)$

transducer, the subsequential transducer $T' = (\Sigma, Q', i', F', \otimes, *, \rho)$ defined as follows will be later proved equivalent to T:

- $Q' \subset 2^{Q \times \Sigma^*}$. In fact the determinization of the transducer is related to the determinization of FSAs in the sense that it also involves a power set construction. The difference is that one has to keep track of the set of states of the original transducer one might be in and also of the words whose emission have been postponed. For instance, a state $\{(q_1, w_1), (q_2, w_2)\}$ means that this state corresponds to a path that leads to q_1 and q_2 in the original transducer and that the emission of w_1 (resp. w_2) was delayed for q_1 (resp. q_2).

- $i' = \{(i, \epsilon)\}$. There is no postponed emission at the initial state.

- the emission function is defined by:

$$S * a = \bigwedge_{(q,u) \in S} \bigwedge_{q' \in d(q,a)} u \cdot \delta(q, a, q')$$

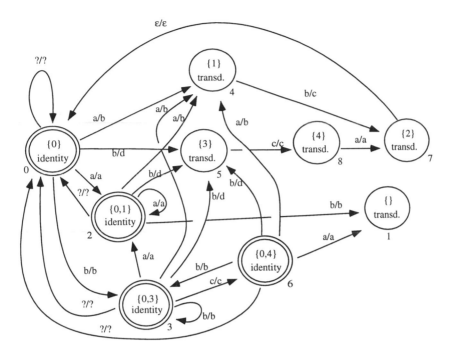

Figure 7.20: Local Extension T_6 of T_3: $T_6 = LocExt(T_3)$

This means that, for a given symbol, the set of possible emissions is obtained by concatenating the postponed emissions with the emission at the current state. Since one wants the transition to be deterministic, the actual emission is the longest common prefix of this set.

- the state transition function is defined by:

$$S \otimes a = \bigcup_{(q,u) \in S} \bigcup_{q' \in d(q,a)} \{(q', (S * a)^{-1} \cdot u \cdot \delta(q, a, q'))\}$$

Given $u, v \in \Sigma^*$, $u \cdot v$ denotes the concatenation of u and v and $u^{-1} \cdot v = w$, if w is such that $u \cdot w = v$, $u^{-1} \cdot v = \emptyset$ if no such w exists.

- $F' = \{S \in Q' | \exists (q, u) \in S \text{ and } q \in F\}$

- if $S \in F'$, $\rho(S) = u$ s.t. $\exists q \in F$ s.t. $(q, u) \in S$. We will see in the proof of correctness that ρ is properly defined.

$LocalExtension(T' = (\Sigma, Q', i', F', E'), T = (\Sigma, Q, i, F, E))$
1 $C'[0] = (\{i\}, identity); q = 0; i' = 0; F' = \emptyset; E' = \emptyset;$
   $Q' = \emptyset; C'[1] = (\emptyset, transduction); n = 2;$
2 do {
3      $(S, type) = C'[q]; Q' = Q' \cup \{q\};$
4   if $(type == identity)$
5          $F' = F' \cup \{q\}; E' = E' \cup \{(q, ?, ?, i')\};$
6   for each $w \in \Sigma \cup \{\epsilon\}$
7   s.t. $\exists x \in S, d(x, w) \neq \emptyset$ and $\forall y \in S, d(y, w) \cap F = \emptyset$
9   if $(\exists r \in [0, n-1]$ s.t. $C'[r] == (\{i\} \cup \bigcup_{x \in S} d(x, w), identity)$
9                  $e = r;$
10   else
11                 $C'[e = n++] = (\{i\} \cup \bigcup_{x \in S} d(x, w), identity);$
12             $E' = E' \cup \{(q, w, w, e)\};$
13   for each $(i, w, w', x) \in E$
14   if $(\exists r \in [0, n-1]$ such that $C'[r] == (\{x\}, transduction)$
15                 $e = r;$
16   else
17                 $C'[e = n++] = (\{x\}, transduction);$
18             $E' = E' \cup \{(q, w, w', e)\};$
19   for each $w \in \Sigma \cup \{\epsilon\}$ s.t. $\exists x \in S \; d(x, w) \cap F \neq \emptyset$
           then $E' = E' \cup \{(q, w, w, 1)\};$
20   else if $(type == transduction)$
21   if $\exists x_1 \in Q$ s.t. $S == \{x_1\}$
22   if $(x_1 \in F)$ then $E' = E' \cup \{(q, \epsilon, \epsilon, 0)\};$
23   for each $(x_1, w, w', y) \in E$
24   if $(\exists r \in [0, n-1]$ such that $C'[r] == (\{y\}, transduction)$
25                     $e = r;$
26   else
27                     $C'[e = n++] = (\{y\}, transduction);$
28                 $E' = E' \cup \{(q, w, w', e)\};$
29   q++;
30}while$(q < n);$

Figure 7.21: Local Extension Algorithm.

The determinization algorithm of Figure 7.23 computes the above subsequential transducer.

Let us now apply the determinization algorithm of Figure 7.23 on the finite-state transducer T_1 of Figure 7.14 and show how it builds the subsequential transducer T_5 of Figure 7.22. Line 1 of the algorithm builds the first state and instantiates it with the pair $\{(0, \epsilon)\}$. q and n respectively denote the current state and the number of states having been built so far. At line 5, one takes all the possible input symbols w; here only a is possible. w' of line 6 is the output symbol, $w' = \epsilon \cdot (\bigwedge_{\bar{q}' \in \{1,2\}} \delta(0, a, \bar{q}'))$, thus $w' = \delta(0, a, 1) \wedge \delta(0, a, 2) = b \wedge c = \epsilon$. Line 8 is then computed as follows: $S' = \bigcup_{\bar{q} \in \{0\}} \bigcup_{\bar{q}' \in \{1,2\}} \{\bar{q}', \epsilon^{-1} \cdot \delta(0, a, \bar{q}')\}$, thus $S' = \{(1, \delta(0, a, 1))\} \cup \{(2, \delta(0, a, 2))\} = \{(1, b), (2, c)\}$. Since no r verifies the condition on line 9, a new state e is created to which the transition labeled $a/w = a/\epsilon$ points and n is incremented. On line 15, the program goes to the construction of the transitions of state 1. On line 5, d and e are then two possible symbols. The first symbol, h, at line 6, is such that w' is $w' = \bigwedge_{\bar{q}' \in d(1,h) = \{2\}} b \cdot \delta(1, h, \bar{q}')) = bh$. Henceforth, the computation of line 8 leads to $S' = \bigcup_{\bar{q} \in \{1\}} \bigcup_{\bar{q}' \in \{2\}} \{(\bar{q}', (bh)^{-1} \cdot b \cdot h)\} = \{(2, \epsilon)\}$. State 2 labeled $\{(2, \epsilon)\}$ is thus added and a transition labeled h/bh that points to state 2 is also added. The transition for the input symbol e is computed the same way.

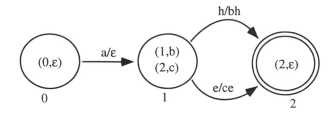

Figure 7.22: Subsequential transducer T_5 such that $|T_5| = |T_1|$

The subsequential transducer generated by this algorithm could in turn be minimized by an algorithm described in (Mohri, 1994a). However, in the case of the part-of-speech tagger, the transducer is nearly minimal.

$DeterminizeTransducer(T' = (\Sigma, Q', i', F', \otimes, *, \rho), T = (\Sigma, Q, i, F, E))$
1 $i' = 0; q = 0; n = 1; C'[0] = \{(0, \epsilon)\}; F' = \emptyset; Q' = \emptyset;$
2 do {
3    $S = C'[q]; Q' = Q' \cup \{q\};$
4   if $\exists(\bar{q}, u) \in S$ s.t. $\bar{q} \in F$ then $F' = F' \cup \{q\}$ and $\rho(q) = u;$
5   foreach w such that $\exists(\bar{q}, u) \in S)$ and $d(\bar{q}, w) \neq \emptyset$ {
6      $w' = \bigwedge\limits_{(\bar{q},u)\in S} \bigwedge\limits_{\bar{q}' \in d(\bar{q},w)} u \cdot \delta(\bar{q}, w, \bar{q}')$

7      $q * w = w';$
8      $S' = \bigcup\limits_{(\bar{q},u)\in S} \bigcup\limits_{\bar{q}' \in d(\bar{q},w)} \{(\bar{q}', w'^{-1} \cdot u \cdot \delta(\bar{q}, w, \bar{q}'))\};$

9   if $\exists r \in [0, n-1]$ such that $C'[r] == S'$
10        $e = r;$
11   else
12        $C'[e = n++] = S';$
13      $q \otimes w = e;$
14   }
15    $q++;$
16 }while($q < n$);

Figure 7.23: Determinization Algorithm

7.9.2 Proof of correctness

Although it is decidable whether a function is subsequential or not (Choffrut, 1977), the determinization algorithm described in the previous section does not terminate when run on a non-subsequential function.

Two issues are addressed in this section. First, the proof of soundness: the fact that if the algorithm terminates, then the output transducer is deterministic and represents the same function. Second, the proof of completeness: the algorithm terminates in the case of subsequential functions.

Soundness and completeness are a consequence of the main proposition which states that if a transducer T represents a subsequential function f, then the algorithm *DeterminizeTransducer* described in the previous section applied on T computes a subsequential transducer representing the same function.

In order to simplify the proofs, we will only consider transducers that do not have ϵ input transitions, that is $E \subseteq Q \times \Sigma \times \Sigma^* \times Q$, and also without loss of generality, transducers that are reduced and that are deterministic in the sense of finite-state automata[18].

In order to prove this proposition, we need to establish some preliminary notations and lemmas.

First we extend the definition of the transition function d, the emission function δ, the deterministic transition function $\otimes$ and the deterministic emission function $*$ on words in the classical way. We then have the following properties:

$$
d(q, ab) = \bigcup_{q' \in d(q,a)} d(q', b)
$$

$$
\delta(q_1, ab, q_2) = \bigcup_{\{q' \in d(q_1,a) \mid q_2 \in d(q',b)\}} \delta(q_1, a, q') \cdot \delta(q', b, q_2)
$$

$$
q \otimes ab = (q \otimes a) \otimes b
$$

$$
q * ab = (q * a) \cdot (q \otimes a) * b
$$

For the following, it useful to note that if $|T|$ is a function, then δ is a function too.

The following lemma states an invariant that holds for each state S built within the algorithm. The lemma will later be used for the proof of soundness.

Lemma 1 *Let $I = C'[0]$ be the initial state. At each iteration of the "do" loop in* DeterminizeTransducer, *for each $S = C'[q]$ and for each $w \in \Sigma^*$ such that $I \otimes w = S$, the following holds:*

(i) $I * w = \bigwedge_{q \in d(i,w)} \delta(i, w, q)$

(ii) $S = I \otimes w = \{(q, u) \mid q \in d(i, w) \text{ and } u = (I * w)^{-1} \cdot \delta(i, w, q)\}$

Proof: (i) and (ii) are obviously true for $S = I$ (since $d(i, \epsilon) = i$ and $\delta(i, \epsilon, i) = \epsilon$) and we will show that given some $w \in \Sigma^*$ if it is true for $S = I \otimes w$ then it is also true for $S_1 = S \otimes a = I \otimes wa$ for all $a \in \Sigma$.

Assuming that (i) and (ii) hold for S and w, then for each $a \in \Sigma$:

$$
\bigwedge_{q \in d(i,w), q' \in d(q,a)} \delta(i, w, q) \cdot \delta(q, a, q')
$$

$$
= (I * w) \cdot \bigwedge_{q \in d(i,w), q' \in d(q,a)} ((I * w)^{-1} \cdot \delta(i, w, q)) \cdot \delta(q, a, q')
$$

---

[18] A transducer defines an automaton whose labels are the pairs "input/output"; this automaton is assumed to be deterministic.

$$= (I * w) \cdot \bigwedge_{(q,u) \in S = I \otimes w, q' \in d(q,a)} u \cdot \delta(q, a, q')$$

$$= (I * w) \cdot (S * a)$$

$$= I * w \cdot (I \otimes w) * a$$

$$= I * wa$$

This proves (i).

We now turn to (ii). Assuming that (i) and (ii) hold for S and w, then for each $a \in \Sigma$, let $S_1 = S \otimes a$; the algorithm (line 8) is such that

$$S_1 = \{(q', u') | \exists (q, u) \in S, q' \in d(q, a)$$
$$\text{and } u' = (S * a)^{-1} \cdot u \cdot \delta(q, a, q')\}$$

Let

$$S_2 = \{(q', u') | q' \in d(i, wa) \text{ and } u' = (I * wa)^{-1} \cdot \delta(i, wa, q')\}$$

We show that $S_1 \subset S_2$. Let $(q', u') \in S_1$, then $\exists (q, u) \in S$ s.t. $q' \in d(q, a)$ and $u' = (S * a)^{-1} \cdot u \cdot \delta(q, a, q')$. Since $u = (I * w)^{-1} \cdot \delta(i, w, q)$, then $u' = (S * a)^{-1} \cdot (I * w)^{-1} \cdot \delta(i, w, q) \cdot \delta(q, a, q')$, that is, $u' = (I * wa)^{-1} \cdot \delta(i, wa, q')$. Thus $(q', u') \in S_2$. Hence $S_1 \subset S_2$.

We now show that $S_2 \subset S_1$. Let $(q', u') \in S_2$, and let $q \in d(i, w)$ be s.t. $q' \in d(q, a)$ and $u = (I * w)^{-1} \cdot \delta(i, w, q)$ then $(q, u) \in S$ and since $u' = (I * wa)^{-1} \cdot \delta(i, wa, q') = (S * a)^{-1} \cdot u \cdot \delta(q, a, q'), (q', u') \in S_1$

This concludes the proof of (ii).   □

The following lemma states a common property of the state S, which will be used in the complexity analysis of the algorithm.

Lemma 2 *Each $S = C'[q]$ built within the "do" loop is s.t. $\forall q \in Q$, there is at most one pair $(q, w) \in S$ with q as first element.*

Proof: Suppose $(q, w_1) \in S$ and $(q, w_2) \in S$, and let w be s.t. $I \otimes w = S$. Then $w_1 = (I * w)^{-1} \cdot \delta(i, w, q)$ and $w_2 = (I * w)^{-1} \cdot \delta(i, w, q)$. Thus $w_1 = w_2$.
□

The following lemma will also be used for soundness. It states that the final state emission function is indeed a function.

Lemma 3 *For each S built in the algorithm, if $(q, u), (q', u') \in S$, then $q, q' \in F \Rightarrow u = u'$*

Proof: Let S be one state set built in line 8 of the algorithm. Suppose $(q, u), (q', u') \in S$ and $q, q' \in F$. According to (ii) of lemma 1, $u =$

$(I * w)^{-1} \cdot \delta(i, w, q)$ and $u' = (I * w)^{-1} \cdot \delta(i, w, q')$. Since $|T|$ is a function and $\{\delta(i, w, q), \delta(i, w, q')\} \in |T|(w)$ then $\delta(i, w, q) = \delta(i, w, q')$, therefore $u = u'$. $\square$

The following lemma will be used for completeness.

Lemma 4 *Given a transducer T representing a subsequential function, there exists a bound M s.t. for each S built at line 8, for each $(q, u) \in S$, $|u| \leq M$.*

We rely on the following theorem proven by Choffrut (1978):

Theorem 5 *A function f on Σ^* is subsequential iff it has bounded variations and for any rational language $L \subset \Sigma^*$, $f^{-1}(L)$ is also rational.*

with the following two definitions:

Definition 25 *The left distance between two strings u and v is*

$$\|u, v\| = |u| + |v| - 2|u \wedge v|$$

Definition 26 *A function f on Σ^* has bounded variations iff for all $k \geq 0$, there exists $K \geq 0$ s.t. $u, v \in dom(f)$, $\|u, v\| \leq k \Rightarrow \|f(u), f(v)\| \leq K$*

Proof of lemma 4: Let $f = |T|$. For each $q \in Q$ let $c(q)$ be a string w s.t. $d(q, w) \cap F \neq \emptyset$ and s.t. $|w|$ is minimal among such strings. Note that $|c(q)| \leq \|T\|$ where $\|T\|$ is the number of states in T. For each $q \in Q$ let $s(q) \in Q$ be a state s.t. $s(q) \in d(q, c(q)) \cap F$. Let us further define

$$
\begin{aligned}
M_1 &= max_{q \in Q} |\delta(q, c(q), s(q))| \\
M_2 &= max_{q \in Q} |c(q)|
\end{aligned}
$$

Since f is subsequential, it is of bounded variations, therefore there exists K s.t. if $\|u, v\| \leq 2M_2$ then $\|f(u), f(v)\| \leq K$. Let $M = K + 2M_1$.

Let S be a state set built at line 8 , let w be s.t. $I \otimes w = S$ and $\lambda = I * w$. Let $(q_1, u) \in S$. Let $(q_2, v) \in S$ be s.t. $u \wedge v = \epsilon$. Such a pair always exists, since if not

$$| \bigwedge_{(q', u') \in S} u'| \; > \; 0$$

thus $|\lambda \cdot \bigwedge_{(q', u') \in S} u'| \; = \; | \bigwedge_{(q', u') \in S} \lambda \cdot u'| > |\lambda|$

Thus, because of (ii) in lemma 1,

$$| \bigwedge_{q' \in d(i, w)} \delta(i, w, q')| > |I * w|$$

which contradicts (i) in lemma 1.

Let $\omega = \delta(q_1, c(q_1), s(q_1))$ and $\omega' = \delta(q_2, c(q_2), s(q_2))$.

Moreover, for any $a,b,c,d \in \Sigma^*$, $\|a, c\| \leq \|ab, cd\| + |b| + |d|$. In fact, $\|ab, cd\| = |ab| + |cd| - 2|ab \wedge cd| = |a| + |c| + |b| + |d| - 2|ab \wedge cd| = \|a, c\| + 2|a \wedge c| + |b| + |d| - 2|ab \wedge cd|$ but $|ab \wedge cd| \leq |a \wedge c| + |b| + |d|$ and since $\|ab, cd\| = \|a, c\| - 2(|ab \wedge cd| - |a \wedge c| - |b| - |d|) - |b| - |d|$ one has $\|a, c\| \leq \|ab, cd\| + |b| + |d|$.

Therefore, in particular, $|u| \leq \|\lambda u, \lambda v\| \leq \|\lambda u \omega, \lambda v \omega'\| + |\omega| + |\omega'|$, thus $|u| \leq \|f(w \cdot c(q_1)), f(w \cdot c(q_2))\| + 2M_1$. But $\|w \cdot c(q_1), w \cdot c(q_2)\| \leq |c(q_1)| + |c(q_2)| \leq 2M_2$, thus $\|f(w \cdot c(q_1)), f(w \cdot c(q_2))\| \leq K$ and therefore $|u| \leq K + 2M_1 = M$. $\square$

The time is now ripe for the main proposition which proves soundness and completeness.

Proposition 11 *If a transducer T represents a subsequential function f, then the algorithm* DeterminizeTransducer *described in the previous section applied on T computes a subsequential transducer τ representing the same function.*

Proof: The lemma 4 shows that the algorithm always terminates if $|T|$ is subsequential.

Let us show that $dom(|\tau|) \subset dom(|T|)$. Let $w \in \Sigma^*$ s.t. w is not in $dom(|T|)$, then $d(i, w) \cap F = \emptyset$. Thus, according to (ii) of lemma 1, for all $(q, u) \in I \otimes w$, q is not in F, thus $I \otimes w$ is not terminal and therefore w is not in $dom(\tau)$.

Conversely, let $w \in dom(|T|)$. There exists a unique $q_f \in F$ s.t. $|T|(w) = \delta(i, w, q_f)$ and s.t. $q_f \in d(i, w)$. Therefore $|T|(w) = (I * w) \cdot ((I * w)^{-1} \cdot \delta(i, w, q_f))$ and according to (ii) of lemma 1 $(q_f, (I*w)^{-1} \cdot \delta(i, w, q_f)) \in I \otimes w$ and since $q_f \in F$, lemma 3 shows that $\rho(I \otimes w) = (I * w)^{-1} \cdot \delta(i, w, q_f)$, thus $|T|(w) = (I * w) \cdot \rho(I \otimes w) = |\tau|(w)$. $\square$

7.9.3 Worst-case complexity

In this section we give a worst-case upper bound of the size of the subsequential transducer in term of the size of the input transducer.

Let $L = \{w \in \Sigma^* \text{ s.t. } |w| \leq M\}$ where M is the bound defined in the proof of lemma 4. Since, according to lemma 2, for each state set Q', for each $q \in Q$, Q' contains at most one pair (q, w), the maximal number N of states built in the algorithm is smaller than the sum of the number of functions from states to strings in L for each state set, that is

$$N \leq \sum_{Q' \in 2^Q} |L|^{|Q'|}$$

we thus have $N \leq 2^{|Q|} \times |L|^{|Q|} = 2^{|Q|} \times 2^{|Q| \times \log_2 |L|}$ and therefore $N \leq 2^{|Q|(1+\log |L|)}$.

Moreover,

$$|L| = 1 + |\Sigma| + \cdots + |\Sigma|^M = \frac{|\Sigma|^{M+1} - 1}{|\Sigma| - 1} \text{ if } |\Sigma| > 1$$

and $|L| = M + 1$ if $|\Sigma| = 1$. In this last formula, $M = K + 2M_1$ as described in lemma 4. Note that if $P = max_{a \in \Sigma} |\delta(q, a, q')|$ is the maximal length of the simple transitions emissions, $M_1 \leq |Q| \times P$, thus $M \leq K + 2 \times |Q| \times P$.

Therefore, if $|\Sigma| > 1$, the number of states N is bounded:

$$N \leq 2^{|Q| \times (1 + \log \frac{|\Sigma|^{(K+2 \times |Q| \times P+1)} - 1}{|\Sigma| - 1})}$$

and if $|\Sigma| = 1$,

$$N \leq 2^{|Q| \times (1 + \log (K + 2 \times |Q| \times P + 1))}.$$

7.10 Subsequentiality of Transformation-Based Systems

The proof of correctness of the determinization algorithm and the fact that the algorithm terminates on the transducer encoding Brill's tagger show that the final function is subsequential and equivalent to Brill's original tagger.

In this section, we prove in general that any transformation-based system, such as those used by Brill, is a subsequential function. In other words, any transformation-based system can be turned into a deterministic finite-state transducer.

We define transformation-based systems as follows.

Definition 27 *A transformation-based system is a finite sequence* $(f_1, \cdots, f_n)$ *of subsequential functions whose domains are bounded.*

Applying a transformation-based system consists of taking the functions f_i, one after the other, and for each of them, one looks for the first position in the input at which it applies, and for the longest string starting at that position, transforms this string, go to the end of this string, and iterate until the end of the input.

It is not true that, in general, the local extension of a subsequential function is subsequential[19]. For instance, consider the function f_a of Figure 7.24.

---

[19] However, the local extensions of the functions we had to compute *were* subsequential.

Figure 7.24: Function f_a

The local extension of the function f_a is not a function. In fact, consider the input string $daaaad$, it can be decomposed either into $d \cdot aaa \cdot ad$ or into $da \cdot aaa \cdot d$. The first decomposition leads to the output $dbbbad$ and the second one to the output $dabbbd$.

The intended use of the rules in the tagger defined by Brill is to apply each function from left to right. In addition, if several decompositions are possible, the one that occurs first is the one chosen. In our previous example, it means that only the output $dbbbad$ is generated.

This notion is now defined precisely.

Let α be the rational function defined by $\alpha(a) = a$ for $a \in \Sigma$, $\alpha([) = \alpha(]) = \epsilon$ on the additional symbols '[' and ']' with α such that $\alpha(u \cdot v) = \alpha(u) \cdot \alpha(v)$.

Definition 28 *Let $Y \subset \Sigma^*$ and $X = \Sigma^* - \Sigma^* \cdot Y \cdot \Sigma^*$, a Y-decomposition of x is a string $y \in X \cdot ([\cdot Y \cdot] \cdot X)^*$ s.t. $\alpha(y) = x$*

For instance, if $Y = dom(f_a) = \{aaa\}$, the set of Y-decompositions of $x = daaad$ is $\{d[aaa]ad, da[aaa]d\}$.

Definition 29 *Let $<$ be a total order on Σ and let $\overline{\Sigma} = \Sigma \cup \{[,]\}$ be the alphabet Σ with the two additional symbols '[' and ']'. Let extend the order $>$ to $\overline{\Sigma}$ by $\forall a \in \Sigma$, '[' $< a$ and $a < $ ']'. $<$ defines a lexicographic order on $\overline{\Sigma}^*$ that we also denote $<$. Let $Y \subset \Sigma^*$ and $x \in \Sigma^*$, the minimal Y-decomposition of x is the Y-decomposition which is minimal in $(\overline{\Sigma}^*, <)$.*

For instance, the minimal $dom(f_a)$-decomposition of $daaaad$ is $d[aaa]ad$. In fact, $d[aaa]ad < da[aaa]d$.

Proposition 12 *Given $Y \subset \Sigma^+$ finite, the function md_Y that to each $x \in \Sigma^*$ associates its minimal Y-decomposition, is subsequential and total.*

Proof: Let dec be defined by $dec(w) = u \cdot [\cdot v \cdot] \cdot dec((uv)^{-1} \cdot w)$ where $u, v \in \Sigma^*$ are s.t. $v \in Y$, $\exists v' \in \Sigma^*$ with $w = uvv'$ and $|u|$ is minimal among such strings. The function md_Y is total because the function dec always returns an output which is a Y-decomposition of w.

We shall now prove that the function is rational and then that it has bounded variations; this will prove according to theorem 5 that the function is subsequential. In the following $X = \Sigma^* - \Sigma^* \cdot Y \cdot \Sigma^*$. The transduction T_Y that generates the set of Y-decompositions is defined by

$$T_Y = \mathrm{Id}_X \cdot (\epsilon/[\cdot \mathrm{Id}_Y \cdot \epsilon/] \cdot \mathrm{Id}_X)^*$$

where Id_X (resp. Id_Y) stands for the identity function on X (resp. Y). Furthermore, the transduction $T_{\overline{\Sigma},>}$ that to each string $w \in \overline{\Sigma}^*$ associates the set of strings strictly greater than w, that is $T_{\overline{\Sigma},>}(w) = \{w' \in \overline{\Sigma}^* | w < w'\}$, is defined by the transducer of Figure 7.25 in which $A = \{(x,x) | x \in \overline{\Sigma}\}$, $B = \{(x,y) \in \overline{\Sigma}^2 | x < y\}$, $C = \overline{\Sigma}^2$, $D = \{\epsilon\} \times \overline{\Sigma}$ and $E = \overline{\Sigma} \times \{\epsilon\}$.[20]

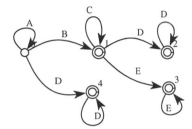

Figure 7.25: Transduction $T_{\overline{\Sigma},>}$

Therefore, the right-minimal Y-decomposition function md_Y is defined by $md_Y = T_Y - (T_{\overline{\Sigma},>} \circ T_Y)$ which proves that md_Y is rational.

Let $k > 0$. Let $K = 6 \times k + 6 \times M$ where $M = max_{x \in Y}|x|$. Let u, $v \in \Sigma^*$ be s.t. $\|u,v\| \leq k$. Let us consider two cases: (i) $|u \wedge v| \leq M$ and (ii) $|u \wedge v| > M$.

(i): $|u \wedge v| \leq M$, thus $|u|, |v| \leq |u \wedge v| + \|u,v\| \leq M + k$. Moreover, for each $w \in \Sigma^*$, for each Y-decomposition w' of w, $|w'| \leq 3 \times |w|$. In fact, Y doesn't contain ϵ, thus the number of [(resp.]) in w' is smaller than $|w|$. Therefore, $|md_Y(u)|, |md_Y(v)| \leq 3 \times (M + k)$ thus $\|md_Y(u), md_Y(v)\| \leq K$.

(ii): $u \wedge v = \lambda \cdot \omega$ with $|\omega| = M$. Let μ, ν be s.t. $u = \lambda \omega \mu$ and $v = \lambda \omega \nu$. Let λ', ω', μ', λ'', ω'' and ν'' be s.t. $md_Y(u) = \lambda'\omega'\mu'$, $md_Y(v) = \lambda''\omega''\nu''$, $\alpha(\lambda') = \alpha(\lambda'') = \lambda$, $\alpha(\omega') = \alpha(\omega'') = \omega$, $\alpha(\mu') = \mu$ and $\alpha(\nu'') = \nu$. Suppose that $\lambda' \neq \lambda''$, for instance $\lambda' < \lambda''$. Let i be the first indice s.t. $(\lambda')_i < (\lambda'')_i$.[21] We have two possible situations: (ii.1) $(\lambda')_i = [$ and $\lambda'' \in \Sigma$ or $(\lambda'')_i =]$. In that case, since the length of the elements in Y is smaller

---

[20]This construction is similar to the transduction built within the proof of Eilenberg's cross section theorem (Eilenberg, 1974).

[21]$(w)_i$ refers to the ith letter in w.

than $M = |\omega'|$, one has $\lambda'\omega' = \lambda_1[\lambda_2]\lambda_3$ with $|\lambda_1| = i$, $\lambda_2 \in Y$ and $\lambda_3 \in \overline{\Sigma}^*$. We also have $\lambda''\omega'' = \lambda_1\lambda'_2\lambda'_3$ with $\alpha(\lambda'_2) = \alpha(\lambda_2)$ and the first letter of λ'_2 is different from [. Let λ_4 be a Y-decomposition of $\alpha(\lambda'_3\nu'')$, then $\lambda_1[\lambda_2]\lambda_4$ is a Y-decomposition of v strictly smaller than $\lambda_1\lambda'_2\lambda'_3\nu'' = md_Y(v)$ which contradicts the minimality of $md_Y(v)$. The second situation is (ii.2): $(\lambda')_i \in \Sigma$ and $(\lambda'')_i =$], then we have $\lambda'\omega' = \lambda_1[\lambda_2\lambda_3]\lambda_4$ s.t. $|\lambda_1[\lambda_2| = i$ and $\lambda''\omega'' = \lambda_1[\lambda_2]\lambda'_3\lambda'_4$ s.t. $\alpha(\lambda'_3) = \alpha(\lambda_3)$ and $\alpha(\lambda'_4) = \alpha(\lambda_4)$. Let λ_5 be a Y-decomposition of $\lambda'_4\nu''$ then $\lambda_1[\lambda_2\lambda_3]\lambda_5$ is a Y-decomposition of v strictly smaller than $\lambda''\omega''\nu''$ which leads to the same contradiction. Therefore, $\lambda' = \lambda''$ and since $|\mu'| + |\nu''| \leq 3 \times (|\mu| + |\nu|) = 3 \times \|u, v\| \leq 3 \times k$, $\|md_Y(u), md_Y(v)\| \leq |\omega'| + |\omega''| + |\mu'| + |\nu''| \leq 2 \times M + 3 \times k \leq K$. This proves that md_Y has bounded variations and therefore that it is subsequential.
□

We can now define precisely what is the effect of a function when one applies it from left to right, as was done in the original tagger.

Definition 30 *If f is a rational function, $Y = dom(f) \subset \Sigma^+$, the right-minimal local extension of f, denoted $RmLocExt(f)$, is the composition of a right-minimal Y-decomposition md_Y with $Id_{\Sigma^*} \cdot ([/\epsilon \cdot f \cdot]/\epsilon \cdot Id_{\Sigma^*})^*$.*

RmLocExt being the composition of two subsequential functions, it is itself subsequential, this proves the following final proposition which states that given a rule-based system similar to Brill's system, one can build a subsequential transducer that represents it:

Proposition 13 *If $(f_1, \cdots, f_n)$ is a sequence of subsequential functions with bounded domains then*
$RmLocExt(f_1) \circ \cdots \circ RmLocExt(f_n)$ is subsequential.

We have proven in this section that our techniques apply to the class of transformation-based systems. We now turn our attention to the implementation of finite-state transducers.

7.11   Implementation of Finite-State Transducers

Once the final finite-state transducer is computed, applying it to an input is straightforward: it consists of following a unique path in the transducer whose left labels correspond to the input. However, in order to have a complexity fully independent of the size of the grammar and in particular, independent of the number of transitions at each state, one should carefully choose an appropriate representation for the transducer. In our implementation, the transitions can be accessed randomly. The transducer is first represented by a two-dimensional table whose rows are indexed by the states and whose columns are indexed by the alphabet of all possible input letters. The content of the table at line q and at column a is the word w such that the transition from q with the input label a outputs w. Since only a few transitions are allowed from many states, this table is very sparse and can be compressed. This compression is achieved using a procedure for sparse data tables following the method given by Tarjan and Yao (1979).

7.12   Acknowledgments

We thank Eric Brill for providing us with the code of his tagger and for many useful discussions. We also thank Aravind K. Joshi, Mark Liberman and Mehryar Mohri for valuable discussions. We thank the anonymous reviewers for many helpful comments that led to improvements in both the content and the presentation of this paper.

7.13   Conclusion

The techniques described in this chapter are more general than the problem of part-of-speech tagging and are applicable to the class of problems dealing with local transformation rules.

We showed that any transformation based program can be transformed into a deterministic finite-state transducer. This yields to optimal time implementations of transformation based programs.

As a case study, we applied these techniques to the problem of part-of-speech tagging and presented a finite-state tagger that requires n steps to tag a sentence of length n, independent of the number of rules and the length of the context they require. We achieved this result by representing the rules acquired for Brill's tagger as non-deterministic finite-state transducers. We composed each of these non-deterministic transducers and turned the resulting transducer into a deterministic transducer. The resulting deterministic transducer yields a part-of-speech tagger which operates in optimal time in the sense that the time to assign tags to a sentence corresponds to the time required to follow a single path in this deterministic finite-state machine. The tagger outperforms in speed both Brill's tagger and trigram-based taggers. Moreover, the finite-state tagger inherits from the rule-based system its compactness compared to a stochastic tagger. We also proved the correctness and the generality of the methods.

We believe that this finite-state tagger will also be found useful combined with other language components, since it can be naturally extended by composing it with finite-state transducers which could encode other aspects of natural language syntax.

References

Brill, Eric. 1992. A simple rule-based part of speech tagger. In *Third Conference on Applied Natural Language Processing*, pages 152–155, Trento, Italy.

Brill, Eric. 1994. A report of recent progress in transformation error-driven learning. In *AAAI'94, Tenth National Conference on Artificial Intelligence*.

Choffrut, Christian. 1977. Une caractérisation des fonctions séquentielles et des fonctions sous-séquentielles en tant que relations rationnelles. *Theoretical Computer Science*, 5:325–338.

Choffrut, Christian. 1978. *Contribution à l'étude de quelques familles remarquables de fonctions rationnelles*. Ph.D. thesis, Université Paris VII (Thèse d'Etat).

Chomsky, N. 1964. *Syntactic Structures*. Mouton and Co., The Hague.

Church, Kenneth Ward. 1988. A stochastic parts program and noun phrase parser for unrestricted text. In *Second Conference on Applied Natural Language Processing*, Austin, Texas.

Clemenceau, David. 1993. *Structuration du Lexique et Reconnaissance de Mots Dérivés*. Ph.D. thesis, Université Paris 7.

Cutting, Doug, Julian Kupiec, Jan Pederson, and Penelope Sibun. 1992. A practical part-of-speech tagger. In *Third Conference on Applied Natural Language Processing*, pages 133–140, Trento, Italy.

DeRose, S.J. 1988. Grammatical category disambiguation by statistical optimization. *Computational Linguistics*, 14:31–39.

Eilenberg, Samuel. 1974. *Automata, languages, and machines*. Academic Press, New York.

Elgot, C. C. and J. E. Mezei. 1965. On relations defined by generalized finite automata. *IBM Journal of Research and Development*, 9:47–65, January.

Francis, W. Nelson and Henry Kučera. 1982. *Frequency Analysis of English Usage*. Houghton Mifflin, Boston.

Kaplan, Ronald M. and Martin Kay. 1994. Regular models of phonological rule systems. *Computational Linguistics*, 20(3):331–378.

Karttunen, Lauri, Ronald M. Kaplan, and Annie Zaenen. 1992. Two-level morphology with composition. In *Proceedings of the 14th International Conference on Computational Linguistics (COLING'92)*.

Kupiec, J. M. 1992. Robust part-of-speech tagging using a hidden Markov model. *Computer Speech and Language*, 6:225–242.

Laporte, Eric. 1993. Phonétique et transducteurs. Technical report, Université Paris 7, June.

Merialdo, Bernard. 1990. Tagging text with a probabilistic model. Technical Report RC 15972, IBM Research Division.

Mohri, Mehryar. 1994a. Minimisation of sequential transducers. In *Proceedings of the Conference on Computational Pattern Matching 1994*.

Mohri, Mehryar. 1994b. On some applications of finite-state automata theory to natural language processing. Technical report, Institut Gaspard Monge.

Pereira, Fernando C. N., Michael Riley, and Richard W. Sproat. 1994. Weighted rational transductions and their application to human language processing. In *ARPA Workshop on Human Language Technology*. Morgan Kaufmann.

Revuz, Dominique. 1991. *Dictionnaires et Lexiques, Méthodes et Algorithmes*. Ph.D. thesis, Université Paris 7.

Roche, Emmanuel. 1993. *Analyse Syntaxique Transformationelle du Français par Transducteurs et Lexique-Grammaire*. Ph.D. thesis, Université Paris 7, January.

Schützenberger, Marcel Paul. 1977. Sur une variante des fonctions sequentielles. *Theoretical Computer Science*, 4:47–57.

Silberztein, Max. 1993. *Dictionnaires Electroniques et Analyse Lexicale du Français — Le Système INTEX*. Masson.

Tapanainen, Pasi and Atro Voutilainen. 1993. Ambiguity resolution in a reductionistic parser. In *Sixth Conference of the European Chapter of the ACL, Proceedings of the Conference*, Utrecht, April.

Tarjan, Robert Endre and Andrew Chi-Chih Yao. 1979. Storing a sparse table. *Communications of the ACM*, 22(11):606–611, November.

Weischedel, Ralph, Marie Meteer, Richard Schwartz, Lance Ramshaw, and Jeff Palmucci. 1993. Coping with ambiguity and unknown words through probabilistic models. *Computational Linguistics*, 19(2):359–382, June.

8 Parsing with Finite-State Transducers

Emmanuel Roche

Accurately parsing natural language sentences requires large scale and detailed lexical grammars. We will see that for the problem of parsing natural language sentences, finite-state models are both efficient and very accurate even in complex linguistic situations. Finite-state transducers should appeal to the linguist looking for precise and natural description of complex syntactic structures while the wide range of formal operations on finite-state transducers provides the designer of parsing programs with powerful tools to improve parsing efficiency. The parsing programs derived from this approach are both simple, precise linguistically and very efficient.

8.1 Introduction

Finite-State methods have recently improved computational efficiency for a wide variety of natural language processing tasks; ranging from morphological analysis (Silberztein, 1993; Karttunen, Kaplan, and Zaenen, 1992; Clemenceau and Roche, 1993) to phonetic and speech processing (Pereira, Riley, and Sproat, 1994; Laporte, 1993; Laporte, 1996).

However, finite-state modeling is usually thought as a necessary evil in the sense that more powerful formalisms such as context-free grammars are more accurate but of intractable size for reasonable efficiency. A clear illustration of this view comes from the field of speech recognition in which grammars are often given in a context-free form but the size of the data and the finite-state nature of most representations (phoneme or word lattice for instance) make it difficult and inefficient to use general algorithms such as the Earley parsing. Complex grammars are therefore approximated by finite-state models (Pereira and Wright, 1996). In these situations, approximations lead to more efficient and simpler parsing strategies at the cost of a lost of accuracy.

We will see here that for the problem of parsing natural language sentences, finite-state models are not an efficient but somewhat inaccurate tool but rather one of the best formalism at hand to represent accurately complex linguistic phenomena. The use of finite-state transducers for parsing should appeal both to the linguist looking for precise and natural description of complex phenomena and to the implementer of efficient parsing programs.

From a computational point of view, finite-state transducers can be used to parse very large scale lexical grammars. Some of the formal characteristics of transducer parsing include:

- very large scale grammars are represented in a compact form. Parts of different rules that are similar are represented only once,

- factorization, determinization and minimization of transducers can be used to generate more efficient parsers (Roche, 1995),

- the grammar compilation, the input sentences and the parsing process use one homogeneous representations,

- parsing and building the grammar are the same operation, i.e. a rational transduction,

- transforming a context-free grammar into a transducer is yet another transduction.

These properties have been described and illustrated on a large coverage grammar of French in Roche (1993).

From a linguistic point of view, we take here a complementary approach to Gross (1996) in this volume which shows that FSA is a very natural framework for the task of designing large coverage and lexicalized grammars. We focus on the process of parsing a sentence, therefore assuming that a very precise grammar is already available. While our main point is not grammar design, the discussion should shed light on several important problems and solutions involved at the grammar building stage.

To illustrate the possible precision of parsing with transducers, we will show that we can tackle one of the main drawback in using context-free grammars in language modeling, namely the inability or the difficulty of handling various types of deletion. Consider the sentence

(1)   *He expected John to buy a new book.*

In the transformational grammar of Z. S. Harris (see Harris (1991) for instance), this sentence is analyzed as the verb *expected* (an *operator*) taking three arguments: (1) the subject *he*, (2) the first complement *John* and (3) the sentence *John buys a new book*; the application of the verb operator deletes the subject of the last argument to transform the sentence into the infinitive clause *to buy a new book*. In order to handle this situation with context-free grammars, each sentence has to be described both with its declarative form, say *N buy N*, and with its infinitive clause form, say *to buy N*. This might not seem to be a difficult problem at first but recall that grammars have to be lexicalized (see Gross (1975) and Boons and Leclere (1976) for instance), that is, each rule should contain an explicit word, and therefore this type of duplication, which is only one duplication among many others, has to be repeated throughout the whole lexicon. It is however possible to stick to a grammatical description that respects this phenomenon.

The next section will give a short background about parsing viewed as a string transformation (the formal definitions of the objects manipulated in this chapter are given in the general introduction of this volume). The following section, describing one of the ways context-free languages can be parsed with finite-state transducers, give the general framework for transducer parsing.

Section 8.4 shows that the interaction between morphology and syntax can be viewed as a simple sequence of finite-state operations. Section 8.5, shows, through a variety of linguistic examples, that transduction parsing is well adapted to transformational grammars and that, in addition to lead to efficient parsing strategies, it also leads to more accurate sentence analysis.

We will see in Section 8.6 that both parsing and grammar design can be viewed as a simple transduction operation; this similarity can be used to precompile the analysis of language sequences that are finite-state in nature.

Section 8.7 details a typical example of tree adjoining grammar to show that there is a natural way of converting a tree adjoining grammar into a single finite-state transducer. The transducer associated to a tree adjoining grammar also defines a parser for this grammar. Since the tree adjoining grammar formalism, which is strictly more powerful than context-free grammars, was designed specifically to render more accurately syntactic phenomena, this is another indication that transducer parsing is a tool well adapted to the complexity of natural language.

8.2 Background

Parsing will be considered here strictly as a string transformation process. Namely, if Σ_g represents the set of symbols, such as (N, N) or $(S$, used to mark the syntactic analysis; if Σ_w is the list of words in the language, then a parser is a mapping

$$\text{parser} : \Sigma_w^* \longrightarrow 2^{(\Sigma_g^* \cdot \Sigma_w^* \cdot \Sigma_g^*)^*}$$

such that, for instance, a sequence of words like:

(2)   *John left this morning.*

is transformed into a set of of outputs representing the analysis of this sentence:

(3)   (S (N *John* N) (V *left* V) (N *this morning* N) S)

Here the set contains only one element but is would contain more than one element if the sentence was syntactically ambiguous.

In practice, parsing will be broken up into two phases: (1) a morphological analysis and (2) the syntactic analysis. In order to simplify the exposition, in the following section as well as in most of this chapter, we will make the assumption that the syntactic analysis applies directly on the words and that morphological information is available when necessary. This simplification is justified in Section 8.4.

8.3   A Top-Down Parser for Context-Free Grammars

One way[1] of parsing context-free grammars with finite-state transducers consists of modeling a top-down analysis. Consider the sentence

(4)   *John thinks that Peter kept the book*

and suppose the we have the syntactic data of Table 8.1.

N *thinks that* S	S
N *kept* N	S
John	N
Peter	N
the book	N

Table 8.1: syntactic dictionary for *John thinks that Peter kept the book*

This data can be seen as a sample of a syntactic dictionary in which the keys are the structures and the information is the type of the structure (sentence structure, noun structure). Such a syntactic dictionary would look like the sample of Figure 8.1[2].

---

[1] Other ways are described in Roche (1993).

[2] This grammatical representation is motivated by the fact that grammatical representations, whatever the formalism they are expressed in, should be lexicalized. The linguistic motivation comes from Z.S. Harris (Harris, 1991) and Maurice Gross (Gross, 1968; Gross, 1975).

$$\begin{array}{|l|}
\hline
\vdots \\
\textbf{N think,}S \\
\textbf{N think that S,}S \\
\vdots \\
\textbf{N say N,}S \\
\textbf{N say that S,}S \\
\textbf{N say N to N,}S \\
\textbf{N say that S to N,}S \\
\textbf{N say to N that S,}S \\
\vdots \\
\textbf{John,}N \\
\vdots \\
\textbf{the book,}N \\
\vdots \\
\hline
\end{array}$$

Figure 8.1: Sample of the Syntactic Dictionary

The first step for building a parser consists of transforming each entry of this syntactic dictionary into a finite-state transducer. The finite-state transducer related to an entry will be the machine responsible for analyzing a sentence with this structure. Here, this will lead to the transducers[3] of Table 8.2. This table can be seen as a dictionary of transducers.

Each transducer represents a transduction from Σ^* to Σ^* where $\Sigma = \Sigma_w \cup \Sigma_g$. For instance, the transducer associated to the structure N *thinks that* S (the first transducer of Table 8.2), that we denote T_{thinks_that}, will map (5) to (6).

(5) [S *John thinks that Peter kept the book* S]
(6) (S [N *John* N] *thinks that* [S *Peter kept the book* S] S)

Formally, $T_{thinks\_that}(5) = (6)$.
Given the dictionary of transducers we define the grammar

$$T_{dic} = \bigcup_{T_i \in dic} T_i$$

as being the union of all the transducers defined in the dictionary. For instance, if dic$_1$ is the dictionary defined in Table 8.2, then T_{dic_1} is the transducer represented of Figure 8.2.

---

[3]On this graph, the symbol *?* stands for any symbol in the alphabet considered and the symbol $<E>$ stands for the empty word ϵ.

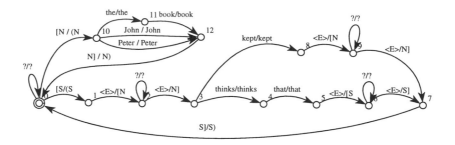

Figure 8.2: Transducer T_{dic_1} representing the syntactic dictionary dic_1

This transducer being given, parsing simply consists of applying the transducer on the input and checking whether the output is different from the input; if it is, then the transducer is applied again. The process is repeated until the input is not modified. Formally,

$$\text{parser} = T_{dic}^{\infty}$$

On the example of the input (5), the parsing is illustrated below:

[S *John thinks that Peter kept the book* S]
$$\downarrow (T_{dic_1})$$
(S [N *John* N] *thinks that* [S *Peter kept the book* S] S)
(S [N *John thinks that Peter* N] *kept* [N *the book* N] S)
$$\downarrow (T_{dic_1})$$
(S (N *John* N) *thinks that* (S [N *Peter* N] *kept* [N *the book* N] S) S)
$$\downarrow (T_{dic_1})$$
(S (N *John* N) *thinks that* (S (N *Peter* N) *kept* (N *the book* N) S) S)

The input sequence is given on top and the first application of T_{dic_1} results in two outputs. We reapply the transducer on each one, the first one leads to the next sequence while the second one has no output. Finally, the latest sequence is:

(7)   (S (N *John* N) *thinks that* (S (N *Peter* N) *kept* (N *the book* N) S) S)

which is also the analysis of the input.

The parsing is described here as the application of a transducer on a string however, in practice, the input strings are represented by FSAs and the transducers therefore apply on these FSAs directly. For instance, the input sentence is initially represented by the flat automaton of Figure 8.3.

Once T_{dic} is available, the parsing algorithm is therefore extremely simple to describe, it is given on Figure 8.4 in which the function *Apply_transducer*,

Figure 8.3: Automaton representing the input sentence

takes a transducer and an automaton as input and outputs an automaton. Each string of this output automaton is an output of a string represented by the input automaton through the transducer.

TransducerParse
Input: T_{dic}, sentence
sent$_1$ = sentence;
while $((\text{sent}_2 = \text{Apply\_transducer}(T_{dic}, \text{sent}1))! = sent_1)$
     sent$_1$ = sent$_2$;
Output: sent$_1$

Figure 8.4: Parsing algorithm

A trace of the parsing of the example above is given on Figure 8.5. The figure shows that each transduction is applied on a finite-state automaton, a directed acyclic graph here, representing a finite set of strings.

8.4 Morphology

The transducers representing the sentence structures in the previous section apply directly on the inflected words like *thinks* or *kept*. Hence, in order to build a full parser, one would have to duplicate each transducer for all the inflected forms of a given noun or verb. For instance, the transducer representing the sentence structure *N kept N* should a priori be duplicated into the transducer representing *N keep N* and *N keeps N*. Obviously, such an approach is highly redundant and space consuming and for languages with higher inflexion variability (French, Italian, Spanish for instance) this type of duplication is not feasible. A more practical approach consists of decomposing the parsing process into a morphological analysis and the syntactic analysis per se. The morphological analysis will map each inflected word into a unique canonical form (the infinitive form for a verb or the singular form for a noun) plus a list of morphological features such as tense, person or number. The individual syntactic transducers will now be described as applying on the

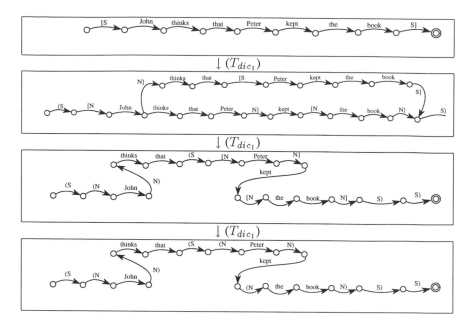

Figure 8.5: Parsing trace of the example

canonical forms rather than on the inflected words.

In first approximation, the morphological analysis is a dictionary lookup which can also be formalized as a string transformation process. Indeed, consider the sentence

(8)   *John left this morning.*

Each of the four words of this sentence should be an entry in a morphological dictionary[4]. The information related to each entry is a list of morphological interpretations for this entry. For instance, the ambiguous string *left* could be a noun, a verb or an adjective and the information associated to *left* should therefore give all these interpretations. More formally, each interpretation can be written as a sequence of symbols. For instance, the interpretation of *left* as the past tense of the verb *to leave* would be the sequence:

(9)   # v pt *leave left*

with the convention that the symbol # marks the starting point of the interpretation, that *v* stands for verb, that *pt* stands for past tense and that the word

---

[4]The precise description of such dictionaries is described in Courtois (1989). See also Silberztein (1993) and Silberztein (1997) in this volume for other kinds of precise treatment of morphological analysis.

leave is the canonical form of the word (infinitive form here) whereas the last symbol is the word itself. With this representation, the entry of the string *left* in the morphological dictionary will be the following[5]:

left	# v pt *leave left*
	# v pp *leave left*
	# ns *left*
	# adv *left*
	# adj *left*

With these conventions, each interpretation is a string of

$$\{\#\} \cdot \Sigma_m^* \cdot \Sigma_w$$

in which

- Σ_w is the list of words and symbols such as *eat, John, left, leave* that can appear in the text being analyzed,

- Σ_m contains symbols representing morphological features (such as *pt, ns* or *adv*) and the canonical forms of the words (such as *leave*).

Moreover, since the information associated to a word is a list of interpretations, the information is an element of

$$2^{(\{\#\} \cdot \Sigma_m^* \cdot \Sigma_w)}$$

and the dictionary lookup is therefore a mapping from words to morphological information, that is:

$$lookup : \Sigma_w^* \longrightarrow 2^{(\{\#\} \cdot \Sigma_m^* \cdot \Sigma_w)}$$

The whole dictionary can therefore be viewed as a string transformation. For instance, the sub-dictionary necessary to analyze Sentence (8) can be represented as follows:

---

[5]We use the additional following conventions: *pp*: past participle, *ns*: singular noun, *adv*: adverb, *adj*: adjective.

$$John \quad \longrightarrow \quad \text{\# pn } John$$

$$left \quad \longrightarrow \quad
\begin{array}{l}
\text{\# v pt } leave\ left \\
\text{\# v pp } leave\ left \\
\text{\# ns } left \\
\text{\# adv } left \\
\text{\# adj } left
\end{array}$$

$$this \quad \longrightarrow \quad
\begin{array}{l}
\text{\# det } this \\
\text{\# det } this
\end{array}$$

$$morning \quad \longrightarrow \quad \text{\# ns } morning$$

The function *lookup* takes individual words as input, it can be generalized into the function *morpho* that associates to each sequence of words, e.g. sentence, its morphological interpretations. Formally,

$$morpho = lookup^*$$

that is,

$$morpho(a \cdot b) = lookup(a) \cdot lookup(b)$$

and therefore *morpho* is a function mapping a sequence of words to a set of sequences of words and morphological information:

$$morpho : \Sigma_w^* \longrightarrow 2^{(\{\#\} \cdot \Sigma_m^* \cdot \Sigma_w)^*}$$

For instance, the following sequence, which is the correct interpretation of (8),

(10)   # pn *John* # v pt *leave left* # det *this* # nn *morning* # .

is an element of *morpho*(8). Obviously, *morpho*(8) doesn't contain the correct morphological interpretation only, it contains all the possible interpretations. At this point it is important to notice that number of interpretations of a sentence is typically very high. For instance (8) contains 5×2 interpretations, and this number tends to grow exponentially with the length of the sentence. Hence, the result of the mapping of *morpho* will not be the explicit list of strings representing each interpretation, this would be unmanageable, but rather a finite-state automaton representing this set of interpretations. For instance, *morpho*(8) will be represented by the automaton of Figure 8.6.

The syntactic analysis will run on the result of the preliminary morphological analysis. In other words, the whole parsing process, which is a mapping:

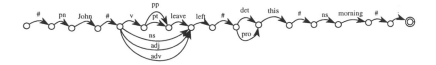

Figure 8.6: Automaton representing a morphological analysis.

$$\text{parser} : \Sigma_w^* \longrightarrow 2^{(\Sigma_g^* \cdot \Sigma_w^* \cdot \Sigma_g^*)^*}$$

will be broken as indicated in the following diagram:

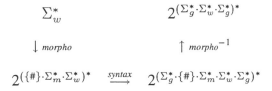

In the example of sentence (8), we can illustrate this decomposition as follows:

John left this morning.
$\downarrow$ (*morpho*)

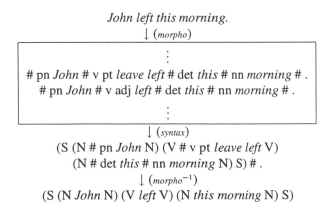

$\downarrow$ (*syntax*)
(S (N # pn *John* N) (V # v pt *leave left* V)
(N # det *this* # nn *morning* N) S) # .
$\downarrow$ (*morpho⁻¹*)
(S (N *John* N) (V *left* V) (N *this morning* N) S)

The morphological analyzer applies directly on the input string to produce a set of morphological interpretations for this sentence. The syntactic analysis is then performed by *syntax* on each morphological interpretation, that is on the automaton representing the set of interpretations. A final stage, denoted *morpho⁻¹*, removes the symbol representing the morphological features as well as the canonical forms introduced by the first step.

In order for the syntactic analysis to apply on the result of the morphological analysis, each syntactic transducer should be adjusted to handle inputs of the correct shape, that is, outputs generated by the morphological analysis. For instance, the transducer T_{kept} (second transducer of Table 8.2) will be replaced by the transducer T'_{keep} of Figure 8.7. In this transducer, the transition *kept/kept* is replaced by a sequence of transitions labeled *#/# v/v ?/? keep/keep ?/?* that will take any string of the shape[6]

$$\# \cdot v \cdot ? \cdot keep \cdot ?$$

Such strings are the morphological interpretation of any form of the verb *to keep*. Note that without a morphological analysis, the grammar should contain, in addition to T_{kept}, two similar transducers T_{keep} and T_{keeps}. By contrast, only T'_{keep} will be used now.

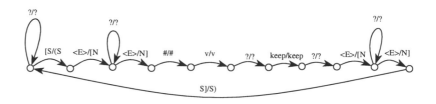

Figure 8.7: Syntactic transducer to be combined with a morphological analysis.

As a by-product of such decomposition, it becomes straight-forward to transform the syntactic analysis into a part-of-speech tagger (i.e. a program that disambiguates each word). In fact, if $morpho^{-1}$ is replaced by a mapping $gram^{-1}$ that removes the syntactic markers instead of the morphological symbols. The final result is a string representing the exact morphological interpretation of each word. In other words, the process defined by the following diagram:

$$\Sigma_w^* \qquad\qquad 2^{(\{\#\}\cdot\Sigma_m^*\cdot\Sigma_w^*)^*}$$

$$\downarrow morpho \qquad\qquad \uparrow gram^{-1}$$

$$2^{(\{\#\}\cdot\Sigma_m^*\cdot\Sigma_w^*)^*} \xrightarrow{\ syntax\ } 2^{(\Sigma_g^*\cdot\{\#\}\cdot\Sigma_m^*\cdot\Sigma_w^*\cdot\Sigma_g^*)^*}$$

will take sentence (8) and process as described on Figure 8.8.

Another natural consequence of this approach is that a local grammar disambiguation can take place between the dictionary lookup and the syntactic

---

[6]Recall that ? stands for any string.

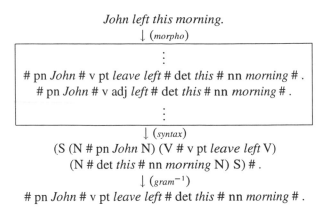

Figure 8.8: Part-of-speech tagging through syntactic analysis

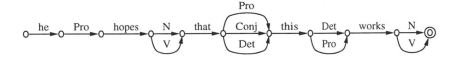

Figure 8.9: Automaton representing the morphological analysis of *he hopes that this works*

analysis. The introduction chapter showed how it is possible to state negative constraints on morphological interpretations of sentences. By doing that, the number of ambiguities decreases significantly. Formally, a set of constraints $C_1, .. \ C_n$, represented each by a finite-state automaton, is applied on the sentence by the following operation:

$$S' = S - \Sigma^* \cdot (C_1 \cup \ldots \cup C_n) \cdot \Sigma^*$$

Recall that for instance, if S is the sentence represented by the automaton of Figure 8.9 and if the constraints are represented by the two automata of Figure 8.10 then S' is given by the automaton of Figure 8.11. Note that this representation is less ambiguous than S.

Using local constraints can improve the speed of the whole process. Such an analyzer can be summarized by the decomposition diagram of Figure 8.12.

Figure 8.10: Automata representing two negative rules.

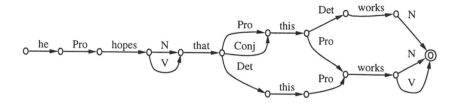

Figure 8.11: Result of the application of the negative rule of Figure 8.10 to Figure 8.9.

8.5   A Parser for Transformation Grammars

In this section, we illustrate the flexibility of the finite-state transducer formalism through a few examples of increasing linguistic complexity. These problems have been studied in greater detail for French and the techniques introduced here are more precisely presented in Roche (1993). See also Mohri (1993) for a closely related discussion. Before looking the examples, let us warn the reader that the complex linguistic problems found in the following examples should not be considered as exceptions and that the level of detail required in the grammar description is not exaggerated (as proved in Gross (1968) and Gross (1975)). In fact, Mohri (1993) shows that, from a linguistic point of view, an even greater level of linguistic detail is required to disambiguate numerous common sentences.

8.5.1   Modal verbs

We will now detail the analysis of the sentence *John should read this book*; the technique uses is general. Before looking at this example, we have to consider the following extension: input sentences, analyzed sentences, and partially analyzed sentences will be written in the same formalism, namely as strings in Σ^*, the transducer associated to each structure will be generalized such that it handles partially analyzed sentences. This extension will make the analysis of apparently very diverse linguistic phenomena homogeneous.

For instance, with the grammar described up to this point, the structure

$$\Sigma_w^* \qquad\qquad 2^{(\Sigma_g^* \cdot \Sigma_w^* \cdot \Sigma_g^*)^*}$$

$$\downarrow morpho \qquad\qquad\qquad \uparrow morpho^{-1}$$

$$2^{(\{\#\} \cdot \Sigma_m^* \cdot \Sigma_w^*)^*}$$

$$\downarrow local$$

$$2^{(\{\#\} \cdot \Sigma_m^* \cdot \Sigma_w^*)^*} \quad \xrightarrow{syntax} \quad 2^{(\Sigma_g^* \cdot \{\#\} \cdot \Sigma_m^* \cdot \Sigma_w^* \cdot \Sigma_g^*)^*}$$

Figure 8.12: Parsing Diagram (Local Grammar included)

(11) N <V *read* V> N

is handled by the transducer $T_{N\_read\_N}$, defined by

$$[S\ a\ read\ b\ S]$$
$$\downarrow$$
$$(S\ [N\ a\ N] <V\ read\ V> [N\ b\ N]\ S)$$

We now extend it such that it recognizes an already partially analyzed sentence. For instance, $T_{N\_read\_N}$ is extended to realize the additional following mappings:

(12) [S [N *a* N] *read b* S] → (S [N *a* N] <V *read* V> [N *b* N] S)
(13) [S [N *a* N] <V *read* V> [N *b* N] S] →
      (S [N *a* N] <V *read* V> [N *b* N] S)
(14) [S N *read* N S] → (S N <V *read* V> N S)

In (12), *a* had already been detected as a noun phrase. In a similar way, in (13), the whole structure has already been recognized and in this case the transduction acts as a recognizer. In (14), the transducer just checks whether the proposed structure is correct with respect to the verb.

In addition to these generalizations, the transducer should be able to handle sentences in which sequences, such as adverbials, have been inserted. They perform the following mappings:

(15) [S *a read b* <OP *c* OP> S] → (S [N *a* N] *read* [N *b* N] <OP *c* OP> S)
(16) [S *a* <OP *d* OP> *read b* S] →
      (S [N *a* N] <OP *d* OP> <V *read* V> [N *b* N] S)

in which the <OP and OP> markers[7] define a sequence that can be ignored

---

[7] OP stands for operator. In fact, Gross (1986) shows that adverbials are often, but not always, analyzed as transformational operators on sentences. In other words, an adverbial is an operator that takes one argument: a sentence.

during parsing. In practice, the sequence of words *c* could be an adverbial like *yesterday* and *d* could be a modal verb such as *could*.

Let us can now consider the following sentence:

(17)   *John should* v *read this book*

in which *v* represents a morphological tag that we suppose results from a morphological analysis. *should* is considered to be an operator that applies on a sentence (Harris, 1991). This operator takes a sentence as input, say

N V W

in which *W* stands for any sequence of complements, and produces the same sentence with *should* inserted:

N *should* V W

From the analysis point of view, if a sequence contains *should* between what could be a subject and a verb, then the same sequence, minus *should*, should be analyzed as a sentence. The analysis of *John should read this book* is done as follows:

$$[S \; John \; should \; read \; \text{v} \; this \; book \; S]$$
$$\downarrow$$
$$[S \; [N \; John \; N] \; <OP \; should \; OP> \; \text{v} \; read \; this \; book \; S]$$
$$\downarrow$$
$$(S \; [N \; John \; N] \; <OP \; should \; OP> \; <V \; \text{v} \; read \; V> \; [N \; this \; book \; N] \; S)$$
$$\downarrow$$
$$(S \; (N \; John \; N) \; <OP \; should \; OP> \; <V \; \text{v} \; read \; V> \; (N \; this \; book \; N) \; S)$$

The second and third transformations are already handled by T_{dic} as described before. The first transformation is a translation of the fact that if *John should read this book* has to be analyzed as a sentence, then *John read this book* should be analyzed as a sentence whose subject is *John* and whose main verb is *read*. To perform this first transformation, we have to add to the grammar a transducer, that we call $T_{N\_should\_W}$, which is associated to the structure N *should* V W in the syntactic dictionary. $T_{N\_should\_W}$ computes the following mapping:

$$[S \; a \; should \; \text{v} \; c \; S]$$
$$\downarrow$$
$$[S \; [N \; a \; N] \; <OP \; should \; OP> \; \text{v} \; c \; S]$$

This mapping keeps the markers [S and S] meaning that the sequence still have to be analyzed as a sentence. The mapping also marks *should* as an operator.

$T_{N\_should\_W}$ should therefore be added to T_{dic}.

The analysis of sentences with the auxiliary verb *to have* can be handled in a similar way. A further addition to T_{dic}, namely $T_{N\_have\_W}$, will include both the following mapping[8]:

(18)   [S *a have* v c S] → [S [N *a* N] <OP *have* OP> v c S]

and this one:

$$[S \text{ [N } a \text{ N] } <OP \ b > OP \ have \ v \ c \ S]$$
$$\downarrow$$
$$[S \text{ [N } a \text{ N] } <OP \ <OP \ b \ OP> \ have \ OP> \ v \ c \ S]$$

The first mapping corresponds to the case were *have* is used as a simple auxiliary, as in *They have accomplished that* and the second mapping corresponds to the case in which *have* is used in conjunction with a modal verb. For instance, a sentence like:

(19)   [S *John should have read this book* S]

will be analyzed as follows:

[S *John should have* v *this book* S]
↓
[S [N *John* N] <OP *should* OP> *have* v *read this book* S]
↓
[S [N *John* N] <OP <OP *should* OP> *have* OP> v *read this book* S]
↓
(S [N *John* N] <OP <OP *should* OP> *have* OP> <V v *read* V> [N *this book* N] S)
↓
(S (N *John* N) <OP <OP *should* OP> *have* OP> <V v *read* V> (N *this book* N) S)

in which, as above, sequences enclosed in <OP and OP> markers, once inserted, are simply ignored at latter stage of the analysis. The result of the parsing, namely the string

(S (N *John* N) <OP <OP *should* OP> *have*OP> <V v *read* V> (N *this book* N) S)

should be interpreted as follows: *John read this book* is the main sentence with *John* as subject, *read* as verb and *this book* as direct object. On this sentence,

---

[8] Whether a verb can take *to have* as an auxiliary can be added in this transducer.

the operator *have* is first applied which leads to the more complex sentence *John has read this book*. Finally, the operator *should* is applied on the previous sentence which leads to the actual sentence *John should have read this book*.

The same strategy can be used to handle discontinuous operators such as *not . . . so much*. Consider the following sentence:

(20)   *John should not read this book so much.*

The first step of the analysis recognizes both *not* and *so much* as being one discontinuous operator. The analysis goes as follows:

$$[S\ John\ should\ not\ v\ this\ book\ that\ much\ S]$$
$$\downarrow$$
$$[S\ [N\ John\ N]\ <OP\ should\ OP>\ not$$
$$v\ read\ this\ book\ not\ that\ much\ S]$$
$$\downarrow$$
$$[S\ [N\ John\ N]\ <OP\ <OP\ should\ OP>\ not\ OP>$$
$$v\ read\ this\ book\ <OP\ \leftarrow not\ that\ much\ OP>\ S]$$
$$\downarrow$$
$$(S\ [N\ John\ N]\ <OP\ <OP\ should\ OP>\ not\ OP>$$
$$<V\ v\ read\ V>\ [N\ this\ book\ N]\ <OP\ \leftarrow not\ that\ much\ OP>\ S)$$
$$\downarrow$$
$$(S\ (N\ John\ N)\ <OP\ <OP\ should\ OP>\ not\ OP>$$
$$<V\ v\ read\ V>\ (N\ this\ book\ N)\ <OP\ \leftarrow not\ that\ much\ OP>\ S)$$

The symbol $\leftarrow not$ is inserted such that the final analysis of the sentence clearly identifies *not . . . so much* as one single operator. To achieve the previous analysis, a transducer $T_{not\_so\_much}$ needs to be added to the whole grammar. $T_{not\_so\_much}$ is defined functionally by:

$$[S\ [N\ a\ N]\ <OP\ b\ OP>\ not\ v\ c\ so\ much\ S]$$
$$\downarrow$$
$$[S\ [N\ a\ N]\ <OP\ <OP\ b\ OP>\ not\ OP>\ v\ b\ <OP\ \leftarrow not\ so\ much\ OP>\ S]$$

8.5.2   Operators on sentential complements

The previous examples show how sentences with modal verbs can be analyzed. The analysis of a sentence with a modal verb is reduced to the analysis of a simpler sentence. A similar approach will be used now for sentences with an infinitive clause. In fact, the analysis of a sentence with an infinitive clause will be reduced to the analysis of two simpler sentences. Consider:

(21) *John expected Mary to come.*

in which the verb *expected* takes three arguments: a noun, namely *John*, a second noun, namely *Mary*, and a sentence, namely *Mary came*. The subject of the second argument is used as first complement and it is deleted from the argument sentence *Mary came*. We want to have a finite-state transducer representing *expected*, or more precisely the structure[9]

N *expected* N *to* ϵN V W

such that nothing has to be changed in the transducer associated to N *come*. In other words, the analysis of *Mary came* should remain as it would be if it where a simple isolated sentence. We achieve this goal with a transducer representing N *expected* N *to* ϵN V W that, not only puts boundary markers around N, but also explicitly adds an N symbol that stands for the deleted noun phrase. For the sentence (21), the transformation is the following:

[S *John expected Mary to come* S]
↓
(S [N *John* N] <V *expected* V> [N *Mary* N] [S N <OP *to* OP> *come* S] S)

and the analysis continues as follows:

(S [N *John* N] <V *expected* V> [N *Mary* N] [S N <OP *to* OP> *come* S] S)
↓
(S (N *John* N) <V *expected* V> (N *Mary* N) (S N <OP *to* OP> <V *come* V> S) S)

This last step is possible because T_{N_come} as been generalized as described at the beginning of this section and the symbol N can be used in place of an actual noun phrase. The sequence enclosed by <OP and OP> is ignored.

For the same sentence, with an additional adverbial:

(22) *John expected Mary to come yesterday.*

the analysis goes as follows:

---

[9]The structure N *expected* N *to* ϵN V W could also be written N *expected* N *to* Vinf W. The fist notation emphasizes the fact that the subject of the second verb is deleted. The second structure, on the other hand, emphasizes the fact that the surface form of the second argument is an infinitive clause.

[S *John expected Mary to come yesterday* S]

↓

(S [N *John* N] <V *expected* V> [N *Mary* N]
[S N <OP *to* OP> *come yesterday* S] S)

↓

(S (N *John* N) <V *expected* V> (N *Mary* N)
(S N <OP *to* OP> *come* <OP *yesterday* OP> S) S)

↓

(S (N *John* N) <V *expected* V> (N *Mary* N)
(S N <OP *to* OP> <V *come* V> <OP *yesterday* OP> S) S)

Note that, simultaneously to this analysis, the parser performs the analysis in which the adverbial *yesterday* is attached to the verb *expected* rather than to the verb *came*. In fact, the sentence is ambiguous and the correct result of a syntactic analysis should provide these two analyses.

8.5.3 Support verb construction

Gross (1988) demonstrates that three categories of sentences have to be considered to build complete grammars. The first category consists of free sentences like *John eats potatoes*, the second one consists of sentences like *John makes concessions*, with complements with a smaller degree of variability. They are called *support verb constructions*. Finally, the third category consists of *frozen sentences*, or *idiomatic expressions*, such as *John kicks the bucket*, in which one or several arguments, e.g. complements, are fixed. The rest of this section presents a few typical problems encountered while handling sentences of one of the last two categories.

The following sentences are examples of *support* (or *light*) verb constructions.

(23)   *John makes concessions to his friend.*
(24)   *John makes a right turn*
(25)   * *John makes a right turn to his friend.*
(26)   *John's concessions to his friend were unexpected.*

If *make* is analyzed as a verb such as *read* then sentences (23) and (24) should be analyzed with the structures

(27) N_0 *makes* N_1 *to* N_2
(28) N_0 *makes* N_1

This analysis takes the verb as the head of the sentence but fails to explain why sentence (25) is forbidden.

Furthermore, (23) is clearly present in sentence (26). In fact, the noun phrase construction *N's N to N* is not general and

(29)   * *John's turn to his friend.*

is clearly forbidden too. These two observations, among others (Giry-Schneider, 1978), lead to analyze sentences such as (23) with the noun (called *predicative noun*) as the real head and the verb, called *support verb* (or *light verb*), as support for the tense. (23) will therefore be described by the structure

(30) N_0 $(V_{sup}$ make $V_{sup})$ $(N_{pred}$ concessions $N_{pred})$ to N_1

The diversity of the following examples, with the support verb *take*, further illustrates that the predicative noun, and not the verb, governs the number and the nature of the arguments.

(31)   *John takes a decision.*
(32)   *John takes a look at this.*
(33)   *John takes advantage of his position.*
(34)   *John takes credible steps toward solving this problem.*
(35)   *The party is not likely to take a backseat.*

To be able to parse such sentences each of the following transducers[10], corresponding respectively to (23), (31), (32) and (33) should be added to the global syntactic dictionary

$[S$ *a make concessions to b S*$]$ $\longrightarrow$
$(S$ [N *a* N] $< V_{sup}$ *make* $V_{sup} > <$ N_{pred} *concessions* $N_{pred} >$ *to* [N *b* N] S$)$

$[S$ *a take a decision S*$]$ $\longrightarrow$
$(S$ [N *a* N] $<V_{sup}$ *take* $V_{sup}> <N_{pred}$ *a decision* $N_{pred}>$ S$)$

$[S$ *a take a look at b S*$]$ $\longrightarrow$
$(S$ [N *a* N] $<V_{sup}$ *take* $V_{sup}> <$ N_{pred} *a look* $N_{pred}>$ *at* [N *b* N] S$)$

$[S$ *a take advantage of b S*$]$ $\longrightarrow$
$(S$ [N *a* N] $< V_{sup}$ *take* $V_{sup} > <$ N_{pred} *advantage* $N_{pred} >$ *of* [N *b* N] S$)$

Figure 8.13 gives the trace of the analysis of sentence (23).

---

[10]Here, the transductions are defined functionally but in practice they are defined by their graph representation.

$$[S \; John \; makes \; concessions \; to \; his \; friend \; S]$$
$$\downarrow$$
$$(S \; [N \; John \; N] \; <V_{sup} \; makes \; V_{sup}> \; N_{pred}< \; concessions \; N_{pred}>$$
$$to \; [N \; his \; friend \; N] \; S)$$
$$\downarrow$$
$$(S \; (N \; John \; N) \; <V_{sup} \; makes \; V_{sup}> \; N_{pred}< \; concessions \; N_{pred}>$$
$$to \; (N \; his \; friend \; N) \; S)$$

Figure 8.13: Trace of a Support Verb Construction Analysis

8.5.4 Support verb and sentential clause

In sentence (34), the construction *John takes credible steps toward* is followed by a sentence clause whose verb's subject is also the subject of the main clause, that is, *John*. The analysis works as follows: the input sequence for the parsing transducer is

(36) $[S \; John \; takes \; credible \; steps \; toward \; V_{ing} \; solving \; the \; problem \; S]$

in which V_{ing} is a marker generated by the morphological analysis[11].

We build the grammar such that the first application of the transduction to (36) leads to the following sequence:

(37) $(S \; [N \; John \; N] \; <V_{sup} \; takes \; V_{sup}> \; <N_{pred} \; credible \; steps \; N_{pred}>$
$toward \; OP_{N_0 \rightarrow NS} \; [S \; N \; V_{(ing)} \; solving \; the \; problem \; S] \; S)$

This performs simultaneously the following eight actions:

- the subject is enclosed into $[N$ and $N]$ brackets,

- the sequence *take credible steps toward* is recognized,

- *take* is marked as a support verb with $<V_{sup}$ and $V_{sup}>$,

- *credible steps* is marked as a predicative noun with $<N_{pred}$ and $N_{pred}>$,

- *solving* is recognized as a verb in *ing* form,

- *solving this problem* is marked as a sentence to be recognized while a subject marker N is added.

- The morphological marker V_{ing} is transformed into the marker $V_{(ing)}$ to signify that although the verb was originally in the *ing* form, it has to be considered as a simple conjugated verb during the rest of the analysis.

---

[11]Recall that, in practice, the transduction doesn't apply on the text directly but to the sequence of words and symbols representing the result of the morphological analysis.

- A marker $OP_{N_0 \to NS}$ is inserted to link the subject of the sentence with the subject of the *ing* clause, that is the subject of *solving*.

This should be interpreted in the context of transformation grammars in which the sentence is analyzed as the operator *John takes credible steps toward* applying to the sentence *John solves the problem*. The subject of the second sentence is deleted within this operation.

The second step of the analysis consists of analyzing *John* as a nominal and $N\ V_{(ing)}$ *solving the problem* as a sentence. The sentence structure N *solve* N should therefore be compiled into a transduction that takes into account both the possibility for the sentence to appear by itself, e.g. *John solves the problem*, or, as in our example, to appear as an *ing* clause. In order to handle both situations, the grammar should perform the following two mappings:

$$[S\ a\ solve\ b\ S] \quad\quad \to \quad (S\ [N\ a\ N] <\text{V}\ solve\ \text{V}> [N\ b\ N]\ S)$$
$$[S\ N\ V_{(ing)}\ solving\ b\ S] \quad \to \quad (S\ N\ V_{(ing)} <\text{V}\ solving\ \text{V}> [N\ b\ N]\ S)$$

The application of the grammar to the sequence of (37), i.e. the second step of the analysis of (36), leads to the following sequence:

(38) $(S\ (N\ John\ N) <V_{sup}\ takes\ V_{sup}> <N_{pred}\ credible\ steps\ N_{pred}>$
       $toward\ OP_{N_0 \to NS}\ (S\ N\ V_{(ing)} <\text{V}\ solving\ \text{V}> [N\ the\ problem$
       $N]\ S)\ S)$

and finall   he analysis

(39) $(S\ (N\ John\ N) <V_{sup}\ takes\ V_{sup}> <N_{pred}\ credible\ steps\ N_{pred}>$
       $toward\ OP_{N_0 \to NS}\ (S\ N\ V_{(ing)} <\text{V}\ solving\ \text{V}> (N\ the\ problem$
       $N)\ S)\ S)$

8.5.5 Support verb recovery in noun clauses

Let us now consider:

(40) $[S\ John's\ concessions\ to\ his\ friend\ were\ unexpected\ S]$

The difficulty is to analyze correctly the nominal *John's concessions to his friend*. Recall that the grammar should not contain a rule that says that the structure $N'sNtoN$ can always form a nominal, this would generate many incorrect analyses. In fact, this type of nominal is made possible here by the underlying support verb construction

(41) *John makes concessions to his friend*

and the analysis should therefore reduce the problem of analyzing the nominal to the analysis of this sentence. The first application of the transducer representing the grammar will transform the original sentence (40) into the following one:

(42) $(S$ $[N$ *John's concessions to his friend* $N]$ $<V$ *were* $V>$ $[$ADJ *unexpected* ADJ] $S)$

Linguistically, a sentence, such as (41), of the shape[12]

(43) N V_{sup} N_{pred} W

can often be transformed into a nominal with the following shape:

(44) N's N_{pred} W

in which the support verb disappears. To cover this phenomenon, the following mapping, corresponding to the nominal structure (44) should be added to the grammar

$$[N \ a \text{'s } concessions \ to \ b \ N]$$
$$\downarrow$$
$$(N \ [S \ a \ V_{sup} \ ? \ concessions \ to \ b \ S] \ N)$$

The transduction representing the structure

(45) N *make concessions to* N

should also perform the two mappings

$$[S \ a \ make \ concessions \ to \ b \ S]$$
$$\downarrow$$
$$[N \ a \ N] < V_{sup} \ make \ V_{sup} > < N_{pred} \ concessions \ N_{pred} >$$
$$to \ [N \ b \ N] \ S)$$

$$[S \ a \ V_{sup} \ make \ concessions \ to \ b \ S]$$
$$\downarrow$$
$$(S \ [N \ a \ N] \ V_{sup} < V_{sup} \ make \ V_{sup} > < N_{pred} \ concessions \ N_{pred} >$$
$$to \ [N \ b \ N] \ S)$$

The first one handles sentences such as (41) and the second one validates the support verb construction hypothesis.

With these mappings, the analysis of (40) is performed as indicated on Figure 8.14. Here again, the underlying support verb sentence is explicitly recovered during parsing and can be extracted from the resulting analysis.

---

[12] W represents any number of arguments; the type and number of arguments depend on the predicative noun N_{pred}.

$$[S \; John's \; concessions \; to \; his \; friend \; were \; unexpected \; S]$$
$$\downarrow$$
$$(S \; [N \; John's \; concessions \; to \; his \; friend \; N] \; <V \; were \; V> \; [ADJ \; unexpected \; ADJ]S)$$
$$\downarrow$$
$$(S \; (N \; [S \; John \; V_{sup} \; ? \; concessions \; to \; his \; friend \; S] \; N) \; <V \; were \; V>$$
$$(ADJ \; unexpected \; ADJ) \; S)$$
$$\downarrow$$
$$(S \; (N \; (S \; [N \; John \; N] \; V_{sup} \; <V_{sup} \; make \; V_{sup}> \; <N_{pred} \; concessions \; N_{pred}>$$
$$to \; [N \; his \; friend \; N] \; S) \; N) \; <V \; were \; V> \; (ADJ \; unexpected \; ADJ) \; S)$$
$$\downarrow$$
$$(S \; (N \; (S \; (NN \; John \; N) \; V_{sup} \; <V_{sup} \; make \; V_{sup}> \; <N_{pred} \; concessions \; N_{pred}>$$
$$to \; (N \; his \; friend \; N) \; S) \; N) \; <V \; were \; V> \; (ADJ \; unexpected \; ADJ) \; S)$$

Figure 8.14: Analysis of the sentence *John's concessions to his friend were unexpected*

8.5.6 Hidden support verb constructions

We now show how FSTs are applied to more complex dependencies within the sentence arguments (the type of linguistic constraints presented below have been extensively studied in Mohri (1993)). Let us now consider the following sentences:

(46) *John asked Peter for an immediate decision*
(47) *John asked Peter for his belongings*
(48) *John asked Peter for a ride*

which share the common surface sentence structure:

(49) N_0 *ask* N_1 *for* N_2

However, describing such sentences only with the surface structure is not sufficient. In fact, such description would not explain why the following sentence

(50) * *They asked Peter for their immediate decision*

is not accepted, contrary to

(51) *They asked Peter for his immediate decision*
(52) *They asked Peter for his belongings*
(53) *They asked Peter for their belongings*

The linguistic explanation is that sentences (46) and (51) are analyzed as transformations of

(54)   *They asked Peter to make (a/his) decision immediately*

whereas (52) and (53) are analyzed as transformations of

(55)   *They asked Peter to give them (his/their) belongings*

Mohri (1993) shows that, in French, complex verbs such as *to ask*, should be described in conjunction with a list of support verbs. The support verbs such as *take* and *give* are then deleted by the constraints they impose remain. The situation is almost identical in English. Here for instance, the infinitive of (54) contains the sentence

(56)   *Peter makes a decision immediately*

or equivalently[13],

(57)   *Peter makes an immediate decision*

The verb *makes* disappears within the transformation. However it is still necessary to know which construction is really used. In fact, the support verb construction allows sentences

(58)   *Peter makes his decision*

in which the word *his* has to refer to the subject of the construction. This explains why (50) is incorrect.

In order to take these properties into account the parsing of (46) works as indicated in the following trace:

$$[S\ \textit{John asks Peter for an immediate decision}\ S]$$
$$\downarrow$$
$$(S\ [N\ \textit{John}\ N]\ <\text{V asks V}>\ [N\ \textit{Peter}\ N]\ \textit{for}\ [S\ N\ <V_{sup}\ (\textit{make/give})\ V_{sup}>$$
$$\textit{an immediate decision}\ S]\ S)$$
$$\downarrow$$
$$S\ (N\ \textit{John}\ N)\ <\text{V asks V}>\ (N\ \textit{Peter}\ N)\ \textit{for}\ (S\ N\ <V_{sup}\ \textit{make}\ V_{sup}>$$
$$<N_{pred}\ \textit{an immediate decision}\ N_{pred}>\ S)\ S)$$

Here again, it is possible, within the parsing program, to introduce hypotheses about several support verb constructions. Some of these hypotheses are invalidated at a later stage of the analysis and the correct support verb is recovered.

---

[13]This transformation, first described by Z.S. Harris (Harris, 1976), is very common an is even on the criterion to identify a support verb construction (see also (Giry-Schneider, 1978; Meunier, 1981)).

8.5.7 Frozen expressions

A recurrent problem when recognizing support verb constructions or frozen expressions is that these sentences also have the surface form of a free expression. For instance, the sentence

(59) $[S \text{ } John \text{ } take \text{ } (a/his) \text{ } seat \text{ } S]$

is going to be parsed in two different ways. First, it will be parsed as a free sentence (by resemblance to $[S \text{ } John \text{ } take \text{ } a \text{ } seat \text{ } S]$) and the resulting analysis will be

(60) $(S \text{ } (N \text{ } John \text{ } N) <V \text{ } take \text{ } V> (N \text{ } a \text{ } seat \text{ } N)$

It will also be parsed as a support verb construction and, in that case, the analysis will be

(61) $(S \text{ } (N \text{ } John \text{ } N) <V_{sup} \text{ } take \text{ } V_{sup}> <N_{pred} \text{ } a \text{ } seat \text{ } N_{pred}>$

Whereas both analysis are possible in principle, the frozen interpretation is usually the correct one. For the analysis to contain the frozen interpretation only, the parser not only has to produce the correct analysis, but it has to delete the incorrect one. In other words the transducer representing the structure N *take a seat* should perform the following two mappings:

$$[S \text{ } a \text{ } take \text{ } a \text{ } seat \text{ } S] \rightarrow$$
$$(S \text{ } [N \text{ } a \text{ } N] <V_{sup} \text{ } take \text{ } V_{sup}> <N_{pred} \text{ } a \text{ } seat \text{ } N_{pred}> S)$$

$$(S \text{ } (N \text{ } a \text{ } N) \text{ } (V \text{ } take \text{ } V) \text{ } (N \text{ } a \text{ } seat \text{ } N) \text{ } S) \quad \rightarrow \quad \emptyset$$

The first mapping handles the analysis per se whereas the second one deletes the improper analysis resulting from the free structure.

The parsing trace of the sentence is then the following:

$$[S \text{ } John \text{ } takes \text{ } a \text{ } seat \text{ } S]$$
$$\downarrow$$
$$(S \text{ } [N \text{ } John \text{ } N] <V \text{ } takes \text{ } V> [N \text{ } a \text{ } seat \text{ } N] \text{ } S)$$
$$(S \text{ } [N \text{ } John \text{ } N] <V_{sup} \text{ } takes \text{ } V_{sup}> <N_{pred} \text{ } a \text{ } seat \text{ } N_{pred}> S)$$
$$\downarrow$$
$$(S \text{ } (N \text{ } John \text{ } N) <V \text{ } takes \text{ } V> (N \text{ } a \text{ } seat \text{ } N) \text{ } S)$$
$$(S \text{ } (N \text{ } John \text{ } N) <V_{sup} \text{ } takes \text{ } V_{sup}> <N_{pred} \text{ } a \text{ } seat \text{ } N_{pred}> S)$$
$$\downarrow$$
$$(S \text{ } (N \text{ } John \text{ } N) <V_{sup} \text{ } takes \text{ } V_{sup}> <N_{pred} \text{ } a \text{ } seat \text{ } N_{pred}> S)$$

In the gradation from free to frozen for the verb *take*, we should also consider sentences such as *The elected candidate takes his seat in the House*. This sentence should be interpreted neither as a free construction with an object complement *his seat* and an adverbial *in the House*, nor as the support verb construction *to take (a/his) seat* with the adverbial *in the House* but rather as the frozen expression *N take POSS seat in the House* in which only the subject may vary. For the parser to achieve this analysis, it should perform three mappings:

$$[S \; a \; take \; his \; seat \; in \; the \; House \; S]$$
$$\downarrow$$
$$(S \; [N \; a \; N] \; <\text{F } take \; his \; seat \; in \; the \; House \; \text{F}> \; S)$$

$$(S \; (N \; a \; N) \; (V \; take \; V) \; (N \; a \; seat \; N) \; (\text{ADV in the House ADV}) \; S)$$
$$\downarrow$$
$$\emptyset$$

$$(S \; (N \; a \; N) \; <V_{sup} \; take \; V_{sup}> \; <N_{pred} \; a \; seat \; N_{pred}>$$
$$(\text{ADV in the House ADV}) \; S)$$
$$\downarrow$$
$$\emptyset$$

The first mapping performs the analysis per se, the second one deletes the free sentence analysis while the third one deletes the support verb construction analysis.

8.6   Finite-State Acceleration

In section 8.5, a sentence with a modal verb such as

(62)   *John should read this book*

was analyzed with two different steps for *should* and *read*. It is also possible to think about *should read* as one single compound verb. This is not linguistically motivated but it might improve parsing efficiency. Such a composite verb could take two arguments: a noun phrase as subject and a noun phrase as direct object. From this point of view, the first of the analysis would be a mapping from

(63)   [S *John should read this book* S]

to

(64)   [S [N *John* N] <V *should read* V> [N *this book* N] S]

The advantage of such an approach obviously is that it shortens the number of analysis phases by one, at the cost of more space requirement for T_{dic}.

Also, longer sequences, such as *should read* here, are recognized through a simple finite-state mechanism. This follows the intuition that some sequences within natural language, such as auxiliary verb sequences, are very well modeled by a simple finite-state automaton. For instance, the set of auxiliary verb sequences could be modeled by the finite-state automaton of Figure 8.15. In this automaton, sequences of auxiliary verbs and verbs are represented with a slightly new convention. Sequences are elements of $(\Sigma_w \cdot \Sigma_{pps})^*$ in which Σ_w is the set of words in the language and Σ_{pps} is a finite set of part-of-speech tags. The tags used here are derived from those used in the Brown Corpus (Francis and Kučera, 1982). *vb* stands for *infinitive form of the verb*, *vbd* stands for the past tense, *vbg* stands for the progressive form, *vbn* stands for the passive form and *vbz* stands for the third person singular of the verb. The symbol *???* matches any other symbol. For instance the sequence

$$??? \cdot vbz$$

stands for a verb conjugated at the third person singular.

From a computational efficiency point of view, it is important to recognize these sequences through a pure finite-state mechanism rather than through more complex parsing procedures. In this section we will see that, by combining some of finite-state transducers derived from the syntactic dictionary, it is possible to obtain a pure finite-state recognition process for these specific sequences while keeping the generality of the grammar. This addresses the following remark: many sequences within natural language sentences seems to be finite-state, however, a pure finite-state modeling cannot model the whole syntax and more powerful, yet less efficient, formalisms, such as context-free grammars, are required.

We now suppose that we have each finite-state transducer associated to each structure of the syntactic dictionary. In particular, we have $T_{N\_read\_N}$ that performs the following matching (among others):

$$[S\ [S\ a\ N]\ <OP\ c\ OP>\ v\ read\ b\ S]$$
$$\downarrow$$
$$(S\ [N\ a\ N]\ <OP\ c\ OP>\ <V\ v\ read\ V>\ [N\ b\ N]\ S)$$

and $T_{N\_should\_V\_W}$ that performs the following matching:

$$[S\ a\ should\ v\ read\ b\ S]$$
$$\downarrow$$
$$[S\ [N\ a\ N]\ <OP\ should\ OP>\ v\ b\ S]$$

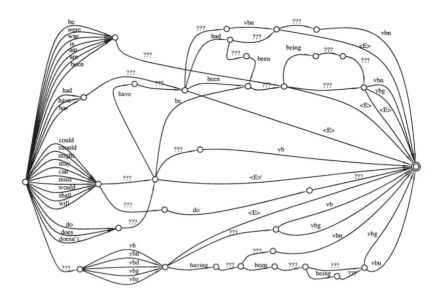

Figure 8.15: Finite-state automaton representing auxiliary verb sequences

and we saw in section 8.5 how these two mappings are combined together to analyze (63). Let us now compose $T_{N\_should\_V\_W}$ and $T_{N\_read\_N}$ into one transducer that we denote $T_{M\_should\_read\_N}$. This transducer performs the following mapping:

$$[\text{S } a \text{ should v } read \text{ } b \text{ S}]$$
$$\downarrow$$
$$(\text{S } [\text{N } a \text{ N}] <\text{OP } should \text{ OP}> <\text{V v } read \text{ V}> [\text{N } b \text{ N}] \text{ S})$$

This maps the input sentence (63) to the following sequence:

(65)   (S [N *John* N] <OP *should* OP> <V v *read* V> [N *this book* N] S)

on which the analysis is continued as in section 8.5.

Formally, if $T_{dic_1} = T_{N\_should\_V\_W} \cup T_2{}^{14}$ then we can build a new finite-state transducer $T_{dic_2} = T_2 \cup (T_{N\_should\_V\_W} \circ T_2)$ for which the analysis of (63) goes as follows:

---

[14]T_2 represents the union of the finite-state transducers associated to each structure.

[S *a should* v *read b* S]
$$\downarrow (T_{dic_2})$$
(S [N *John* N] <OP *should* OP> <V v *read* V> [N *this book* N] S)
$$\downarrow (T_{dic_2})$$
(S (N *John* N) <OP *should* OP> <V v *read* V> (N *this book* N) S)

By using T_{dic_2} instead of T_{dic}, we achieve our goal of recognizing the sequence *should read* through a pure finite-state process while obtaining the exact same analysis: *should* is still analyzed as an modal operator on the whole sentence and *read* is also still analyzed as the main verb. Formally, T_{dic_2} has the property that:

$$T_{Dic_2}^{\infty} = T_{dic}^{\infty}$$

which guarantees that the language recognized and the analysis are identical for T_{dic} and T_{dic_2}. The cost of such speed improvement however, is that T_{dic_2} will take more space than T_{dic}.

8.7 A Transducer Parser for Tree-Adjoining Grammars

In this section we will see on a formal example that the finite-state transducer framework is not restricted to context-free grammars and that it can in fact be used to parse tree-adjoining grammars (TAGs). Since the original motivation to introduce Tree-Adjoining Grammars was to better reflect linguistic analysis, this further illustrates the relevance of finite-state transducers to natural language parsing.

Tree-adjoining grammars (Joshi, Levy, and Takahashi, 1975; Joshi, 1985) is a formalism in which elementary trees are combined through an operation of adjunction. This formalism allows many linguistic properties to be encoded in a natural way (Kroch and Joshi, 1985). We will not develop here linguistic examples but rather illustrate the transducer approach on a formal language typical of tree adjoining grammars.

Let us consider the following tree adjoining grammar:

$$G_1 = (\{a, b, c, d, e\}, \{S\}, \{\alpha_1\}, \{\alpha_2\}, S)$$

in which $\{a, b, c, d, e\}$ is the alphabet of terminal symbols, $\{S\}$ is the alphabet of non terminal symbols, $\{\alpha_1\}$ is the set of initial trees (α_1 is represented on Figure 8.16, left), $\{\alpha_2\}$ is the set of auxiliary trees (α_2 is represented on Figure 8.16, right) and S is the root. This grammar generates the language

$$L_1 = \{a^n b^n e c^n d^n | n \geq 1\}$$

(Schabes, 1991). This language is not context-free, that is, there exists no context-free grammar G such that $L(G) = L_1$. L_1 is generated through a mechanism we now describe informally.

The main composition operation of TAGs is called *adjoining* or *adjunction*; it builds a new tree from an auxiliary tree, α_2 here, and any other tree. For instance, because α_1 contains a node labeled S and the root node of α_2 is also labeled S, it is possible to make the adjunction of α_2 on α_1. The resulting tree, β_1 of Figure 8.17, obtained by adjoining α_2 to α_1 at the root node root$_{\alpha_1}$ of α_1 is built as follows:

- the sub-tree of α_1 dominated by root$_{\alpha_1}$, called t, is excised, leaving a copy of root$_{\alpha_1}$,

- the auxiliary tree α_2 is attached at the copy of root$_{\alpha_1}$ and its root node is identified with the copy of root$_{\alpha_1}$,

- the sub-tree t is attached to the foot node of α_2 and the root node of t, i.e. root$_{\alpha_1}$, is identified with the foot node of α_2

In addition, when the special symbol NA is used to label a node, no adjunction is allowed on this node. For instance, for β_1, the adjunction can take place only at the medium node S and therefore β_2 is the only tree that can be derived from β_1 through a single adjunction. The language defined by a set of trees is built by taking the sequences generated by the leaves of each tree. For instance α_1, β_1 and β_2 respectively generate the strings e, *abecd* and *aabbeccdd*.

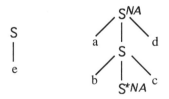

Figure 8.16: *left:* α_1, *right:* α_2

We can consider, as we did for context-free grammars in Section 8.3, that the grammar, is a syntactic dictionary. Each entry in this dictionary is a tree of the grammar and each of these trees will be converted into a transducer. As

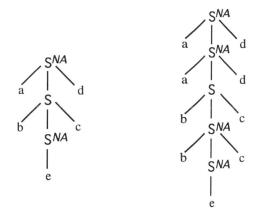

Figure 8.17: *left:* β_1, *right:* β_2

for context-free grammars, the core of transducer parsing for tree adjoining grammars consists of building a dictionary of finite-state transducers. The transducer representing the union of each individual transducer will then be used to parse input sentences.

Formally, we can define two general mappings[15] TAG-FST$_{ini}$ and TAG-FST$_{aux}$. TAG-FST$_{ini}$ will take any initial tree as input and will build a finite-state transducer associated to this tree; if γ is an initial tree, TAG-FST$_{ini}(\gamma)$ will denote the transducer associated to γ. Similarly, TAG-FST$_{aux}$ will convert any auxiliary tree into a finite-state transducer; if ω is an auxiliary tree, we denote by TAG-FST$_{aux}(\omega)$ the finite-state transducer associated to ω. A tree adjoining grammar being given, the transducer representing the whole grammar will be built by taking each initial tree and each auxiliary tree and by converting each one into a finite-state transducer. The final transducer is then the union of all individual transducers derived that way. In other words, the transducer T_G associated to a grammar G is equal to:

$$\bigcup_{\text{tree}_i \in ini(G)} \text{TAG-FST}_{ini}(\text{tree}_i) \cup \bigcup_{\text{tree}_i \in aux(G)} \text{TAG-FST}_{aux}(\text{tree}_i)$$

in which $ini(G)$ and $aux(G)$ respectively denote the set of initial and auxiliary tree of G. At this point the parser of a tree adjoining grammar G can be defined by

$$\text{parser} = T_G^\infty$$

---

[15] Not detailed here.

meaning, as for context-free grammars, that the syntactic analysis of a sequence w of the language $L(G)$ generated by G is the fixed-point of $(T_G^n(w))_{n\geq 0}$. Therefore, in practice, the parsing process consists of applying the transducer T_G to the input sequence, then to the result of the first application and to continue until the automaton representing the set of sequences stays unmodified.

To illustrate this, consider again the grammar G_1. In this grammar, only two transducers have to be built: (1) the transducer $T_{\alpha_1} = \text{TAG-FST}_{ini}(\alpha_1)$ representing the initial tree α_1 and (2) the transducer $T_{\alpha_2} = \text{TAG-FST}_{aux}(\alpha_2)$ representing the auxiliary tree α_2.

Figure 8.18 illustrates the parsing of the input string *aabbeccdd*. As for context-free grammars, the input of the transducer parsing will be the string to be parsed enclosed into the markers $[S$ and $S]$. Here, this will be the sequence $[S$ *aabbeccdd* $S]$ and it will be represented by a finite-state automaton (represented at the top of Figure 8.18) for more efficiency.

The transducer T_{α_1} representing the tree α_1 is defined functionally as follows:

$$T_{\alpha_1}:$$
$$w_1 \; [S \; w_2 \; e \; w_3 \; S] \; w_4$$
$$\downarrow$$
$$(1) \; w_1 \; [[S \; w_2 \; \{S \; e \; S\} \; w_3 \; S]] \; w_4 \text{ if } w_2 \neq \epsilon \text{ and } w_3 \neq \epsilon$$
$$(2) \; w_1 \; (S \; e \; S) \; w_4 \text{ if } w_2 = w_3 = \epsilon.$$
$$(3) \; \emptyset \text{ otherwise}$$

in which w_1, w_2, w_3 and w_4 are elements of Σ^* in which $\Sigma = \{a, b, c, d, e\}$ is a finite alphabet. This transducer takes sequences in which the markers $[S$ and $S]$ are used, it has three different types of output depending on the shape of the input string: (1) if the string enclosed between the markers $[S$ and $S]$ is of the shape w_2ew_3 in which both w_2 and w_3 are not the empty string then the markers $[S$ and $S]$ are transformed into $[[S$ and $S]]$ while two markers $\{S$ and $S\}$ are inserted around e. This transformation indicates that the string should be regarded as the tree α_1 on which some adjunction has been made. The markers $[[S, S]]$, $\{S$ and $S\}$ indicate the position of the possible adjunction within the input string. (2) If the string is such that the sequence enclosed within $[S$ and $S]$ is the simple character e then the $[S$ and $S]$ are respectively transformed into $(S$ and $S)$ to indicate that the input sequence was recognized as the sequence of leaves of α_1, i.e. the symbol e. (3) If the input string is not of the previous two shapes then the input sequence cannot be parsed with the tree α_1.

The transducer T_{α_2} representing the tree α_2 is defined functionally as follows:

$$w_1 \; [[S \; a \; w_2 \; b \; \{S \; w_3 \; S\} \; w_4 \; d \; S]] \; w_5 \longrightarrow$$

(1) w_1 (S a [[S w_2 {S b (S w_3 S) c S} w_4 S]] d S) w_5
if $w_1, w_5, w_3 \in (\Sigma \cup \{(S, S)\})^*$ and
$w_2, w_4 \in \Sigma^+$

(2) w_1 (S a (S b (S w_3 S) c S) d S) w_5
if $w_1, w_5, w_3 \in (\Sigma \cup \{(S, S)\})^*$ and $w_2 = w_4 = \epsilon$

(3) $\emptyset$ otherwise

in which w_1 to w_5 are strings of Σ^*. The input string of such a transduction contains the markers $[[S, S]]$, $\{S$ and $S\}$, meaning that the sequence has been parsed with an adjunction. A sequence of the shape

$$w_1 \; [[S \; a \; w_2 \; b \; \{S \; w_3 \; S\} \; w_4 \; d \; S]] \; w_5$$

indicates that w_1, w_3 and w_5 have been recognized and that the part appearing between $[[S$ and $\{S$, on one hand, and between $S\}$ and $S]]$, on the other hand, should be analyzed as the adjunction of one or several auxiliary trees. The transduction can generate three different types of output depending on the shape of the input. (1) If w_2 and w_4 are not the empty string then the tree α_2 has been adjoined and at least one other adjunction has also taken place, therefore, the transducer converts the symbols $[[S, S]]$, $\{S$ and $S\}$ to indicate that an adjunction of α_2 has been recognized. At the same time, new symbols $[[S, S]]$, $\{S$ and $S\}$ are introduced to indicate the possibility for another adjunction. (2) If the sequence of symbols to be analyzed with an adjunction has exactly the shape $a \cdot b \cdot c \cdot d$ then the markers $[[S, S]]$, $\{S$ and $S\}$ are replaced by the markers $(S$ and $S)$ to indicate that an adjunction of α_2 has been recognized and that the analysis is completed. (3) the transducer outputs the empty set in all other circumstances.

The process is best illustrated by the analysis of a simple example. The transducer associated to G_1 is defined by:

$$T_{G_1} = T_{\alpha_1} \cup T_{\alpha_2}$$

T_{G_1} is represented on Figure 8.19. In addition to the convention used previously, a transition labeled by A/A stands for a set of transitions labeled respectively by a/a, b/b, c/c, d/d and e/e. Recall also that if a state q has an outgoing transition labeled $?/?$, this transition stands for all the pairs s/s such that there is no other outgoing transition from q whose input label is s.

Let us now come back to the analysis of the sequence *aabbeccdd* illustrated on Figure 8.18. The first input of T_{G_1} is the singleton

$$\{[S \; aabbeccdd \; S]\}$$

represented by the top finite-state automaton of Figure 8.18. The markers [S and S] indicate that the enclosed sequence has to be analyzed as a sentence. The first application of T_{G_1} to this input automaton leads to the second automaton from the top, this automaton represents the singleton

$$\{[[Saabb\{SeS\}ccdd \; S]]\}$$

The only part of T_{G_1} which leads to a non empty output comes from T_{α_1}. The resulting automaton is pruned before applying the transducer T_{G_1} a second time. The second application of T_{G_1} leads to the third automaton from the top, this automaton represents the singleton

$$\{(Sa[[Sab\{Sb(SeS)cS\}cdS]]dS)\}$$

The part of T_{G_1} which leads to a non empty string corresponds this time to T_{α_2}. This automaton is pruned and the transducer is applied again which leads to the bottom automaton which represents the singleton

$$\{(Sa(Sa(Sb(Sb(SeS)cS)cS)dS)dS)\}$$

Here again, the active part of T_{G_1} corresponds to T_{α_2}. Finally, this last automaton is pruned. Since, another application of T_{G_1} does not modify the input, this last automaton is a fixed-point of T_{G_1} and therefore the result of the analysis of [S *aabbeccdd* S]. Note that this last automaton represents the tree β_1 of Figure 8.17.

This short example is only an illustration of the flexibility of transducer parsing and the proof of the correctness of the previous example is left to the reader[16]. The practical efficiency of transducer parsing for tree adjoining grammar can only be evaluated by comparing this parsing method with others (in particular with the algorithms described in Schabes (1991)) on realistic data (both input strings and grammars). Such experiments should be done on very large lexical grammars.

---

[16]We also leave to the reader the interesting exercise of proving that any tree adjoining grammar G is equivalent to a transducer T_G that analyzes the same language, i.e. such that $L(G) = \{w | T^\infty(w) \neq \emptyset\}$.

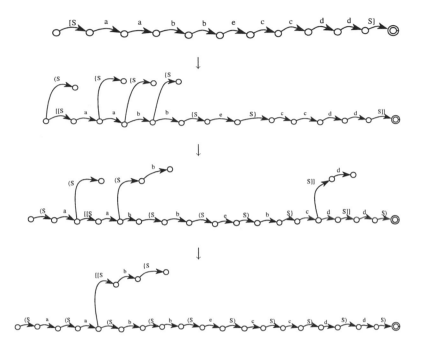

Figure 8.18: Example of Analysis.

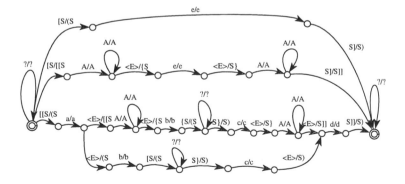

Figure 8.19: T_{G_1}

8.8   Conclusion

We saw that finite-state transducers can be used to parse context-free grammars and that they are especially relevant for large lexicalized grammars. However, parsing with finite-state transducers does not have to follow the context-free framework. In fact, finite-state transducers can describe and handle more complex linguistic situations in a efficient and accurate manner. In addition, the homogeneity of the analysis, reducing every complex sentence analysis to the analysis of simpler sentences, thus following the transformational grammar theory, also provides clarity and some strong linguistic motivation; This is essential for any large grammars designed to handle real word sentences.

References

Boons, Jean-Paul, Alain Guillet and Christian Leclere. 1976. *La structure des phrases simples en français, Constructions Intransitives.* Librairie Droz, Geneve-Paris.

Clemenceau, David and Emmanuel Roche. 1993. Enhancing a large scale dictionary with a two-level system. In *EACL-93, proceedings of the conference.*

Courtois, Blandine. 1989. Delas: Dictionnaire electronique du ladl pour les mots simples du français. Technical report, Université Paris 7.

Francis, W. Nelson and Henry Kučera. 1982. *Frequency Analysis of English Usage.* Houghton Mifflin, Boston.

Giry-Schneider, Jacqueline. 1978. *Les preédicats nominaux en français, les phrases simples à verb support.* Droz, Genève, Paris.

Gross, Maurice. 1968. *Grammaire transformationnelle du Français,1. Syntaxe du verbe.* Cantilène.

Gross, Maurice. 1975. *Méthodes en syntaxe,régime des constructions complétives.* Hermann.

Gross, Maurice. 1986. *Grammaire transformationnelle du Français,3. Syntaxe de l'adverbe.* Cantilène.

Gross, Maurice. 1988. Les limites de la phrase figée. *Langages*, (90):7–22, June.

Gross, Maurice. 1996. The construction of local grammars. In *this volume.*

Harris, Zellig. 1976. *Notes du cours de syntaxe.* Seuil, Paris.

Harris, Zellig. 1991. *Theory of Language and Information.* Oxford University Press.

Joshi, Aravind K., L. S. Levy, and M. Takahashi. 1975. Tree adjuct grammars. *Journal of Computer and System Sciences*, 10(1).

Joshi, Aravind K. 1985. How much context-sensitivity is necessary for characterizing structural descriptions - tree adjoining grammars. In D. Dowty, L. Karttunen, and A. Zwicky, editors, *Natural Language Processing - Theortical, Computational and Psychological Perspectives.* Cambridge University Press.

Karttunen, Lauri, Ronald M. Kaplan, and Annie Zaenen. 1992. Two-level morphology with composition. In *Proceedings of the 14th International Conference on Computational Linguistics (COLING'92).*

Kroch, Anthony and Aravind K. Joshi. 1985. Linguistic relevance of tree adjoining grammars. Technical Report MS-CIS-85-18, Department of Computer and Information Science, University of Pennsylvania, April.

Laporte, Eric. 1993. Phonétique et transducteurs. Technical report, Université Paris 7.

Laporte, Eric. 1996. Rational transductions for phonetic conversion and phonology. In *this volume.*

Meunier, Annie. 1981. *Nominalisations d'adjectifs par verbs supports.* Ph.D. thesis, Université Paris 7.

Mohri, Mehryar. 1993. *Analyse et Représentation par Automates de Structures Syntaxiques Composees.* Ph.D. thesis, Université Paris 7, January.

Pereira, Fernando and Rebecca N. Wright. 1996. Finite state approximation of phrase structure grammars. In *this volume.*

Pereira, Fernando C. N., Michael Riley, and Richard W. Sproat. 1994. Weighted rational transductions and their application to human language processing. In *ARPA Workshop on Human Language Technology.* Morgan Kaufmann.

Roche, Emmanuel. 1993. *Analyse Syntaxique Transformationnelle du Français par Transducteurs et Lexique-Grammaire.* Ph.D. thesis, Université Paris 7, January.

Roche, Emmanuel. 1995. Smaller representations for finite-state transducers. In *Lecture Notes in Computer Science, Combinatorial Pattern Matching, Fifth Annual Symposium, Helsinki, Finland, Proceedings.*

Schabes, Yves. 1991. *Mathematical and Computational Aspects of Lexicalized Grammars, Processing with Lexicalized Tree-Adjoining Grammars.* Ph.D. thesis, University of Pennsylvania.

Silberztein, Max. 1993. *Dictionnaires Electroniques et Analyse Lexicale du Français— Le Système INTEX.* Masson.

Silberztein, Max. 1997. The lexical analysis of natural languages. In *this volume.*

S	N *thinks that* S	[S *a* thinks that *b* S] →
		(S [N *a* N] <V *thinks* V> *that* [S *b* S] S)

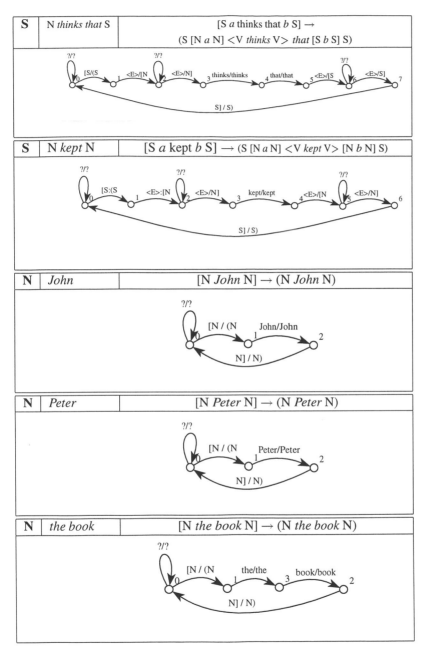

S	N *kept* N	[S *a* kept *b* S] → (S [N *a* N] <V *kept* V> [N *b* N] S)

N	*John*	[N *John* N] → (N *John* N)

N	*Peter*	[N *Peter* N] → (N *Peter* N)

N	*the book*	[N *the book* N] → (N *the book* N)

Table 8.2: Transducers associated to each structure

9 Designing a (Finite-State) Parsing Grammar

Atro Voutilainen

This paper discusses the design of a parsing grammar from a linguistic point of view. Attention is paid (i) to the specification of the *grammatical representation* that can be viewed as the linguistic task definition of the parser, and (ii) the design of the *parsing grammar* and the *heuristic data-driven component*. Illustrations are given from an emerging English grammar.

9.1 Introduction

The purpose of this paper is to examine, from a bird's-eye perspective, the design of the knowledge base of a parser intended for the syntactic analysis of running English text. The main observations are meant to be applicable to parsing grammar design in general, so the discussion may be of interest to a wider readership than those involved in finite-state parsing.

My perspective is linguistic rather than algorithmic. Certain descriptive desiderata are outlined and even formalised; how these formal representations should actually be implemented, e.g. as finite state parsers, is left to the computer scientist. Koskenniemi and Tapanainen (this volume) discuss algorithmic aspects related to this work.

The main topics are:

- design of a grammatical representation (the linguistic task definition of the parser), and

- design of the formal grammar and the data-driven heuristics.

As illustration, reference is made to ongoing work on an English finite-state grammar (Voutilainen and Tapanainen, 1993; Voutilainen, 1994; Voutilainen, 1995) which draws on the author's collaboration with Koskenniemi and Tapanainen (cf. also (Koskenniemi, 1990; Koskenniemi and Voutilainen, 1991;

Tapanainen, 1991; Koskenniemi, Tapanainen and Voutilainen, 1992)). This joint work is related to and partly derived from another brand of reductionistic surface-syntactic parsing called Constraint Grammar (Karlsson, 1990; Voutilainen, Heikkilä and Anttila, 1992; Karlsson *et al.* (eds.), 1995).

9.2   Framework

9.2.1   Representation of sentences

Linguistic structure can be represented with different notations, e.g. phrase structure bracketing and feature structures. We use word tags for indicating morphological and syntactic properties. To each word in the utterance, a base form and several tags are associated, e.g.

```
The      the      DET        @>N           <wb>
red      red      A ABS      @>N           <wb>
car      car      N NOM SG   @SUBJ         <wb>
is       be       V PRES     @MAINVERB     <wb>
in       in       PREP       @ADVL         <wb>
the      the      DET        @>N           <wb>
garden   garden   N NOM SG   @PREPCOMP     <wb>
.
```

Here *red* is analysed as an adjective in the absolutive (A ABS) that syntactically is a premodifier of a nominal (@>N). The noun *car* is a subject (@SUBJ); *is* is a present tense verb that syntactically is a main verb, and so on. The symbol <wb> represents word boundaries.

Our grammatical tags indicate dependency-oriented functions of words in an underspecific way. For instance, adverbials are left unattached; this often saves the parser from processing structurally unresolvable ambiguities.

One of the two inputs of the finite-state parser is the morphologically analysed, typically ambiguous, sentence that is represented as a *regular expression* (cf. Tapanainen's chapter in this volume; cf. also (Tapanainen, 1991)). Here is a simplified representation of the above sentence before parsing:

```
The      the      DET        @>N                              <wb>
red      red      [[A ABS    [@>N | @SUBJCOMP]] |
                  [V ING     @MAINVERB]]                       <wb>
car      car      N NOM SG   [@SUBJ | @OBJ | @PREPCOMP]        <wb>
is       be       V PRES     [@MAINVERB | @AUX]                <wb>
in       in       [[PREP     [@ADVL | @N<]] |
                  [ADV       @ADVL]]                           <wb>
the      the      DET        @>N                              <wb>
```

```
garden    garden    N NOM SG [@SUBJ  | @OBJ  | @PREPCOMP] <wb>
.
```

Here "[" and "]" indicate grouping and "|" indicates disjunction. Some of the words are given more than one alternative analyses, e.g. *garden* gets three syntactically different analyses. At the sentence level, this representation contains $1 * 3 * 3 * 2 * 3 * 1 * 3 = 162$ readings, such as:

```
The       the       DET          @>N          <wb>
red       red       V ING        @MAINVERB    <wb>
car       car       N NOM SG     @OBJ         <wb>
is        be        V PRES       @AUX         <wb>
in        in        PREP         @N<          <wb>
the       the       DET          @>N          <wb>
garden    garden    N NOM SG     @SUBJ        <wb>
.
```

This sentence reading is obviously an analysis that we do not wish to accept, e.g. the main verb reading of *red* directly follows the determiner *The*. The task of the reductionistic parser is to discard inappropriate readings like these. Indeed, no structure building is required from the parser because the correct syntactic analysis is already among the alternatives. In the analysis of the above sentence, a successful grammar will discard all sentence readings but the appropriate one:

```
The       the       DET          @>N          <wb>
red       red       A ABS        @>N          <wb>
car       car       N NOM SG     @SUBJ        <wb>
is        be        V PRES       @MAINVERB    <wb>
in        in        PREP         @ADVL        <wb>
the       the       DET          @>N          <wb>
garden    garden    N NOM SG     @PREPCOMP    <wb>
.
```

Before parsing proper starts, the regular expression that represents the sentence is transformed into a finite-state automaton.

9.2.2 Rule formalism

In our finite-state framework (Koskenniemi, 1983; Koskenniemi, 1990; Koskenniemi and Voutilainen, 1991; Tapanainen, 1991; Koskenniemi, Tapanainen and Voutilainen, 1992; Voutilainen and Tapanainen, 1993; Voutilainen, 1994; Voutilainen, 1995), parsing means first introducing grammatical descriptors as alternatives during lexical analysis, and then eliminating illegitimate sentence readings. The correct syntactic analysis is already in the lexically analysed ambiguous input, so no new descriptors are introduced by the parser.

Technically, parsing is the intersection of two kinds of finite-state automata: the sentence automaton and the grammar automata. The parse consists of those sentence readings that all of the grammar automata accept.

The grammarian does not directly operate with automata; rather, the sentence representation as well as the grammar rules are expressed as *extended regular expressions* (Tapanainen, 1991) that can be translated into finite-state automata.

The grammar can employ *constants*, *predicates* and so-called *implication rules*.

- A constant is a shorthand for a regular expression. For instance, it may be expedient to define a constant for nominals:

  ```
  Nominal = [N | ABBR | NUM | PRON] ;
  ```

  Thus *Nominal* accepts any of the alternatives – nouns, abbreviations, numerals and pronouns.

  Another useful constant is *dot*[1] "." that stands for a sequence of tokens (e.g. base forms and morphological tags) within a single word (Koskenniemi, Tapanainen and Voutilainen, 1992):

  ```
  . = \[@@ | @/ | @< | @>];
  ```

  The *backslash* "\" denotes any sequence of tokens not containing occurrences of its argument (which here contains all types of word and clause boundaries).

  Still another much-used constant is *dotdot* that represents a sequence of tokens within the same clause (that may contain centre-embedded clauses):

  ```
  @<> = @< [. | @ | @/]* @>;
  .. = [. | @ | @<>];
  ```

  The *asterisk* "*" denotes any number of its arguments (in this case: any number of word analyses or plain word boundaries or iterative clause boundaries).

---

[1] The definitions for *dot*, *dotdot* and "nowhere(X)" have been borrowed from the finite-state parser written by Tapanainen 1990–1993. The implication rule dates back to the two-level rule formalism (Koskenniemi, 1983).

- Predicates (or parameterised constants) can be used in or as rules, and the grammarian can define new ones, e.g. the "nowhere(X)" predicate:

```
nowhere(X) = \X ;
```

The "nowhere(X)" predicate can be used as a grammar rule, e.g.

```
nowhere(DET . <wb> . VFIN) ;
```

This rule forbids all determiner – finite verb sequences.[2]

- The implication rule is of the form

```
X =>
LC1 _ RC1,
LC2 _ RC2,
LCn _ RCn;
```

where *X*, *LC1*, *RC1*, *LC2* etc. are regular expressions. The rule reads: '*X is legitimate only if it occurs in context* LC1 _ RC1 *or in context* LC2 _ RC2 .. *or in context* LCn _ RCn'. At least one of the alternative context conditions has to be satisfied for sentence readings containing the *X* part; otherwise that sentence reading is rejected.[3]

Linguistically, the implication rule seems to be the most natural type of rule for expressing distributional generalisations. The distributional category is clearly identified, and its legitimate syntactic contexts can be represented at an intuitive level of abstraction using the context mechanism. Linguistically, the rule is a positive distributional description, yet the desired disambiguation effect comes out as a side effect in parsing (for a contrast, cf. the "nowhere(X)" predicate above).

Grammar rules are compiled into finite-state automata before parsing. No attempt is made to compile these grammar rules into one automaton because, with a non-trivial grammar, that intersection would be huge. Rather, in the spirit of Two-level Morphology (Koskenniemi, 1983), grammar rules are represented as several smaller automata.

---

[2] In spirit, this type of rule resembles a typical Constraint Grammar rule (Karlsson *et al.* (eds.), 1995): superficially, it specifies an illegitimate tag sequence rather than a legitimate one. Indeed, the present rule formalism does not 'force' the grammarian to express grammatical generalisations as positive distributional generalisations. The choice is left to the grammarian.

[3] Note however that the parser can optionally be 'forced' to yield an analysis for every input, including ill-formed ones; optimally this analysis is the 'least' ungrammatical of the alternatives.

9.3   Grammatical Representation

This section motivates and outlines a method for specifying a grammatical representation for parsing purposes. Finally, an illustration is given from English syntax.

9.3.1   Motivation

The central task of a parser is to assign grammatical descriptions onto input sentences. Designing a computational lexicon and grammar as well as evaluating and using a parser's output presupposes a predefined, parser-independent specification of the grammatical representation.

With "grammatical representation" we mean a set of grammatical descriptors (e.g. tags) and their application guidelines – (i) general principles and (ii) detailed instructions for constructions where the general principles do not seem unambiguously applicable. Our usage of 'grammatical representation' agrees with Sampson's definition of 'parsing scheme',

> ... a statement of just what range of structures and categories will be used ... and which among various analyses in terms of those structures and categories will be regarded as correct for any debatable construction ... (Sampson, 1987)

Is it always clear what *is* the 'correct analysis'? Language structure can be described in many different ways, and sometimes there is no consensus about a preferred analysis. Even part-of-speech assignment, let alone analysis at a higher level of description, is a theoretical matter, and, without an agreed-upon grammatical representation, the appropriate analysis of several constructions is all but obvious. For example, consider the part-of-speech analysis of *than* in *Alice lived longer than Jane*. Is *than* a preposition or a subordinating conjunction? Arguments for both analyses could be given:

1. "A preposition has a noun phrase as its complement; *Jane* is a noun phrase; therefore *than* is a preposition."

2. "A subordinating conjunction introduces a clause; *Jane* introduces a clause, an elliptical one where the predicate has been omitted; therefore *than* is a subordinating conjunction."

Neither analysis may seem immediately preferable. A practical way to deal with problems like this is to make an explicit commitment (i.e. specify a grammatical representation; cf. the above quotation).[4]

---

[4] Voutilainen and Järvinen (1995) report on double-blind experiments at the level of morpholog-

9.3.2 Method

A grammatical representation can be specified by creating a *grammar definition corpus*, a representative collection of utterances consistently analysed using a fixed set of grammatical descriptors.

A grammar definition corpus ideally accounts for all constructions in the object language. A carefully documented comprehensive grammar definition corpus should provide an unambiguous answer to the question how to analyse any utterance in the object language.

How to collect a representative inventory of sample sentences? Consulting a large descriptive grammar seems a natural starting point. In the present work, *A Comprehensive Grammar of the English Language* (Quirk et al., 1985) was used, and about 2,000 sentences representing various grammatical constructions were extracted, e.g:

```
;;p.764
These kind of parties are dangerous.
These sort of parties are dangerous.
These type of parties are dangerous.
;;p.765
A large number of people have applied for the job.
The majority are Moslems.
Lots of the stuff is going to waste.
;;p.766
Neither you, nor I, nor anyone else knows the answer.
Either my wife or I am going.
;;p.767
My child is an angel.
My children are angels.
I consider my child an angel.
I consider my children angels.
My only hope for the future is my children.
My only hope for the future are my children.
More nurses is the next item on the agenda.
More nurses are the next item on the agenda.
Their principal crop is potatoes.
Good manners are a rarity these days.
Good manners is a rarity these days.
The younger children are a problem.
```

Then these sentences were semi-automatically annotated (by the author), e.g.

---

ical and shallow syntactic annotation. Their main result is that specifying a shallow grammatical representation can be carried out consistently, i.e. interjudge agreement can be reached at least at the level of surface syntactic analysis.

```
;; number agreement (S/V)
                                                      @@
Good good <*> A ABS                    @>N            @
manners manner N NOM PL                @SUBJ          @
is be <SVC/N> <SVC/A> V PRES SG3       @MV MAINC@     @
a a <Indef> DET CENTRAL ART SG         @>N            @
rarity rarity N NOM SG                 @SC            @
these this DET CENTRAL DEM PL          @>N            @
days day N NOM PL                      @ADVL          @
@fullstop                                             @@
```

Also some documentation was produced, especially when the descriptive solutions differ from those in (Quirk et al., 1985).

At this stage we (hopefully) have a representative inventory of grammatical constructions in English, for each of which a (usually) unique analysis using the available descriptors has been determined. On the basis of (i) these annotated examples and (ii) written documentation (basically, tag application guidelines), new utterances (to be used for e.g. creating and evaluating parsing grammars) should be possible to analyse with a high degree of consistency.

Compiling a systematic inventory of sentences has the additional advantage that also possible compromises in the specification of the object language can be conveniently identified. A comprehensive descriptive grammar is likely to contain constructions accounting for which would negatively affect the accuracy of the parser. Some examples:

```
;; PP as subject??
?? In the evenings is best for me.
;; vocatives
?? Play on my side, Mary.
?? John, you listen to me!
```

For instance, the English grammar under development is likely to ignore formally very untypical subjects, such as subject prepositional phrases, in order to avoid constantly introducing structurally acceptable but extremely unlikely analyses (e.g. analysing *In that case* as a subject and *the meeting* as an apposition in the sentence *In that case the meeting may end*).

In addition to a systematic collection of "inventory" sentences, it is useful to include large samples of annotated running text from different genres for representing phenomena less adequately covered in conventional descriptive grammars (punctuation, sentence fragments, calendar expressions etc.). In the present work, a corpus of running text has been semiautomatically annotated by a research assistant (Ms. Pirkko Paljakka), at a speed of about 400 words per hour. The present annotated running text corpus (over 200,000 words) contains texts from newspapers, novels, manuals, scientific magazines and encyclopaedias.

9.3.3 A representation for English syntax

The grammatical representation[5] used in my current work is an extension of the representation used in the English Constraint Grammar system (Voutilainen, Heikkilä and Anttila, 1992; Karlsson *et al.* (eds.), 1995). Surface-syntactic grammatical relations are encoded with dependency-oriented functional tags. Functional representation of phrases and clauses has been introduced to facilitate expressing syntactic generalisations. The representation is introduced in (Voutilainen and Tapanainen, 1993; Voutilainen, 1994) and the tags are listed with examples in the appendix. Here, only the main characteristics are presented.

- Each word boundary is represented as one of five alternatives:

  - the sentence boundary "@ @"
  - the boundary separating juxtaposed finite clauses "@/"
  - centre-embedded (sequences of) finite clauses are flanked with "@<" (beginning) and "@>" (end of centre-embedding)
  - the plain word boundary "@"

- Each word is furnished with a tag indicating a surface-syntactic function (subject, premodifier, auxiliary, main verb, adverbial, etc.). Unlike other categories, all main verbs are furnished with *two* syntactic tags, one indicating its main verb status, the other indicating the function of the clause in question.

- An explicit difference is made between finite clauses (that contain a finite verb chain) and nonfinite clauses (that contain a nonfinite verb chain (Quirk et al., 1985, pp. 149–151)). Members in nonfinite clauses are coded with lower case tags. Syntactic tags in the upper case are reserved for members in finite clauses and for those categories for which no distinction with regard to finiteness is made (e.g. adverbials).

- In addition to syntactic tags, also morphological, e.g. part-of-speech tags are provided for each word. An illustration with a simplified example:

```
                                    @@
Mary        N       @SUBJ           @
```

---

[5]This subsection is taken almost as such from (Voutilainen, 1995).

```
told        V      @MV       MC@     @
the         DET    @>N               @
fat         A      @>N               @
butcher's   N      @>N               @
wife        N      @IOBJ             @
and         CC     @CC               @
daughters   N      @IOBJ             @/
that        CS     @CS               @
she         PRON   @SUBJ             @
remembers   V      @MV       OBJ@    @
seeing      V      @mv       OBJ@    @
a           DET    @>N               @
dream       N      @obj              @
last        DET    @>N               @
night       N      @ADVL             @
@fullstop                            @@
```

Here *Mary* is a subject in a finite clause (hence the upper case); *told* is a main verb in a main clause; *the*, *fat* and *butcher's* are premodifiers; *wife* and *daughters* are indirect objects; *that* is a subordinating conjunction; *remembers* is a main verb in a finite clause that serves the Object role in a finite clause; *seeing* is a main verb in a nonfinite clause (hence the lower case) that also serves the Object role in a finite clause; *dream* is an object in a nonfinite clause; *night* is an adverbial.

Because only boundaries separating finite clauses are indicated, there is only one sentence-internal clause boundary, "@/" between *daughters* and *that*. In principle, also nonfinite clauses could be identified with different boundary symbols. In practice, the lower case syntactic tags used for nonfinite clause members may suffice. Item order in nonfinite clauses usually is so rigid in nonfinite clauses that identifying these stereotypical patterns using the lower case tags alone is likely to succeed easily enough. (Stereotypical linguists's counter-examples like the topicalised *Who* in *Who did Mary want John to see?* seem to be negligibly uncommon in our text corpora.)

This kind of representation seeks to be (i) sufficiently expressive for stating grammatical generalisations in an economical and transparent fashion and (ii) sufficiently underspecific to make for a structurally resolvable grammatical representation. For example, the present way of functionally accounting for clauses enables the grammarian to express rules about the coordination of formally different but functionally similar entities. For instance, both *This* and *what you call a clause* are coordinated subjects in the sentence *This and what you call a clause are subjects* though they are formally different categories, the former being a noun phrase, the other being a finite clause.

Regarding the resolvability requirement, certain kinds of structurally unresolvable distinctions are never introduced. For instance, the premodifier tag *@>N* only indicates that its head is a nominal in the right hand context.

9.4   Sample Rule

The task of the grammarian is determining (i) distributional categories and (ii) their necessary syntactic contexts. For illustration, let us sketch a partial description of subjects, as given in (Quirk et al., 1985).

With regard to internal structure, a subject can be a noun phrase, a nonfinite clause, or even a finite clause. Also the constructions in which subjects can occur are of two main kinds: finite and nonfinite clauses. In the present paper we shall only be concerned with the most typical kind of subject: *noun phrase subject in finite clauses*. This type of subject has the most variable distribution of all four main types of subject, so describing the other types of subject will be more straightforward than what is the case here.

Noun phrase subjects in finite clauses are marked with the tag *@SUBJ* that is attached to the head of the noun phrase (and, in the case of coordination, to the head of each coordinate noun phrase). For instance, consider *boys* and *girls* in

```
                              @@
all     DET    @>N             @
the     DET    @>N             @
boys    N      @SUBJ           @
and     CC     @CC             @
girls   N      @SUBJ           @
will    V      @AUX            @
be      V      @MV     MAINC@  @
there   ADV    @ADVL           @
.       FULLSTOP               @@
```

The use of upper case in the tag indicates that the construction serves a function in a finite clause, and the existence of "@" at the beginning of the tag indicates that the functional category is a phrase rather than a clause. If we need more specific information e.g. about the part of speech of the subject, we can of course consult the morphological features. For instance, a noun acting as a subject in a finite clause can be expressed as the following regular expression:

```
N  .  @SUBJ
```

Note in particular that we need not be concerned about the internal structure of a category whose distribution we are trying to express, because a comprehensive grammar will in any case account for the distribution of e.g. determiners and modifiers with other rules. What has been said once in a grammar need not be repeated elsewhere.

The grammarian's other task is to determine the distribution of the construction. Again, a natural starting point is a comprehensive grammar, and perhaps extensive corpora as well. The type of subjects we are concerned with occur e.g. in declarative clauses with 'normal' word order, for instance:

```
                        @@
sam    N      @SUBJ           @
was    V      @MV    MAINC@   @
a      DET    @>N            @
man    N      @SC            @
.      FULLSTOP              @@
```

In this kind of clause, the subject is followed by a finite verb chain – main verb @*MV* and/or auxiliary @*AUX*. This generalisation can be expressed as the following expression:

```
@SUBJ  ..  [@MV  |  @AUX]
```

The *dotdot* "`..`" is a constant that accepts anything within the same clause, centre-embedded clauses included. So this expression accepts not only the sentence *Sam was a man* but also sentences like

```
                        @@
the     DET    @>N            @
man     N      @SUBJ          @<
who     PRON   @SUBJ          @
came    V      @MV    N<@     @
here    ADV    @ADVL          @/
when    ADV    @ADVL          @
he      PRON   @SUBJ          @
was     V      @MV    ADVL@   @
on      PREP   @ADVL          @
duty    N      @P<<           @
last    DET    @>N            @
time    N      @ADVL          @>
is      V      @MV    MAINC@  @
her     PRON   @>N            @
father  N      @SC            @
.       FULLSTOP              @@
```

Here *man*, which is the subject, is followed by *is*, the main verb of the clause, and the above expression recognises them as parts of the same clause although there is an intervening centre-embedding.

A declarative clause may also have other word orders. For instance, the clause may start with an adverbial or a 'formal subject' like *there*, continue with the finite verb chain, and end with the subject, e.g.

```
                          @@
here  ADV    @ADVL            @
is    V      @MV    MAINC@    @
my    PRON   @>N              @
bus   N      @SUBJ            @
.     FULLSTOP                @@
```

```
                            @@
there    ADV   @F-SUBJ          @
used=to  V     @AUX             @
be       V     @MV    MAINC@    @
a        DET   @>N              @
school   N     @SUBJ            @
on       PREP  @ADVL/N<         @
the      DET   @>N              @
island   N     @P<<             @
.        FULLSTOP               @@
```

This construction can be expressed with the following regular expression:

```
[@ADVL | @F-SUBJ] .. [@MV | @AUX] .. @SUBJ
```

A subject can occur in other constructions too. Here are some examples and the corresponding regular expressions ("..." ("\@@") accepts anything save a sentence boundary):

```
WH .. @MV .. @SUBJ ...        @question
Why    is    Sally so cruel   ?

[be | have | do] . @MV .. @SUBJ
Is                  Sally so cruel?
Did                 Italy win the match?
Were                she here, she would die.
```

Now we have seen how to express the constructions where a given distributional category can occur. The main point is to keep the formalisations sufficiently general. It suffices to explicitly represent the necessary contextual conditions; the rest of the (intervening) context can be represented in less detail, e.g. by using the *dotdot* constant. A little underspecificity in one rule is not harmful as long as the missing information is given somewhere else.

Our next move is to combine the distributional category and its contexts into an implication rule. Consider the skeleton of an implication rule:

```
X =>
LC1 _ RC1,
LC2 _ RC2,
LCn _ RCn;
```

We replace *X* with the regular expression that corresponds to the distributional category (*@SUBJ* in this case) and in the place of the context conditions *LC1 _ RC1* to *LCn _ RCn*, we list the regular expressions that correspond to the constructions in which the distributional category is legitimate. In the place of the *X* part, an underscore is inserted. The following formulation is based on the above-mentioned syntactically tagged grammar definition corpus.

```
# Defs
... = \@@;
FinChain = [@MV | @AUX];
@qu = @question;
@ex = @exclamation;
TooAd = [too . @ADVL];

# Rule
                        @SUBJ =>
                             _ .. FinChain,                    #1
    [@ADVL | @FSUBJ] .. FinChain .. _,                         #2
                        WH .. @MV .. _ ... @qu | @ex,          #3
            [be | have | do] . @MV .. _,                       #4
@/ . @comma . @ . @AUX .. PRON . _ .. @qu,                    #5
            @/ .. <Vcog> . @MV .. _,                           #6
    @/ . [@comma | @dash | @CC] .. _ .. @SC | @OBJ | TooAd,#7
@/ . [as|than] . @CS .. @AUX .. _;                            #8
```

Some comments:

- The first context states probably the most frequent case where the finite verb chain follows the subject. An auxiliary is given as an option to account for elliptical clauses like *Go where* YOU *will*[6] where the subject *you* is followed only by the modal auxiliary *will*.

---

[6]Here the relevant subjects are written in SMALL CAPS.

- The third context also allows exclamation marks, e.g. *How strange is his* APPEARANCE*!*.

- The fourth context accounts for several special cases having to do with the verbs "be", "have" and "do":

    - Direct questions, e.g. *Is* SHE *a tall girl?* and *Has* HE *any money?*

    - Questions in coordinations, e.g. *Did* ITALY *win the match, or did* BRAZIL*?*

    - "Be"-conditionals, e.g. *Were* SHE *here, she would support the motion.*

    - Certain topicalisations, e.g. *He has no need to make speeches, so impregnable is his* POSITION.

- The fifth context accounts for tag questions, e.g. *It is warm, isn't* IT*?*.

- The sixth context accounts for certain kinds of parenthetical clauses used in reporting speech, e.g. *"Inefficient cultures die hard," said one Wall Street securities* ANALYST where *said* gets the lexical tag "<Vcog>".

- The seventh context accounts for ellipses in clause coordinations, witness sentences like *Pushkin was Russia's greatest poet, and* TOLSTOY *her greatest novelist.*

- The eighth context accounts for certain kinds of comparative clauses beginning with she conjunction "as" or "than" and where the auxiliary precedes the subject, e.g. *Oil costs less than would atomic* ENERGY.

Some more general observations:

- The contexts could be more restrictive, e.g. ".." is probably too permissive in many cases. More restrictive formulations could use the "..not(X)" predicate instead of "..". The predicate "..not(X)" is defined[7] as follows:

    ```
    ..not(X) = -[.. X ..] & .. ;
    ```

    "..not(X)" accepts token sequences in a clause not containing occurrences of "X".

    Note, however, much of the effect of using "..not(X)" comes as a 'side product' of other rules. For instance, rules about the form of the noun phrase impose further restrictions on tags sequences accepted by ".." in our rule on NP subjects.

---

[7]The definition is borrowed from Tapanainen's parser implementation.

- The rule does not account for coordination of subjects. Further restrictions can be imposed with rules about coordinating conjunctions.

- The rule contains many contexts. Compiling a complicated rule into an automaton can be a very expensive operation. Possibilities for automatically splitting a rule into smaller ones should perhaps be explored.

Finally, a note on rule validation. A rule should be true and effective: true in the sense that it does not disallow a legitimate construction; effective in the sense that it reduces ambiguity.

Introspection may not alone suffice for ensuring that a rule in the parsing grammar is true and effective. Empirical test benches are also needed. One useful resource is the grammar definition corpus. As shown above, the grammar definition corpus contains a collection of (manually) analysed sentences that represent the syntactic structures in the object language. Now testing is simple: the candidate grammar rule can be applied to the grammar definition corpus, and if it accepts all sentences in the corpus, it is likely to be true. If the rule rejects a sentence in the corpus, the rejected sentence reading can be used as a diagnostic, and the 'leak' in the rule can be easily mended.

As for the effectiveness requirement: it is possible to enrich the grammar definition corpus with all initial ambiguities. This ambiguous corpus can then be used as a test bench for the modified grammar rule. It may for instance happen that a rule relaxed somewhat may leave much more ambiguity in the analyses than originally; this information is likely to be useful e.g. in the design of heuristics.

9.5   Heuristic Techniques

The present grammatical representation avoids introducing certain structurally unresolvable distinctions connected with modifier scope, attachment and coordination. Still, some kinds of structurally unresolvable distinction remain to bother the parser. For instance, consider the following three alternative parses:

```
                                @@
remove    V      @MV    MAINC@   @
the       DET    @>N             @
lower     A      @>N             @
clutch    N      @>N             @
housing   PCP1   @>N             @
bolts     N      @OBJ            @
and       CC     @CC             @
the       DET    @>N             @
cover     N      @OBJ            @
```

```
.         FULLSTOP              @@

                                @@
remove    V       @MV    MAINC@  @
the       DET     @>N            @
lower     A       @>N            @
clutch    N       @OBJ           @
housing   PCP1    @mv    @N<     @
bolts     N       @obj           @
and       CC      @CC            @
the       DET     @>N            @
cover     N       @OBJ           @
.         FULLSTOP              @@

                                @@
remove    V       @MV    MAINC@  @
the       DET     @>N            @
lower     A       @>N            @
clutch    N       @OBJ           @
housing   PCP1    @mv    @N<     @
bolts     N       @obj           @
and       CC      @CC            @
the       DET     @>N            @
cover     N       @obj           @
.         FULLSTOP              @@
```

On the basis of structural information, all three readings are structurally acceptable: *clutch housing bolts* can be analysed as a simplex noun phrase, or *housing* can be the main verb of a nonfinite construction that takes as object either *bolts* or *bolts and the cover*.

A grammar should minimally make a distinction between what is structurally acceptable in a language and what is not. In a realistic application, however, this may not always suffice: a grammar that accounts for (virtually) every construction in the language is likely to assign uncomfortably many analyses onto some of the input sentences, even with a relatively resolvable grammatical representation. Therefore a robust parsing system will also benefit from properly used less categorical generalisations.

Next, we sketch some possible ways of using heuristics.

9.5.1 Hand-written heuristics

One option is to define heuristic rules on the basis of the linguist's "rule of thumb". In the present implementation these heuristics can be expressed in the form of penalties for regular expressions:

```
heuristic{

1:      @APP;
        PL  .  @>N;

2:      AdjectiveAsNPHead;


        }
```

Different penalties can be imposed for different regular expressions. Given the above heuristics, a sentence reading containing one apposition reading and two adjectival noun phrase heads would be assigned $1 + 2 + 2 = 5$ penalty points. When heuristics are used, the parser returns the least penalised analyses first.

A problem with the purely artisanal approach is that considerable expertise is needed for imposing optimal penalties. My personal experience even suggests that writing (almost) true grammar rules seems easier than writing intentionally untrue but still useful rules (or heuristics).[8]

9.5.2   Data-driven techniques

Using corpus-based frequencies may be preferable. The general idea is to choose the most likely alternative syntactic analysis from those accepted by the strict grammar rules. Frequencies can be calculated at different levels of granularity. The more coarse-grained the variables, the smaller needs the tagged training corpus be. However, using few variables, e.g. only part-of-speech and syntactic tags, may result in coarse-grained classifications that may lead to many wrong overall predictions about the best syntactic analysis. Therefore also techniques are proposed for using a higher number of variables, especially frequency patterns for the syntactic behaviour of lexemes (or lexical classes). These lexico-grammatical frequencies may require some manual work in addition to large amounts of corpus data, so a pragmatic solution might be to derive lexico-grammatical frequencies only for the high and medium frequency lexemes, and use the lexically less distinctive frequencies as a 'fall-back' for the remaining cases.

Let us sketch some possible data-driven heuristic techniques.

1. Unigram probabilities can be counted from tagged corpora. Probabilities can be counted for different levels of representation, e.g.

   • word-form – morphological category (or part of speech)

---

[8]This, of course, with the reservation that a properly documented grammar definition corpus is accessible.

- morphological category – syntactic category
- word-form – syntactic category

Because there are already accurate and fast morphological taggers available, there is no shortage of annotated data for counting these lexical probabilities. Rough estimates for the mappings from morphology to syntax can be derived from the present syntactically annotated 200,000-word corpus. The last item on the list would probably need a very large syntactically annotated corpus for all but the most frequent words, so its present potential seems to be very limited.

These probabilities can in principle be used with the present heuristic penalty mechanism (see above): the least likely mappings get the highest penalties, and vice versa.

2. Also contextual probabilities may be useful. One possible starting point is the implication rules in the grammar. Given the sample rule

```
X =>
   A _ B,
   C _ D,
   E _ F;
```

frequencies could be counted for the different constructions listed in the rule, namely "A X B", "C X D" and "E X F", from the grammar definition corpus. During parsing, the penalty mechanism would assign the highest penalties onto the least frequent constructions.[9]

3. Another possibility is to take a more lexical perspective on determining syntactic preferences. Determining syntactic preferences for a large part of the lexicon may require a very large annotated corpus, and, as noted above, we do not have a sufficiently large syntactic corpus for these purposes. An alternative is using a very shallow but accurate parser for annotating a large corpus which would be a source for semiautomatically derived lexico-syntactic preferences.

A potential tool for this kind of work is a very shallow but accurate parser. For instance, consider *NPtool* (Voutilainen, 1993). The system employs a parser that recognises simple phrases (noun phrases, prepositional phrases, adverbials) as well as active and passive verb chains. It produces the following kind of output:

---

[9]Note in passing that these probabilities would not be limited to an artificial window of two or three words, as is often the case with statistical taggers. Rather, these heuristics would estimate the *relevant* contextual properties, local or global.

```
e_V she_PH would_V    learn_VA a_D> new_A> poem_NH every
s_NH as=well=as_CC    learn_VA a_D> new_A> set_NH of_<P
e_V require_V to_V    learn_VA a_D> new_A> text_NH pract
very_D> morning_NH    learn_VA a_D> poem_NH @lparen whil
P> school_NH we_PH    learn_VA a_D> poem_NH a_D> week_NH
              i_PH    learn_VA a_D> professor_N> higgins
bill_N> clinton_NH    learn_VA a_D> sharp_A> lesson_NH t
     @dquote to_V     learn_VA a_D> skill_NH @comma four
@comma so_CS he_PH    learn_VA a_D> speech_NH from_P st_
s_NH @comma and_CC    learn_VA a_D> stack_NH of_<P new_A
_NH @comma could_V    learn_VA a_D> thing_NH or_CC two_A
N> lawyers_NH be_V    learn_VA a_D> thing_NH or_CC two_A
ifferent_AH from_P    learn_VA a_D> trade_NH @fullstop
comma we_PH must_V    learn_VA a_D> vital_A> lesson_NH f
gs_NH he_PH have_V    learn_VA about_AH @comma jan_NH ge
in=there_AH and_CC    learn_VA about_AH sin_NH @fullstop
he_PH begin_V to_V    learn_VA about_P a_D> different_A>
ins_NH have_V be_V    learn_VA about_P act_NH i_NH @full
the_D> children_NH    learn_VA about_P anatomy_NH @comma
V unlikely_AH to_V    learn_VA about_P courtesy_NH from_
H of_<P germans_NH    learn_VA about_P democratic_A> pra
            we_PH     learn_VA about_P everything_PH tha
he_D> last_PH to_V    learn_VA about_P fraudulent_A> dea
e_V little_AH to_V    learn_VA about_P loch_N> ness_NH @
V a_D> lot_NH to_V    learn_VA about_P office_N> politic
e_V what_PH you_PH    learn_VA about_P office_N> work_NH
 perks_NH first_AH    learn_VA about_P opting_NH out_AH
```

This sample study concerns the local syntactic context of the verb "learn". For each occurrence of the verb, the base form is given, along with the tag _VA, which signifies a main verb in an active verb chain. The tag _D> signifies a determiner, i.e. the beginning of a noun phrase, and the tag _P signifies a preposition, i.e., there is a PP in the right hand context. From these clues we can determine, probably with a moderate amount of human effort, the following kind of statistics:

```
learn_VA              1000  # size of ``learn'' corpus
learn_VA + OBJ         400
learn_VA + about/P      60
```

In parsing, information about typical local syntactic contexts can help in resolving structurally genuine ambiguities in favour of typical analyses. This technique could be employed using a credit point mechanism: the more typical the local context of the word, the more credit points the sentence analysis would get.

This last technique could be seen as related to ideas inherent to *local grammars* (see other papers by Roche, Silberztein, Mohri and Gross, in this volume). Here, though, local syntactic information is not used in the form of absolute rules but rather as a mechanism for heuristically ranking analyses that have already been identified as structurally well-formed by global syntactic rules. Therefore the syntactic analyses of the present system are likely to make sense also at the sentence level, which is not guaranteed in a system that uses only local information.

9.6 Final Remarks

Some observations on the present English finite-state grammar and the parser may be of interest.

How many grammar rules are needed in a comprehensive parsing grammar of the kind outlined above? – Probably about two hundred implication rules. However, the present grammar contains almost 800 rules, purely because of technical problems: compiling big rules (those with something like 5-10 contexts) into automata is presently rather problematic, therefore the grammarian had to express the distributional statements in a more fragmentary fashion. New techniques are needed for using big rules.

The present grammar also contains about 200 hand-written heuristics of the kind outlined above. In future work on resolving structurally genuine (though often unlikely) ambiguities, more effort will be spent on data-driven techniques.

With regard to completeness: the grammar is no longer trivial, but it is also obvious that many further rules remain be written.

How much time does writing a comprehensive parsing grammar for this kind of representation take?

One part of the effort is the creation of the grammatical representation, the grammar definition corpus, and annotated running text. Probably about one person year is needed for this alone, if the syntactically annotated running text corpus is to contain 200,000 words or more. (Even with this time schedule, this semiautomatic annotation method requires shallow parsers like ENGCG (Karlsson *et al.* (eds.), 1995).)

Writing and testing a rule like the above about NP subjects probably requires less than a day, given the availability of sufficient test corpora and utilities[10]. Two hundred implication rules might mean a six months' effort.

The descriptive work is still underway, so giving any figures on the system's present accuracy seems premature. Probably the present system is not as

---

[10]These utilities could include a mechanism for automatically replacing "."'s with maximally restrictive "..not(X)"'s.

accurate as some other, more mature systems (like McCord's English Slot Grammar parser (McCord, 1990)).

As pointed above, the accuracy of the system can be improved by adding new rules to the grammar. Another more technical problem is that the parser, using the above outlined grammatical representation and parsing grammar, cannot always produce a parse for a long sentence (above 40 words) even though the present setup uses a Constraint Grammar style parser as a kind of preprocessor for resolving some of the easiest morphological and syntactic ambiguities (Voutilainen, 1995). During the intersection of the grammar automata with the ambiguous sentence automaton, the intermediary results sometimes become prohibitively large, so the parser sometimes produces no analyses even though the grammar accepted some (and only some) of the alternative sentence analyses. Jussi Piitulainen is investigating techniques for approximating intersection of automata so that readings are removed while the size of the intermediate sentence representation is kept in control (Piitulainen, 1995).

Appendix

This appendix lists those syntactic tags used in the present grammar definition corpus. For each item, a sample application is given. The word to which the tag would be assigned is written in SMALL CAPS. In the case of clause function tags, also the clause boundaries are indicated with the square brackets "[" and "]". These samples are by no means exhaustive; often the tags could also be applied to somewhat different constructions. A more exhaustive documentation of the grammatical representation is under preparation.

- @@   sentence boundary

- @   plain word boundary

- @/   boundary between consecutive finite clauses

- @<   beginning of centre-embedded finite clause

- @>   end of centre-embedded finite clause

    - @@ *John* @< *who* @ *died* @/ *when* @ *Sue* @ *was* @ *here* @>
      was @ *buried* @ *yesterday* @ *.* @@

- @P<<   preposition complement

    - *John is in the* KITCHEN.

- @>>P   complement of a deferred preposition

    – WHAT *are you talking about?*

- P<<@   clause as preposition complement

    – *John is in [what we* CALL *a kitchen].*

- @>A   adverb as premodifier

    – *It is* EXTREMELY *odd.*

- @A<   adverb as postmodifier

    – *She sings well* ENOUGH.

- @>N   determiner or modifier of a nominal in the right-hand context

    – THE RED *car is there.*

- @N<   determiner or modifier of a nominal in the left-hand context

    – *Something* ODD *happened yesterday.*

- N<@   postmodifying clause

    – *This is the car [that John* BOUGHT*].*

- @CC   coordinating conjunction

    – *John* AND *Mary got married.*

- @>CC   introducer of a coordination ("either", "neither", "both")

    – BOTH *John and Mary got married.*

- @CS   subordinating conjunction

    – *Get married* IF *necessary.*

- @AUX   auxiliary in a finite verb chain

    – *John* HAS BEEN *drinking coffee again.*

- @aux   auxiliary in a nonfinite verb chain

    – HAVING *said that, he died.*

- @MV   main verb in a finite verb chain

    – *John has been* DRINKING *coffee again.*

- @mv   main verb in a nonfinite verb chain

    – *Having* SAID *that, he died.*

- @ADVL   adverbial

    – *John has been drinking coffee* AGAIN IN *the cupboard.*

- ADVL@   adverbial clause

    – *He came [when she* LEFT*].*

- @APP   apposition

    – *John, a* FRIEND *of Bill's, is there.*

- APP@   appositive clause

    – *We were faced with the demand [that this tax* BE *abolished].*

- @SUBJ   subject in a finite clause

    – JOHN *is here.*

- @subj   subject in a nonfinite clause

    – *I dislike* JOHN'S *being here.*

- SUBJ@   clause as subject in a finite clause

    – *[What I* DISLIKE*] is John's presence.*

- @FSUBJ   formal subject in a finite clause

    – THERE *was a car on the street.*

- @fsubj   formal subject in a nonfinite clause

    – THERE *being a car on the street doesn't bother me.*

- @FOBJ   formal object in a finite clause

    – *I consider* IT *odd that she resigned.*

- **@SC**   complement of a finite clause subject

      – *John is my* FRIEND.

- **@sc**   complement of a subject in a nonfinite clause

      – *John being my* FRIEND *doesn't bother me.*

- **SC@**   clause as complement of a finite clause subject

      – *John is [what I* CALL *my friend].*

- **sc@**   clause as complement of a subject in a nonfinite clause

      – *John being [what I* CALL *my friend] doesn't bother me.*

- **@OBJ**   object in a finite clause

      – *John saw a* CAR.

- **@obj**   object in a nonfinite clause

      – *Seeing a* CAR *was appalling.*

- **OBJ@**   clause as object in a finite clause

      – *I know that [seeing a car* IS *appalling].*

- **obj@**   clause as object in a nonfinite clause

      – *Knowing that [seeing a car* IS *appalling] doesn't bother me.*

- **@IOBJ**   indirect object in a finite clause

      – *John gave* MARY *an apple.*

- **@iobj**   indirect object in a nonfinite clause

      – *Giving* MARY *an apple is no sin.*

- **IOBJ@**   clause as indirect object in a finite clause

      – *You can tell [whoever is* WAITING*] that I'll be back in ten minutes.*

- @OC   complement of a finite clause object

  – *He called Mary a* FOOL.

- @oc   complement of an object in a nonfinite clause

  – *Calling Mary a* FOOL *was foolish.*

- OC@   clause as complement of a finite clause object

  – *You can call me [whatever you* LIKE*].*

- @nh   stray noun phrase head

  – INTRODUCTION

- MAINC@   finite main clause

  – *[John* IS *a fool.]*

- mainc@   nonfinite main clause

  – *[How to* WRITE *a book]*

- PAREN@   finite parenthetical clause

  – *I found in the kitchen the letter [I* THOUGHT*] I had burned.*

Acknowledgements

I wish to thank Fred Karlsson, Lauri Karttunen, Kimmo Koskenniemi, Jussi Piitulainen and Pasi Tapanainen for useful discussions on surface parsing.

References

Fred Karlsson. 1990. Constraint Grammar as a Framework for Parsing Running Text. In H. Karlgren (ed.), *Papers presented to the 13th International Conference on Computational Linguistics, Vol. 3*. Helsinki. 168-173.

Fred Karlsson, Atro Voutilainen, Juha Heikkilä and Arto Anttila (eds.). 1995. *Constraint Grammar: a Language-Independent System for Parsing Unrestricted Text*. Berlin and New York: Mouton de Gruyter.

Kimmo Koskenniemi. 1983. *Two-level Morphology. A General Computational Model for Word-form Production and Generation.* Publication No. 11, Department of General Linguistics, University of Helsinki.

Kimmo Koskenniemi. 1990. Finite-state parsing and disambiguation. In Hans Karlgren (ed.) *COLING-90. Papers presented to the 13th International Conference on Computational Linguistics, Vol. 2.* Helsinki, Finland. 229–232.

Kimmo Koskenniemi and Atro Voutilainen. 1991. Finite-state parsing and disambiguation. Unpublished manuscript. Department of General Linguistics, University of Helsinki.

Kimmo Koskenniemi, Pasi Tapanainen and Atro Voutilainen. 1992. Compiling and using finite-state syntactic rules. In *Proceedings of the fifteenth International Conference on Computational Linguistics. COLING-92, Vol. I.* Nantes, France. 156–162.

Michael McCord. 1990. A System for Simpler Construction of Practical Natural Language Grammars. In R. Studer (ed.), *Natural Language and Logic. Lecture Notes in Artificial Intelligence 459.* Berlin: Springer Verlag. 118-145.

Jussi Piitulainen. 1995. Locally tree-shaped sentence automata and resolution of ambiguity. In K. Koskenniemi (ed.), *Proceedings of the 10th Nordic Conference of Computational Linguistics (NODALIDA-95), Helsinki May 29-30 1995.* Helsinki.

Randolph Quirk, Sidney Greenbaum, Geoffrey Leech and Jan Svartvik. 1985. *A Comprehensive Grammar of the English Language.* London and New York: Longman.

Geoffrey Sampson. 1987. The grammatical database and grammatical representation. In Garside, Leech and Sampson (eds.) 1987. Garside, R., Leech, G. and Sampson, G. *The Computational Analysis of English.* London and New York: Longman. 82-96.

Pasi Tapanainen. 1991. Äärellisinä automaatteina esitettyjen kielioppisääntöjen soveltaminen luonnollisen kielen jäsentäjässä (Natural language parsing with finite-state syntactic rules). Master's thesis. Department of Computer Science, University of Helsinki.

Atro Voutilainen. 1993. *NPtool*, a detector of English noun phrases. In *Proceedings of the Workshop on Very Large Corpora, June 22, 1993.* Ohio State University, Ohio, USA.

Atro Voutilainen. 1994. *Three studies of grammar-based surface parsing of unrestricted English text.* Doctoral dissertation. Publications, Nr. 24, Department of General Linguistics, University of Helsinki. Helsinki.

Atro Voutilainen. 1995. A syntax-based part of speech analyser. In *Proceedings of the Seventh Conference of the European Chapter of the Association for Computational Linguistics.* Association for Computational Linguistics. Dublin.

Atro Voutilainen and Timo Järvinen. 1995. Specifying a shallow grammatical representation for parsing purposes. In *Proceedings of the Seventh Conference of the European Chapter of the Association for Computational Linguistics.* Association for Computational Linguistics. Dublin.

Atro Voutilainen, Juha Heikkilä and Arto Anttila. 1992. *Constraint Grammar of English: A Performance-Oriented Introduction.* Publication No. 21, Department of General Linguistics, University of Helsinki.

Atro Voutilainen and Pasi Tapanainen. 1993. Ambiguity Resolution in a Reductionistic Parser. In *Proceedings of the Sixth Conference of the European Chapter of the Association for Computational Linguistics.* Association for Computational Linguistics. Utrecht.

10 Applying a Finite-State Intersection Grammar

Pasi Tapanainen

We present some methods to intersect an acyclic finite-state automaton with a set of cyclic finite-state automata in a framework of a shallow syntactic analyser of a natural language.

10.1 Introduction

In this paper I discuss applying the rules of a finite-state intersection grammar to a morphologically analysed sentence. More information about the finite-state intersection grammar can be found in the article of Atro Voutilainen in this same volume and in (Koskenniemi, 1990; Koskenniemi et al., 1992; Tapanainen, 1992; Voutilainen and Tapanainen, 1993; Voutilainen, 1994).

I use some specific terminology in this paper:

- A *sentence automaton* denotes an acyclic finite-state automaton that initially represents all the possible analyses that a morphological analyser has given to words of the sentence. After the rules have been applied, only a subset of analyses remain in the sentence automaton.

- A *rule automaton* denotes a (cyclic) automaton that represents some linguistic generalisation. It is similar to a morphological two-level rule in that it constraints the occurence of some symbol or a sequence of symbols by the context.

- *Applying a rule* means intersecting the sentence automaton and the specific rule automaton.

- The *amount of remaining ambiguity* is in principle the number of analyses (strings) accepted by the corresponding sentence automaton. (It is always finite because the sentence automaton is acyclic.)

10.1.1   Text samples

We demonstrate the performance of the algorithms by using two sentences. The first one is short and the second one more complex. Both the sentences are analysed morphologically (and partly disambiguated) and syntactic ambiguity is introduced. The syntactic ambiguity that can be easily rejected by close context is not present anymore when the sentence is feed into the finite-state intersection parser. In principle, more ambiguity could be present in the sentences if all the syntactic ambiguity were introduced blindly to all the appropriate morphological readings.

The first sentence is:

God is a puzzling and elusive notion, by no means easy to define.

Initially, it is presented by a finite-state automaton of 89 states. 236 rules are used for parsing this sentence. The result contains 93 states and the following two analyses:

```
@@
<*god> god <*> N NOM SG @SUBJ @
<is> be <SV> <SVC/N> <SVC/A> V PRES SG3 VFIN @MV MAINC@ @
<a> a <Indef> DET CENTRAL ART SG @>N @
<puzzling> puzzle <SVO> <SV> PCP1 @>N @
<and> and <>N> CC @CC @
<elusive> elusive A ABS @>N @
<notion> notion <Cog> N NOM SG @SC @ @comma @
<by=no=means> by=no=means ADV ADVL @ADVL @
<easy> easy A ABS @ADVL @
<to> to INFMARK> @aux @
<define> define <as/SVOC/A> <SVO> <SV> V INF @mv N<@ @
@fullstop @@

@@
<*god> god <*> N NOM SG @SUBJ @
<is> be <SV> <SVC/N> <SVC/A> V PRES SG3 VFIN @MV MAINC@ @
<a> a <Indef> DET CENTRAL ART SG @>N @
<puzzling> puzzle <SVO> <SV> PCP1 @SC @
<and> and <SC> CC @CC @
<elusive> elusive A ABS @>N @
<notion> notion <Cog> N NOM SG @SC @ @comma @
<by=no=means> by=no=means ADV ADVL @ADVL @
<easy> easy A ABS @ADVL @
<to> to INFMARK> @aux @
<define> define <as/SVOC/A> <SVO> <SV> V INF @mv N<@ @
@fullstop @@
```

The second sentence is:

> Ooldea used to be a railway siding on the east-west line that
> connects Perth with Adelaide, but the little fettlers' cottages and
> the old station were pushed to one side by bulldozers in the
> Fifties and now all that is left to mark the site is a few piles of
> rubble and a white concrete memorial for Mrs Bates, standing
> forlorn close to the line.

Initially, it is presented by an automaton of 508 states. The result contains 809 states. 577 rules are used for parsing this sentence.

10.1.2   The rules

There are 986 rules represented by 986 finite-state automata. Most of the rules are small finite-state automata (see Table 10.1) and the number of the rule automata could be decreased by intersecting some of the rules. It is not likely that all the rules can be combined into a big finite-state machine because in the worst case the size of the intersection of two automata of size n and m states is $n \times m$ states. The size of all the rule automata could thus be in the worst case as big as the product of the sizes of all the rule automata. That is about 10^{1050}.

size	frequency
1-5 states	255
6-10 states	309
11-20 states	204
21-50 states	105
51-100 states	42
101-1000 states	66
over 1000 states	5

Table 10.1: The distribution of the sizes of the rule automata

10.2   Straight Intersection

The intersection algorithm is roughly the following for two automata. Let $Q_1 = \{q_1, q_2, \ldots, q_m\}$ be the state set of the first automaton and $Q_2 = \{s_1, s_2, \ldots, s_n\}$ the state set of the second. The intersection result is the Cartesian product $Q_1 \times Q_2$ of those two state sets, so that there is an arc with label $\lambda \in \Sigma$ from state $q_i \times s_j$ to state $q_k \times s_l$ if and only if there are arcs with label λ from the state q_i to the state q_k and from the state s_j to the state s_l.

The state $q_i \times s_j$ is a final state if and only if both the state q_i and the state s_j are final states. The start state is the state $q_\alpha \times s_\beta$ where the states q_α and s_β are start-states of the original automata.

This may be easily generalised to n automata by using the product $Q_1 \times Q_2 \times \ldots \times Q_n$ and the method above.

Another way to intersect a set of n automata, is to take two automata from the set, intersect them, put the result back to the set, and repeat this until there is only one automaton left.

10.3   Sequential Methods

10.3.1   Randomised intersection

In this section we use a trivial way to apply all the rules. We take the sentence automaton and one of the rules. We intersect them. Then we take another rule and intersect it with previous intersection result. We repeat this until all the rules have been intersected. The order of the intersection does not have an effect on the result and we do not pay any attention to the ordering in the parsing algorithm.

The simple sentences can be easily parsed using this method but it turns out that the longer and more complex sentences tend to produce huge intermediate results.

Let S be an acyclic automaton that represents all the possible analyses of the sentence and R be a set of automata, $R = \{r_1, r_2, \ldots, r_n\}$, that represents a set of the rules. We take randomly an automaton r_i out of the set R and compute the intersection $S_1 = S \cap r_i$. Next, we take the next automaton r_j and compute the intersection $S_j = S_{j-1} \cap r_j$. This is repeated until all the rules are applied. The result is S_n.

With an easy sentence this method may work as can be seen in Figure 10.1. There are two runs in the figure. In the both cases the next rule to be applied is selected randomly. There is relatively big difference between the maximal intermediate sizes. Although the sizes are quite small.

Figure 10.2 shows the sizes of the intermediate results of randomly selected orderings of the rules with the longer sentence. We can see that the intermediate results grow very rapidly. In all the cases the intermediate size of the sentence automaton has grown beyond 100000 states before 35 rules out of 600 have been applied. This suggests that it is not a good idea to intersect the rules with the sentence automaton in a random order.

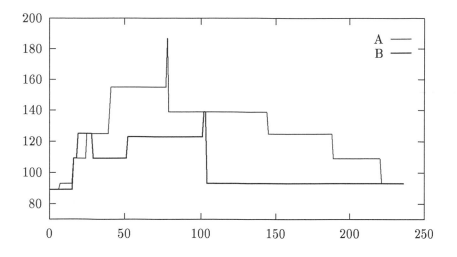

Figure 10.1: The sizes of intermediate results in two runs with the easy sentence.

10.3.2 "The best next" -methods

The experiment with randomly ordered rules raises a question: is there an ordering of the rules that do not produce this kind of blow-up in intermediate results. And if there is, how can we find it.

Next, we use simple heuristics to obtain smaller intermediate results. This is a greedy algorithm, and it is quite simple. In each step we test each rule against the current intermediate result and select the rule that provides the smallest result[1] in the next step.

The result with the short sentence is surprising. As seen in Figure 10.3 the maximal intermediate size does not get above the size of the final size. The long sentence has much bigger intermediate results, as seen in Figure 10.4 but it also stays relatively small all the time.

Although the maximal size of the intermediate result (in this case) is tolerable, the problem is the massive computing that is needed to intersect the sentence automaton with all the remaining rule automata in every step. To compute the intersection of n automata requires $O(n^2)$ intersection operations.

---

[1] Also a variation where we select the rule that removes the biggest amount of ambiguity gives interesting results.

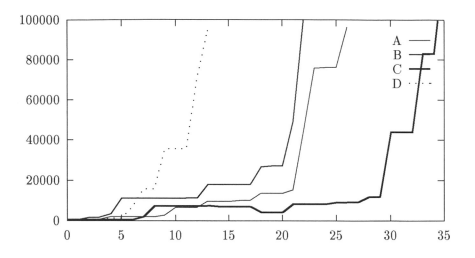

Figure 10.2: The sizes of intermediate results in four runs with the difficult sentence.

10.3.3   Approximated "best next" ordering

Knowing that there may be a better ordering of the rules than just some random order, we try to find a method to approximate this before-hand to avoid unnecessary computing. What we do is simply that we first intersect the original sentence automaton with each rule automaton, and determine the ordering of the rules by the sizes of these obtained networks. Alternatively we can determine the ordering by the amount of ambiguity still remaining in these networks. Then we apply the rules according to this predefined ordering.

In Figure 10.5 we see that the size is still tolerable[2] but significantly bigger than in previous algorithm. Here we need only $2n$ intersection operations, which makes this operation faster than the previous method. If we could make an universal approximation of the ordering, we would not need to do the first step at all, and only n intersection operations would be needed.

---

[2]The tolerable intermediate result size is here a little bit fuzzy expression, but 10 000 states should still fit to memory of any modern computer and much time is not required to compute it.

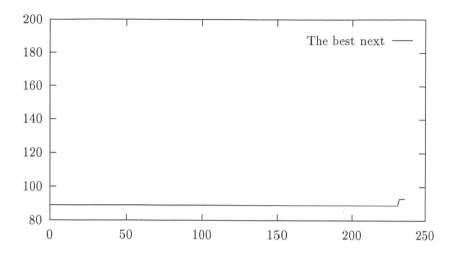

Figure 10.3: The *best next* method for the short sentence.

10.3.4 Improving the approximated ordering

We can improve the ordering by using the approximate ordering like above but instead of always selecting the first rule in queue (especially if it increases much the size) we try also some of the following rules, and select the best one. This is thus a combination of the methods above. We use an approximate ordering but also try to approximate the result in run-time.

In Figure 10.6 we tried this method with a window size of three and five.

10.3.5 Run-time compression

An interesting way to try to handle the size of the intermediate results is to add some ambiguity back to the sentence to produce a sentence automaton that accepts more analyses for the sentence but requires less space.

One way to compress the sentence automaton is to transform the sentence-based readings to word-based readings and back to sentence-based readings. This means that some information is lost but the size of the sentence automaton has some upper boundary. For example the analyses of the short sentence in Section 10.1.1 can be represented as the following:

@@

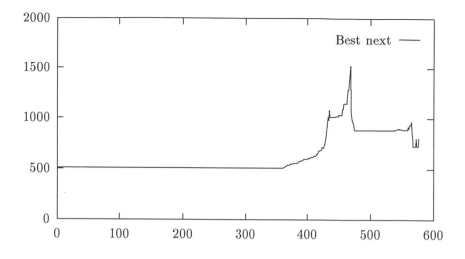

Figure 10.4: The *best next* method for the long sentence.

```
<*god> god <*> N NOM SG @SUBJ @

<is> be <SV> <SVC/N> <SVC/A> V PRES SG3 VFIN @MV MAINC@ @

<a> a <Indef> DET CENTRAL ART SG @>N @

<puzzling> puzzle <SVO> <SV> PCP1 @>N @
<puzzling> puzzle <SVO> <SV> PCP1 @SC @

<and> and <>N> CC @CC @
<and> and <SC> CC @CC @

<elusive> elusive A ABS @>N @

<notion> notion <Cog> N NOM SG @SC @ @comma @

<by=no=means> by=no=means ADV ADVL @ADVL @

<easy> easy A ABS @ADVL @

<to> to INFMARK> @aux @
```

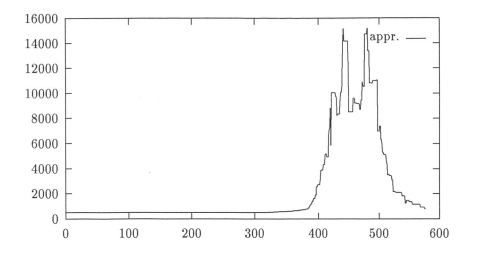

Figure 10.5: The approximated best ordering for the long sentence.

```
<define> define <as/SVOC/A> <SVO> <SV> V INF @mv N<@ @

@fullstop @@
```

This notion loses the information how the two ambiguous words *puzzling* and *and* are related and introduces thus some new ambiguity.

In Figure 10.7 it is demonstrated how this method works with the short sentence. In the figure the sentence automaton is compressed every time the size of the intermediate result exceeds 100 states. The kind of behaviour that this rule order would have without compression, can be seen in Figure 10.1.

The long sentence does not have as nice behaviour as the short one as can be seen in Figure 10.8. In the beginning the size tends to grow very rapidly (like in Figure 10.2) and much compression is needed. Finally enough size-growing ambiguity is removed from the sentence and in the second round (there are about 600 rules) the intermediate results do not grow much.

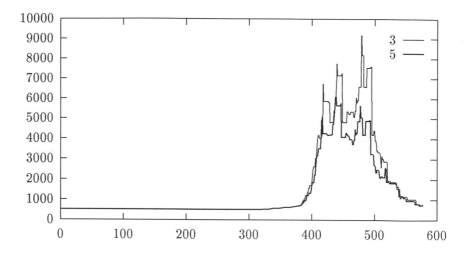

Figure 10.6: The approximated best ordering with the selection of the best in a 3 and 5 rule window.

10.4   Parallel Intersection

A parallel intersection algorithm can be generalised from the algorithm for two automata by using state set $Q_1 \times Q_2 \times \ldots \times Q_n$. In general, the maximal size is as large as in the sequential case. Parallel intersection may be slower than the sequential method, because the sequential application allows minimisation after every step.

Although parallel intersection may not offer an advantage in the general case, it can be superior if we have an acyclic automaton among the automata to be intersected and we also know that the result should be relatively small. A similar observation is made in (Karttunen, 1994) with respect to composing a lexicon with a set of rule automata. The method of parallel intersection alone and the intersecting composition are closely related.

10.4.1   Depth-first search

We can transform the intersection problem to a search problem. This is done by selecting the sentence automaton to present the search tree and starting from the start-state of the sentence automaton. In each state an arc is visited and

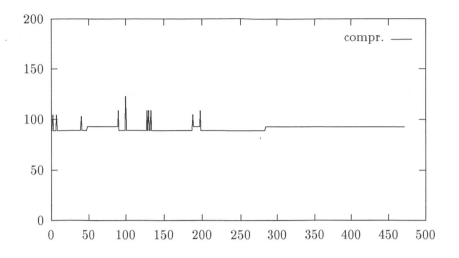

Figure 10.7: Compressing the short sentence. The limit is 100 states.

and after that the subtree beginning from that arc. When the subtree is totally explored the next arc is selected and the new subtree is then explored. In each step all the rule automata are run in parallel, and whenever it is known that a rule automaton rejects the string, the search is halted and the process backtracks.

In the worst case all the alternative analyses are needed to enumerate. If the average ambiguity rate per word is k this means k^n different leaves in the search tree. The worst case time requirement is thus $O(e^n)$. On the other hand, in the best case, only one path is need what makes the time requirement $O(n)$.

In practise this method may be faster than sequential methods when the grammar restricts well the possible paths and cuts the search tree rapidly. The sequential methods are likely to be better when the number of the rule automata is small and their sizes are relatively small.

10.5   Hybrid Intersection-Search Method

While the problems with the straight intersection is the large intermediate result and with the search-based method the enourmous search tree, we can combine the methods to minimise their bad-side effects.

The method is the following. We select a couple of rules that reduce the

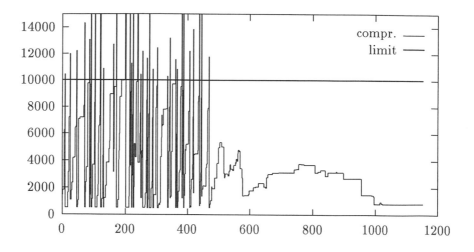

Figure 10.8: Compressing the long sentence. The limit is 10000 states.

ambiguity most and intersect them with the sentence automaton. We do not intersect so many rules that the intermediate result would become too large. After that we apply all the remaining rule automata in parallel. Because the first step has removed a big part of the ambiguity, the search tree is significantly reduced. This usually shortens the search time.

10.6   A Small Comparison

We tested some of the methods with a test sample of sentences and rules (Voutilainen and Tapanainen, 1993). Intersection in random order (Chapter 10.3.1) takes 31 000 seconds. With the approximation of ordering (Chapter 10.3.3), the required time drops to 730 seconds. The depth-first search (Chapter 10.4.1) is somewhat slower, namely 1500 seconds. When the methods are combined (Chapter 10.5) the required time drops to 500 seconds. The process can be speeded up further by using a method that quickly selects the relevant rules (Tapanainen, 1992) and by combining some rules.

10.7 Theoretical Worst-Case Study

10.7.1 Premises

Let us first make a simplified assumption that each word may have exactly two alternative tags. This makes the ambiguous sentence originally look like the automaton in Figure 10.9.

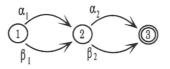

Figure 10.9: A simplified sentence automaton.

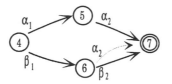

Figure 10.10: A simplified sentence automaton when a rule is applied.

When we apply a rule the number accepted analyses decreases, but the size of the network may grow. The Figure 10.10 presents a hypotetical result that may be achieved by applying a rule.

Later on, we suppose that, in each step, the parsing algorithm produces a minimal deterministic finite-state automaton that accepts all the analyses that do not violate any of the applied rules. No new analyses that do not belong to the original set of alternatives are created by this process.

Our question is how big can this intermediate result in the worst case. We have here two different approaches. The first one does not restrict the grammar in any way. The latter presupposes that the grammar is represented by finite-state automata and it is defined before the parsing.

10.7.2 Variable Grammar

Definition 31 *An* initial sentence automaton *is a minimal deterministic finite-state automaton M with states $S = \{s_0, s_1, \ldots, s_n\}$, final states $F = \{s_n\}$ and arcs are $\delta(s_i, w) = s_{i+1}$ where w is a letter in alphabet Σ and $0 \le i < n$ an integer. In addition, we suppose that for all $0 \le i < n$ there exist at least one letter $w \in \Sigma$ so that $\delta(s_i, w) = s_{i+1}$ holds.*

Definition 32 *A sentence automaton is a minimal deterministic finite-state automaton M with states* $S = s_{0,0}, s_{n,0} \cup S_1 \cup \cdots \cup S_{n-1}$ *where* S_i *is a level (i.e. distance from the start-state) of states* $S_i = \{s_{i,0}, s_{i,1}, \ldots, s_{i,n_i}\}$ *and* $n_i \geq 1$ *holds. The set of final states is* $F = \{s_{n,0}\}$ *and arcs are* $\delta(s_{i,k}, w) = s_{i+1,l}$ *where* w *is a letter in alphabet* Σ, *and* $0 \leq i < n$ *and* $0 \leq k < n_i$ *integers.*

An initial sentence automaton is always also a sentence automaton. In the parsing process the initial sentence automaton expresses all the alternative parses that the morphological analysis may produce. The sentence automaton contains some of them. It may be produced by applying the rules to the corresponding initial sentence automaton.

Next, let us concider how big the sentence automaton may be. We can proceed in two ways: computing the maximal amount of states at each level when started from the start-state $s_{0,0}$ or from the final-state $s_{n,0}$.

In the first level we always have only one state, that is $S_0 = \{s_{0,0}\}$. In general, number of states in the level i is bound to the leaving arcs from the level $i - 1$. This means that a state $s_{i-1,k}$ may produce, at most, n_{i-1} states to the level i. This gives us a recursive worst-case definition for the number of the states in each level S_i:

$$f(S_i) = \begin{cases} 1 & \text{when } i = 0 \\ n_{i-1} f(S_{i-1}) & \text{otherwise} \end{cases} \tag{10.1}$$

$$= \begin{cases} 1 & \text{when } i = 0 \\ \prod_{j=0}^{i-1} n_j & \text{otherwise} \end{cases} \tag{10.2}$$

On the other hand, there is only one final state, because the sentence automaton is minimal and none of the final states has leaving arcs, and thus all of them accept the same language. This means that Formula 10.1 is bound by this restriction.

We can compute also the maximum number of the possible states in level $n - 1$. In this case none of the states in level $n - 1$ can accept the same language because the automaton would not be minimal otherwise. This means, that the maximal size of the level S_{n-1} is then $S_{n-1} = 2^{n_{i-1}} - 1$ because the number of all the appropriate label subsets is $2^{n_{i-1}}$, and the empty set should be excluded.

In general, we need to consider also possible destinations of the arcs. This means that if we have selected k labels, we have $|S_{i+1}|^k$ ways to arrange them. Thus, we get that in the level S_i there can be at most following amount of states:

$$f'(S_i) = \begin{cases} 1 & \text{when } i = n \\ \sum_{k=1}^{n_i} \binom{n_i}{k} f'(S_{i+1})^k & \text{otherwise} \end{cases} \tag{10.3}$$

The formule 10.1 and 10.3 define together the maximal size of a sentence automaton with more than two ambiguous words:

$$\sum_{i=0}^{n} \min(f(S_i), f'(S_i)) = \sum_{i=0}^{k} f(S_i) + \sum_{i=k+1}^{n} f'(S_i) \tag{10.4}$$

where $0 < k < n$ is an index that holds $f(S_k) \leq f'(S_k)$ and $f(S_{k+1}) \geq f'(S_{k+1})$. Function f is growing and f' is decreasing function.

We may derive a lower bound of the size by reducing the ambiguity to two in maximum. Then we get formula

$$\sum_{i=0}^{k} f(S_i) + \sum_{i=k+1}^{n} f'(S_i) \geq \sum_{i=0}^{n} \begin{cases} 1, \text{ if } i = 0 \text{ or } i = n \\ \prod_{j=0}^{i-1} n_j, \text{ if } i \leq k \\ \sum_{j=1}^{n_i} \binom{n_i}{j} f'(S_{i+1})^j, \text{ otherwise} \end{cases} \tag{10.5}$$

$$\geq \prod_{j=0}^{k-1} n_j + \sum_{j=1}^{n_i} \binom{n_i}{j} f'(S_{k+2})^j \text{ where } k \text{ is a constant} \tag{10.6}$$

Let there be α the number of ambiguous words before the kth word (including the kth word) and β the number of ambiguous words after.

$$\prod_{j=0}^{k-1} n_j + \sum_{j=1}^{n_i} \binom{n_i}{j} f'(S_{k+2})^j \geq 2^\alpha + 3^{2^{\beta-1}} \tag{10.7}$$

$$\geq \begin{cases} 2^{(\alpha+\beta)/2} = \sqrt{2}^{\alpha+\beta} & \text{if } \alpha > \beta \\ 3^{2^{(\alpha+\beta-1)/2}} = 3\sqrt{2}^{\alpha+\beta-1} & \text{otherwise} \end{cases} \tag{10.8}$$

We finally obtain a lower bound for the worst case. The lower bound is clearly exponential to the number of ambiguous words $\alpha + \beta$.

10.7.3 Fixed finite-state grammar

Here we discuss the time requirement of applying all the n rules to a sentence, when the grammar is given.

The intersection of the sentence automaton S and the rule automata $R = \{r_1, r_2, \ldots, r_n\}$ may be computed in the following way. Before the intersection the rules are preprocessed and intersected with together. The new automaton $R' = r_1 \cap r_2 \cap \ldots \cap r_n$ is computed. Now we know that the intersection of $S \cap R'$ can be computed in time $O(|S| \times |R'|)$ where $|S|$ and $|R'|$ denote the number of the states of automata S and R' respectively. The size of the automaton R' is constant and may be replaced by constant C. Thus the time requirement is $O(|S|) = O(C|S|)$. And the grammar can be applied in linear time according to the size of the automaton S. We suppose the size of automaton S is linear according to the length of the original sentence. This is the case if we have an upper bound for the number of tags t for a word and maximal amount of ambiguity m for a word, then we know that each word can be presented with $m(t + 1)$ states. Thus a sentence of w words requires $wm(t + 1)$ states in maximum. The algorithm does not need then more than a linear time according to number of words in the sentence.

A big drawback here is that the constant C may be huge. I would approximate that with the grammar earlier in this paper the constant C may be 10^{1000}. Also, the size of the automaton R' may be, in the worst case, as big as $|R'| \leq |r_1| \times |r_2| \times \ldots \times |r_n|$.

10.8   Conclusion

In this paper we discussed some methods to intersect an acyclic finite-state automaton with a set of cyclic finite-state automata. The trivial way to do it may works in easy cases but in the framework of natural language processing we quickly encounter examples that are too hard for the most trivial algorithms.

There are many ways to pass this problem. Here we tried to cope with this problem by reordering the rules and intersecting some of the rules sequentially and some parallel. These optimisations do not affect the final result but there may be a big difference on run-time perfomance as seen when Figures 10.2 and 10.4 are compared. These methods may also be combined so that as many rules as possible (or some specific ones) are intersected with the sentence and the remaining rules are applied in parallel afterwards.

References

Lauri Karttunen. 1994. Constructing Lexical Transducers. in the proceedings of *The 15th International Conference on Computational Linguistics* (COLING'94). International Comittee on Computational Linguistics, Kyoto, 1994.

Kimmo Koskenniemi. 1990. Finite-state parsing and disambiguation. In *proceedings of Coling-90. Papers presented to the 13th International Conference on Computational Linguistics*. Vol. 2, pages 229–232. Helsinki, 1990.

Kimmo Koskenniemi, Pasi Tapanainen and Atro Voutilainen. 1992. Compiling and using finite-state syntactic rules. In the proceedings of The *Fourteenth International Conference on Computational Linguistics* (COL-

ING'92). Vol. I, pages 156-162. International Comittee on Computational Linguistics, Nantes, 1992.

Pasi Tapanainen. 1992. Äärellisiin automaatteihin perustuva luonnollisen kielen jäsennin. Lisensiaattityö. Department of computer science, University of Helsinki.

Atro Voutilainen. 1994. *Three studies of grammar-based surface parsing of unrestricted English text* Publications 24, Department of General Linguistics, University of Helsinki.

Atro Voutilainen and Pasi Tapanainen. 1993. Ambiguity resolution in a reductionistic parser. In the proceedings of the *Sixth Conference of the European Chapter of the Association for Computational Linguistics* (EACL'93). pages 394-403. Association for Computational Linguistics, Utrecht, 1993.

11 The Construction of Local Grammars

Maurice Gross

11.1 Introduction

Grammar, or, as it has now been called, linguistic theory, has always been driven by a quest for complete generalizations, resulting invariably in recent times in the production of abstract symbolism, often semantic, but also algorithmic. This development contrasts with that of the other Natural Sciences such as Biology or Geology, where the main stream of activity was and is still now the search and accumulation of exhaustive data. Why the study of language turned out to be so different is a moot question. One could argue that the study of sentences provides an endless variety of forms and that the observer himself can increase this variety at will within his own production of new forms; that would seem to confirm that an exhaustive approach makes no sense. As a simple computation shows, there are more than 10^{50} sentences having at most 20 words, a number which seems to deprive of any meaning the possibility of performing a systematic inquiry. However, the same could be said in Astronomy, Botany or Entomology, since the potential number of observations of individual stars, plants or butterflies is also limitless. Note that nonetheless, establishing catalogs of objects (and devising suitable criteria to do so) remains an important part of the activity in these fields. It is not so in linguistics, even if lexicographers do accumulate and classify words very much as in the other sciences. But grammarians operating at the level of sentences seem to be interested only in elaborating general rules and do so without performing any sort of systematic observation and without a methodical accumulation of sentence forms to be used by further generations of scientists. It is not necessary to stress that such an accumulation in any science is made possible by constructing and using suitable equivalence relations to eliminate what are deemed to be accidental variations, irrelevant to the specified goal of the catalog.

The approach in linguistics leads all too easily to overgeneralization. To take a well-known example, using the grammatical categories of Classical Greek (as taught in high schools) to describe exotic languages is more often than not utterly irrelevant. Another example is the way in which models of grammars have been introduced in linguistics. The earliest models of language dealt with sequences of grammatical categories, i.e. they formalized sentence forms where each word is replaced by its grammatical category. Such models succeeded in capturing in a natural way gross positional features such as the place of articles and adjectives on the left of their noun. Owing to its conceptual simplicity, this model has been repeatedly introduced under different names. It might be proper to call it the Markovian model, since its essential ingredients were introduced by Markov to study phonetic sequences. Such crude models do not go very far. At a more refined level, phrase structure models directly reflect the grammatical analyses taught in high school. N. Chomsky 1957 formalized them under the name of context-free grammars and demonstrated some of their fundamental inadequacies on the basis of carefully selected examples. In fact, as early as 1952, Z.S. Harris had proposed transformational grammars, which constituted a vast improvement over the Markovian and phrase structure models. But again, any of these types of grammar can be shown to have its validity restricted to the description of the linear order of words or grammatical categories with rather simple dependencies holding between them. Detailed attempts of systematic applications have revealed an endless number of subclasses of exceptions, each of them require a special treatment.

Short range constraints between words in sentences are crudely accounted for by Markovian models. But since Chomsky's mathematical proof of the inadequacy of the models (N. Chomsky 1956, M. Gross 1972), they have been totally neglected, and the interest has shifted to the essential problems of long range constraints between words and phrases.

An exception is the model of W. Woods 1970, which, however has not been used to attempt a full scale analysis of the language. This is precisely our present programme. It could be viewed as an attempt to revive the Markovian model, but this would be wrong, because previous Markovian models were aimed at giving a global description of a language, whereas the model we advocate, and which we call it finite-state for short, is of a strictly local nature. In this perspective, the global nature of language results from the interaction of a multiplicity of local finite-state schemes which we call finite-state local automata.

Our goal we repeat is very specifically to account for all the possible sentences within a given corpus, and this, with no exception. The apparent obstruction evoked above to the realization of such a programme is avoided by the complexity of the various automata necessary for the description of the corpus. Examples will show what we mean by this admittedly loose presentation. It turns out that the long range constraints are taken care of automatically, so to say, by the interaction of the automata within the complete structured schema. We will see that these individual automata can be reused to describe other corpora. This is somewhat similar to the way small molecules combine to produce much larger ones in organic chemistry. To start with, we give elementary examples where the finite constraints can be exhaustively described in a local way, that is, without interferences from the rest of the grammar.

Consider some examples of adverbs. The following sentence form, where an adverb and an elementary sentence are combined, is not accepted:

(1)　　* *Democratically, Bob is authoritarian*

but the same form with an adjunction to the same adverb is accepted:

(2)　　*Democratically speaking, Bob is authoritarian*

Many adverbs derived from adjectives are systematically accepted in the left context of *speaking* and of no other forms. The same adverbs are forbidden in the context of *saying, calling, talking*, although such words are morphologically and semantically similar to *speaking*. Alongside these productive forms, we observe combinations that are considered as frozen, such as:

(3)　　*(broadly + generally + roughly) speaking*

These two phenomena are clearly of a finite-state nature.

Another analogous phenomenon involving adverbial contexts is found in the pairs:

(4)　　*(Stupidly + Surprisingly), Bob drank his beer*
(5)　　*(Stupidly + Surprisingly) enough, Bob drank his beer*

The word *enough* optionally modifies some adverbs in a constrained way. For example, the combination is forbidden with the adverbs *initially, actually*, etc. We also observe frozen combinations such as *sure enough, true enough*. Representing such families of constraints by finite automata is quite natural.

In the same way, a noun phrase such as an *English speaking student* can be generalized in the following way:

- in the position of *English* one finds the name of any language,

- in the position of *student* any human noun may occur, whether nouns of individuals (e.g. *child, grocer*) or of groups (e.g. *Parliament*),

- the word *speaking* is obligatory; neighbouring words such as *talking*, *discussing* are not allowed.

Once the nouns of the lexicon of the langage have been classified by features such as: **Language**[1], **Human**, **HumanGroup**, the combinatorial productivity of these phrases is captured by a simple finite automaton in a most natural fashion.

We have grouped these three examples in Figure 11.1.

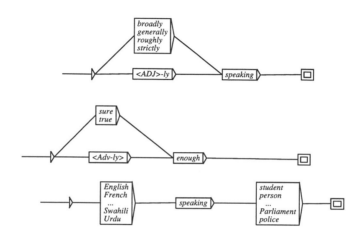

Figure 11.1: Three adverbials.

---

[1]This category should be subdivided in **Modern Languages** and **Ancient Languages** (no longer spoken).

Notations:

1. The *graphs* of Figure 11.1 represent finite-state automata. Each has one initial state (left-most arrow) and one final state (right-most square). This representation has been devised in order to facilitate the effective construction of grammars by linguists.[2] It departs from classical representations in that states are not overtly represented: the nodes are not the states, there is no symbol for them. Arrows are labelled by the alphabet of the automaton, that is English words and/or their grammatical categories. The notation $<N:Hum;s>$ corresponds to any human noun (**Hum**) in the singular (**s**), $<E>$ is the null string. A word between angle brackets corresponds to all the members of its inflectional class: $<a>$ corresponds to the variant articles *a* and *an*. Inflected words and grammatical categories are defined by an electronic dictionary (EDELA) of about 50,000 entries (simple words), inflected in a set of about 100,000 words with their grammatical attributes. To avoid multiplying parallel paths with words having identical roles, labels are grouped in boxes, hence a box of *n* words labels *n* arrows in the classical representation. Shaded boxes contain subautomata that are called into the graph by their name.

2. *Structures*. We note sentence patterns in the following way: N_0 V N_1 *Prep* N_2 represents the structure subject-verb-two complements; the N_is are noun phrases. But in the graphs, phrase boundaries are not always marked. One way of formalizing phrases is by describing them in separate automata, which requires attributing a name to each automaton, hence to the corresponding phrases. This name is used in the automata where the phrase occurs. The unit of description is the sentence, and as a first step, declarative simple sentences, i.e. the sentence forms subject-verb-complement(s). We will discuss their transformational equivalence.

We will describe here a more complex example than those in Figure 11.1 and we will use it to show how a general method of representation can be developed for precise and complex data. The corpus we have chosen is the description of the activity of a Stock Exchange, as reported daily in newspapers. The texts are short and they seem to be repetitive, using fixed phrases that recur constantly, differing only in numerical variations.

Such a point of departure is highly subjective. Firstly the choice of the domain is completely semantic and secondly, it is determined by the intuition that the set of expressions is restricted, perhaps closed. The perusal of texts, over a period of several months, has given the impression that the vocabulary,

---

[2]M. Silberztein 1993 has written a graph editor for this purpose: FSGRAPH.

the constructions and the style of the domain are limited. Such a hypothesis needs to be verified carefully, and can only be confirmed experimentally. After all, it might be the case that the family of texts considered special contain in fact all the sentences of English. Namely, the general sentences of the language appear rarely, but by accumulating them, albeit slowly, the whole of English would be covered. We did not perform any a priori study, consisting for example in building the lexicon of a series of texts and comparing them chronologically. Instead, we decided to analyze syntactically the sentences and the phrases of the texts and to classify them in order to fit the representation. Once these local grammars are built, it is easy to use them to parse the texts and to verify their rate of success.[3]

11.2   Linguistic Modules

Typical sentences dealt with are the following:

(6)   *Advancing issues outnumbered decliners, 1,016 to 861*
(7)   *The Dow Jones Industrial Average fell 15.40 points Friday*
(8)   *The Dow Jones industrial average closed below 4,000*

It is clear that (6) on the one hand and (7)-(8) on the other describe entirely different facts. Hence, they will be described by disjoint local grammars. Such separations are crucial in the sense they allow a modular construction of the grammar of the field. In this case, the separation is obvious, but we will see that in other situations, one must introduce both semantic and syntactic criteria to obtain separations. Moreover, ergonomic limitations such as the size of computer screens also intervene as boundary conditions in the effective construction of local grammars.

11.2.1   Example 1

In Figure 11.2, we give a local grammar of the sentences that are used to express the meaning of (6). The graph contains independent modules which we discuss now.

Module 1. The shaded right-most box is called AdvUnchanged. It represents an embedded local grammar that describes phrases such as:

(9)   *with 230 stocks left unchanged*

---

[3]M. Silberzstein's FSGRAPH program incorporates a generator that provides a parser for each graph. D. Maurel 1990 has written an extensive f.-s. grammar for time adverbials. E. Roche 1993 has built general parsers for full sentences and E. Laporte has used related transducers to resolve various types of ambiguity.

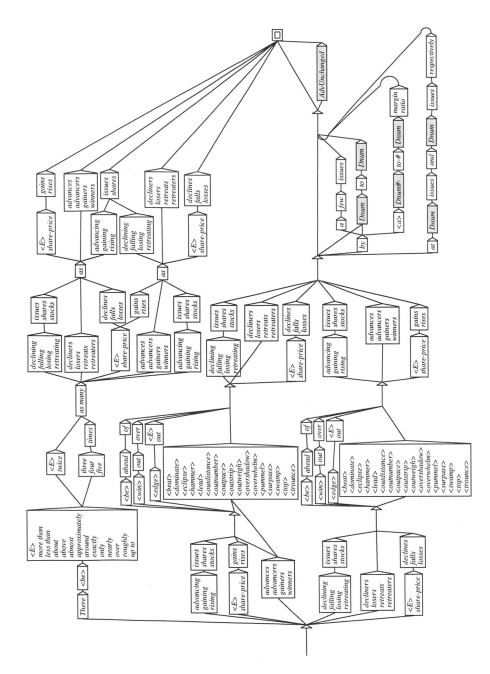

Figure 11.2: IssuesTop.

We provide this subgrammar in Figure 11.3.

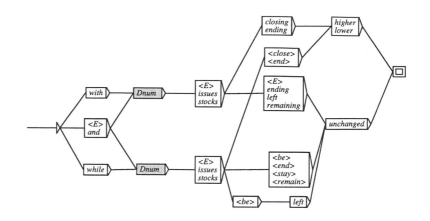

Figure 11.3: AdvUnchanged.

Module 2. In the right lower part, we have another subgrammar, which is clearly isolated by arrows corresponding to empty (flattened) nodes of the automaton. For example, the forms represented are the adverb or apposition:

(10) *Dnum to Dnum* specified as: *1,016 to 861*

Both shaded boxes Dnum represent an automaton of numerals in two forms, digits as above or literal as in:

(11) *one thousand and sixteen to eight hundred and sixty one*

Module 3. The upper part of the graph is occupied by sentences of the form There are X:

(12) *There are twice as many decliners as advances*

In these sentences, the numerical information is given by a comparative expression. Note that other sentences should be added to this subgrammar, namely other comparative sentences of the type:

(13) *There were (more + less) decliners than advances*

Module 4. The lower left-most part contains the core of sentences (6). They all have the syntactic form: subject-verb-complement, noted $N_0 V N_1$ for the exact structure of (6), and $N_0 V Prep N_1$ for the three prepositional cases given in separate boxes. Modules 1 and 2 are adverbials that can be added to these structures. They provide precise numbers, whereas numerical information was rounded in the *There are* sentences. This is a feature we will observe in other situations.

The constructions are symmetrical, in the sense that subjects and objects are identical from a morpho-syntactic point of view. Some are simple words: *decliners*, *winners*, others are compound nouns, more or less elliptical: *declining shares* vs. *share-price declines*. All are in the plural. Identical phrases are observed in module 3. Semantically, these phrases are separated into two groups: **Share-prices which gain** and **Share-prices which lose**. This description results from a decision taken about incorporating semantics into the grammar. As a consequence, the subgrammar is composed of two independent submodules, one for each sentence group:

(14) *Decliners topped advancers*
(15) *Advancers topped decliners*

The same is true in module 3, except that a common part *There are ...* is factored out to the left.[4]

We could have decided to limit ourselves to a syntactic description, ignoring the two semantic types. In this case, we would have considered only one type of phrase, in which would be grouped *advances* and *decliners* in the same distributional class; the content of this class would then appear both in the subject and complement positions. On the one hand, this representation is more economical since there is no longer any need for distinct submodules. On the other hand, a unique module such as this generates forms of the type:

(16) *Decliners topped decliners*
(17) *Decliners topped share-price losses*

which are forbidden as nonsensical. An often-heard argument in favor of the limitation of the description to strict syntactic data consists in claiming that forms such as (16)-(17) will never occur in texts, hence will not have to be recognized by a parser. We oppose this stand for two reasons:

- forms such a (16)-(17) may indeed be found when, in the process of parsing a sentence, systematic hypotheses about the words and phrases of the sentence are made;

- the local grammars we build are neutral with respect to the parsing and synthesizing of sentences. For sentence generation, a grammar where all paths are meaningful is certainly easier to use.

However, the semantic adjustment we have just argued for is not sufficient, for there are syntactic differences. In each of the two semantic groups we have

---

[4]Notice that the situation is similar in module 4 where the adverbials are right factors common to both submodules.

distinguished three separate types of nouns: simple nouns (e.g. *decliners*) and compounds of two types: *share price declines* and *declining shares*. This last type of compound has the pronominal form *declining ones* which is allowed in complement positions only when the subject is one of the two compound forms:

(18) *Declining shares topped advancing ones*
(19) **(Decliners + declines) topped advancing ones*

Hence, we cannot simply add *ones* to the boxes which contain *issues, shares, stocks* in complement positions, in which case the grammar would generate (19). To adjust this subject-object dependency, we have to duplicate the four corresponding subgraphs, doubling the size of this local grammar. We must realize that the size of the computer screen is such that a duplication of the given graph cannot 'physically' be performed: two separate graphs (with two names) will be needed. At this point, we would separate the *There are* sentences from the other type.

11.2.2   Example 2

Our second example is a grammar of the sentences that express the variations of a Stock Exchange Index, say one of the Dow Jones indexes. Examples of sentences indicating positive and negative variations are:

(20) *The Dow Jones industrial average (gained + lost) 15.40 points at 3,398.37*
(21) *The Dow Jones Industrial average finished with a (gain + loss)*
(22) *The Dow Jones Industrial average broke an all-time record of 5,000 points*

The sentences present common syntactic features:

(i)   the subject is an **Index**: (cf. Figures 11.5-11.6-11.7),
(ii) a verb (Figure 11.4) or a verbal phrase (Figure 11.8) expresses the direction of the variation,
(iii) two complements contain numerals which provide:

- a relative variation, namely the difference with the previous quotation day: 15.40 in (8). The variation is always a positive number, the sign being expressed by the verb,

- and then, the full value of the Index: 3,398.37 or 5,000.

In (21), the complement of relative variation (**RelChange**)[5] is obligatory, and the complement of Index value is optional. In (20), both complements are optional.

A full description of these sentences requires at lest 50 graphs corresponding to different sentence types. We will discuss here the two types given in Figures 11.4 and 11.8.

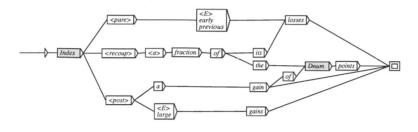

Figure 11.4: NVNUp.

Let us comment on some of the features of these graphs.

11.2.2.1 Subjects

The box **Index** may be filled by any index name from any stock market. In the Figures 11.5-11.6-11.7, we give the names of the main indexes used in New York City, London and Tokyo. These graphs are typical of compound nouns, whether technical terms or proper names. Such utterances have abbreviations of various types: acronyms, omission of parts, and they also have lexical variants, either limited to parts of the term or morphemically unrelated synonyms. Finite automata represent these variations in a natural way. Note that, depending on the content of the automaton, we may want to name them grammars or lexicons. Beyond the representation of strings, incorporation into the same automaton constitutes a statement of equivalence for these strings. In many cases, semantic equivalence is the natural relation that holds between the strings and at the same time, it is the most useful relation for our descriptive program. However, there is leeway for refinements linked to the discussion above (see Section 11.2.1, Module 4) about the amount of semantics we want to include in graphs, under the general proviso that finite-state models are appropriate.

We shall consider the various numerals involved. **Dnum** is the name of the graph that describes numerals. The numerical value of an index is given by the variable **Dnum** appearing in six shaded boxes with the same interpretation. **Dnum** has already been used in Figure 11.2 and in Figure 11.3

---

[5]This subgraph corresponds to forms such as *15.40 points or 0.50 %*, etc.

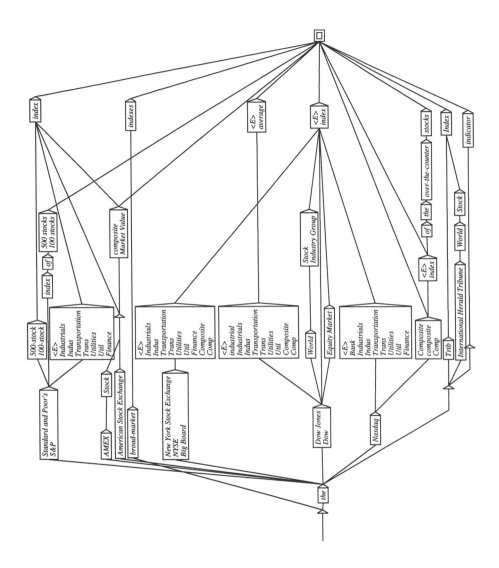

Figure 11.5: IndexNY.

(cf. Section 11.2.1 Module 2), but there, **Dnum** corresponds to numbers of
stock names and as such, ranges between a few units and the thousands.[6]

---

[6]This number depends on the number of issues quoted in each stock market.

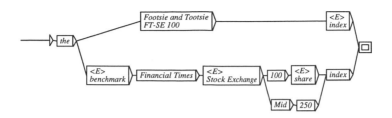

Figure 11.6: IndexLondon.

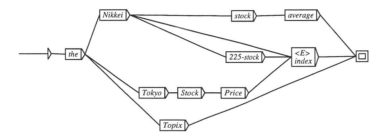

Figure 11.7: IndexTokyo.

When **Dnum** corresponds to volumes of trading (i.e. number of shares sold), it ranges in the millions, and when **Dnum** corresponds to the Dow Jones Average, numerals oscillate around the 4.000 (in 1995), whereas the FST index and the Nikkei have different ranges. The grammar **Dnum** covers all of these numbers, the question is then whether we want to adjust the numerals to the terms they bear on.

The solution given in Figure 11.4 consists in having a unique graph **Index**, which is a union of the various Exchange graphs. Since the numerical range of all the indexes is wide, the general grammar **Dnum** covers all cases, except that numerals in the millions are not relevant. A different solution consists in having as many graphs of the type of Figure 11.4 as there are indexes and in using one specific grammar of numerals for each index (e.g. **DnumNikkei** for **IndexTokyo**). This dilemma has no solution within present linguistic and formal frameworks. The choice may depend on applications (e.g. for banks, for brokers) and will vary accordingly.

Another way of discussing this issue is in terms of the modularity of the subgraphs. Adjusting numerals to indexes amounts to introducing constraints

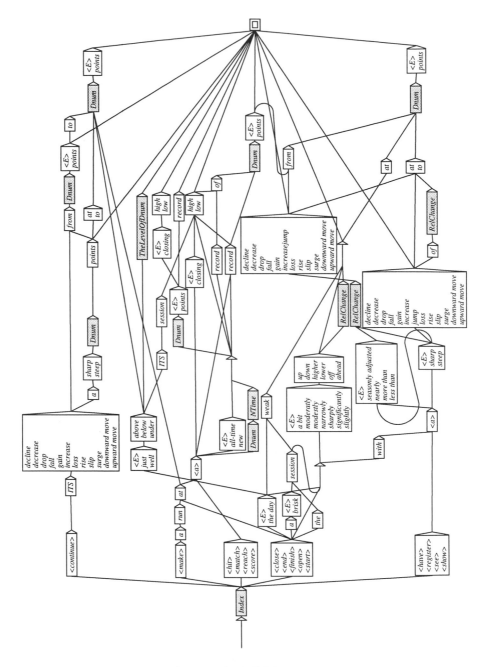

Figure 11.8: NVNUpDown.

between the box **Index** and the boxes **Dnum**. These constraints are superimposed on the existing paths that link these boxes, but they are independent of these paths. If we represent them directly, we change the formal method of representation (e.g. to graphs with colored edges), and this goes beyond the natural use of the finite-state model. In the other solutions evoked, we use a different method for representing the constraint:

- in the solution of Figure 11.4, all shaded boxes are independent; no fine-tuning of the numerals is performed,

- in the solution where we refine the lexicons involved (i.e. lexicons of indexes and lexicons of numerals), subgraphs such as **IndexTokyo** and **DnumNikkei** become autonomous, that is, the modularity of the various components is preserved.

Finally, let us mention another solution for this adjustment problem. We could describe the combinations index-numerals as free at the syntactic level, which is roughly what we have done in Figure 11.4. The adjustment of the numerals would be treated in a separate semantic component. We hinted at this solution for the percentage numerals by appending a subscript: < 100. In this case, the variation range is $0 < \mathbf{Dnum} < 100$. Such information could be either 'manually' introduced into the graph or in some cases constructed from the context (i.e. the paths involving the box **Dnum**). Then a separate component of the system would use this indication to restrict **Dnum** to the relevant range of variation.

11.2.2.2   Verbs

In principle, the verbs appearing in Figure 11.4 are polarized, indicating an upward movement of the index. This semantic feature often has a syntactic consequence, for sentences without any complement informally indicate the trend, as in:

(23)   *The Dow Jone (advanced + jumped + grew)*

as opposed to verbs indicating the opposite trend:

(24)   *The Dow Jones (slid + declined + slumped)*

In Figure 11.4, complements are adverbials, close to locatives; in a sense they are not essential whereas in Figure 11.8, they are similar to objects and the verbs are not polarized.

11.2.2.3 Complements

The growth of the index is made explicit in complements which provide a numerical value of the index:

(25)   *The Dow Jones advanced to 3,425 points*

This minimal information is often enhanced by recalling the former value of the index; various forms can then be used:

(26)   *The Dow Jones advanced from 3,213 to 3,425 points*
(27)   *The Dow Jones advanced to 3,425 points up from 3,213*

Other complements or parts of these numerical complements are more stylistic than informative. For example, nouns such as *level, peak, record* or *psychologically important high* are classifiers for the numerical value of the index. They are semantically redundant, and as a consequence (Z.S. Harris 1988) can be zeroed in certain contexts.

The graph of Figure 11.4 contains additional information:

- relative changes, including percentages of variation, which indicate indirectly the value of the index on the previous quotation day (cf. 1.2.1);

- time indication of duration: the subautomaton **AdjTime** corresponds to phrases such as *six week* (e.g. *a six week record high*), indication of date: the subautomaton (i.e. lexicon) **Day's** contains the five working days of the week (e.g. *from Tuesday's close*).

11.2.3   Verbal compounds

The graph of Figure 11.8 named **NVNUpDown** corresponds to sentences describing both upward and downward movements of an index. The motivation for having such a graph distinct from the graph of Figure 11.4 is both syntactic and semantic: the verbs in figure 4 all carry a meaning of directed movement. In Figure 11.8, the same movements are expressed by combinations of verbs and complements and the verbs by themselves are not polarized. For example in:

(28)   *The Dow Jones hit a new (high + low)*

the verb *hit* does not carry any information, it is the nouns *high* and *low* that are significant.This situation is common with support verb constructions (M. Gross 1994) introduced in the nominalizations of verbs as in:

(29)   *to (have + register + show) a (decline + gain + loss + ...)*

(30) $= to\ (decline + gain + lose + ...\ )$

or with support verbs and stand-alone nouns as in:

(31)   *to (hit + reach) a record*

Most of these verbal compounds take the same numerical complements as those of simple verbs. There are however a few differences:

- with simple verbs, numerical complements are all of an adverbial type;

- in support constructions the numerical complement sometimes becomes a noun complement of the supported noun:

(32)   *The Dow Jones hit a record high of 4.000 points*

The subgrammar of Figure 11.9 bears similarities to that of Figure 11.8 with respect to localization of meaning. The meaning of variation is even less localized in Figure 11.9, for it is given by metaphorical and idiomatic expressions:

(33)   *The Dow Jones ended on a firm note*
(34)   *The Dow Jones gathered steam*

The sentences we have listed are all different, except for a few variations for a small group. Most of them can receive additional information, for example the general numerical appositions:

(35)   *The Dow Jones ended on a firm note, at 3,425 points up 1 % from 3,213*

Such examples hint at the definition of a numerical module which would appear in several graphs, avoiding duplication. But it should be noticed that two very similar modules of this kind may be needed:

- one for upward movements:

(36) *The Dow Jones advanced to 3,425 points up from 3,213*
(37) **The Dow Jones advanced to 3,213 points up from 3,425*

- one for downward movements:

(38) *The Dow Jones fell to 3,213 points, down from 3,425*
(39) **The Dow Jones fell to 3,425 points, down from 3,213*

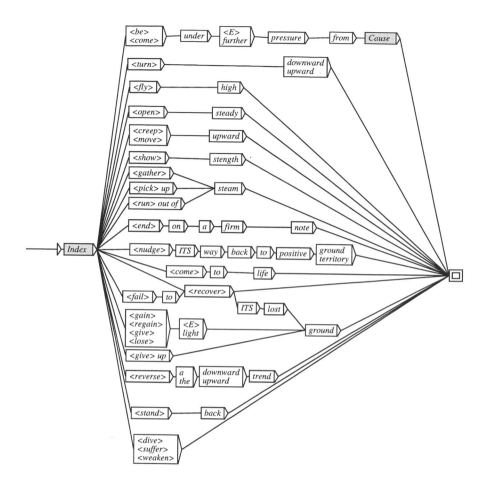

Figure 11.9: NVNUpDownIdiomatic.

The adjustment realized by these modules is semantic; the two values of the index have to be ordered correctly. But a lexical feature is also involved, for the adverbs *down* and *up* depend on the verbs:

(40)   *The Dow Jones advanced to 3,425 points, down from (3,213 + 3,645)

Some verbs are not polarized (*to stay*, *to trade*) and accept both complements. They are described in a different graph. In Figure 11.10, we describe

a non polarized range of variations expressed by an adverbial complement
BetweenPoints, as in:

(41) *The Dow Jones hovered between 3,213 and 3,425 points*
(42) *The Dow Jones hovered between 3,425 and 3,213 points*

where both constructions, with reversed order of the numerals, are accepted.
Hence there is no need here for an arithmetical constraint between the two
values. Polarized complements are of a similar type and share many of the
components of this family of phrases.

11.2.4 Practical limitations

When constructing local grammars, the complexity of the graphs of Figures 11.2, 11.4 and 11.8 is maximal, from an ergonomic viewpoint:

- first, the format of the screen of the graph editor does not allow many
  more boxes,

- second, the complexity of the chains of elements is high, to the point
  where the linguist[7] who builds the graph becomes prone to errors.

These practical limitations can be overcome is various ways:

- by using larger computer screens and appropriate software;

- paths in Figure 11.4 are composed of straight segments. Hence the
  reading of a sentence from the initial state to the final state is kept left-
  to-right, that is, natural. The graph editor allows right-to-left reading of
  paths, as in Figure 11.8. It then becomes possible to lengthen the paths,
  and at the same time more dependencies may be introduced, adding to
  the perceptual complexity of the graph.[8]

As a general solution to these problems, we use several techniques:

- firstly, we systematically have recourse to modularity, that is, to **semantically** defined subgraphs which are embedded into a graph, and then
  occupy one small box of the graph;

---

[7]Grammars should not be individual pieces of work. Their construction is sufficiently explicit
to allow specialists other than the author to use and modify graphs.

[8]Of course, in the case of loops, right-to-left reading is a necessity.

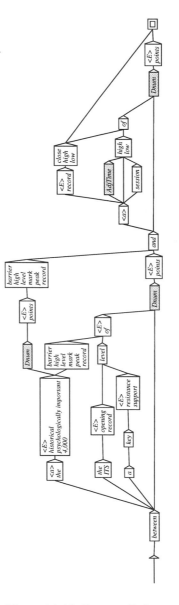

Figure 11.10: BetweenPoints

- secondly, we divide the sets of utterances according to **syntactic** criteria. We then construct separate subgrammars for specific syntactic forms.[9]

---

[9]Since different syntactic forms may involve different lexical items, the separation of graphs should also be viewed as based on lexical criteria.

In Section 11.2.3, we discussed examples of this approach,

- thirdly, we attempt to draw graphs in a way that preserves syntactic similarities between the sentences of the graph. For example, sentences are mostly analyzed into sequences of categories such as:

  - *Determiner* followed by a *Noun*, (for the subject)
  - *Verb*
  - *Preposition, Determiner* followed by a *Noun*, (for the complements)

Nouns can be modified on their left or on their right. Since most sentences contain these basic elements, we attempt to place them in the same vertical zones. Although such zones are not materially indicated in the graph, they can be clearly observed for verbs and for some complements in most of our examples. Such a display, when feasible, introduces linguistic clarity for the dependencies among the various parts.

Not totally independent of such attempts is a more subjective notion of elegance or beauty of the graph. It is based on local and global symmetries, sometimes those of classical typography. For example, we avoid cutting boxes by arrows, and in general, we try to reduce the number of intersections of paths. In some cases, such results are achieved through the use of empty nodes whose only function is to redirect paths outside of an encumbered area of the graph. In other situations, we duplicated certain paths to avoid a web of intersecting arrows going to one area of the graph. These procedures are uneconomical in terms of number of states[10], but general algorithms of determinization and minimization can be applied to these redundant graphs in order to provide compact forms for use by parsers.

Graphs possessing the qualities discussed are definitely more readable and easier to maintain.

11.3 Transformations

Many transformations affect word order. Finite automata can compactly represent sets of strings that differ by variant substrings including the null variant, but they cannot well represent pairs of strings that differ by a permutation. In other terms, the two substrings uv and vu of the strings $AuvB$ and $AvuB$ have to be considered as totally distinct, hence represented by two different

---

[10]A general way of representing the ambiguity of a given string is by generating it through as many different paths as there are meanings, very much in the way constitutent trees are used. Duplicating paths prevents the use of this convention.

paths with common factors A and B. This observation has consequences for the description of sentence forms.

In some cases, duplications are not costly. For example, in Figure 11.8 we had to duplicate paths that include boxes with the nouns: *decline, ... , upward move*, because of variants such as:

(43)   *a 3 % decline, a decline of 3 %*

The situation is different for inserts, that is adverbials and sentential inserts such as: *at the end of the session, as it seemed* or *as confirmed by Federal authorities*. Given the syntactic form:

(44) N_0 *Aux V* N_1 *Prep* N_2

that is, a typical sentence form with an auxiliary and two complements, most inserts may occur either at the beginning or at the end of the sentence, or at any of the four spaces separating the constituents:

(45)   **Without any reason,** *the Dow Jones has lost 100 points at 3.000*
(46)   *The Dow Jones,* **without any reason,** *has lost 100 points at 3.000*
(47)   *The Dow Jones has,* **without any reason,** *lost 100 points at 3.000*
      etc.

One way of handling this situation is by making six copies of the sub-grammar (e.g. **NVNUpDown**) corresponding to (44) and by introducing a box **Insert** in each of the six mentioned positions. Since these six subgrammars are semantically and syntactically equivalent, they could be put in the same graph. Merging these graphs does not have to be a trivial union, for common parts exist that can be factorized out, for example, as in Figure 11.11.

Passive forms are another example of the problems raised by the representation of permitted forms. The following sentence is a Passive transform of one of the active sentences of Figure 11.8:

(48)   *An all-time record of 4,000 points was reached by the Dow Jones Index*

One of the problems we have to solve is the systematic derivation of Passive forms from active ones. The transformational rule:

(49) N_0 *V Prep* N_1 = N_1 *be Vpp Prep by* N_0 (with *Prep* possibly zero)

is not general, and its application depends on the lexical choice of *V* and on the nature of *Prep* N_1. Hence, it does not seem possible to construct a Passive graph automatically from an Active one such as the graph of Figure 11.8, which contains well-identified complements, that is a priori passivizable forms. However, the sentences with main verb *to have, to register* behave differently:

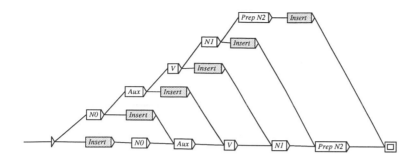

Figure 11.11: SInsert.

(50) *A steep decline was had by the Dow Jones*
(51) *A steep decline was registered by the Dow Jones*

With the sentences of the type:

(52) *The Dow Jones continued its fall*

the situation is more complex because of the pronoun ITS obligatorily coreferent to the subject. Passive forms are all unacceptable:

(53) *Its fall was continued*

Note that the Middle transformation that also brings the object into the subject position is allowed, but only if the pronoun is replaced by its source:

(54) *The fall of the Dow Jones continued*

As a consequence of the numerous irregularities observed, the only possibility is to build the graph of the Passive forms 'by hand'. This observation is true for all unary transformations.

By definition, the unary transformations are those that preserve an invariant of meaning. In this respect, a sentence and its transforms belong to the same class of equivalence (Z.S. Harris 1968). We can construct this class by taking the union of the corresponding automata, say Active, Passive and Middle. Among others, a subclass that needs to be added to this class should be mentioned. The sentences described in Figure 11.8 and 11.9 are semantically simple. Alongside them there exist similar sentences of a higher complexity: the corresponding causative sentences. For example, associated with:

(55)   *The Dow Jones moved up to a record 4,000 points*

we find the sentence with a causative subject:

(56)   *The fall of interest rates sent the Dow Jones up to a record 4,000 points*

This sentence has a passive form, where the agent can be omitted, yielding:

(57)   *The Dow Jones was sent up to a record 4,000 points*

This is a sentence equivalent to (55), that is, which will have to belong to the same class as (55).

These remarks show that the coverage of a local grammar for an initially simple notion may become considerable. But at the same time, it should be clear that many of the modules built for such a special purpose will be of use in a general grammar.

11.4   Conclusion

For obvious reasons, grammarians and theoreticians have always attempted to describe the general features of sentences. This tendency has materialized in sweeping generalizations intended to facilitate language teaching and recently to construct mathematical systems. But beyond these generalities lies an extremely rigid set of dependencies between individual words, which is huge in size; it has been accumulated over the millenia by language users, piece by piece, in micro areas such as those we began to analyze here. We have studied elsewhere what we call the lexicon-grammar of free sentences. The lexicon-grammar of French is a description of the argument structure of about 12,000 verbs. Each verbal entry has been marked for the transformations it accepts (J.-P. Boons, A. Guillet, C. Leclère 1976; A. Guillet, C. Leclère 1992; M. Gross 1975, 1994). It has been shown that every verb had a unique syntactic paradigm. The lexicon-grammar has been extended to frozen sentences, that is, to sentences with at least one constant argument (e.g. the idiomatic form: *N take the bull by the horns* has two constant arguments). We have shown that the lexicon-grammar of frozen sentences is several times larger than the one for free sentences: so far it covers 25,000 idiomatic-like sentences and it is far from having the coverage the lexicon-grammar of free forms has. Moreover, we exclude from this count an even larger number of sentences with main verbs *être* (to be), *avoir* (to have, to get), *faire* (to do, to make).

What we have presented here is the natural generalization of lexicon-grammar. The enormity of the number of dependencies between words is itself a compelling reason to consider the sort of fixed-string free-slot theory that finite-state local grammars suggest. Most of all, the notion of local grammar constitutes a generalization of the notion of equivalence classes of transformed sentences and allows the practical construction of classes of semantically equivalent utterances. We leave to another discussion the implications for theoretical linguistics of the need, and hopefully, of the validity of such a model.

Acknowledgements

I am indebted to Morris Salkoff and M.-P. Schützenberger for important suggestions that improved this article.

References

Boons Jean-Paul, Guillet Alain, Leclère Christian. 1976. *La structure des phrases simples en français: Les verbes intransitifs*. Droz: Geneva.

Chomsky, Noam. 1956. Three models for the description of language. *IRE Transactions on Information Theory*, IT-2, pp.113-124.

Gross Maurice. 1972. *Mathematical Methods in Linguistics*. Englewood Ciffs N.J.: Prentice Hall Inc., 159 p.

Gross, Maurice. 1975. *Méthodes en syntaxe*. Paris: Hermann, 412 p.

Gross, Maurice. 1994. Constructing Lexicon-Grammars. In B.T.S. Atkins and A. Zampolli, editors, *Computational Approaches to the Lexicon*. Oxford: Oxford University Press, pp. 213-263.

Guillet Alain, Leclère Christian. 1992. *La structure des phrases simples en français: constructions transitives locatives*. Droz: Geneva.

Harris, Zellig. 1968. *Mathematical Structures of Language*. New York: Interscience Publishers, John Wiley and Sons, 230 p.

Harris, Zellig. 1988. *Language and Information*. New York: Columbia University Press, 119 p.

Laporte, Eric. 1994. Experiments in Lexical Disambiguation Using Local Grammars. In *Papers in Computational Lexicography (COMPLEX)*. Budapest: Research Institute for Linguistics, Hungarian Academy of Sciences, pp.163-172.

Maurel, Denis. 1990. Adverbes de date: étude préliminaire à leur traitement automatique. *Lingvisticae Investigationes*, XIV:1, Amsterdam-Philadelphia: J. Benjamins Pub. Co., pp. 31-63.

Roche, Emmanuel. 1993. Une représentation par automate fini des textes et des propriétés transformationnelles des verbes. *Lingvisticae Investigationes*, XVII:1, Amsterdam-Philadelphia: J. Benjamins Pub. Co., pp. 189-222.

Silberztein, Max. 1993. *Dictionnaires électroniques et analyse automatique de textes: le système INTEX*. Paris: Masson, 233 p.

Woods, W.A. 1970. Transition network grammars for natural language. *CACM*, 13(10), pp. 591-606.

12 On the Use of Sequential Transducers in Natural Language Processing

Mehryar Mohri

Finite-state machines have been used in various domains of natural language processing. We here consider the use of a type of transducers that supports very efficient programs: deterministic or sequential transducers. We recall classic theorems and give new ones characterizing the class of sequential transducers. We then examine several areas of computational linguistics. For each, we briefly describe and discuss the advantages offered by these transducers: they allow very high speed performance and they can be minimized by algorithms we describe and illustrate.

12.1 Introduction

The use of finite-state machines in language processing is very natural and can be justified by both linguistic and computational arguments. Indeed, linguistically, the use of finite automata is very convenient since they allow one to describe easily most of the relevant local phenomena encountered in the empirical study of language. They often provide a compact representation of lexical rules or idioms and clichés which appears as natural to linguists (Gross, 1989; Gross, 1991). Graphic tools also allow one to visualize and modify automata. This helps in correcting and completing a grammar. Other more general phenomena such as parsing context-free or context-sensitive grammars can also be dealt with using finite-state machines. Moreover, the underlying mechanisms in most of the methods used in parsing are related to automata.

From the computational point of view, the use of finite-state machines is mainly motivated by considerations of time and space efficiency. Time efficiency is usually achieved by using deterministic automata. The output of deterministic machines depends, in general linearly, only on the input size and can therefore be considered as optimal from this point of view. Space efficiency is achieved with classical minimization algorithms (Aho, Hopcroft, and Ullman, 1974; Revuz, 1991) for deterministic automata. Applications such as compiler construction have shown deterministic finite-state automata to be very efficient in practice (Aho, Sethi, and Ullman, 1986; Perrin, 1990).

We shall here extend the use of deterministic automata to deterministic transducers, that is machines that produce output strings in addition to accepting (deterministically) input. Thus, we shall describe methods consistent with the initial reasons for using finite-state machines, in particular the time efficiency of deterministic machines, and the space efficiency achievable with a new minimization algorithm for deterministic transducers.

Both time and space concerns are important when dealing with language. Indeed, one of the trends which clearly come out of new studies of language is a large increase in the size of data. Lexical approaches have shown to be the most appropriate in many areas of computational linguistics ranging from large-scale dictionaries in morphology to large lexical grammars in syntax. The effect of the size increase on time and space efficiency is probably the main computational problem one needs to face in language processing.

The use of finite-state machines in natural language processing is certainly not new. Limitations of the corresponding techniques, however, are very often pointed out more than their advantages. In the following, we shall briefly consider several areas of computational linguistics and show that not only sequential transducers can be used to perform all of the computational tasks needed in those areas but also that they often achieve those tasks very efficiently. In order to help the reader become familiar with sequential machines, we start with an extended description of these devices and several mathematical characterizations.

12.2   Definitions

12.2.1   Sequential transducers

We consider here *sequential* transducers, namely transducers with a deterministic input. At any state of such transducers, at most one arc is labeled with a given element of the alphabet. Figure 12.1 gives an example of a sequential transducer. Notice that output labels might be strings. The output of a sequential transducer is not necessarily deterministic. The one in figure 12.1 is not since two distinct arcs with output labels b for instance leave the state 0.

Sequential transducers are computationally very interesting because their

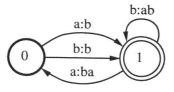

Figure 12.1: Example of a sequential transducer.

use on a given input does not depend on the size of the transducer but only on that of the input. Since that use consists in following the only path corresponding to the input string and in writing consecutive output labels along this path, the total computational time is linear in the size of the input. We here consider that the cost of copying out each output label does not depend on the length of the string label. This can be realized using an appropriate representation of these labels. In fact, a convenient approach consists in representing the set of labels by a weighted acceptor. We will develop this remark in the last section.

More formally, a sequential transducer T is a 7-tuple which can be represented by $(V, i, F, A, B^*, \delta, \sigma)$, where:
- V is the set of states;
- $i \in V$ the initial state;
- $F \subseteq V$ the set of final states;
- A and B finite sets corresponding respectively to the input and output alphabets of the transducer;
- δ the state transition function which maps $V \times A$ to V;
- σ the output function which maps $V \times A$ to B^*.

The functions δ and σ can be extended to map $V \times A^*$, by the following classic recursive relations:
$$\forall s \in V, \forall w \in A^*, \forall a \in A, \quad \delta(s, \epsilon) = s, \delta(s, wa) = \delta(\delta(s, w), a);$$
$$\sigma(s, \epsilon) = \epsilon, \sigma(s, wa) = \sigma(s, w)\sigma(\delta(s, w), a).$$

Thus, a word $w \in A^*$ is accepted by T iff $\delta(i, w) \in F$, and in that case the output of the transducer is $\sigma(i, w)$.

12.2.2 Subsequential and p-subsequential transducers

Sequential transducers can be generalized by introducing the possibility of generating an additional output string at final states (Schützenberger, 1977). The application of the transducer to a string can then possibly end up with the concatenation of such an output string to the usual output. Such transducers are called *subsequential* transducers. Language processing often requires a

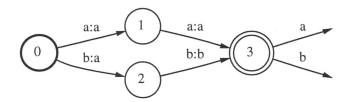

Figure 12.2: Example of 2-subsequential transducer τ_1.

more general extension. Indeed, the ambiguities encountered in language cannot be taken into account using sequential or subsequential transducers. In order to deal with ambiguities one can introduce p-subsequential transducers (Mohri, 1994a), namely transducers provided with at most p additional output strings at each final state. Figure 12.2 gives an example of 2-subsequential transducer. Here the input string $w = aa$ gives two distinct outputs aaa and aab. Since one cannot find any reasonable case in language in which the number of ambiguities would be infinite, p-subsequential transducers seem to be sufficient for describing linguistic ambiguities.

Composition is one of the convenient operations transducers allow. Following the definitions above it is easy to prove the following theorem which shows that the classes of sequential and p-subsequential functions[1] are closed under composition.

Theorem 1 *Let* $f : A^* \rightarrow B^*$ *be a sequential (resp. p-subsequential) and* $g : B^* \rightarrow C^*$ *be a sequential (resp. q-subsequential) function, then* $g \circ f$ *is sequential (resp. pq-subsequential).*

Analogous theorems stand for the union of sequential or p-subsequential transducers. In particular, the union of a p-subsequential function and a q-subsequential function is $(p + q)$-subsequential[2].

Figure 12.3 gives an example of a 1-subsequential or subsequential transducer τ_2. The result of the composition of the transducers τ_1 and τ_2 is shown in figure 12.4. States in the transducer τ_3 correspond to pairs of states of τ_1

---

[1] This last result generalizes the theorems given by Choffrut (1978) and Berstel (1979). We use the expression p-subsequential in two ways here. One means that a finite number of ambiguities is admitted (the closure under composition matches this case), the second indicates that this number equals exactly p.

[2] See (Mohri, 1994c) for a full description of the algorithm permitting one to obtain directly the $(p + q)$-subsequential transducer union of a p-subsequential and a q-subsequential transducer.

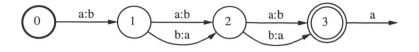

Figure 12.3: Example of a 1-subsequential transducer τ_2.

and τ_2. The composition consists essentially in making the intersection of the outputs of τ_1 with the inputs of τ_2.

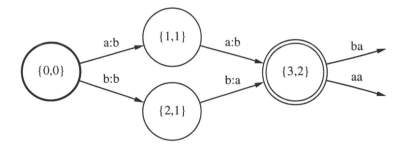

Figure 12.4: 2-Subsequential transducer τ_3, obtained by composition of τ_1 and τ_2.

12.3 Characterization and Extensions

Their linear recognition complexity makes sequential or p-subsequential transducers both mathematically and computationally of particular interest. However, not all rational functions can be represented by these transducers. Consider for instance the function f associated with the classical transducer represented in figure 12.5. f can be defined by[3]:

$$\forall w \in \{x\}^+, \quad f(w) = \quad a^{|w|} \quad if \ |w| \ is \ even, \qquad (12.1)$$
$$= \quad b^{|w|} \quad else$$

This function is not sequential, that is, it cannot be realized by any sequential transducer. Indeed, in order to start writing the output associated with an input string $w = x^n$, a or b according to whether n is even or odd, one needs to finish reading the whole input string w, which can be arbitrarily long. Sequential

---

[3] Here, $|w|$ stands for the length of the string w.

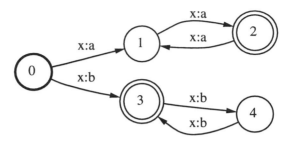

Figure 12.5: Transducer T with no equivalent sequential representation.

functions, namely functions which can be represented by sequential transducers do not allow such unbounded delays. More generally, sequential functions can be characterized among rational functions by the following theorem (Ginsburg and Rose, 1966; Berstel, 1979; Perrin, 1989).

Theorem 2 *Let f be a rational function mapping A^* to B^*. f is sequential iff there exists a positive integer K such that for all u in A^* and a in A:*

$$ua \in Dom(f) \Rightarrow \exists w \in A^*, \ |w| \le K \ and \ f(ua) = f(u)w \quad (12.2)$$

In other words, for any string u and any element of the alphabet a, $f(ua)$ is equal to $f(u)$ concatenated with some bounded string. Notice that this implies that $f(u)$ is always a prefix of $f(ua)$, and more generally that if f is sequential then it preserves prefixes.

The fact that not all rational functions are sequential could reduce the interest of sequential transducers. The following theorem due to Elgot and Mezei (1965) shows however that rational transducers are exactly compositions of left and right sequential transducers.

Theorem 3 *Let f be a partial function mapping A^* to B^*. f is rational iff there exist a right sequential function $r : A^* \to C^*$ and a left sequential function $l : C^* \to B^*$ such that $f = r \circ l$.*

Left sequential functions or transducers are those we previously defined. Their application to a string proceeds from left to right. Right sequential functions apply to strings from right to left. According to the theorem, considering a new sufficiently large alphabet C permits one to define two sequential functions l and r decomposing a rational function f. This result considerably increases the importance of sequential functions in the theory of finite-state machines as well as in the practical use of transducers. Berstel (1979) gives

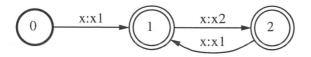

Figure 12.6: Left to right sequential transducer L

an easy and constructive proof of this theorem. Given a finite-state transducer T, one can easily construct a left sequential transducer L and a right sequential transducer R such that $L \circ R = T$. Intuitively, the extended alphabet C keeps track of the local ambiguities encountered when applying the transducer from left to right. A distinct element of the alphabet is assigned to each of these ambiguities. The right sequential transducer can be constructed in such a way that these ambiguities can then be resolved from right to left. Figures 12.6 and 12.7 give a decomposition of the non sequential transducer T of Figure 12.5. The symbols of the alphabet $C = \{x1, x2\}$ store information about the size of the input string w. The output of L ends with $x1$ iff $|w|$ is odd. The right sequential function R is then easy to construct. Sequential transducers offer

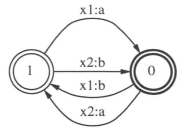

Figure 12.7: Right to left sequential transducer R

other theoretical advantages. In particular, while several important tests such as the equivalence are undecidable with general rational transducers, sequential transducers have the following decidable property.

Theorem 4 *Let T be a transducer mapping A^* to B^*. It is decidable whether T is sequential.*

The proof of this theorem was given by Choffrut (1978). This proof is constructive and can be directly implemented. Other characterizations have been given for subsequential functions by Choffrut (1978). They can be expressed by means of a distance on A^*. Denote by $u \wedge v$ the longest common prefix of two words u and v in A^*. It is easy to verify that the following defines a distance on any free monoïd A^*:

$$d(u, v) = |u| + |v| - 2|u \wedge v| \tag{12.3}$$

The following theorem describes this characterization of subsequential functions.

Theorem 5 *Let f be a partial function mapping A^* to B^*. f is subsequential iff:*
1- f has bounded variation (according to the distance defined above).
2- for any rational subset Y of B^*, $f^{-1}(Y)$ is rational.

The notion of bounded variation[4] can be roughly understood here in the following way: if two words x and y are close enough, namely if the prefix they share is long enough compared to their lengths, then the same is true for their images $f(x)$ and $f(y)$. This theorem can be extended to describe the case of p-subsequential functions by defining a distance d_∞ on $(B^*)^p$. For any $u = (u_1, ..., u_p)$ and $v = (v_1, ..., v_p) \in (B^*)^p$,

$$d_\infty(u, v) = \max_{1 \leq i \leq p} d(u_i, v_i) \tag{12.4}$$

The following generalizes the Choffrut (1978) theorem.

Theorem 6 *Let $f = (f_1, ..., f_p)$ be a partial function mapping A^* to $(B^*)^p$. f is p-subsequential iff:*
1- f has bounded variation (using the distances d on A^* and d_∞ on $(B^*)^p$).
2- for all i ($1 \leq i \leq p$) and any rational subset Y of B^*, $f_i^{-1}(Y)$ is rational.

Indeed, if these conditions hold, then each component f_i ($1 \leq i \leq p$) of f has bounded variation (condition 1). Condition 2 combined with the previous theorem imply then that each f_i is subsequential. One obtains a transducer representing f by making the union of the subsequential transducers representing f_i's. Hence, f is p-subsequential. Conversely, if $f = (f_1, ..., f_p)$ is p-subsequential then each component f_i is subsequential. The previous theorem implies then that 2 is verified. Given the definition of d_∞ the condition 1 is

---

[4]It can be proved that a rational function f has bounded variation iff it is Lipstchizian (Lothaire, 1990).

also verified. A proof of this theorem analogous to that of Choffrut (1978) can be given and this characterization can be used to give a constructive algorithm for determining whether a given transducer is p-subsequential. One can also prove this theorem using the previous one. Indeed, if f is p-subsequential each of its component f_i is clearly subsequential since f_i admits no ambiguity. This implies the condition 2 and that each f_i has bounded variation using the previous theorem. By definition of d_∞, f has bounded variation. Conversely, if the first condition holds, a fortiori each f_i has bounded variation. The second condition implies that each f_i is subsequential. As a union of the p subsequential transducers f_i, f is p-subsequential.

One can also give a characterization of p-subsequential transducers independant from the choice of their components. Let d'_p be the semi-distance defined by:

$$d'_p(u,v) = \max_{1 \le i,j \le p} d(u_i, v_j) \tag{12.5}$$

Then the following theorem can be interesting in practice to prove that a function is p-subsequential.

Theorem 7 *Let f be a rational function mapping A^* to $(B^*)^p$. f is p-subsequential iff it has bounded variation (using the semi-distance d'_p on $(B^*)^p$).*

The proof is an adaptation of Berstel's (1979) for subsequential functions. According to the previous theorem the condition is sufficient since: $\forall (u,v) \in (A^*)^2, d_\infty(u,v) \le d'_p(u,v)$. Conversely if f is p-subsequential, let $T = (V, i, F, A, B^*, \delta, \sigma, \Phi)$ be a p-subsequential transducer representing f, where Φ is the output function mapping V to $(B^*)^p$. Let N and M be defined by:

$$N = \max_{q \in F, 1 \le i,j \le p} |\Phi_i(q)| \ and \ M = \max_{a \in A, q \in V} |\sigma(q,a)| \tag{12.6}$$

Let $k \ge 0$ and $(u_1, u_2) \in [dom(T)]^2$ such that $d(u_1, u_2) \le k$. Then, there exists $u \in A^*$ such that:

$$u_1 = uv_1, \ u_2 = uv_2, \ and \ |v_1| + |v_2| \le k \tag{12.7}$$

Hence,

$$\sigma(i, u_1) = (\sigma(i,u)\sigma(\delta(i,u), v_1)\Phi_j(\delta(i,u_1)))_{1 \le j \le p} \tag{12.8}$$
$$\sigma(i, u_2) = (\sigma(i,u)\sigma(\delta(i,u), v_2)\Phi_j(\delta(i,u_2)))_{1 \le j \le p}$$

Let $K = kM + 2N$. We have:

$$
\begin{aligned}
d'(\sigma(i,u_1), \sigma(i,u_2)) &\le M(|v_1| + |v_2|) \\
&\quad + d'([\Phi(\delta(i,u_1))]_j, [\Phi(\delta(i,u_2))]_j) \\
&\le kM + 2N = K
\end{aligned}
\tag{12.9}
$$

Thus, f has bounded variation using d'_p.

We briefly mentioned several theoretical and computational properties and advantages of sequential and p-subsequential transducers. In the following we shall consider the use of these transducers in several areas of computational linguistics.

12.4   Phonology and Morphology

Kaplan and Kay (1994) showed that phonological rules can be represented by finite-state transducers. These tools are currently widely used in compiling phonological or morphological rules (Koskenniemi, 1985; Karttunen, Kaplan, and Zaenen, 1992; Sproat, 1992). However, time and space efficiency of such methods could become serious concerns depending on the way these transducers are computed and used.

One might be more specific about the type of transducers needed for such representations. Indeed, notice that the rules considered by Kaplan and Kay (1994) basically involve deterministic transducers. Compositions and unions of the transducers corresponding to such rules might introduce ambiguities. But, the degree of ambiguity seems bounded. In fact, we could not find a single serious case in which a morphological or phonological rule could not be represented by a p-subsequential transducer.

These transducers could be used to compile phonological rules more efficiently. But, in general, the computation described in Kaplan and Kay (1994) for compiling rules leads to non-sequential transducers. The corresponding transducers can however be determinized (Mohri, 1994c). The determinization algorithm is close to the classic powerset determinization of non-deterministic automata. When several transitions labeled with the same input element a leave the states of a given subset, a new transition is created in the resulting transducer with input label a. The output of this transition is the same as those of the initial transitions if they are all identical. If not, the longest common prefix of the output labels is associated with the transition of the resulting transducer.

Figures 12.8 and 12.9 illustrate this determinization in a concrete case. Figure 12.8 represents a transducer involved in the description of the morphophonemic rules of English (Kaplan and Kay, 1994). It corresponds to the rule which states that the abstract phoneme N should be realized as m if followed by a labial, and by n otherwise[5].

Figure 12.9 shows an equivalent subsequential transducer obtained by determinization. Two transitions labeled with the input N leave the state 0 of the non-sequential transducer. The outputs associated with these transitions are

---

[5]We have denoted here by @ any letter not in $\{b, m, p, n, N\}$.

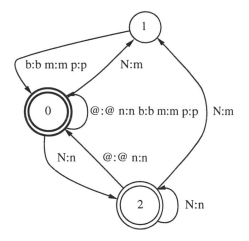

Figure 12.8: Example of a transducer τ_0 representing a morphophonemic rule.

distinct. Only the empty word ϵ can therefore be output when reading N and the output strings need to be stored in memory. This explains the transition from the state 0 to $\{(0, m), (1, n)\}$. Since 2 is a final state, the remaining string n associated with 2 can be freed as a final output. The next steps of the construction of the sequential transducer are analogous.

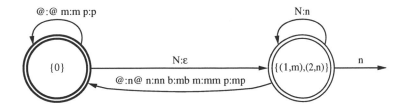

Figure 12.9: Subsequential transducer τ_0' equivalent to τ_0.

12.5 Representation of Large Dictionaries

p-Subsequential transducers can also be used to construct efficient representations of large scale dictionaries (Mohri, 1994a; Mohri, 1994c). Indeed, dictionaries such as pronunciation or morphological dictionaries consist of pairs of strings. Transducers can then be considered as very natural for the representation of such double column lists, since they allow one to associate members of one column with those of the other without imposing any direction in this association.

Dictionary lookup using p-subsequential transducers is optimal since the lookup time only depends on the size of the input. The size of the representation of dictionaries using these devices can also be limited. More precisely, each sequential function admits a minimal sequential transducer realizing it (Choffrut, 1978; Reutenauer, 1993; Mohri, 1994b). We have designed a minimization

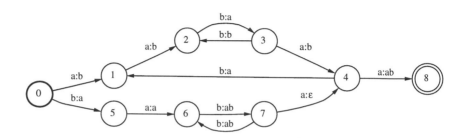

Figure 12.10: Sequential transducer T_1.

algorithm permitting one to obtain a minimal subsequential transducer from a given subsequential transducer (Mohri, 1994b). The first stage of the algorithm consists in pushing output labels towards the initial state as much as possible. Consider for instance the transducer T_1 of figure 12.10. Notice that this transducer cannot be minimized if considered as an automaton over the alphabet $A \times B$.

The application of the first stage of the algorithm to this transducer gives the transducer T_2 represented in Figure 12.11. More precisely, let $T_1 = (V, i, F, A, B^*, \delta, \sigma)$ be the initial sequential transducer[6] the first stage of the minimization leads to a another transducer $T_2 = (V, i, F, A, B^*, \delta, \sigma_2)$ which has the same transitions as T_1 except that its outputs have been modified in the following way:

$$\forall s \in V, \ \sigma_2(s, a) = [P(s)]^{-1} \sigma(s, a) P(\delta(s, a)) \tag{12.10}$$

where the function P is defined by:

$$\forall s \in F, \quad P(s) = \epsilon; \tag{12.11}$$

---

[6]For the sake of clarity, we shall define the algorithm for sequential transducers and assume that the longest common prefix of the outputs at the initial state is ϵ. Notice that if this were not the case, then this string could always be output before any attempt to match the input.

$$\forall s \in V - F, \quad P(s) = \bigwedge_{a \in A} \sigma(s, a) \, P(\delta(s, a))$$

For any state s, $P(s)$ corresponds to the longest common prefix of the strings

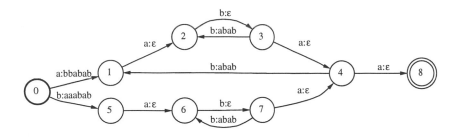

Figure 12.11: Sequential transducer T_2 obtained from T_1 by prefixation.

associated with the paths leaving s and reaching a final state. The expression of line 12.10 is thus well defined. Indeed, according to this definition, for any state s and any a in A, $[P(s)]$ is a prefix[7] of $\sigma(s, a)P(\delta(s, a))$. This operation of prefixation is not trivial. It requires the computation of the strongly connected components of the graph, and solving a system of word equations for each of these components (Mohri, 1994b). We shall give below a brief description of this algorithm.

The transducer of figure 12.11 can be considered as an automaton over the alphabet $A \times B$. The second stage of the algorithm can be reduced to the minimization of the transducer considered as such, namely the minimization in the sense of automata (Aho, Hopcroft, and Ullman, 1974). The resulting transducer is shown on figure 12.12. This transducer is a minimal sequential transducer representing the same language as T_1 in the sense of transducers. The step corresponding to the transformation of the output labels of a transducer does not affect the input labels, therefore we can simplify the presentation of the algorithm by considering a non-deterministic automaton $G = (V, i, F, A^*, \delta)$ where:

- V is the set of states or vertices;

- $i \in V$ the initial state;
- $F \subseteq V$ the set of final states;
- A a finite alphabet;

---

[7] The notation used here corresponds to the one generally adopted for monoids. In particular, for any string u and v, $u^{-1}(uv) = v$.

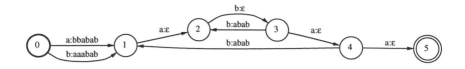

Figure 12.12: Minimal sequential transducer T_3.

- δ the state transition function which maps $V \times A^*$ to the set of subsets of V.[8]
We denote by

- G^T the transpose of G, namely the automaton obtained from G by reversing each transition;
- $Trans[q]$ the set of transitions leaving $q \in V$;
- $Trans^T[q]$ the set of transitions entering $q \in V$;
- $t.v$ the vertex reached by (resp. source of) t and $t.l$ its label, for any transition t in $Trans[q]$ (resp. in $Trans^T[q]$), $q \in V$;
- $out - degree[q]$ the number of edges leaving $q \in V$;
- $in - degree[q]$ the number of edges entering $q \in V$;
- E the set of edges of G.

In the following, we shall consider automata with no non-coaccessible state, that is such that from any state there exists at least one path leading to a final state. As in previous equations, we denote by $x \wedge y$ the longest common prefix of two strings x and y in A^*, and by ϵ the empty word of A^*. Let J be the function mapping V to A^* defined by the following:

$$
\begin{array}{lll}
\text{if } q \in F & J(q) = & \epsilon, \\
\text{else} & J(q) = & \text{longest common prefix of the labels of all paths} \\
& & \text{leading to } F \text{ from } q.
\end{array}
$$

J is well defined since for any q in V there exists at least one path leading from q to F. This path is finite, hence the longest common prefix of the labels of all paths leading from $q \in V - F$ to F is well defined and in A^*. J can be equivalently defined by the following recursive definition:

$$\forall q \in F \quad J(q) = \quad \epsilon \tag{12.12}$$

$$\forall q \in V - F \quad J(q) = \bigwedge_{t \in Trans[q]} t.l \, J(t.v)$$

The algorithm then consists in pushing the labels of this automaton towards the initial state as much as possible. Given a non-deterministic automaton G,

---

[8]Notice that the input alphabet of G is A^*. Hence, labels of transitions can be words.

we define $p(G)$, *the prefix of* G, as the non-deterministic automaton resulting from the application of this operation to G. $p(G)$ has the same set of vertices and edges as G, the same initial state and final states. It differs from G by the labels of its transitions in the following way: for any edge $e \in E$ with starting state q and destination state[9] r,

$$label_{p(G)}(e) = label_G(e)J(r) \qquad if \ q = i, \qquad (12.13)$$
$$label_{p(G)}(e) = [J(q)]^{-1}label_G(e)J(r) \qquad else,$$

where $label_{p(G)}(e)$ is the label of the edge e in $p(G)$ and $label_G(e)$ its label in G. $p(G)$ is well defined since $J(q)$ is by definition a prefix of $label_G(e)J(r)$. It is not hard to show that $p(G)$ recognizes the same language as G.

The recursive definition of J indicates one way of obtaining $p(G)$ from G. It consists in computing J for all states of the adjacent list of $q \in V$ before calculating $J(q)$. However, this method cannot be applied in general since in case G contains cycles there does not exist an ordering of the states such that if the adjacent list of q contains r, then r appears before q in the ordering. Two states can indeed belong to the same cycle. Hence, J cannot be computed in such a way.

In case G is a directed acyclic graph such an ordering exists. The reverse ordering of a *topological sort* of a dag meets this condition. This ordering can be obtained in linear time $O(|V| + |E|)$ since it corresponds to the increasing ordering of the finishing times in a depth-first search. Therefore, in case G is acyclic, states can be considered in such an order and the longest common prefix can be computed for each according to the recursive definition of J above. In this way, the longest common prefix computation is performed at most once for each state of G. The computation of the automaton $p(G)$ from G can be performed in a similar way by considering the states of G in the same ordering.

In case G is not acyclic, we consider strongly connected components (SCC's) of G. There exists a linear ordering of SCC's such that if the adjacent list of a state in a SCC scc_1 contains a state of another SCC scc_2, then scc_2 appears before scc_1 in the ordering: the reverse ordering of a topological sort of the dag G^{SCC}, the *component graph* of G. Recall that the component graph of G is the dag which contains one state for each SCC of G, and which contains a transition $(q, a, r) \in V \times A^* \times V$ if there exists a transition from the SCC of G corresponding to q, to the SCC of G corresponding to r. It can be obtained in linear time $O(|E| + |V|)$ like strongly connected components of G (Aho, Hopcroft, and Ullman, 1974).

In order to compute $p(G)$ from G, one can gradually modify the transitions

---

[9]Notice that there can be several edges with starting state r and destination state r in G. Besides, these edges can bear the same labels.

of G by considering its SCC's according to this ordering. Each time a SCC scc is considered, all the transitions leaving states of scc are transformed into those of $p(G)$, and all the transitions from another SCC entering a state q of scc are modified in a way such that:

$$\forall t \in Trans^T[q], \quad t.l = label_G(t)\, J(q). \tag{12.14}$$

Thanks to the choice of the ordering, these transformations are operated only once for each SCC. Once all SCC's of G have been considered one obviously obtains $p(G)$.

Now we still need to describe the way these transformations are performed. Suppose all the SCC's visited before scc have been correctly modified. This is necessarily true for the first SCC considered since no transition leaves it to join a distinct SCC. Then, according to the definition of the function J, the following system of equations holds:

$$\forall q \in scc, \quad X_q = \Big(\bigwedge_{\substack{t \in Trans[q] \\ t.v \in scc}} t.l\, X_{t.v} \Big) \wedge \Big(\bigwedge_{\substack{t \in Trans[q] \\ t.v \notin scc}} t.l \Big), \tag{12.15}$$

and it has a unique solution corresponding to the longest common prefixes of each state of scc ($\forall q \in scc, X_q = J(q)$). To solve this system, we can proceed in the following way:

1- For each q in scc, we compute π_q, the longest common prefix of all its leaving transitions:

$$\pi_q \leftarrow \Big(\bigwedge_{\substack{t \in Trans[q] \\ t.v \in scc}} t.l\, X_{t.v} \Big) \wedge \Big(\bigwedge_{\substack{t \in Trans[q] \\ t.v \notin scc}} t.l \Big) \quad if \ q \notin F \tag{12.16}$$

$$\pi_q \leftarrow \epsilon \qquad\qquad\qquad\qquad\qquad\qquad\qquad else$$

2- If $\pi_q \neq \epsilon$, we can make a change of variables: $Y_q \leftarrow \pi_q\, X_q$.
This second step is equivalent to storing the value π_q and solving the system modified by the following operations:

2'- $\forall t \in Trans[q], \quad t.l \leftarrow \pi_q^{-1}\, t.l$
$\forall t \in Trans^T[q], \quad t.l \leftarrow t.l\, \pi_q.$

We can limit the number of times these two operations are performed by storing in a array N the number of empty labels leaving each state q of scc. As long as $N[q] \neq 0$, there is no use performing these operations since the value of π_q is ϵ. Also, if $N[q] = 0$ right after the computation of π_q, then π_q will remain equal to ϵ, because changes of variables will only affect suffixes of the transitions leaving q. We can store this information using an array F, in order to avoid performing step 1 in such situations or when q is a final state. We use a queue Q containing the set of states q with $N[q] = F[q] = 0$ for which the two operations above need to be performed, and an additional array INQ indicating for each state q whether it is in Q.

We start the above operations by initializing N and F to 0 for all states in scc, and by enqueuing in Q an arbitrarily chosen state q of scc. Each time the transition of a state r of $Trans^T[q]$ is modified, r is added to Q if $N[r] = F[r] = 0$. The property of SCC's and the initialization of N and F guarantee that each state of scc will be enqueued at least once. Steps 1 and 2' are operated until $Q = \emptyset$. This necessarily occurs since, except for the first time, step 1 is performed for a state q if $N[q] = 0$.

PREFIX(G)
```
1     for each r ∈ V(G^SCC)      ▷ considered in order of increasing finishing times
                                     of a DFS of G^SCC
2        do   for each r ∈ SCC[q]
3                do N[r] ← INQ[r] ← F[r] ← 0
4                Q ← r                ▷r arbitrarily chosen in SCC[q]
5                INQ[r] ← 1
6                while Q ≠ ∅
7                   do   r ← head[Q]
8                        DEQUEUE(Q)
9                        INQ[r] ← 0
10                       p ← LCP(G, r)
11                       for each t ∈ Trans^T[r]
12                          do   if (p ≠ ε)
13                               then   if (t.v ∈ SCC[r] and N[t.v] > 0 and
                                              t.l = ε and F[t.v] = 0)
14                                      then N[t.v] ← N[t.v] − 1
15                                      t.l ← t.l p
16                               if (N[t.v] = 0 and INQ[t.v] = 0 and F[t.v] = 0)
17                               then   ENQUEUE(Q, t.v)
18                                      INQ[t.v] = 1
```

After the computation of the longest common prefix we have or $N[q] = 0$ and then q will never be enqueued again, or $N[q] \neq 0$ and a new non empty factor π_q of $J(q)$ has been identified. Thus, each state q is enqueued at most $(|J(q)|+2)$ times in Q. Let J_{max} be the maximum of the lengths of the longest common prefixes of all paths leaving states q, $J_{max} = max_{q \in V} |J(q)|$. Then, after at most $(|J_{max}| + 2)$ steps we have $Q = \emptyset$. Once $Q = \emptyset$, it is easy to notice that the system of equations has a trivial solution: $\forall q \in scc, X_q = \epsilon$. As noticed above, it has a unique solution. Therefore, the system is resolved. Concatenating the factors π_q involved in the changes of variables corresponding to the state q gives the value of $J(q)$. The set of operations $2'$ are thus equivalent to multiplying the label of each transition joining the states q and r, ($r \in scc$), at right by $J(r)$ and at left by $[J(q)]^{-1}$ if q is in scc. This shows that the transformations described above do modify the transitions leaving or entering states of scc as desired. Thus, the pseudocode above gives an algorithm computing $p(G)$ from G.

In this pseudocode, $V(G^{SCC})$ represents the set of the states of the component graph of G, and, for each q in $V(G^{SCC})$, $SCC[q]$ stands for the strongly connected component corresponding to q. The function $LCP(G, q)$ called in the algorithm is such that it returns p the longest common prefix of all the transitions leaving q ($p = \epsilon$ if $q \in F$), replaces each of these transitions by dividing them at left by p, counts and stores in $N[q]$ the number of empty transitions, and, if $N[q] = 0$ after the computation of the longest common prefix or if q is a final state gives $F[q]$ the value 1.

This algorithm can be easily extended to deal with the more general case of p-subsequential transducers. This extension allowed us to obtain very compact and time efficient representations of large scale dictionaries. As an example, it took us about 9 minutes to construct a p-subsequential transducer from a dictionary of more than 670,000 lines[10] of 21.2 Mb using an HP/9000 755, including I/O time. The size of the pronunciation dictionary was reduced this way to 870 Kb (Mohri, 1994c). Lookup time using this transducer reached about 80 words per second. Analogous experiments were carried out with several large-scale dictionaries, in particular with the large morphological dictionaries of LADL (Courtois, 1989; Karlsfeld, 1991). They confirm that p-subsequential transducers combine both efficiency in time and space.

12.6   Syntax

The use of finite-state transducers is very useful and can be very efficient in syntax. Most of the local linguistic phenomena (Church, 1983; Gross, 1989) as well as many complex sentences (Mohri, 1993) can indeed be described by finite-state machines. Finite-state machines can then be considered as convenient tools for the representation of such local constraints. Their application can be efficient in disambiguation for tagging, or in building a lexical analyzer (Silberztein, 1993) as well as in syntax (Roche, 1993; Mohri, 1994d; Karlsson et al., 1995). Here again, an interesting property of these transducers is that they correspond to p-subsequential functions. The number of ambiguities is indeed not infinite, therefore the corresponding transducers can be determinized

---

[10]Because of several factorizations, the number of lines of the file is superior to the number of entries.

as described in previous sections and put in the shape of p-subsequential transducers. Since these transducers also allow minimization, they permit us to obtain an efficient and compact device for parsing or disambiguating, at least locally, in many applications. Figure 12.13 provides an example of a local grammar represented by a sequential transducer. It can be used in disambiguating the sequence *s'* in French. Indeed, *s'* can be both a conjunction and a pronoun. When followed by the pronoun *en*, *s'* is necessarily a pronoun and when followed by *il* a conjunction. The transducer of Figure 12.13 provides an equivalent expression for these rules[11].

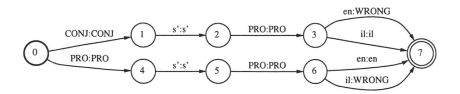

Figure 12.13: Local grammar represented by a sequential transducer.

The application of such local grammars represented by a transducer T involves however the construction of another transducer $(Id_{A^*\backslash_T} T)^*$, where $Id_{A^*\backslash_T}$ represents the identity transducer restricted to the strings not recognized by T. Indeed, the corresponding transducer can be used to operate the required syntactic substitutions whenever an entry of T appears. An efficient construction of the corresponding transducer involves the use of failure functions in a way close to what has been described for the application of local grammars represented by automata (Mohri, 1994d; Mohri, 1995).

Finite-state automata approximations of context-free grammars provide helpful tools for parsing in some applications (Pereira and Wright, 1991). In addition to approximations, the use of finite-state machines in parsing is essential. Indeed, the problem of parsing is often considered to be solved thanks to efficient algorithms such as those of Graham *et al.* (1980) and Earley (1970) from the complexity point of view and maybe that of Tomita (1986) in practice. The complexity of these algorithms in terms of the size of the grammar is generally not considered as relevant[12]. Grammars with large coverage such

---

[11] The output WRONG indicates that the corresponding sequence is not part of a sentence

[12] The complexity with respect to the size of the grammar is linear in the case of the parser of Graham *et al.* (1980) and for efficient implementations of Earley's algorithm. Recall that at least the root of the grammar size appears as an exponential factor in the complexity of Tomita's algorithm (Johnson, 1972).

as the lexicon-grammar of LADL prove however that the size of the grammar should be the main concern when dealing with syntax. While the size of the input n, namely a sentence, could be about 30 in languages such as English and French, the size of a precise grammar G for these languages which would take into account lexical restrictions can easily exceed 10^7. Obviously in the complexity of these algorithms the size of the input is therefore not the issue $(n^3 << |G|)$. The space complexity of these algorithms also involves the size of the grammar and this is also rarely mentioned as a problem.

Finite-state machines provide an elegant solution to these problems. The rules of a context-free grammar can indeed be represented by automata or transducers (Woods, 1970). Consider for example the context-free grammar G with with productions:

$$
\begin{aligned}
S &\rightarrow aAc \\
A &\rightarrow Abb|b
\end{aligned}
\tag{12.17}
$$

It can be represented by the transducer of figure 12.14. Cascaded application of such transducers can be used in parsing (Roche, 1994). The complexity of the algorithms described by Roche (1994) is exponential in time and space with respect to the size of the input. We shall not consider here the problem of the improvement of the complexity of the use of these transducers[13]. We shall

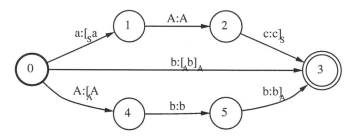

Figure 12.14: Transducer representing the grammar G.

assume here that algorithms analogous to those of Earley for instance can also be simulated using these transducers. This has been shown to be the case at least for RTN automata (Woods, 1970). The major interest of the use of finite-state machines is then that the number of rules of a context-free grammar is no more involved as a parameter in the complexities. Instead, only the size of the transducer used to store the set of rules of this grammar is then a factor in these

---

[13] Methods close to those used by Woods (1970; 1980) lead to much more efficient complexities. We are also currently defining a method based on the use of a class of pushdown transducers which leads to better complexities (see Choffrut and Culik for a formal study of the corresponding classes of languages (1983)).

complexities. In the worst case, the size of the grammar $|G|$, that is the sum of the lengths of all paths of a transducer representing G, is exponential in the size of the transducer. Thus, one can hope to obtain important improvements of the parsing complexities using automata or transducers.

Given a transducer representing a context-free grammar, the problem consists in reducing its size to reduce its contribution to algorithm complexity, and also in improving its application. Notice that the corresponding transducer cannot allow an infinite number of ambiguities since such cases are not encountered in syntax. Thus we may assume that the corresponding function has a bounded number of ambiguities p. The following generalizes the theorem of Elgot and Mezei (1965) and helps to make clear that p-subsequential transducers can be used in parsing.

Theorem 8 *Let T be a rational transducer with input alphabet A and output alphabet B having p ambiguities. There exist a left sequential transducer L with corresponding alphabets A and C and a right p-subsequential transducer R with alphabets C and B such that $T = L \circ R$.*

We shall not give the proof of this theorem here since it is long and complex, but mention that it provides an effective algorithm for the construction of the transducers L and R. As pointed out previously, these transducers can be minimized. The corresponding minimized transducers can then be considered as compact and efficient representations of a given context-free grammar.

12.7 Speech Processing

Transducers also lead to efficient tools in speech processing. Their use in text-to-speech systems has been described by Sproat (1995). Transducers allow us to represent in a uniform manner many of the components of text-to-speech systems. In addition to the modularity it supports, this approach leads to improved efficiency. In fact, most of the system modules use transducers as described in previous sections since they correspond for instance to morphology, the application of local grammars, etc. A considerable part of the text-to-speech system can therefore also be represented as a composition of p-subsequential transducers, thus as a single p-subsequential transducer.

These transducers need however to be completed by adding weights to arcs or transitions in order to take into account the various possibilities encountered in applied speech processing. Weighted transducers have been shown by Pereira, Riley, and Sproat (1994) to be an appropriate theoretical basis for representing speech to text algorithms and dealing with the corresponding issues. Some of these transducers correspond in fact to p-subsequential functions. Thus, once again this type of transducers appears in language processing.

One of the major problems often encountered in this field is however the one of the size of the machines. Typically, the corresponding transducers may have several million states and transitions. Reducing the size of these machines clearly requires further investigation and probably should be considered as a crucial theoretical and practical issue in speech recognition. Here, we shall give a simple example of the adaptation of the minimization algorithm described above to reducing the size of weighted finite-state machines. Some of the

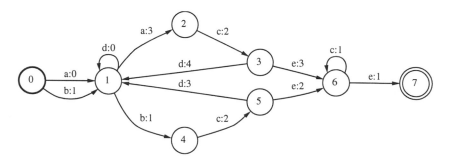

Figure 12.15: Language transducer T_1'.

weighted machines involved in this application can be considered as sequential or p-subsequential transducers from a given alphabet[14] A to numbers. When applied to an input string, these machines generate numbers generally by adding or multiplying the numbers encountered on the path. Figure 12.15 shows an example of such a transducer.

When applied to the input *abcece*, this transducer ouputs $0 + 1 + 2 + 2 + 1 + 1 = 7$. In most practical cases, this number can be interpreted as a non normalized probability for this string to appear. Finite-state language models have typically this shape since they commonly correspond to n-gram models. Notice that here the minimization of automata does not help to reduce the size of the graph. No two states are equivalent if it is considered as an automaton for which the alphabet consists of pairs composed of a letter and an integer. The labels of this transducer can however be changed in a way similar to the one described when outputs are made of strings. The output numbers can be *pushed up* to the initial state. In other words, the maximum possible output is extracted from the outleaving paths. The transducer of Figure 12.16 represents the result of this process. Here again, this process should not be considered as trivial. Though easier than in the case where outputs are strings, this requires in general the computation of the strongly connected components of the graph, and the application of this process for each of these. This transducer

---

[14]This alphabet can be the cross-product of the two alphabets B and V. Therefore, this includes the case of transducers and also weighted transducers.

can then be minimized using classic algorithms for automata. The resulting transducer (Figure 12.17) is a minimal sequential transducer representing the same language as T_1'. In practical cases in speech recognition, weights are real

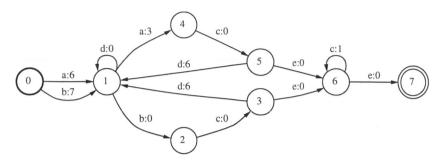

Figure 12.16: Transducer T_2' obtained from T_1' by left extraction.

numbers. The above algorithm does not exactly handle these cases. The first stage of left extraction of the algorithm remains unchanged. But minimization needs to be modified. Indeed, at this stage, that two labels bear the same real-number output is not very likely. However, the difference between these outputs can be irrelevant in many cases since one is mainly interested in the best path of the resulting graph. Thus, approximations can be made at this step. Namely, two states can be merged if the outleaving paths are identical apart from a small ϵ difference in their outputs. In practice, many other considerations may need to be taken into account to keep the soundness of the whole system. In particular, these approximations should be compatible with any pruning method used in the recognition. The algorithm we just illustrated can be used to minimize any

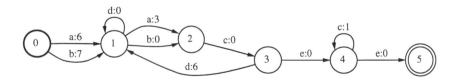

Figure 12.17: Transducer T_3' obtained by minimization of T_1'.

sequential transducer with integer outputs. One of the applications where this algorithm can also be used is in associating ranks with strings and the reverse. Indeed, consider a list of strings with their associated ranks. The corresponding association can be represented by a transducer of the type described above. Such a transducer is interesting in indexation since when used from numbers to strings it provides the string associated with a given number and the reverse. Using the minimization method we just described permits one not only to reduce the size of this machine but also to optimize it when used with integer inputs. Indeed, in general, one of the effects of the minimization method we described is to provide a pseudo-determinization of the output, here the integer side of the transducer (Mohri, 1994a). Since the output numbers are pushed towards the initial state, the disambiguation is made as soon as possible[15].

12.8   Conclusion

We have briefly presented the use of a set of devices which seem to fit the complexity of language and provide efficiency in space and time. Finite-state sequential machines can be used efficiently in many other areas of computational linguistics. In particular, sequential machines permit to achieve efficient results in indexation (Crochemore, 1986; Mohri, 1994c). Still, their possible role in computational semantics needs to be made precise. More generally, their use in theoretical computer science and other connected areas has been described by Perrin (1993). Some extensions of sequential or p-subsequential transducers can be used in computational linguistics. In particular, we have started to examine the minimization of *poly-subsequential transducers*, finite-state machines introduced by Schützenberger (1987). The use of these devices appears also as very natural in other fields. In particular, integer division can be represented by a poly-subsequential transducer. There seem to be reasons to use these machines in natural language processing too.

12.9   Acknowledgments

I thank Fernando Pereira and Richard Sproat helpful comments on earlier drafts of this work.

References

Aho, Alfred V., John E. Hopcroft, and Jeffrey D. Ullman. 1974. *The design and analysis of computer algorithms*. Addison Wesley: Reading, MA.

Aho, Alfred V., Ravi Sethi, and Jeffrey D. Ullman. 1986. *Compilers, Principles, Techniques and Tools*. Addison Wesley: Reading, MA.

---

[15]The resulting transducer can be considered as a *perfect hasher* (Revuz, 1991). Notice that one can use these transducers to efficiently represent the alphabet of other transducers or automata.

Berstel, Jean. 1979. *Transductions and Context-Free Languages*. Teubner Studienbucher: Stuttgart.

Choffrut, Christian. 1978. *Contributions à l'étude de quelques familles remarquables de fonctions rationnelles*. Ph.D. thesis, (thèse de doctorat d'Etat), Université Paris 7, LITP: Paris, France.

Choffrut, Christian and Karel Culik. 1983. Properties of finite and pushdown transducers. *SIAM Journal of Computing*, 12.

Church, Kenneth W. 1983. A finite-state parser for use in speech recognition. In 21st *Meeting of the Association for Computational Linguistics (ACL 83), Proceedings of the Conference*. ACL.

Courtois, Blandine. 1989. DELAS: Dictionnaire électronique du LADL pour les mots simples du français. Technical report, LADL: Paris, France.

Crochemore, Maxime. 1986. Transducers and repetitions. *Theoretical Computer Science*, 45.

Earley, Jay. 1970. An efficient context-free parsing algorithm. *Communications of the Association for the Computational Machinery*, 14.

Elgot, C. C. and J. E. Mezei. 1965. On relations defined by generalized finite automata. *IBM Journal of Research and Development*, 9.

Ginsburg, S. and G. F. Rose. 1966. A characterization of machine mappings. *Canadian Journal of Mathematics*, 18.

Graham, S. L., M. A. Harrison, and W. L. Ruzzo. 1980. An improved context-free recognizer. *ACM Transactions on Programming Languages and Systems*, 2.

Gross, Maurice. 1989. The use of finite automata in the lexical representation of natural language. *Lecture Notes in Computer Science*, 377.

Gross, Maurice, 1991. "Computational Approaches to the Lexicon". chapter Constructing Lexicon-Grammars. Oxford University Press: Oxford, England.

Johnson, Mark, 1991. "Generalized LR Parsing". chapter The Computational Complexity of GLR Parsing. Kluwer Academic Publishers.

Kaplan, Ronald M. and Martin Kay. 1994. Regular models of phonological rule systems. *Computational Linguistics*, 20(3).

Karlsfeld, Gaby. 1991. Dictionnaire morphologique de l'anglais. Technical report, LADL: Paris, France.

Karlsson, Fred, Atro Voutilainen, Juha Heikkila, and Atro Anttila. 1995. *Constraint Grammar, A language-Independent System for Parsing Unrestricted Text*. Mouton de Gruyter.

Karttunen, Lauri, Ronald M. Kaplan, and Annie Zaenen. 1992. Two-level morphology with composition. In *Proceedings of the fifteenth International Conference on Computational Linguistics (COLING'92), Nantes, France*. COLING.

Koskenniemi, Kimmo. 1985. Compilation of automata from morphological two-level rules. In *Proceedings of the Fifth Scandinavian Conference of Computational Linguistics, Helsinki, Finland*.

Koskenniemi, Kimmo. 1990. Finite-state parsing and disambiguation. In *Proceedings of the thirteenth International Conference on Computational Linguistics (COLING'90), Helsinki, Finland*. COLING.

Lothaire, M. 1990. *Mots*. Hermès: Paris, France.

Mohri, Mehryar. 1993. *Analyse et représentation par automates de structures syntaxiques composées*. Ph.D. thesis, Université Paris 7: Paris, France.

Mohri, Mehryar. 1994a. Compact representations by finite-state transducers. In 32nd *Meeting of the Association for Computational Linguistics (ACL 94), Proceedings of the Conference, Las Cruces, New Mexico*. ACL.

Mohri, Mehryar. 1994b. Minimization of sequential transducers. *Lecture Notes in Computer Science*, 807.

Mohri, Mehryar. 1994c. On some applications of finite-state automata theory to natural language processing: Representation of morphological dictionaries, compaction, and indexation. Technical Report IGM 94-22, Institut Gaspard Monge, Noisy-le-Grand.

Mohri, Mehryar. 1994d. Syntactic analysis by local grammars automata: an efficient algorithm. In *Proceedings of the International Conference on Computational Lexicography (COMPLEX 94)*. Linguistic Institute, Hungarian Academy of Science: Budapest, Hungary.

Mohri, Mehryar. 1995. Matching patterns of an automaton. *Lecture Notes in Computer Science*, to appear.

Pereira, Fernando C. N., Michael Riley, and Richard Sproat. 1994. Weighted rational transductions and their application to human language processing. In *ARPA Workshop on Human Language Technology*. Advanced Research Projects Agency.

Pereira, Fernando C. N. and Rebecca N. Wright. 1991. Finite-state approximation of phrase structure grammars. In *29th Annual Meeting of the Association for Computational Linguistics (ACL 94), Proceedings of the Conference, Berkeley, California*. ACL.

Perrin, Dominique. 1989. Automates et algorithmes sur les mots. In *Annales des Télécommunications 44*. Centre Nationale d'études des télécommunications.

Perrin, Dominique. 1990. Finite automata. In J. Van Leuwen, editor, *Handbook of Theoretical Computer Science, Volume B: Formal Models and Semantics*. Elsevier, Amsterdam, pages 1–57.

Perrin, Dominique. 1993. Les débuts de la théorie des automates. Technical Report LITP 93.04, Institut Blaise Pascal, Paris, France.

Reutenauer, Christophe. 1993. Subsequential functions: Characterizations, minimization, examples. In *Proceedings of the International Meeting of Young Computer Scientists, Lecture Notes in Computer Science*. Springer-Verlag: Berlin-New York.

Revuz, Dominique. 1991. *Dictionnaires et lexiques, méthodes et algorithmes*. Ph.D. thesis, Université Paris 7: Paris, France.

Roche, Emmanuel. 1993. *Analyse syntaxique transformationnelle du français par transducteur et lexique-grammaire*. Ph.D. thesis, Université Paris 7: Paris, France.

Roche, Emmanuel. 1994. Two parsing methods by means of finite state transducers. In *Proceedings of the sixteen International Conference on Computational Linguistics (COLING'94), Kyoto, Japan*. COLING.

Schützenberger, Marcel Paul. 1977. Sur une variante des fonctions séquentielles. *Theoretical Computer Science*.

Schützenberger, Marcel Paul. 1987. Polynomial decomposition of rational function. In *Lecture Notes in Computer Science 386*. Lecture Notes in Computer Science, Springer-Verlag: Berlin Heidelberg New York.

Schützenberger, Marcel Paul and Christophe Reutenauer. 1991. Minimization of rational word functions. *SIAM Journal of Computing*, 20(4).

Silberztein, Max. 1993. *Dictionnaires électroniques et analyse automatique de textes: le système INTEX*. Masson: Paris, France.

Sproat, Richard. 1992. *Morphology and Computation*. The MIT Press.

Sproat, Richard. 1995. A finite-state architecture for tokenization and grapheme-to-phoneme conversion in multilingual text analysis. In *Proceedings of the ACL SIGDAT Workshop, Dublin, Ireland*. ACL.

Tomita, Masaru. 1986. *Efficient Parsing for Natural Language: A Fast Algorithm for Practical Systems*. Kluwer, Boston.

Woods, W.A. 1970. Transition network grammars for natural language analysis. *Communications of the Association for the Computational Machinery*, 13(10).

Woods, W.A. 1980. Cascaded ATN grammars. *Computational Linguistics*, 6(1).

13 FASTUS: A Cascaded Finite-State Transducer for Extracting Information from Natural-Language Text

Jerry R. Hobbs, Douglas Appelt, John Bear, David Israel, Megumi Kameyama, Mark Stickel, and Mabry Tyson

FASTUS is a system for extracting information from natural language text for entry into a database and for other applications. It works essentially as a cascaded, nondeterministic finite-state automaton. There are five stages in the operation of FASTUS. In Stage 1, names and other fixed form expressions are recognized. In Stage 2, basic noun groups, verb groups, and prepositions and some other particles are recognized. In Stage 3, certain complex noun groups and verb groups are constructed. Patterns for events of interest are identified in Stage 4 and corresponding "event structures" are built. In Stage 5, distinct event structures that describe the same event are identified and merged, and these are used in generating database entries. This decomposition of language processing enables the system to do exactly the right amount of domain-independent syntax, so that domain-dependent semantic and pragmatic processing can be applied to the right larger-scale structures. FASTUS is very efficient and effective, and has been used successfully in a number of applications.

13.1 Introduction

FASTUS is a (slightly permuted) acronym for Finite-State Automaton Text Understanding System. It is a system for extracting information from free text in English, Japanese, and potentially other languages as well, for entry into a database and for other applications. It works essentially as a set of cascaded, nondeterministic finite-state transducers. Successive stages of processing are applied to the input, patterns are matched, and corresponding composite structures are built. The composite structures built in each stage provide the input to the next stage.

In Section 2 we describe the information extraction task, especially as exemplified by the Message Understanding Conference (MUC) evaluations (Sundheim 1992, 1993), which originally motivated the system design. We also discuss the important distinction between information extraction systems and text understanding systems. Section 3 is a review of previous finite-state approaches to natural language processing. Section 4 describes the overall architecture of the FASTUS system, and Sections 5 through 9 describe the individual stages. Section 10 describes the history of the system, including its principal applications and its performance in the MUC evaluations. Section 11 summarizes the advantages of the FASTUS approach.

13.2   The Information Extraction Task

There are a large number of applications in which a large corpus of texts must be searched for particular kinds of information and that information must be entered into a database for easier access. In the applications implemented so far, the corpora have typically been news articles or telegraphic military messages. The task of the system is to build templates or database entries with information about who did what to whom, when and where.

This task has been the basis of the successive MUC evaluations. In MUC-1 in June 1987, and MUC-2 in May 1989, the corpora were telegraphic messages about naval operations. The task definition for the evaluations took shape over the course of these two efforts.

The corpus for MUC-3 in June 1991 and MUC-4 in June 1992 consisted of news articles and transcripts of radio broadcasts, translated from Spanish, from the Foreign Broadcast Information Service. The focus of the articles was Latin American terrorism. The articles ranged from one third of a page to two pages in length. The template-filling task required identifying, among other things, the perpetrators and victims of each terrorist act described in an article, the occupations of the victims, the type of physical entity attacked or destroyed, the date, the location, and the effect on the targets. Many articles described multiple incidents, while other texts were completely irrelevant.

The following are some relevant excerpts from a sample terrorist report (TST2-MUC4-0048).

> San Salvador, 19 Apr 89 (ACAN-EFE) – [TEXT] Salvadoran
> President-elect Alfredo Cristiani condemned the terrorist killing

of Attorney General Roberto Garcia Alvarado and accused the Farabundo Marti National Liberation Front (FMLN) of the crime.

. . .

Garcia Alvarado, 56, was killed when a bomb placed by urban guerrillas on his vehicle exploded as it came to a halt at an intersection in downtown San Salvador.

. . .

Vice President-elect Francisco Merino said that when the attorney general's car stopped at a light on a street in downtown San Salvador, an individual placed a bomb on the roof of the armored vehicle.

. . .

According to the police and Garcia Alvarado's driver, who escaped unscathed, the attorney general was traveling with two bodyguards. One of them was injured.

Some of the corresponding database entries are as follows:

Incident: Date	- 19 Apr 89
Incident: Location	El Salvador: San Salvador (city)
Incident: Type	Bombing
Perpetrator: Individual ID	"urban guerrillas"
Perpetrator: Organization ID	"FMLN"
Perpetrator: Organization Confidence	Suspected or Accused by Authorities: "FMLN"
Physical Target: Description	"vehicle"
Physical Target: Effect	Some Damage: "vehicle"
Human Target: Name	"Roberto Garcia Alvarado"
Human Target: Description	"attorney general": "Roberto Garcia Alvarado"
	"driver"
	"bodyguards"
Human Target: Effect	Death: "Roberto Garcia Alvarado"
	No Injury: "driver"
	Injury: "bodyguards"

Fifteen sites participated in MUC-3, and seventeen in MUC-4. A development corpus of 1500 texts, together with their corresponding templates and an automatic scoring program, were made available. The systems were tested on a new set of 100 messages from the same time slice as the development messages, and in MUC-4 on a test set of 100 messages from a new time slice.

The task in MUC-5 in July 1993 was to extract information about joint ventures from business news, including the participants in the joint venture, the resulting company, the ownership and capitalization, and the intended activity. A typical text is the following:

> Bridgestone Sports Co. said Friday it has set up a joint venture in Taiwan with a local concern and a Japanese trading house to produce golf clubs to be shipped to Japan.
>
> The joint venture, Bridgestone Sports Taiwan Co., capitalized at 20 million new Taiwan dollars, will start production in January 1990 with production of 20,000 iron and "metal wood" clubs a month.

This text is used as an example in the description below of the FASTUS system.

The information to be extracted from this text is shown in the following templates:

TIE-UP-1:

Relationship:	TIE-UP
Entities:	"Bridgestone Sports Co."
	"a local concern"
	"a Japanese trading house"
Joint Venture Company:	"Bridgestone Sports Taiwan Co."
Activity:	ACTIVITY-1
Amount:	NT$20000000

ACTIVITY-1:

Activity:	PRODUCTION
Company:	"Bridgestone Sports Taiwan Co."
Product:	"iron and 'metal wood' clubs"
Start Date:	DURING: January 1990

Seventeen sites participated in MUC-5. It was conducted in conjunction with the ARPA-sponsored Tipster program, whose objective has been to encourage development of information extraction technology and to move it into the user community.

The principal measures for information extraction tasks are recall and precision. *Recall* is the number of answers the system got right divided by the number of possible right answers. It measures how complete or comprehensive the system is in its extraction of relevant information. *Precision* is the number of answers the system got right divided by the number of answers the system gave. It measures the system's correctness or accuracy. For example, if there are 100 possible answers and the system gives 80 answers and gets 60 of them right, its recall is 60% and its precision is 75%.

In addition, a combined measure, called the F-score, is often used. It is an approximation to the weighted geometric mean of recall and precision. The F-score is defined as follows:

$$F = \frac{(\beta^2+1)PR}{\beta^2 P + R}$$

where P is precision, R is recall, and β is a parameter encoding the relative importance of recall and precision. If $\beta = 1$, they are weighted equally. If $\beta > 1$, precision is more significant; if $\beta < 1$, recall is.

It is important to distinguish between two types of natural language systems: *information extraction* systems and *text understanding* systems. In information extraction,

- generally only a fraction of the text is relevant; for example, in the case of the MUC-4 terrorist reports, probably only about 10% of the text was relevant;

- information is mapped into a predefined, relatively simple, rigid target representation; this condition holds whenever entry of information into a database is the task;

- the subtle nuances of meaning and the writer's goals in writing the text are of at best secondary interest.

This contrasts with text understanding, where

- the aim is to make sense of the entire text;

- the target representation must accommodate the full complexities of language;

- one wants to recognize the nuances of meaning and the writer's goals.

The task in the MUC evaluations has been information extraction, not text understanding. When SRI participated in the MUC-3 evaluation in 1991, we used TACITUS, a text-understanding system (Hobbs et al., 1992a; Hobbs et al., 1993). Using it for the information extraction task gave us a high precision, the highest of any of the sites. However, because it was spending so much of its time attempting to make sense of portions of the text that were irrelevant to the task, the system was extremely slow. As a result, development time was slow, and consequently recall was mediocre.

FASTUS, by contrast, is an information extraction system, rather than a text understanding system. Our original motivation in developing FASTUS was to build a system that was more appropriate to the information extraction task.

Although information extraction is not the same as full text understanding, there are many important applications for information extraction systems, and the technology promises to be among the first genuinely practical applications of natural language processing.

13.3   The Finite-State Approach

The inspiration for FASTUS was threefold. First, we were struck by the strong performance in MUC-3 that the group at the University of Massachusetts got out of a fairly simple system (Lehnert et al., 1991). It was clear they were not doing anything like the depth of preprocessing, syntactic analysis, or pragmatics that was being done by the systems at SRI, General Electric, or New York University. They were not doing a lot of processing. But they were doing the *right* processing for the task.

The second source of inspiration was Pereira's work on finite-state approximations of grammars (Pereira, 1990). We were especially impressed by the speed of the implemented system.

Our desire for speed was the third impetus for the development of FASTUS. It was simply too embarassing to have to report at the MUC-3 conference that it took TACITUS 36 hours to process 100 messages. FASTUS brought that time down to less than 12 minutes.

Finite-state models are clearly not adequate for full natural language processing. However, if context-free parsing is not cost-effective when applied to real-world text, then an efficient text processor might make use of weaker language models, such as regular or finite-state grammars. Every computational linguistics graduate student knows, from the first textbook that introduces the Chomsky hierarchy, that English has constructs, such as center embedding, that cannot be described by any finite-state grammar. This fact biased researchers away from serious consideration of possible applications of finite-state grammars to difficult problems.

Church (1980) was the first in recent years to advocate finite-state grammars as a processing model for language understanding. He contended that, although English is clearly not a regular language, memory limitations make it impossible for people to exploit that context-freeness in its full generality, and therefore a finite-state mechanism might be adequate in practice as a model of human linguistic performance. A computational realization of memory limitation as a depth cutoff was implemented by Black (1989).

Pereira and Wright (1991) developed methods for constructing finite-state grammars from context free grammars that overgenerate in certain systematic ways. The finite-state grammar could be applied in situations, for example, as the language model in a speech understanding system, where computational considerations are paramount.

At this point, the limitations of the application of finite-state grammars to natural-language processing have not yet been determined. We believe our research has established that these simple mechanisms can achieve a lot more than had previously been thought possible.

13.4   Overview of the FASTUS Architecture

The key idea in FASTUS, the "cascade" in "cascaded finite-state automata", is to separate processing into several stages. The earlier stages recognize smaller linguistic objects and work in a largely domain-inde-
pendent fashion. They use purely linguistic knowledge to recognize that portion of the syntactic structure of the sentence that linguistic methods can determine reliably, requiring little or no modification or augmentation as the system is moved from domain to domain. These stages have been implemented for both English and Japanese.

The later stages take these linguistic objects as input and find domain-dependent patterns among them.

The current version of FASTUS may be thought of as using five levels of processing:

1. Complex Words: This includes the recognition of multiwords and proper names.

2. Basic Phrases: Sentences are segmented into noun groups, verb groups, and particles.

3. Complex Phrases: Complex noun groups and complex verb groups are identified.

4. Domain Events: The sequence of phrases produced at Level 3 is scanned for patterns for events of interest to the application, and when they are found, structures are built that encode the information about entities and events contained in the pattern.

5. Merging Structures: Structures arising from different parts of the text are merged if they provide information about the same entity or event.

As we progress through the five levels, larger segments of text are analyzed and structured.

This decomposition of the natural-language problem into levels is essential to the approach. Many systems have been built to do pattern matching on strings of words. One of the crucial innovations in our approach has been dividing that process into separate levels for recognizing phrases and recognizing event patterns. Phrases can be recognized reliably with purely syntactic information, and they provide precisely the elements that are required for stating the event patterns of interest.

Various versions of the system have had other, generally preliminary stages of processing. For the MUC-4 system we experimented with spelling correction. The experiments indicated that spelling correction hurt, primarily because novel proper names got corrected to other words, and hence were lost.

The MUC-4 system also had a preliminary stage in which each sentence was first searched for trigger words. At least one, generally low-frequency trigger word was included for each pattern of interest that had been defined. For example, in the pattern

take <HumanTarget> hostage

"hostage" rather than "take" is the trigger word. Triggering reduced the processing time by about a third, but since it is hard to maintain in a way that does not reduce recall and since the system is so fast anyway, this stage has not been a part of subsequent versions of the system.

We currently have a version of the system, a component in the Warbreaker Message Handler System, for handling military messages about time-critical targets, which has a preliminary stage of processing that identifies the free and formatted portions of the messages, breaks the free text into sentences, and identifies tables, outlines, and lists. The table processing is described in Tyson et al. (to appear).

At one point we investigated incorporating a part-of-speech tagger into the system. This turned out to double the run-time of the entire system, and it made similar mistakes to those that the basic phrase recognition stage made. Consequently, we have not used this component.

Every version of the system we have built has included a postprocessing stage that converts the event structures into the format required by the application or evaluation.

The system is implemented in CommonLisp and runs on Sun workstations. Several partial implementations of FASTUS in C++ have been built.

13.5   Complex Words

The first level of processing identifies multiwords such as "set up", "trading house", "new Taiwan dollars", and "joint venture", and company names like "Bridgestone Sports Co." and "Bridgestone Sports Taiwan Co.". The names of people and locations, dates, times, and other basic entities are also recognized at this level.

Languages in general are very productive in the construction of short, multiword fixed phrases and proper names employing specialized microgrammars, and this is the level at which they are recognized.

Not all names can be recognized by their internal structure. Thus, there are rules in subsequent stages for recognizing unknown possible names as names of specific types. For example, in

> XYZ's sales
> Vaclav Havel, 53, president of the Czech Republic,

we might not know that XYZ is a company and Vaclav Havel is a person, but the immediate context establishes that.

13.6   Basic Phrases

The problem of syntactic ambiguity is AI-complete. That is, we will not have systems that reliably parse English sentences correctly until we have encoded much of the real-world knowledge that people bring to bear in their language comprehension. For example, noun phrases cannot be reliably identified because of the prepositional phrase attachment problem. However, certain syntactic constructs can be reliably identified. One of these is the noun group, that is, the head noun of a noun phrase together with its determiners and other left modifiers. Another is what we are calling the "verb group", that is, the verb together with its auxiliaries and any intervening adverbs. Moreover, an analysis that identifies these elements gives us exactly the units we most need for domain-dependent processing.

Stage 2 in FASTUS identifies noun groups, verb groups, and several critical word classes, including prepositions, conjunctions, relative pronouns, and the words "ago" and "that". Phrases that are subsumed by larger phrases are discarded. Pairs of overlapping, nonsubsuming phrases are rare, but where they occur both phrases are kept. This sometimes compensates for an incorrect analysis in Stage 2.

The first sentence in the sample joint venture text is segmented by Stage 2 into the following phrases:

Company Name:	Bridgestone Sports Co.
Verb Group:	said
Noun Group:	Friday
Noun Group:	it
Verb Group:	had set up
Noun Group:	a joint venture
Preposition:	in
Location:	Taiwan
Preposition:	with
Noun Group:	a local concern
Conjunction:	and
Noun Group:	a Japanese trading house
Verb Group:	to produce
Noun Group:	golf clubs
Verb Group:	to be shipped
Preposition:	to
Location:	Japan

"Company Name" and "Location" are special kinds of noun group.

Noun groups are recognized by a finite-state grammar that encompasses most of the complexity that can occur in English noun groups, including numbers, numerical modifiers like "approximately", other quantifiers and determiners, participles in adjectival position, comparative and superlative adjectives, conjoined adjectives, and arbitrary orderings and conjunctions of prenominal nouns and noun-like adjectives. Thus, among the noun groups recognized are

approximately 5 kg
more than 30 people
the newly elected president
the largest leftist political force
a government and commercial project

Verb groups are recognized by a finite-state grammar that tags them as Active, Passive, Gerund, and Infinitive. Verbs are sometimes locally ambiguous between active and passive senses, as the verb "kidnapped" in the two sentences,

Several men kidnapped the mayor today.
Several men kidnapped yesterday were released today.

These are tagged as Active/Passive, and Stage 4 resolves the ambiguity if necessary.

Predicate adjective constructions are also recognized and classified as verb groups.

The grammars for noun groups and verb groups used in MUC-4 are given in Hobbs et al. (1992b); although these grammars have subsequently been augmented for domain-specific constructs, the core remains essentially the same.

Unknown or otherwise unanalyzed words are ignored in subsequent processing, unless they occur in a context that indicates they could be names.

The breakdown of phrases into nominals, verbals, and particles is a linguistic universal. Whereas the precise parts of speech that occur in any language can vary widely, every language has elements that are fundamentally nominal in character, elements that are fundamentally verbal or predicative, and particles or inflectional affixes that encode relations among the other elements (Croft, 1991).

13.7 Complex Phrases

In Stage 3, complex noun groups and verb groups that can be recognized reliably on the basis of domain-independent, syntactic information are recognized. This includes the attachment of appositives to their head noun group,

> The joint venture, Bridgestone Sports Taiwan Co.,

the construction of measure phrases,

> 20,000 iron and "metal wood" clubs a month,

and the attachment of "of" and "for" prepositional phrases to their head noun groups,

> production of 20,000 iron and "metal wood" clubs a month.

Noun group conjunction,

> a local concern and a Japanese trading house,

is done at this level as well.

In the course of recognizing basic and complex phrases, entities and events of domain interest are often recognized, and the structures for these are constructed. In the sample joint-venture text, entity structures are constructed for the companies referred to by the phrases "Bridgestone Sports Co.", "a local concern", "a Japanese trading house", and "Bridgestone Sports Taiwan Co." Information about nationality derived from the words "local" and "Japanese" is recorded. Corresponding to the complex noun group "The joint venture, Bridgestone Sports Taiwan Co.," the following relationship structure is built:

Relationship:	TIE-UP
Entities:	–
Joint Venture Company:	"Bridgestone Sports Taiwan Co."
Activity:	–
Amount:	–

Corresponding to the complex noun group "production of 20,000 iron and 'metal wood' clubs a month", the following activity structure is built up:

Activity:	PRODUCTION
Company:	–
Product:	"iron and 'metal wood' clubs"
Start Date:	–

When we first implemented the Complex Phrase level of processing, our intention was to use it only for complex noun groups, as in the attachment of "of" prepositional phrases to head nouns. Then in the final week before an evaluation, we wanted to make a change in what sorts of verbs were accepted by a set of patterns; this change, though, would have required our making extensive changes in the domain patterns. Rather than do this at such a late date, we realized it would be easier to define a complex verb group at the Complex Phrase level. We then immediately recognized that this was not an *ad hoc* device, but in fact the way we should have been doing things all along. We had stumbled onto an important property of language–complex verb groups— whose exploitation would have resulted in a significant simplification in the rules for the Stage 4 patterns.

Consider the following variations:

GM *formed* a joint venture with Toyota.
GM *announced it was forming* a joint venture with Toyota.
GM *signed an agreement forming* a joint venture with Toyota.
GM *announced it was signing an agreement to form* a joint venture
  with Toyota.

Although these sentences may differ in significance for some applications, they were equivalent in meaning within the MUC-5 application and would be in many others. Rather than defining each of these variations, with all their syntactic variants, at the domain pattern level, the user should be able to define complex verb groups that share the same significance. Thus, "formed", "announced it was forming", "signed an agreement forming", and "announced it was signing an agreement to form" are all equivalent, at least in this application, and once they are defined to be so, only one Stage 4 pattern needs to be expressed.

Various modalities can be associated with verb groups. In

GM will form a joint venture with Toyota.

the status of the joint venture is "Planned" rather than "Existing". But the same is true in the following sentences.

GM plans to form a joint venture with Toyota.
GM expects to form a joint venture with Toyota.
GM announced plans to form a joint venture with Toyota.

Consequently, as patterns are defined for each of these complex verb groups, the correct modality can be associated with them as well.

Verb group conjunction, as in

Terrorists *kidnapped and killed* three people.

is handled at this level as well.

Our current view is that this stage of processing corresponds to an important property of human languages. In many languages some adjuncts are more tightly bound to their head nouns than others. "Of" prepositional phrases are in this category, as are phrases headed by prepositions that the head noun subcategorizes for. The basic noun group together with these adjuncts constitutes the complex noun group. Complex verb groups are also motivated by considerations of linguistic universality. Many languages have quite elaborate mechanisms for constructing complex verbs. One example in English is the use of control verbs; "to conduct an attack" means the same as "to attack". Many of these higher operators shade the core meaning with a modality, as in "plan to attack" and "fail to attack".

13.8   Domain Events

The input to Stage 4 of FASTUS is a list of complex phrases in the order in which they occur. Anything that is not included in a basic or complex phrase in Stage 3 is ignored in Stage 4; this is a significant source of the robustness of the system. Patterns for events of interest are encoded as finite-state machines, where state transitions are effected by phrases. The state transitions are driven off the head words in the phrases. That is, each pair of relevant head word and phrase type— such as "company-NounGroup", "formed-PassiveVerbGroup", "bargaining-NounGroup", and "bargaining-PresentParticipleVerbGroup"— has an associated set of state transitions.

In the sample joint-venture text, the domain event patterns

<Company/ies> <Set-up> <Joint-Venture> with <Company/ies>

and

<Produce> <Product>

are instantiated in the first sentence, and the patterns

<Company> <Capitalized> at <Currency>

and

<Company> <Start> <Activity> in/on <Date>

are instantiated in the second. These four patterns result in the following four structures being built:

Relationship:	TIE-UP
Entities:	"Bridgestone Sports Co."
	"a local concern"
	"a Japanese trading house"
Joint Venture Company:	–
Activity:	–
Amount:	–

Activity:	PRODUCTION
Company:	–
Product:	"golf clubs"
Start Date:	–

Relationship:	TIE-UP
Entities:	–
Joint Venture Company:	"Bridgestone Sports Taiwan Co."
Activity:	–
Amount:	NT$20000000

(This is an augmentation of the previous relationship structure.)

Activity:	PRODUCTION
Company:	"Bridgestone Sports Taiwan Co."
Product:	–
Start Date:	DURING: January 1990

Although subjects are always obligatory in main clauses, it was determined in the MUC-4 evaluation that better performance in both recall and precision were obtained if the system generated an event structure from a verb together with its object, even if its subject could not be determined.

A certain amount of "pseudo-syntax" is done in Stage 4. The material between the end of the subject noun group and the beginning of the main verb group must be read over. There are patterns to accomplish this. Two of them are as follows:

> Subject {Preposition NounGroup}* VerbGroup
>
> Subject Relpro {NounGroup | Other}* VerbGroup {NounGroup | Other}* VerbGroup

The first of these patterns reads over prepositional phrases. The second over relative clauses. The verb group at the end of these patterns takes the subject noun group as its subject. There is another set of patterns for capturing the content encoded in relative clauses, of the form

> Subject Relpro {NounGroup | Other}* VerbGroup

The finite-state mechanism is nondeterministic. With the exception of passive clauses subsumed by larger active clauses, all events that are discovered in this stage of processing are retained. Thus, the full content can be extracted from the sentence

> The mayor, who was kidnapped yesterday, was found dead today.

One branch discovers the incident encoded in the relative clause. Another branch marks time through the relative clause and then discovers the incident in the main clause. These incidents are then merged.

A similar device is used for conjoined verb phrases. The pattern

> Subject VerbGroup {NounGroup | Other}* Conjunction Verb-
> Group

allows the machine to nondeterministically skip over the first conjunct and associate the subject with the verb group in the second conjunct. That is, when the first verb group is encountered, all its complements and adjuncts are skipped over until a conjunction is encountered, and then the subject is associated with a verb group, if that is what comes next. Thus, in the sentence

> Salvadoran President-elect Alfredo Cristiani condemned the ter-
> rorist killing of Attorney General Roberto Garcia Alvarado
> and accused the Farabundo Marti National Liberation Front
> (FMLN) of the crime.

one branch will recognize the killing of Garcia and another the fact that Cristiani accused the FMLN.

In addition, irrelevant event adjuncts in the verb phrase are read over while relevant adjuncts are being sought.

Many subject-verb-object patterns are of course related to each other. The sentence

GM manufactures cars.

illustrates a general pattern for recognizing a company's activities. But the same semantic content can appear in a variety of ways, including

Cars are manufactured by GM.
... GM, which manufactures cars...
... cars, which are manufactured by GM...
... cars manufactured by GM ...
GM is to manufacture cars.
Cars are to be manufactured by GM.
GM is a car manufacturer.

These are all systematically related to the active form of the sentence. Therefore, there is no reason a user should have to specify all the variations. The FASTUS system is able to generate all of the variants of the pattern from the simple active (S-V-O) form.

These transformations are executed at compile time, producing the more detailed set of patterns, so that at run time there is no loss of efficiency.

Various sorts of adjuncts can appear at virtually any place in these patterns:

Cars were manufactured last year by GM.
Cars are manufactured in Michigan by GM.
The cars, a spokesman announced, will be manufactured in California and Tennessee by General Motors.

Again, these possibilities are systematic and predictable, so there is no reason that the user should be burdened with defining separate patterns for them. Adjuncts are thus added automatically to patterns, and the information, say, about date and place, is extracted from them.

In this way, the user, simply by observing and stating that a particular S-V-O triple conveys certain items of information, is able to define dozens of patterns in the run-time system.

This feature is not merely a clever idea for making a system more convenient. It rests on the fundamental idea that underlies generative transformational grammar, but is realized in a way that does not impact the efficiency of processing.

The Stage 4 level of processing corresponds to the basic clause level that characterizes all languages, the level at which in English Subject-Verb-Object (S-V-O) triples occur, and thus again corresponds to a linguistic universal. This is the level at which predicate-argument relations between verbal and nominal elements are expressed in their most basic form.

13.9 Merging Structures

The first four stages of processing all operate within the bounds of single sentences. The final level of processing operates over the whole text. Its task is to see that all the information collected about a single entity or relationship is combined into a unified whole. This is one of the primary ways the problem of coreference is dealt with in our approach.

The three criteria that are taken into account in determining whether two structures can be merged are the internal structure of the noun groups, nearness along some metric, and the consistency, or more generally, the compatibility of the two structures.

In the analysis of the sample joint-venture text, we have produced three activity structures. They are all consistent because they are all of type PRO-DUCTION and because "iron and 'metal wood' clubs" is consistent with "golf clubs". Hence, they are merged, yielding

Activity:	PRODUCTION
Company:	"Bridgestone Sports Taiwan Co."
Product:	"iron and 'metal wood' clubs"
Start Date:	DURING: January 1990

Similarly, the two relationship structures that have been generated are consistent with each other, so they are merged, yielding,

Relationship:	TIE-UP
Entities:	"Bridgestone Sports Co."
	"a local concern"
	"a Japanese trading house"
Joint Venture Company:	"Bridgestone Sports Taiwan Co."
Activity:	–
Amount:	NT$20000000

Both of these cases are examples of identity coreference, where the activities or relationships are taken to be identical. We also handle examples of inferential coreference here. A joint venture has been mentioned, a joint venture implies the existence of an activity, and an activity has been mentioned. It is consistent to suppose the activity mentioned is the same as the activity implied, so we do. The Activity field of the Tie-Up structure is filled with a pointer to the Activity structure.

For a given domain, there can be fairly elaborate rules for determining whether two noun groups corefer, and thus whether their corresponding entity structures should be merged. A name can corefer with a description, as "General Motors" with "the company", provided the description is consistent with the other descriptions for that name. A precise description, like "automaker", can corefer with a vague description, such as "company", with the precise description as the result. Two precise descriptions can corefer if they are semantically compatible, like "automaker" and "car manufacturer". In MUC-4 it was determined that if two event structures had entities with proper names in some of the role slots, they should be merged only if there was an overlap in the names.

13.10   History of the FASTUS System

FASTUS was originally conceived, in December 1991, as a preprocessor for TACITUS that could also be run in a stand-alone mode. It was only in the middle of May 1992, considerably later in our development, that we decided the performance of FASTUS on the MUC-4 task was so high that we could make FASTUS our complete system.

Most of the design work for the FASTUS system took place during January 1992. The ideas were tested out on finding incident locations and proper names in February. With some initial favorable results in hand, we proceeded with the implementation of the system in March. The implementation of Stages 2 and 3 was completed in March, and the general mechanism for Stage 4 was completed by the end of April. On May 6, we did the first test of the FASTUS system on a blind test set of 100 terrorist reports, which had been withheld as a fair test, and we obtained a score of 8% recall and 42% precision. At that point we began a fairly intensive effort to hill-climb on all 1300 development texts then available, doing periodic runs on the fair test to monitor our progress. This effort culminated in a score of 44% recall and 57% precision in the wee hours of June 1, when we decided to run the official test. The rate of progress was rapid enough that even a few hours of work could be shown to have a noticeable impact on the score. Our scarcest resource was time, and our supply of it was eventually exhausted well before the point of diminishing returns.

We were thus able, in three and a half weeks, to increase the system's F-score by 36.2 points, from 13.5 to 49.7.

In the actual MUC-4 evaluation, on a blind test of 100 texts, we achieved a recall of 44% with precision of 55% using the most rigorous penalties for missing and spurious fills. This corresponds to an F-score ($\beta = 1$) of 48.9. On the second blind test of 100 texts, covering incidents from a different time span than the training data, we observed, surprisingly, an identical recall score of 44%; however our precision fell to 52%, for an F-score of 47.7. It was reassuring to see that there was very little degradation in performance when moving to a time period over which the system had not been trained.

Out of the seventeen sites participating in MUC-4, only General Electric's system performed significantly better (a recall of 62% and a precision of 53% on the first test set), and their system had been under development for over five years (Sundheim, 1992). Given our experience in bringing the system to its current level of performance in three and a half weeks, we felt we could achieve results in that range with another month or two of effort. Studies indicate that human intercoder reliability on information extraction tasks is in the 65-80% range. Thus, we believe this technology can perform at least 75% as well as humans.

And considerably faster. One entire test set of 100 messages, ranging from a third of a page to two pages in length, required 11.8 minutes of CPU time on a Sun SPARC-2 processor. The elapsed real time was 15.9 minutes, although observed time depends on the particular hardware configuration involved.

In more concrete terms, this means that FASTUS could read 2,375 words per minute. It could analyze one text in an average of 9.6 seconds. This translates into 9,000 texts per day.

The FASTUS system was an order of magnitude faster than the other leading systems at MUC-4.

This fast run time translates directly into fast development time, and was the reason we could improve the scores so rapidly during May 1992.

A new version of the FASTUS system was developed in the following year, and it was used for the MUC-5 evaluation. The most significant addition was a convenient graphical user interface for defining rules, utilizing SRI's Grasper system (Karp et al., 1993). This made it much easier to specify the state transitions of the finite-state machines defined for the domain application. In addition, it was at this point that Stages 2 and 3 were made separate stages of processing.

SRI entered the Japanese task in MUC-5 as well as the English. We had during the year developed a Japanese version of FASTUS for use in a conference room reservation task for a commercial client. This system read and extracted the relevant information from romanji input, and was later developed into a real-time spontaneous dialogue summarizer (Kameyama et al., 1995). For MUC-5 we converted this to handle kanji characters as well, and used the Grasper-based interface to define rules for recognizing joint ventures in both

English and Japanese business news.

In the English portion of the evaluation, FASTUS achieved a recall of 34% and a precision of 56%, for an F-score ($\beta = 1$) of 42.67. In the Japanese task, the system achieved a recall of 34% and a precision of 62%, for an F-score of 44.21. Four of the sites were part of the Tipster program, and as such received funding and several extra months to work on the domain; SRI was not at that point in the Tipster program. FASTUS outperformed all of the other non-Tipster systems. Of the four Tipster systems, only two outperformed FASTUS, and only one significantly so.

In early 1994 we developed a declarative specification language called Fast-Spec. If the Grasper-based specification interface is like augmented transition networks, then FastSpec is like unification grammar. The patterns are specified by regular grammars, the applicability of the rules is conditioned on attributes associated with the terminal symbols, and attributes can be set on the objects constructed.

This new version of FASTUS has been used for a number of applications. For one commercial client, we helped in the conversion of parts of the FASTUS system to C++ for the purposes of name recognition. For another commercial client, a pilot version of FASTUS was included in a document analysis system to aid researchers in discovering the ontology underlying complex Congressional bills, thereby ensuring the consistency of laws with the regulations that implement them.

In collaboration with E-Systems, SRI has developed the Warbreaker Message Handling System, for extracting information about time-critical targets from a large variety of military messages. This incorporates FASTUS as the component for handling the free text portions of the messages.

For the dry run of the MUC-6 evaluation in April 1995, we implemented a set of FastSpec rules for recognizing information about labor negotiations, their participants, and the status of the talks.

SRI has also been involved in the second phase of the Tipster program. As part of this effort, we have made FASTUS compliant with the Tipster architecture, aimed at enabling several different document detection and information extraction systems to interact as components in a single larger system.

The successive versions of FASTUS represent steps toward making it more possible for the nonexpert user to define his or her own patterns. This effort is continuing in our current projects.

13.11   Conclusions

Finite-state technology is sometimes characterized as *ad hoc* and as *mere* pattern-matching. However, our approach of using a *cascade* of finite-state machines, where each level corresponds to a linguistic natural kind, reflects important universals about language. It was inspired by the remarkable fact that very diverse languages all show the same nominal element - verbal element - particle distinction and the basic phrase - complex phrase distinction. Organizing a system in this way lends itself to greater portability among domains and to the possibility of easier acquisition of new patterns.

The advantages of the FASTUS system are as follows:

- It is conceptually simple. It is a set of cascaded finite-state automata.

- It is effective. It has been among the leaders in recent evaluations.

- It has very fast run time.

- In part because of the fast run time, it has a very fast development time. This is also true because the system provides a direct link between the texts being analyzed and the data being extracted.

FASTUS is not a text understanding system. It is an information extraction system. But for information extraction tasks, it is perhaps the most convenient and most effective system that has been developed.

One of the lessons to be learned from our FASTUS experience is that many information extraction tasks are much easier than anyone ever thought. Although the full linguistic complexity of the texts is often very high, with long sentences and interesting discourse structure problems, the relative simplicity of the information-extraction task allows much of this linguistic complexity to be bypassed—indeed much more than we had originally believed was possible. The key to the whole problem, as we see it from our FASTUS experience, is to do exactly the right amount of syntax, so that pragmatics can take over its share of the load. For many information extraction tasks, we think FASTUS displays exactly the right mixture.

While FASTUS is an elegant achievement, the whole host of linguistic problems that were bypassed are still out there, and will have to be addressed eventually for more complex tasks, and to achieve higher performance on simple tasks. We have shown one can go a long way with simple techniques. But the hard problems cannot be ignored forever, and scientific progress requires that they be addressed.

Acknowledgments

The FASTUS system was originally built under SRI internal research and development funding. Specific applications and improvements have been funded by the (Defense) Advanced Research Projects Agency under Office of Naval

Research contract N00014-90-C-0220, Office of Research and Development contract 94-F157700-000, and Naval Command, Control and Ocean Surveilliance Center contract N66001-94-C-6044, and by the US Army Topographic Engineering Center under contract no. DACA76-93-L-0019. Specific developments have also been funded by commercial contracts.

References

Appelt, Douglas E., Jerry R. Hobbs, John Bear, David Israel, Megumi Kameyama, and Mabry Tyson, 1993a. "The SRI MUC-5 JV-FASTUS Information Extraction System", *Proceedings*, Fifth Message Understanding Conference (MUC-5), Baltimore, Maryland, August 1993.

Appelt, Douglas E., Jerry R. Hobbs, John Bear, David Israel, and Mabry Tyson, 1993b. "FASTUS: A Finite-State Processor for Information Extraction from Real-World Text", *Proceedings*. IJCAI-93, Chambery, France, August 1993.

Black, Alan W., 1989. "Finite State Machines from Feature Grammars," in Tomita, ed., *International Workshop on Parsing Technologies,* pp. 277–285.

Church, Ken W., 1980. *On Memory Limitations in Natural Language Processing*, MIT Laboratory of Computer Science Technical Report MIT/LCS/TR-245.

Croft, William, 1991. *Syntactic Categories and Grammatical Relations: The Cognitive Organization of Information*, University of Chicago Press, Chicago, Illinois.

Hobbs, Jerry R., Douglas E. Appelt, John Bear, Mabry Tyson, and David Magerman, 1992a. "Robust Processing of Real-World Natural-Language Texts", in *Text-Based Intelligent Systems: Current Research and Practice in Information Extraction and Retrieval*, P. Jacobs, editor, Lawrence Erlbaum Associates, Hillsdale, New Jersey, pp. 13-33.

Hobbs, Jerry R., Douglas E. Appelt, John Bear, David Israel, and Mabry Tyson, 1992b. "FASTUS: A System for Extracting Information from Natural-Language Text", SRI Technical Note 519, SRI International, Menlo Park, California, November 1992.

Hobbs, Jerry R., Douglas E. Appelt, John Bear, David Israel, Megumi Kameyama, and Mabry Tyson, 1992c. "FASTUS: A System for Extracting Information from Text", *Proceedings*, Human Language Technology, Princeton, New Jersey, pp. 133-137, March 1993.

Hobbs, Jerry R., Mark Stickel, Douglas Appelt, and Paul Martin, 1993. "Interpretation as Abduction", *Artificial Intelligence*, Vol. 63, Nos. 1-2, pp. 69-142. Also published as SRI International Artificial Intelligence Center Technical Note 499, December 1990.

Kameyama, Megumi, Goh Kawai, and Isao Arima, 1995. "A Real-Time System for Summarizing Human-Human Spontaneous Spoken Dialogues", *Proceedings* of the Fourth International Conference on Spoken Language Processing (ICSLP-96), Philadelphia, PA, October 1996.

Karp, Peter D., John D. Lowrance, Thomas M. Strat, David E. Wilkins, 1993. "The Grasper-CL Graph Management System", Technical Note No. 521, Artificial Intelligence Center, SRI International, January 1993.

Lehnert, Wendy, Claire Cardie, David Fisher, Ellen Riloff, and Robert Williams, 1991. "Description of the CIRCUS System as Used for MUC-3", *Proceedings*, Third Message Understanding Conference (MUC-3), San Diego, California, pp. 223-233.

Magerman, D., and C. Weir, "Probabilistic Prediction and Picky Chart Parsing," Proceedings of the Fifth DARPA Workshop on Speech and Natural Language, February, 1992.

Pereira, Fernando, 1990. "Finite-State Approximations of Grammars", *Proceedings*, DARPA Speech and Natural Language Workshop, Hidden Valley, Pennsylvania, pp. 20-25.

Pereira, Fernando, and R. Wright, 1991. "Finite-State Approximation of Phrase Structure Grammars", *Proceedings*, 29th Meeting of the Association for Computational Linguistics, Berkeley, California, pp. 246–255.

Sundheim, Beth, ed., 1991. *Proceedings*, Third Message Understanding Conference (MUC-3), San Diego, California, May 1991. Distributed by Morgan Kaufmann Publishers, Inc., San Mateo, California.

Sundheim, Beth, ed., 1992. *Proceedings*, Fourth Message Understanding Conference (MUC-4), McLean, Virginia, June 1992. Distributed by Morgan Kaufmann Publishers, Inc., San Mateo, California.

Sundheim, Beth, ed., 1993. *Proceedings*, Fifth Message Understanding Conference (MUC-5), Baltimore, Maryland, August 1993. Distributed by Morgan Kaufmann Publishers, Inc., San Mateo, California.

Tipster Text Program (Phase I), 1993. *Proceedings*, Advanced Research Projects Agency, September 1993.

Tyson, W. Mabry, Douglas Appelt, Jerry R. Hobbs, John Bear, David Israel, and Megumi Kameyama, to appear. "Recognizing and Interpreting Tables".

Weischedel, Ralph, et al., 1993. "BBN PLUM: MUC-5 System Description", in Sundheim, ed., *Proceedings*, Fifth Message Understanding Conference (MUC-5), Baltimore, Maryland, August 1993.

14 Rational Transductions for Phonetic Conversion and Phonology

Éric Laporte

Phonetic conversion, and other conversion problems related to phonetics, can be performed by finite-state tools. We present a finite-state conversion system, BiPho, based on transducers and bimachines, two mathematical notions borrowed from the theory of rational transductions. The linguistic data used by this system are described in a readable format and actual computation is efficient. With adequate data, BiPho constitutes the first comprehensive spelling-to-phonetics conversion system for French to take the form of transducers or bimachines.

14.1 Introduction

Spelling-to-phonetics conversion is one of the most classical problems in natural language processing. Several other conversion problems related to phonetics are interesting in themselves or for their applications. For example, phonetics-to-spelling decoding is a real challenge and has applications in speech processing. Appropriate computational solutions for these conversion problems are provided by finite-state tools: transducers (i.e. automata with input and output) and bimachines, two notions borrowed from the theory of rational transductions. We present a conversion system, BiPho, based on transducers and bimachines. This conceptual and computational framework has two major advantages: the description of linguistic data is carried out in a readable format, and the speed of the conversion algorithm is independent of the size of the set of conversion rules and dominated by the length of input strings. With spelling-to-phonetics conversion data for French, BiPho constitutes the first comprehensive spelling-to-phonetics conversion system for French to take the

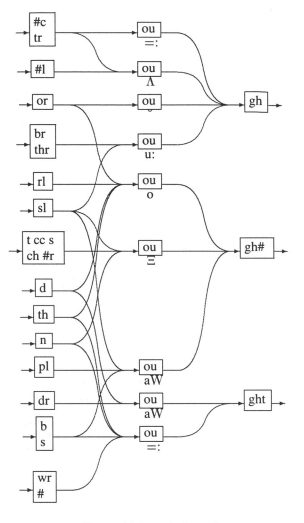

Figure 14.1: *ou* before *gh*.

form of transducers or bimachines.

14.2   An Introductory Example

English has one of the most difficult spelling systems. Figure 14.1 shows the phonetic transcription of *ou* before *gh*. It is a directed acyclic graph which reads from left to right. This graph is a representation of a finite transducer. A transducer is an automaton where each transition is labelled by an input label and an output label. In this figure, input labels are displayed inside the boxes and output labels under the boxes. Input labels are spellings of word parts, output labels are phonetic transcriptions. Since the figure concentrates on the pronunciation of *ou* before *gh*, a phonetic transcription is displayed only under those boxes which contain *ou*. The other boxes contain the left or right contexts. The special symbol ♯ stands for word limit or morpheme boundary. This graph is rather readable for people but it can also be used in order to compute phonetic transcriptions of words. This type of representation has several advantages.

1. Readability. An error in a graph like that of Figure 14.1 is easy to detect even for a non-specialist if a word which is an exception to the rules comes across his mind. Metalanguage and conventions are reduced to a minimum and take a graphical form.

2. Formalization. The formal meaning of this type of representation is defined mathematically.

3. Compactness. Various contexts are taken into account in Figure 14.1, but when similar contexts for different pronunciations are considered, several paths in the graph can often share their common part. For example, final *gh*, i.e. *gh♯*, appears once for *though, enough, bough* and *thorough*; *th* appears once for *though* and *thought*. When long lists of words or word elements are to be listed, avoiding the repetition of common parts is a substantial economy, whereas making such lists without automata is discouraging and error-prone. The mathematical properties of automata that underlie this practical advantage are minimality properties.

4. Cumulativity. Figure 14.1 deals with a very specific issue. It should be associated with many other graphs in order to make up the complete data of a phonetic conversion system. The formal meaning of the combination of finite-state transducers can be designed and defined so that the contents of a given graph will not interfere with the contents of another when they are combined. This feature is an improvement upon hierarchies of rules and exceptions which are traditionally used for spelling-to-phonetics conversion: a modification on a particular rule or exception in a hierarchy may have non-local effects.

5. Generality. This introductory example only deals with spelling-to-phonetics conversion of English text. However, the same type of formalism applies to more exotic conversion tasks, involving other languages, phonemics-to-phonetics conversion, phonetics-to-spelling decoding, etc.

6. Efficiency. Finite-state transducers, including ones with dozens of thousands of states, are also an efficient computational tool if they are wisely implemented. This feature is of the utmost importance since the size of the data at stake, in the final analysis, depends on the number of words in the language.

As a matter of fact, this paper describes theoretical and practical work done in this framework on several conversion problems related to phonetics. The phonetic conversion system BiPho exploits complete data for phonetic conversion in French(Laporte, 1993). French spelling is as irregular as English spelling. The output of the conversion constitutes the 600,000-inflected-word phonetic dictionary of LADL[1].

Section 14.3 states which conversion problems are concerned. Section 14.4 deals with the problem of designing a transducer to specify a given transduction and points out the consequences of decisions made at that stage. Section 14.5 introduces mathematical properties that relevant transductions usually have and mathematical tools that underly our implementation. Section 14.6 specifies a readable mode of representing transductions related to phonetics, defines its formal meaning, and describes an efficient implementation of it.

14.3   Transductions Related to Phonetics

In this section, we have a linguistic standpoint about a number of problems for which we will claim that finite-state devices are appropriate formal and computational tools. The prototypical example of these problems is that of spelling-to-phonetics conversion. A given speech utterance can be transcribed orthographically or phonetically; spelling and phonetics can thus be considered as two levels of representation of language. Spelling-to-phonetic conversion refers to two types of problems. First, one is faced with a descriptive problem: which spelling transcriptions are in relation with which phonetic transcriptions? Then, two computational problems can be contemplated: given a spelling transcription, what phonetic transcriptions can be in relation with it? and the reverse problem. In order to pose this kind of problems in an accurate way, we discuss a few issues about some of the levels of representations of speech. The reader who is only interested in formal or computational aspects can go to section 14.4, page 413.

Spelling needs not be defined, at least for English and other European languages with well-documented, standardized writing systems. Spelling can be considered as a practical level of linguistic representation. It appears as a formal system: transcriptions are coded as sequences of symbols. The set of

---

[1] Laboratoire d'automatique documentaire et linguistique, University of Paris 7, France.

symbols, the alphabet, is finite. We will consider only lowercase letters and a special symbol ♯ standing for word boundary. The size of the alphabet is thus less than 30 in English. It must be extended for other languages, due to accents and other diacritics. In French, spelling is highly ambiguous with respect to pronunciation, so we use as an intermediate level a disambiguating alphabet where e.g. intervocalic *s* is marked as s_{15} when it is pronounced [s], like in *paras$_{15}$ol* (in most words, intervocalic *s* is pronounced [z]). This disambiguating alphabet has 315 symbols. This method could give interesting results in English also.

The definition of a phonetic level of representation is not so simple. It is connected with three theoretical issues:

- the principle of using a finite set of symbols and of building linear sequences of symbols, is a far from neutral choice linguistically;

- it is usually considered that the elementary units at a phonetic level are not the symbols in the phonetic alphabet but binary feature-value pairs which serve to define these symbols;

- we will make a distinction between narrow transcriptions, which are an observational account of pronunciation, and abstract transcriptions, which are a means of taking into account phonetic variations in the phonology of languages.

14.3.1 Linear sequences are simple structures

Using an alphabet, i.e. a finite set of symbols, and building linear sequences of symbols, is a familiar principle, but it is not a neutral linguistic choice when it is used to represent speech. If we consider speech as a combination of acoustic and articulatory events, this combination is much more complex than phonetic transcriptions of speech: in the duration of one or two phonetic segments, dozens of acoustic events happen, their chronological order may vary, most of them are continuous variations of continuous parameters, and those which are instantaneous are hardly ever simultaneous. In other words, the most accurate phonetic transcription is only an approximate, partial and imperfect description of speech. However, phonetic transcriptions are an excellent descriptive tool. It is standardized to quite a reasonable degree among linguists, and it is successfully used for speech synthesis (e.g. synthesis by diphones) when associated with prosodic information. This is why we stick to linear sequences of phonetic symbols as one of the convenient and useful representations of pronunciation.

With the development of non-linear phonology, many linguists shifted from one-dimensional to multi-dimensional abstract representations of speech. For example, in spite of the fact that time is essentially one-dimensional, it is unquestionable that some phonetic variations or phenomena involve embedded structures in speech: syllables, coda, etc. However, the level of recursion of such structures has very restrictive bounds, so that they can be coded in linear strings which are a simpler structure than trees.

14.3.2   Phonetic symbols are readable

The symbols in the phonetic alphabet are usually defined by binary feature-value pairs. In this view, the elementary units at a phonetic level are not the phonetic symbols but the binary features. Phonetic and phonological descriptions make an intensive use of binary features. A set of phonetic symbols, e.g. {pbfv}, may be expressed as [+*labial* −*son*], which is less redundant. One can also replace a few rules by one. Generative phonology is traditionally much concerned about redundancy, since the best possible grammar should be the least redundant. Using binary features brings about some decrease in redundancy, but also a dramatic decrease in readability: for a human reader, series like {pbfv} are more readable than binary-feature specifications. For such a practical purpose as actual linguistic description, readability and compactness are as important as redundancy. The work described in this paper does not take any advantage of binary features, but the same formal framework could undoubtedly be adapted with only minor modifications in order to express rules by means of features.

Since we use linear strings on a finite alphabet, and we study the relations between these strings, the appropriate formal framework for this study is that of transductions, i.e. relations over two sets of strings. Basic definitions about transductions in the context of phonetics and phonology are given in Kaplan and Kay (1994).

14.3.3   Phonetics or phonemics

It seems difficult to actually carry out any extensive description of phonetic forms in a language without taking into account the traditional distinction between narrow and abstract transcriptions. Narrow transcriptions are an observational account of pronunciation, whereas abstract transcriptions aim at taking into account phonetic variations in the phonology of languages. For example, the final *s* is pronounced differently in *seats* and *seizes*, and narrow transcriptions reflect this difference: [si:ts], [si:ziz]. If we consider that this [s] and this [iz] are variants of the [z] heard in *sees* [si:z], we can transcribe them by means of the same symbol /z/ in abstract transcriptions: /si:tz/, /si:zz/, /si:z/. We will use the terms *phonetic level* to refer to the level of narrow transcriptions, *phonemic level* to refer to that of abstract ones, and *phonemes* to refer to the elements of the alphabet of the phonemic level.

Phonemic transcriptions are also useful to describe free phonetic variations. For example, in French, *lier* 'link' admits a monosyllabic phonetic form [lje] and a disyllabic one [lije]: we transcribe both as /li+e/ (Laporte, 1989). Several phonetic variants are produced from a phonemic form by a multiple-output transduction. Multiple-output transductions are often defined with optional rules, but the notion of several-output transduction is more general than that of optional rule. For example, if we transcribe *lier* with the phonemic form /lje/ and if we produce the variant [lije] with an optional rule that inserts [i], this rule might produce a wrong variant *[pije] for *pied* [pje] 'foot'. On the other hand, if we transcribe *lier* with the phonemic form /lije/ and if we produce the variant [lje] with an optional rule that deletes [i], this rule might produce a wrong variant *[pje] for *piller* [pije] 'plunder'. Finally, the phonemic form /li+e/ contains an unpronounceable variation mark /+/, so the rule that produces [lje] and [lije] from /li+e/ has to be obligatory.

14.3.4   From a level to another

Spelling, phonetics and phonemics are three levels of linguistic representation: there are six ways of going from one of them to another, thus six conversion problems for each language. Our experiments on spelling-to-phonemics and phonemics-to-phonetics in French showed that these two problems have much in common: the same computational framework gave good results for both. Another type of conversion problem is also probably very close: the simulation of phonetic changes from a historical state of a language to another or to its present state.

In the following, the transductions whose definition was outlined in this section will be referred to as 'transductions related to phonetics'.

14.4   Construction of the Transductions

A transduction is an abstract object. A transducer or another formal device that 'realizes' a transduction is an abstract machine that specifies it in a more concrete way, though it does not specify a particular algorithm to perform the conversion. Automata theory provides various mathematically equivalent ways of recognizing the same set or realizing the same transduction. In such a practical enterprise as ours, we have to choose a particular device to realize a transduction. This choice is not neutral:

- the success of the operation depends on the theoretical expressive power of the device;

- this choice may facilitate or hinder the descriptive aspect of the work, namely the elaboration of the conversion rules;

- it may lead to more or less efficient implementations of the computation.

Let us examine the consequences of those requirements on the problem of designing and implementing transducers.

14.4.1 Alignments

What we will call an alignment of a transduction is a correspondence between input symbols and output symbols in strings. A transduction in itself does not specify any alignment between input symbols and output symbols. However, transducers and other devices do specify an alignment of the transduction they realize. Several transducers that realize the same transduction may specify different alignments, as in Figure 14.2. The symbol <E> is the empty se-

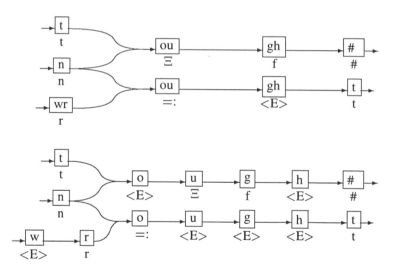

Figure 14.2: Two alignments of the same transduction.

quence which is made of no symbols at all. Rational expressions and other mathematical constructs used to define rational transductions also specify an alignment. In the case of the transductions related to phonetics mentioned in section 14.3, page 410, the time correspondence between input and output is a meaningful alignment for all of them, but specifying it in the smallest detail sometimes involves arbitrary decisions. For example, Figure 14.2 specifies two alignments between spelling and phonetic transcription. They differ only in details and both of them are quite sensible. In order to take full advantage of the partial regularity of spelling-to-phonetics transduction, the transducer that performs the conversion must at least approximately follow the natural alignment.

In a transducer, input and output labels are strings over the input or output alphabet. They can comprise zero, one or several symbols. A reasonable simplification of the problem is to consider alignments where each separate input symbol in the input string has its own counterpart in the output; the output for a given input symbol may still be composed of zero, one or several symbols. Formally, we will say that a device that realizes a transduction is strictly alphabetic if and only if it associates with each symbol in input strings a factor of the corresponding output string. The second transducer of Figure 14.2 is strictly alphabetic, i.e. each input label is an isolated input symbol. In the case of transductions related to phonetics, a strictly alphabetic alignment is always possible and is usually close to the most natural alignment.

14.4.2   Divide and conquer

Describing a complex transduction is an intricate task, we need to split it into smaller tasks. The finite-state formal framework provides ways to do that. Individual transductions can be devised for independent subtasks, and combined into a larger transduction that solves the original problem. Two simple principles will help us implement this strategy.

14.4.2.1   Simultaneous combination

The rules for translating a symbol are often very different from those for translating another. When it is the case, the transduction that will apply to the first symbol can be described independently of the other. Assume a transduction t_1 translates a given input pattern, leaving all the rest unchanged, and a transduction t_2 translates another input pattern that does not overlap the other and also leaves the rest unchanged. Then t_1 and t_2 apply to different places in input strings and can apply (conceptually) simultaneously. In other words, t_1 and t_2 can be implemented (conceptually) in parallel. In section 14.6, page 422, we will give a formal definition of the 'simultaneous combination' $t_1 + t_2$ of transductions t_1 and t_2 provided that they apply either to different input strings or in different contexts. The result of the simultaneous combination of transductions is independent of the order in which the transductions are given.

14.4.2.2   Sequential combination or composition

Transductions related to phonetics frequently have a natural expression as a composition of simpler transductions: one describes a finite sequence of transductions in a definite order, and the output of each of them will serve as input for the next. This amounts to defining intermediate levels of representation and going from each level to the next. Expressing a transduction as a composition of simpler ones is a basic method in generative phonology. This concept is called 'rule ordering'. If the output of t_1 serves as input for t_2, the composition of t_1 and t_2 will be noted $t_1 \circ t_2$.

14.4.3   Deterministic computation

When a transducer is strictly alphabetic, one can make an automaton out of it by deleting all output labels. This automaton is called the projection of the transducer. The projection of a strictly alphabetic transducer may be deterministic or not. If it is, the output strings for a given input string can be produced by a deterministic computation using the transducer. A deterministic computation is more direct, and therefore usually simpler and more efficient than a non-deterministic computation. We say that a transducer is deterministic if it is strictly alphabetic and has a deterministic projection[2]. The transducer of Figure 14.3 is non-deterministic: when we build the projection by deleting

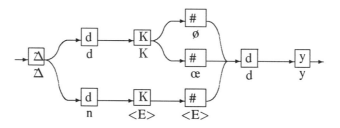

Figure 14.3: A non-deterministic transducer.

the output labels [d] and [n], we leave two transitions with the same label /d/ and different targets. In fact, if we wish to have this transduction realized by a deterministic finite transducer, we will not find any with the same alignment. However, in phonemics-to-phonetics conversion, when this problem occurs, the transduction can usually be expressed as a combination of transductions realized by deterministic transducers. The combination may involve simultaneous or sequential combinations or both (cf. above). The fact that this simplification of the problem is usually possible is an empirical observation

---

[2]This terminology is not traditional. There is no standard definition of deterministic transducers.

which is not predicted by phonological theories. In the following, we assume it is always the case. For example, the transducer of Figure 14.3 can be expressed as $t_1 \circ (t_2 + t_3)$. In this expression, t_1, t_2 and t_3 are the deterministic transducers of Figure 14.4, the symbol $\circ$ refers to sequential combination and + refers to simultaneous combination. An advantage of this representation is that t_1, t_2 and t_3 represent separately three unrelated phenomena. Note that t_1 produces two variants, but is deterministic: when we build the projection by deleting the output labels [K] and <E>, the two original transitions merge into one transition since they have the same input label [K] and the same target.

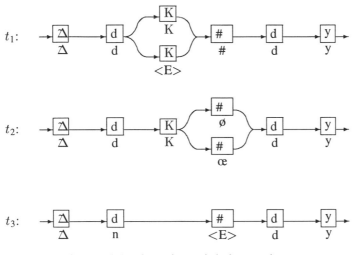

Figure 14.4: Three deterministic transducers.

The phonetic conversion data used with BiPho for French involve 13 levels of representation: the first is spelling, the sixth is phonemics and the last is phonetics. The overall transduction is thus implemented as the composition of 12 transductions. Each of them is in turn the simultaneous combination of 6 to 231 simple transductions realized by deterministic transducers. We need a few more mathematical notions before describing how these elementary transductions are represented, how they are combined, and how the actual conversion is performed.

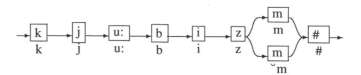

Figure 14.5: A transduction which is not a function.

14.5   Mathematical Properties

The transductions mentioned in section 14.3 page 410 are usually rational transductions. A transduction[3] over alphabets A and B is rational if it can be specified by a rational expression over $A^\star \times B^\star$. Equivalently, a transduction is rational if it can be realized by a finite transducer. The fact that phonological transductions are usually rational is far from new. It was first noticed by Johnson (1972). It is stated in more standard terms by Kaplan and Kay (1994). In what follows we examine other mathematical properties of transductions related to phonetics. The interested reader will find more details about definitions and algorithms in handbooks of automata theory, e.g. Berstel (1979) or Perrin (1990).

14.5.1   Transductions realized by deterministic transducers

In a transduction, an input string can be in relation with several output strings. In the case of transductions related to phonetics, this allows us to describe phonetic variants. For example, in Figure 14.5, the phonemic string /kju:bizm/ is in relation with two phonetic strings, [kju:bizm] and [kju:biz\u{}m].

When every input string is in relation with at most one output string, the transduction is said to be a function. A transduction realized by a deterministic finite transducer is not necessarily a function (examples: Figures 14.4 and 14.5), but it is easy to prove that it is the composition of a rational function and a finite substitution. A finite substitution σ over alphabets A and B is a transduction such that:

- for each $a \in A$, $\sigma(a)$ is a finite subset of $B^\star$,

- $\sigma(<E>) = <E>$ and

- for each $u, v \in A^\star$, $\sigma(uv) = \sigma(u)\sigma(v)$.

Finite substitutions are rational transductions. Figure 14.6 shows the decom-

---

[3]In automata theory, the terminology *rational* is preferred to *regular* because it emphasizes the analogy with the theory of rational functions in classical analysis and of rational power series in commuting variables.

rational
function:

finite substitution:

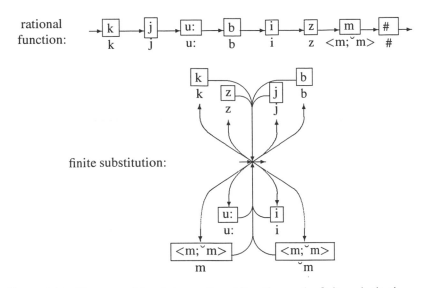

Figure 14.6: Decomposition into a rational function and a finite substitution.

position of the transduction of Figure 14.5 into a rational function and a finite substitution which is represented as a one-state transducer in the figure. Recall that transductions related to phonetics can usually be expressed as a combination of transductions realized by deterministic finite transducers. When they can, it follows that they can also be expressed as a combination of rational functions and finite substitutions, which are simple cases of rational transductions. The computational interest of this decomposition stems from the fact that rational functions and finite substitutions can be realized by well-known, simple devices for which efficient implementations are known. Finite substitutions are realized by one-state transducers. Rational string functions are realized by bimachines.

14.5.2 Bimachines

The notion of bimachine was introduced by Schützenberger (1961). It is a strictly alphabetic, deterministic variant of the notion of finite transducer. The set of transductions realized by bimachines is the set of rational string functions (Eilenberg, 1974). Any bimachine can be compiled into an equivalent transducer with the same alignment.

A bimachine over alphabets A and B is composed of two finite sets $\overrightarrow{Q}, \overleftarrow{Q}$, two initial states $\overrightarrow{q_-} \in \overrightarrow{Q}$, $\overleftarrow{q_-} \in \overleftarrow{Q}$, two transition functions $\overrightarrow{\delta} : \overrightarrow{Q} \times A \to \overrightarrow{Q}$ and

$\overleftarrow{\delta} : \overleftarrow{Q} \times A \rightarrow \overleftarrow{Q}$, and an output function

$$\gamma : \overrightarrow{Q} \times A \times \overleftarrow{Q} \rightarrow B^{\star}.$$

In fact, $\overrightarrow{Q}$, $\overrightarrow{q_-}$ and $\overrightarrow{\delta}$ constitute a left-to-right deterministic automaton without final states, and $\overleftarrow{Q}$, $\overleftarrow{q_-}$ and $\overleftarrow{\delta}$ constitute a right-to-left deterministic automaton without final states. The transition functions are extended to $\overrightarrow{Q} \times A^{\star}$ and $\overleftarrow{Q} \times A^{\star}$ by setting $\overrightarrow{\delta}\ (\overrightarrow{q}, <\mathrm{E}>) = \overrightarrow{q}$, $\overleftarrow{\delta}\ (\overleftarrow{q}, <\mathrm{E}>) = \overleftarrow{q}$, $\overrightarrow{\delta}\ (\overrightarrow{q}, ua) = \overrightarrow{\delta}\ (\overrightarrow{\delta}\ (\overrightarrow{q}, u), a)$, $\overleftarrow{\delta}\ (\overleftarrow{q}, ua) = \overleftarrow{\delta}\ (\overleftarrow{\delta}\ (\overleftarrow{q}, u), a)$. For an input string $a_1 a_2 \ldots a_n$, the output for a_i is defined as

$$\gamma(\overrightarrow{\delta}\ (\overrightarrow{q_-}, a_1 a_2 \ldots a_{i-1}), a_i, \overleftarrow{\delta}\ (\overleftarrow{q_-}, a_n a_{n-1} \ldots a_{i+1}))$$

The output string for $a_1 a_2 \ldots a_n$ is the concatenation of the output strings for $a_1, a_2, \ldots a_n$. Thus, a bimachine realizes a string function.

Bimachines are a convenient tool both for linguistic description and computation.

The linguistic description of a transduction related to phonetics generally takes the form of a set of conversion rules. Usual rules comprise a 'context part', which recognizes whether the rule applies, and an 'action part', which translates symbols. Rules are often stated in the form $a \longrightarrow u/L\_\_\_R$, where the context part is $L\_\_\_R$ and the action part is $a \longrightarrow u$. In the usual sense, the context refers to the input string, which is known before the rules apply, and not to the output string. This is the most straightforward convention and makes rules readable and easy to design.

The structure of a bimachine is quite similar. The two deterministic automata correspond to the left and right context parts of the rule, and the output function constitutes the action part; the context part refers to the input string only. In section 14.6, page 422, we describe a readable, graphic mode of representation of bimachines, and algorithms for loading a bimachine from this format and running it.

The structure of a finite transducer is not so directly similar to that of a usual rule. Contexts and actions are mixed up in transition labels. Since transition labels combine input and output symbols, contexts may refer both to input and output labels (see Koskenniemi (1983), Kaplan and Kay (1994) for examples).

The computation of a bimachine is deterministic, hence simpler than that of a non-deterministic device. On the other hand, the inversion of a transduction (swapping input and output) is probably easier to implement on a transducer than on a bimachine.

14.5.3 Locality

The translation of a symbol usually depends on its context, but this dependency is usually very local. This is probably the reason why phonologists are so fond of counter-examples with unbounded dependencies. Intuitively, a conversion rule is local if the length of the context needed to apply the rule is bounded for all input strings. Typical values of this bound are small, about ten or even five symbols. Contexts of unbounded length are frequently used by phonologists, but in most cases they are easy to replace with bounded contexts. For example, <Cons>* in a context apparently matches any number of consonants, but since sequences of consonants with no intervening vowel hardly go beyond five symbols in French, the pattern of Figure 14.7 has the same effect as a rule that converts /e/ into [ ] before <Cons><Cons>*#.

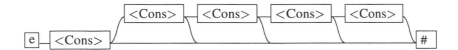

Figure 14.7: Bounded context for sequences of consonants.

Formally, the notion of locality is defined with respect to automata. Let s, d be positive integers such that $0 \leq d \leq s$. An automaton is (s, d)-local if for each pair of paths of length s, $(q_0, a_1, q_1, \ldots a_s, q_s)$ and $(q'_0, a_1, q'_1, \ldots a_s, q'_s)$, labelled by the same sequence $a_1 a_2 \ldots a_s$, we have $q_d = q'_d$. An automaton is local if there exist s and d such that it is (s, d)-local. If so, the smallest possible value for s is called the scope of the automaton.

This notion of locality applies to the left-to-right and right-to-left deterministic automata of a bimachine. Let l, r be positive integers. We say that a bimachine is (l, r)-local if its left-to-right automaton is (l, l)-local and its right-to-left automaton is (r, r)-local. The maximal length of relevant left contexts is l and the maximal length of relevant right contexts is r. If a bimachine is (l, r)-local, the function that it realizes is also realized by a finite transducer whose projection is an $(l + r, l)$-local automaton.

Recall that with BiPho, the transduction is expressed as a combination of rational functions and finite substitutions (cf. page 419). In the phonetic conversion data for French, this decomposition of the problem could be done in such a way that all rational functions are realized by local bimachines, i.e. all contexts have bounded length.

14.6   Implementation

The rational functions used by BiPho are realized by local bimachines. They are created in a graphic form like that of Figure 14.8, which comprises a context part which recognizes whether the rule applies and an action part which translates symbols. Each batch of graphs that must apply simultaneously is read and combined into a bimachine. The resulting bimachines apply sequentially to input strings. The finite substitutions that should apply to the output of the bimachines are not implemented yet.

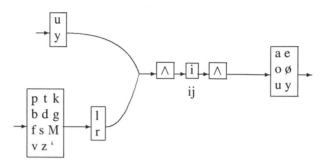

Figure 14.8: A conversion rule.

14.6.1   Construction of a bimachine from a rule

The conversion rule of Figure 14.8 reads as follows. The left and right context parts are delimited from the action part of the rule by the symbol ∧. The left and right contexts take the form of finite automata that read from left to right. The transitions in the context parts are boxes with only input labels (inside the boxes). The action part is the only transition which has both an input label and an output label (below the box). The input label is one input symbol, but the output label may be a string of zero, one or several output symbols. In case of variants, the output label stands for the list of variants. The semantics of the rule is straightforward: whenever the input label of the action part occurs between the left and right contexts, substitute the output label for it, otherwise leave it unchanged. This rule converts /i/ into /ij/ in certain contexts, e.g. for *plier* [plije] 'fold', it converts /plie/ into /plije/.

The context part of the graph contains only the part of the context which is relevant to the transduction; if the action part of the rule must take place no matter what the left context is, then the left context part of the graph is empty. The left and right context parts of the automaton are converted into finite automata which are then determinized and minimized with the aid of standard algorithms. Let L (resp. R) be the set of sequences recognized by the left (resp. right) context part of the graph: the left-to-right deterministic automaton of the bimachine must recognize $A^\star L$, and the right-to-left automaton must recognize $A^\star \tilde{R}$, where the elements of $\tilde{R}$ are the elements of R read in reverse order. The only algorithm needed for the construction of these automata is the construction of a finite automaton recognizing $A^\star L$ from an automaton recognizing L, and the same for $\tilde{R}$. Since relevant contexts are bounded in length, L and R are finite. We apply to them a variant of the algorithm of Aho and Corasick (1975). The original version of this algorithm makes use of the set of prefixes of a finite set L. This set can be replaced with the set of states of the minimal deterministic finite automaton recognizing L. The algorithm has to be adapted (Mohri, 1994), but it produces an automaton with less states than in the original version. However, the resulting automaton is not necessarily minimal, so we minimize it. There is no notion of final states in a bimachine. In our implementation, the automata for $A^\star L$ and $A^\star \tilde{R}$ do have final state sets: they are used in the definition of the output function.

The output function γ of the bimachine is defined as follows: if $a \in A$ is the input label of the action part, and if $u \in B^\star$ is the output label, then

$$\gamma(\overrightarrow{q}, b, \overleftarrow{q}) :=$$

```
    if b = a and →q is final and ←q is final
        then u
        else b
```

The two deterministic automata are implemented with two-dimensional tables whose rows are indexed by states and whose columns are indexed by input symbols. The content of the table at line $\overrightarrow{q}$ and at column a is the state $\overrightarrow{\delta}(\overrightarrow{q}, a)$.

14.6.2   Simultaneous combination of bimachines

Several transductions realized by bimachines can apply simultaneously to the same input provided that they do not conflict. A conflict is defined as follows. Let $a_i \longrightarrow u_i / L_i \underline{\quad} R_i$, for $1 \le i \le n$, be n bimachines over A and B defined as above: $L_i \subset A^\star$ and $R_i \subset A^\star$ are the left and right context parts, $a_i \in A$ is the input label of the action part and $u_i \in B^\star$ is the output label of the action part. A conflict arises if and only if two bimachines apply to the same input symbol of an input string, i.e. if there are two indices i and j, with $1 \le i < j \le n$, such that $A^\star L_i \cap A^\star L_j \ne \emptyset$, $a_i = a_j$ and $R_i A^\star \cap R_j A^\star \ne \emptyset$. This condition is checked for each pair of rules by computing the intersections of contexts.

If there are no conflicts, the simultaneous combination is possible. Let $\overrightarrow{Q_i}$, $\overleftarrow{Q_i}$ be the state sets of the n bimachines, $\overrightarrow{q_{i,-}} \in \overrightarrow{Q_i}$, $\overleftarrow{q_{i,-}} \in \overleftarrow{Q_i}$ the initial states, $\overrightarrow{\delta_i} : \overrightarrow{Q_i} \times A \to \overrightarrow{Q_i}$ and $\overleftarrow{\delta_i} : \overleftarrow{Q_i} \times A \to \overleftarrow{Q_i}$ the transition functions, and $\gamma_i : \overrightarrow{Q_i} \times A \times \overleftarrow{Q_i} \to B^\star$ the output function. Then the combined bimachine is defined as follows:

$$\overrightarrow{Q} = \overrightarrow{Q_1} \times \overrightarrow{Q_2} \times \ldots \times \overrightarrow{Q_n}, \ \overleftarrow{Q} = \overleftarrow{Q_1} \times \overleftarrow{Q_2} \times \ldots \times \overleftarrow{Q_n},$$

$$\overrightarrow{q_-} = (\overrightarrow{q_{1,-}}, \overrightarrow{q_{2,-}}, \ldots \overrightarrow{q_{n,-}}), \ \overleftarrow{q_-} = (\overleftarrow{q_{1,-}}, \overleftarrow{q_{2,-}}, \ldots \overleftarrow{q_{n,-}}),$$

$$\overrightarrow{\delta} ((\overrightarrow{q_1}, \ldots \overrightarrow{q_n}), a) = (\overrightarrow{\delta_1} (\overrightarrow{q_1}, a), \ldots \overrightarrow{\delta_n} (\overrightarrow{q_n}, a)),$$

$$\overleftarrow{\delta} ((\overleftarrow{q_1}, \ldots \overleftarrow{q_n}), a) = (\overleftarrow{\delta_1} (\overleftarrow{q_1}, a), \ldots \overleftarrow{\delta_n} (\overleftarrow{q_n}, a)).$$

With this definition, $\overrightarrow{Q}$ and $\overleftarrow{Q}$ may contain states which cannot be reached from the initial states, but it is not necessary to actually create such states. Before defining the output function, note that for each $u, v \in A^\star$ such that $\overrightarrow{\delta} (\overrightarrow{q_-}, u) = \overrightarrow{\delta} (\overrightarrow{q_-}, v)$,

$$\forall i \in [1, n] \ (u \in A^\star L_i \iff v \in A^\star L_i).$$

For each state $\overrightarrow{q} = \overrightarrow{\delta} (\overrightarrow{q_-}, u)$ we can therefore define

$$\texttt{left}(\overrightarrow{q}) := \{i \in [1, n] \mid u \in A^\star L_i\}.$$

Similarly, for each $\overleftarrow{q} = \overleftarrow{\delta} (\overleftarrow{q_-}, u)$

$$\texttt{right}(\overleftarrow{q}) := \{i \in [1, n] \mid u \in R_i A^\star\}.$$

Now let $\overrightarrow{q} \in \overrightarrow{Q}$, $a \in A$ and $\overleftarrow{q} \in \overleftarrow{Q}$. There is at most one $i \in [1, n]$ such that $i \in \texttt{left}(\overrightarrow{q})$, $a = a_i$ and $i \in \texttt{right}(\overleftarrow{q})$. (If there were two, take $\overrightarrow{q} = \overrightarrow{\delta} (\overrightarrow{q_-}, u)$ and $\overleftarrow{q} = \overleftarrow{\delta} (\overleftarrow{q_-}, v)$: there would be two i's such that $u \in A^\star L_i$, $a = a_i$ and $v \in R_i A^\star$, in contradiction with the fact that there are no conflicts.) If there exists such an i, define $\gamma(\overrightarrow{q}, a, \overleftarrow{q}) = u_i$, otherwise $\gamma(\overrightarrow{q}, a, \overleftarrow{q}) = a$. This completes the definition of the combined bimachine which will simulate the behaviour of the n bimachines whenever one of them applies to an input symbol.

For example, let us combine the rules of Figures 14.8 and 14.9. The rule of Figure 14.9 converts /i/ into /j/ in certain contexts, e.g. for *allier* [alje] 'ally', it converts /alie/ into /alje/. The minimal deterministic automaton for $A^\star L_1$ is in Figure 14.10 and the one for $A^\star L_2$ is in Figure 14.11.

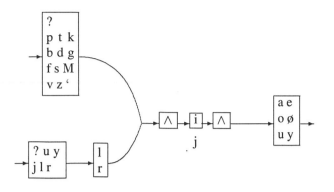

'?' stands for all symbols except p t k b d g f s M v z ' l r j u y.

Figure 14.9: A conversion rule.

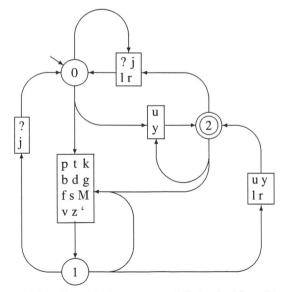

'?' stands for all symbols except p t k b d g f s M v z ' l r j u y.

Figure 14.10: The minimal deterministic automaton for $A^\star L_1$.

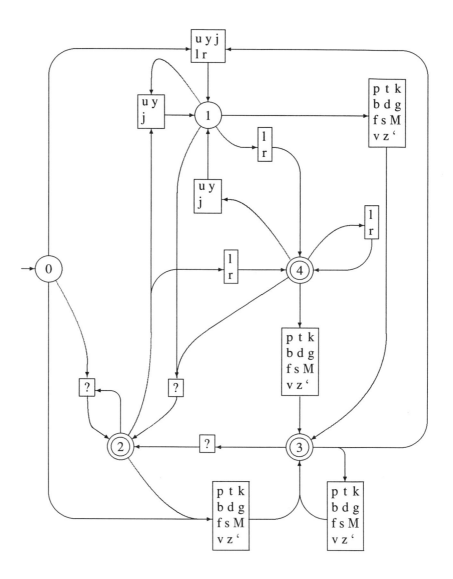

'?' stands for all symbols except p t k b d g f s M v z ' l r j u y.

Figure 14.11: The minimal deterministic automaton for $A^{\star}L_2$.

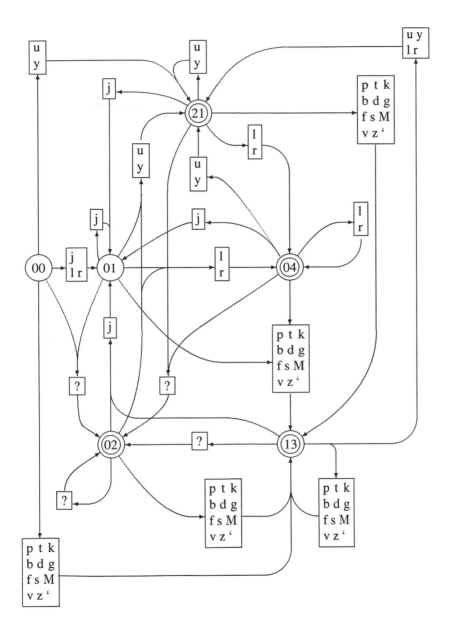

Figure 14.12: The left-to-right automaton of the simultaneous combination.

These rules do not conflict. If you build their simultaneous combination, you will obtain the left-to-right automaton of Figure 14.12,

and a two-state right-to-left automaton. The states $\vec{q}$ which are marked as final in Figure 14.12 are those for which `left(`$\vec{q}$`)` is nonempty. With the French phonetic conversion data for BiPho, the deterministic automata of the 12 bimachines have 3 to 144 states. The output function is implemented with two tables, `BimSet` and `Output`. `BimSet` is a two-dimensional table whose rows are indexed by left-to-right states and whose lines are indexed by right-to-left states. The content of the table at line $\vec{q}$ and at column $\overleftarrow{q}$ is a key that gives access to the set `left(`$\vec{q}$`)`$\cap$`right(`$\overleftarrow{q}$`)`. `Output` is a two-dimensional table whose rows are indexed by the keys of the sets `left(`$\vec{q}$`)`$\cap$`right(`$\overleftarrow{q}$`)`, and whose lines are indexed by input symbols. The content of the table at line k and at column a is the output sequence $\gamma(\vec{q}, a, \overleftarrow{q})$ defined in section 14.6.2.

14.6.3   Running the bimachine

When running the bimachine on an input string, the string is first processed in reverse order: we compute the values of the states of the right-to-left automaton for each symbol in the input string and store them in a one-dimensional array. Then, for each symbol from left to right, the state of the left-to-right automaton is computed. This value is used with the value of the right-to-left state, the input symbol and the tables `BimSet` and `Output` in order to retrieve the output sequence. The complexity of this algorithm is independent of the number of states and transitions of the bimachine: the time of the conversion is dominated by the length of the input sequence.

14.7   Conclusion

The finite-state formal devices described in this chapter and tested in the context of phonetics and phonology proved to be both convenient for linguistic description and adapted for efficient implementation. The conversion system BiPho was tested with complete phonetic conversion data for French. Since phonetic conversion of most languages is simpler than for French, and since BiPho makes only minimal assumptions about the mathematical properties of the conversion, we believe that it can be used for virtually any conversion task related to phonetics.

References

Aho, Alfred and Margaret Corasick. 1975. Efficient string matching: an aid to bibliographic search. *CACM*, 18(6):333–340.

Berstel, Jean. 1979. *Transductions and Context-Free Languages*. Teubner, Stuttgart.

Eilenberg, Samuel. 1974. *Automata, Languages and Machines*, volume A. Academic Press, New York/San Francisco/London.

Johnson, C. Douglas. 1972. *Formal Aspects of Phonological Description*. Mouton.

Kaplan, Ronald M. and Martin Kay. 1994. Regular models of phonological rule systems. *ACL*, 20(3):331–378.

Koskenniemi, Kimmo. 1983. *Two-level morphology: a general computational model for word-form recognition and production*. Publication no. 11. Dept. of General Linguistics, University of Helsinki.

Laporte, Éric. 1989. Quelques variations phonétiques en français. *Lingvisticae Investigationes*, XIII(1):43–116.

Laporte, Éric. 1993. Phonétique et transducteurs. Technical report, Université Paris 7-Denis-Diderot, June.

Mohri, Mehryar. 1994. Syntactic Analysis by Local Grammars Automata: an Efficient Algorithm. Papers in Computational Lexicography (COMPLEX). Research Institute for Linguistics, Hungarian Academy of Sciences, Budapest, pp. 179–191.

Perrin, Dominique. 1990. Finite automata. In J. van Leeuwen, editor, *Handbook of Theoretical Computer Science*. Elsevier, chapter 1, pages 3–57.

Schützenberger, Marcel-Paul. 1961. A remark on finite transducers. *Inform. and Control*, 4:185–196.

15 Speech Recognition by Composition of Weighted Finite Automata

Fernando C. N. Pereira and Michael D. Riley

We present a general framework based on weighted finite automata and weighted finite-state transducers for describing and implementing speech recognizers. The framework provides a uniform representation for the information sources and data structures used in recognition, including context-dependent units, pronunciation dictionaries, language models and lattices. Furthermore, general but efficient algorithms can used for combining information sources in actual recognizers and for optimizing their application. In particular, a single *composition* algorithm is used both to combine in advance information sources such as language models and dictionaries, and to combine acoustic observations and information sources dynamically during recognition.

15.1   Introduction

Many problems in speech processing can be usefully analyzed in terms of the "noisy channel" metaphor: given an observation sequence o, find which intended message w is most likely to generate that observation sequence by maximizing

$$P(w, o) = P(o|w)P(w),$$

where $P(o|w)$ characterizes the *transduction* between intended messages and observations, and $P(w)$ characterizes the message generator. More generally, the transduction between messages and observations may involve several *stages* relating successive *levels* of representation:

$$P(s_0, s_k) = P(s_k|s_0)P(s_0)$$
$$P(s_k|s_0) = \sum_{s_1,\ldots,s_{k-1}} P(s_k|s_{k-1}) \cdots P(s_1|s_0) \tag{15.1}$$

Each s_j is a sequence of units of an appropriate representation, for instance phones or syllables in speech recognition. A straightforward but useful observation is that any such a cascade can be factored at any intermediate level

$$P(s_j|s_i) = \sum_{s_l} P(s_j|s_l)P(s_l|s_i) \tag{15.2}$$

For computational reasons, sums and products in (15.1) are often replaced by minimizations and sums of negative log probabilities, yielding the approximation

$$\begin{aligned}\tilde{P}(s_0, s_k) &= \tilde{P}(s_k|s_0) + \tilde{P}(s_0)\\ \tilde{P}(s_k|s_0) &\approx \min_{s_1,\ldots,s_{k-1}} \sum_{1 \le j \le k} \tilde{P}(s_j|s_{j-1})\end{aligned} \tag{15.3}$$

where $\tilde{X} = -\log X$. In this formulation, assuming the approximation is reasonable, the most likely message s_0 is the one minimizing $\tilde{P}(s_0, s_k)$.

In current speech recognition systems, a transduction stage is typically modeled by a finite-state device, for example a hidden Markov model (HMM). However, the commonalities among stages are typically not exploited, and each stage is represented and implemented by "ad hoc" means. The goal of this paper is to show that the theory of weighted rational languages and transductions can be used as a general framework for transduction cascades. Levels of representation will be modeled as weighted languages, and transduction stages will be modeled as weighted transductions.

This foundation provides a rich set of operators for combining cascade levels and stages that generalizes the standard operations on regular languages, suggests novel ways of combining models of different parts of the decoding process, and supports uniform algorithms for transduction and search throughout the cascade. Computationally, stages and levels of representation are represented as weighted finite automata, and a general automata *composition* algorithm implements the relational composition of successive stages. Automata compositions can be searched with standard best-path algorithms to find the most likely transcriptions of spoken utterances. A "lazy" implementation of composition allows search and pruning to be carried out concurrently with composition so that only the useful portions of the composition of the observations with the decoding cascade is explicitly created. Finally, finite-state minimization techniques can be used to reduce the size of cascade levels and thus improve recognition efficiency (Mohri, 1997).

Weighted languages and transductions are generalizations of the standard notions of language and transduction in formal language theory (Berstel, 1979; Harrison, 1978). A weighted language is a mapping from strings over an alphabet to weights, while a weighted transduction is a mapping from pairs of strings over two alphabets to weights. For example, when weights represent probabilities and assuming appropriate normalization, a weighted language is just a probability distribution over strings, and a weighted transduction a conditional probability distribution between strings. The weighted *rational* languages and transducers are those that can be represented by weighted finite-state acceptors (WFSAs) and weighted finite-state transducers (WFSTs), as described in more detail in the next section. In this paper we will be concerned with the weighted rational case, although some of the theory can be profitably extended more general language classes closed under intersection with regular languages and composition with rational transductions (Lang, 1989; Teitelbaum, 1973).

The notion of weighted rational transduction arises from the combination of two ideas in automata theory: rational transductions, used in many aspects of formal language theory (Berstel, 1979), and weighted languages and automata, developed in pattern recognition (Booth and Thompson, 1973; Paz, 1971) and algebraic automata theory (Berstel and Reutenauer, 1988; Eilenberg, 1974; Kuich and Salomaa, 1986). Ordinary (unweighted) rational transductions have been successfully applied by researchers at Xerox PARC (Kaplan and Kay, 1994) and at the University of Paris 7 (Mohri, 1994a; Mohri, 1994b; Roche, 1993; Silberztein, 1993), among others, to several problems in language processing, including morphological analysis, dictionary compression and syntactic analysis. HMMs and probabilistic finite-state language models can be shown to be equivalent to WFSAs. In algebraic automata theory, rational series and rational transductions (Kuich and Salomaa, 1986) are the algebraic counterparts of WFSAs and WFSTs and give the correct generalizations to the weighted case of the standard algebraic operations on formal languages and transductions, such as union, concatenation, intersection, restriction and composition. We believe our work is the first application of these generalizations to speech processing.

While we concentrate here on speech recognition applications, the same framework and tools have also been applied to other language processing tasks such as the segmentation of Chinese text into words (Sproat et al., 1994). We explain how a standard HMM-based recognizer can be naturally viewed as equivalent to a cascade of weighted transductions, and how the approach requires no modification to accommodate context dependencies that cross higher-level unit boundaries, for instance cross-word context-dependent models. This is an important advantage of the transduction approach over the usual, but more limited "substitution" approach used in existing to speech recognizers. Substitution replaces a symbol at a higher level by its defining language at a lower level, but, as we will argue, cannot model directly the interactions between context-dependent units at the lower level.

15.2 Theory

15.2.1 The weight semiring

As discussed informally in the previous section, our approach relies on associating *weights* to the strings in a language, the string pairs in a transduction and the transitions in an automaton. The operations used for weight combination should reflect the intended interpretation of the weights. For instance, if the weights of automata transitions represent transition probabilities, the weight assigned to a path should be the product of the weights of its transitions, while the weight (total probability) assigned to a set of paths with common source and destination should be the sum of the weights of the paths in the set. However, if the weights represent negative log-probabilities and we are operating under the Viterbi approximation that replaces the sum of the probabilities of alternative paths by the probability of the most probable path, path weights should be the sum of the weights of the transitions in the path and the weight assigned to a set of paths should be the minimum of the weights of the paths in the set. Both of these weight structures are special cases of *commutative semirings*, which are the basis of the general theory of weighted languages, transductions and automata (Berstel and Reutenauer, 1988; Eilenberg, 1974; Kuich and Salomaa, 1986).

In general, a *semiring* is a set K with two binary operations, *collection* $+_K$ and *extension* $\times_K$, such that:

- collection is associative and commutative with identity 0_K;

- extension is associative with identity 1_K;

- extension distributes over collection;

- $a \times_K 0_K = 0_K \times_K a = 0$ for any $a \in K$.

The semiring is *commutative* if extension is commutative.

Setting $K = \mathbf{R}^+$ with $+$ for collection, $\times$ for extension, 0 for 0_K and 1 for 1_K we obtain the *sum-times* semiring, which we can use to model probability calculations. Setting $K = \mathbf{R}^+ \cup \{\infty\}$ with min for collection, $+$ for extension, ∞ for 0_K and 0 for 1_K we obtain the *min-sum* semiring, which models negative log-probabilities under the Viterbi approximation.

In general, weights represent some measure of "goodness" that we want to optimize. For instance, with probabilities we are interested in the highest weight, while the lowest weight is sought for negative log-probabilities. We thus assume a total order on weights and write $\max_x f(x)$ for the optimal value of the weight-valued function f and $\operatorname{argmax}_x f(x)$ for some x that optimizes

$f(x)$. We also assume that extension and collection are monotonic with respect to the total order.

In what follows, we will assume a fixed semiring K and thus drop the subscript K in the symbols for its operations and identity elements. Unless stated otherwise, all the discussion will apply to any commutative semiring, if necessary with a total order for optimization. Some definitions and calculations involve collecting over potentially infinite sets, for instance the set of strings of a language. Clearly, collecting over an infinite set is always well-defined for *idempotent* semirings such as the min-sum semiring, in which $a + a = a \ \forall a \in K$. More generally, a *closed* semiring is one in which collecting over infinite sets is well defined. Finally, some particular cases arising in the discussion below can be shown to be well defined for the plus-times semiring under certain mild conditions on the weights assigned to strings or automata transitions (Booth and Thompson, 1973; Kuich and Salomaa, 1986).

15.2.2 Weighted transductions and languages

In the transduction cascade (15.1), each stage corresponds to a mapping from input-output pairs (r, s) to probabilities $P(s|r)$. More formally, stages in the cascade will be *weighted transductions* $T : \Sigma^* \times \Gamma^* \to K$ where Σ^* and Γ^* are the sets of strings over the alphabets Σ and Γ, and K is the weight semiring. We will denote by T^{-1} the *inverse* of T defined by $T(t, s) = T(s, t)$.

The right-most step of (15.1) is not a transduction, but rather an information source, the language model. We will represent such sources as *weighted languages* $L : \Sigma^* \to K$.

Each transduction $S : \Sigma^* \times \Gamma^* \to K$ has two associated weighted languages, its its *first* and *second projections* $\pi_1(S) : \Sigma^* \to K$ and $\pi_2(S) : \Gamma^* \to K$, defined by

$$\pi_1(S)(s) = \sum_{t \in \Gamma^*} S(s, t)$$
$$\pi_2(S)(t) = \sum_{s \in \Sigma^*} S(s, t)$$

Given two transductions $S : \Sigma^* \times \Gamma^* \to K$ and $T : \Gamma^* \times \Delta^* \to K$, we define their *composition* $S \circ T$ by

$$(S \circ T)(r, t) = \sum_{s \in \Gamma^*} S(r, s) \times T(s, t) \tag{15.4}$$

For example, if S represents $P(s_l|s_i)$ and T $P(s_j|s_l)$ in (15.2), $S \circ T$ represents $P(s_j|s_i)$.

A weighted transduction $S : \Sigma^* \times \Gamma^* \to K$ can be also *applied* to a weighted language $L : \Sigma^* \to K$ to yield a weighted language $S[L]$ over Γ:

$$S[L](s) = \sum_{r \in \Sigma^*} L(r) \times S(r, s) \tag{15.5}$$

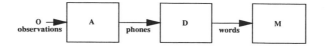

Figure 15.1: Recognition Cascade

We can also identify any weighted language L with the identity transduction restricted to L:

$$L(r, r') = \begin{cases} L(r) & \text{if } r = r' \\ 0 & \text{otherwise} \end{cases}$$

Using this identification, application is transduction composition followed by projection:

$$\begin{aligned} \pi_2(L \circ S)(s) &= \sum_{r \in \Sigma^*} \sum_{r' \in \Sigma^*} L(r, r') \times S(r', s) \\ &= \sum_{r \in \Sigma^*} L(r, r) \times S(r, s) \\ &= \sum_{r \in \Sigma^*} L(r) \times S(r, s) \\ &= S[L](s) \end{aligned}$$

From now on, we will take advantage of the identification of languages with transductions and use ∘ to express both composition and application, often leaving implicit the projections required to extract languages from transductions. In particular, the *intersection* of two weighted languages $M, N : \Sigma^* \to K$ is given by

$$\pi_1(M \circ N)(s) = \pi_2(M \circ N)(s) = M(s) \times N(s) \tag{15.6}$$

It is easy to see that composition is associative, that is, the result of any transduction cascade $R_1 \circ \cdots \circ R_m$ is independent of order of application of the composition operators.

For a more concrete example, consider the transduction cascade for speech recognition depicted in Figure 15.1, where A is the transduction from acoustic observation sequences to phone sequences, D the transduction from phone sequences to word sequences (essentially a pronunciation dictionary) and M a weighted language representing the language model. Given a particular sequence of observations o, we can represent it as the trivial weighted language O that assigns 1 to o and 0 to any other sequence. Then $O \circ A$ represents the acoustic likelihoods of possible phone sequences that generate o, $O \circ A \circ D$ the acoustic-lexical likelihoods of possible word sequences yielding o, and $O \circ A \circ D \circ M$ the combined acoustic-lexical-linguistic probabilities of word sequences generating o. The word string w with the highest weight in $\pi_2(O \circ A \circ D \circ M)$ is the most likely sentence hypothesis generating o.

Composition is thus the main operation involved in the construction and use of transduction cascades. As we will see in the next section, composition can

	Transduction
singleton	$\{(u, v)\}(w, z) = 1$ iff $u = w$ and $v = z$
scaling	$(kT)(u, v) = k \times T(u, v)$
sum	$(S + T)(u, v) = S(u, v) + T(u, v)$
concatenation	$(ST)(t, w) = \sum_{rs=t, uv=w} S(r, u) \times T(s, v)$
power	$T^0(\epsilon, \epsilon) = 1$
	$T^0(u \neq \epsilon, v \neq \epsilon) = 0$
	$T^{n+1} = TT^n$
closure	$T^* = \sum_{k \geq 0} T^k$

Table 15.1: Rational Operations

be implemented as a suitable generalization of the usual intersection algorithm for finite automata. In addition to composition, weighted transductions (and languages, given the identification of languages with transductions presented earlier) can be constructed from simpler ones using the operations shown in Table 15.1, which generalize in a straightforward way the regular operations well-known from traditional automata theory (Harrison, 1978). In fact, the rational languages and transductions are exactly those that can be built from singletons by applications of scaling, sum, concatenation and closure.

For example, assume that for each word w in a lexicon we are given a rational transduction D_w such that $D_w(p, w)$ is the probability that w is realized as the phone sequence p. Note that this allows for multiple pronunciations for w. Then the rational transduction $\left(\sum_w D_w\right)^*$ gives the probabilities for realizations of word sequences as phone sequences if we leave aside cross-word context dependencies, which will be discussed in Section 15.3.

15.2.3 Weighted automata

Kleene's theorem states that regular languages are exactly those representable by finite-state acceptors (Harrison, 1978). Generalized to the weighted case and to transductions, it states that weighted rational languages and transductions are exactly those that can be represented by weighted finite automata (Eilenberg, 1974; Kuich and Salomaa, 1986). Furthermore, all the operations on languages and transductions we have discussed have finite-automata counterparts, which we have implemented. Any cascade representable in terms of those operations can thus be implemented directly as an appropriate combination of the programs implementing each of the operations.

A K-*weighted finite automaton* A is given by a finite set of states Q_A, a set of *transition labels* Λ_A, an initial state i_A, a *final weight* function F_A :

$Q_A \to K$, [1] and a finite set $\delta_A \subset Q_A \times \Lambda_A \times K \times Q_A$ of *transitions* $t = (t.\text{src}, t.\text{lab}, t.\text{w}, t.\text{dst})$. The label set Λ_A must have with an associative *concatenation* operation $u \cdot v$ with identity element ϵ_A. A *weighted finite-state acceptor* (WFSA) is a K-weighted finite automaton with $\Lambda_A = \Sigma^*$ for some finite alphabet Σ. A *weighted finite-state transducer* (WFST) is a K-weighted finite automaton such that $\Lambda_A = \Sigma^* \times \Gamma^*$ for given finite alphabets Σ and Γ, its label concatenation is defined by $(r, s) \cdot (u, v) = (ru, sv)$, and its identity (null) label is (ϵ, ϵ). For $l = (r, s) \in \Sigma^* \times \Gamma^*$ we define $l.\text{in} = r$ and $l.\text{out} = s$. As we have done for languages, we will often identify a weighted acceptor with the transducer with the same state set and a transition $(q, (x, x), k, q')$ for each transition (q, x, k, q') in the acceptor.

A *path* in an automaton A is a sequence of transitions $p = t_1, \ldots, t_m$ in δ_A with $t_i.\text{src} = t_{i-1}.\text{dst}$ for $1 < i \leq k$. We define the *source* and the *destination* of p by $p.\text{src} = t_1.\text{src}$ and $p.\text{dst} = t_m.\text{dst}$, respectively.[2] The *label* of p is the concatenation $p.\text{lab} = t_1.\text{lab} \cdot \cdots \cdot t_m.\text{lab}$, its *weight* is the product $p.\text{w} = t_1.\text{w} \times \cdots \times t_m.\text{w}$ and its *acceptance weight* is $F(p) = p.\text{w} \times F_A(p.\text{dst})$. We denote by $P_A(q, q')$ the set of all paths in A with source q and destination q', by $P_A(q)$ the set of all paths in A with source q, by $P_A^u(q, q')$ the subset of $P_A(q, q')$ with label u and by $P_A^u(q)$ the subset of $P_A(q)$ with label u.

Each state $q \in Q_A$ defines a weighted transduction (or a weighted language):

$$L_A(q)(u) = \sum_{p \in P_A^u(q)} F(p) \qquad . \tag{15.7}$$

Finally, we can define the weighted transduction (language) of a weighted transducer (acceptor) A by

$$\llbracket A \rrbracket = L_A(i_A) \qquad . \tag{15.8}$$

The appropriate generalization of Kleene's theorem to weighted acceptors and transducers states that under suitable conditions guaranteeing that the inner sum in (15.7) is defined, weighted rational languages and transductions are exactly those defined by weighted automata as outlined here (Kuich and Salomaa, 1986).

Weighted acceptors and transducers are thus faithful implementations of rational languages and transductions, and all the operations on these described above have corresponding implementations in terms of algorithms on automata.

---

[1] The usual notion of final state can be represented by $F_A(q) = 1$ if q is final, $F_A(q) = 0$ otherwise. More generally, we call a state *final* if its weight is not 0. Also, we will interpret any non-weighted automaton as a weighted automaton in which all transitions and final states have weight 1.

[2] For convenience, for each state $q \in Q_A$ we also have an *empty path* with no transitions and source and destination q.

In particular, composition is implemented by the automata operation we now describe.

15.2.4 Automata composition

Informally, the composition of two automata A and B is a generalization of NFA intersection. Each state in the composition is a pair of a state of A and a state of B, and each path in the composition corresponds to a pair of a path in A and a path in B with compatible labels. The total weight of the composition path is the extension of the weights of the corresponding paths in A and B. The composition operation thus formalizes the notion of coordinated search in two graphs, where the coordination corresponds to a suitable agreement between path labels.

The more formal discussion that follows will be presented in terms of transducers, taking advantage the identifications of languages with transductions and of acceptors with transducers given earlier.

Consider two transducers A and B with $\Lambda_A = \Sigma^* \times \Gamma^*$ and $\Lambda_B = \Gamma^* \times \Delta^*$. Their composition $A \bowtie B$ will be a transducer with $\Lambda_{A \bowtie B} = \Sigma^* \times \Delta^*$ such that:

$$[\![A \bowtie B]\!] = [\![A]\!] \circ [\![B]\!] \qquad . \tag{15.9}$$

By definition of $L.(\cdot)$ and $\circ$ we have for any $q \in Q_A$ and $q' \in Q_B$:

$$
\begin{aligned}
& (L_A(q) \circ L_B(q'))(u, w) \\
&= \textstyle\sum_{v \in \Gamma^*} (\sum_{p \in P_A^{(u,v)}(q)} F(p)) \times (\sum_{p' \in P_B^{(v,w)}(q')} F(p')) \\
&= \textstyle\sum_{v \in \Gamma^*} \sum_{p \in P_A^{(u,v)}(q)} \sum_{p' \in P_B^{(v,w)}(q')} F(p) \times F(p') \\
&= \textstyle\sum_{(p,p') \in J(q,q',u,w)} F(p) \times F(p')
\end{aligned}
\tag{15.10}
$$

where $J(q, q', u, w)$ is the set of pairs (p, p') of paths $p \in P_A(q)$ and $p' \in P_B(q')$ such that $p.\text{lab.in} = u$, $p.\text{lab.out} = p'.\text{lab.in}$ and $p'.\text{lab.out} = w$. In particular, we have:

$$([\![A]\!] \circ [\![B]\!])(u, w) = \sum_{(p,p') \in J(i_A, i_B, u, w)} F(p) \times F(p') \qquad . \tag{15.11}$$

Therefore, assuming that (15.9) is satisfied, this equation collects the weights of all paths p in A and p' in B such that p maps u to some string v and p' maps v to w. In particular, on the min-sum weight semiring, the shortest path labeled (u, w) in $[\![A \bowtie B]\!]$ minimizes the sum of the costs of paths labeled (u, v) in A and (v, w) in B, for some s.

We will give first the construction of $A \bowtie B$ for ϵ-free transducers A and B, that is, those with transition labels in $\Sigma \times \Gamma$ and $\Gamma \times \Delta$, respectively. Then $A \bowtie B$ has state set $Q_{A \bowtie B} = Q_A \times Q_B$, initial state

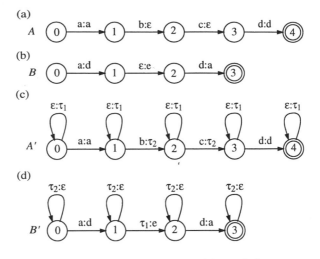

Figure 15.2: Transducers with ϵ Labels

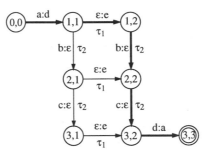

Figure 15.3: Composition with Marked ϵs

$i_{A \bowtie B} = (i_A, i_B)$ and final weights $F_{A \bowtie B}(q, q') = F_A(q)F_B(q')$. Furthermore, there is a transition $((q, q'), (x, z), k \times k', (r, r')) \in \delta_{A \bowtie B}$ iff there are transitions $(q, (x, y), k, r) \in \delta_A$ and $(q', (y, z), k', r') \in \delta_B$. This construction is similar to the standard intersection construction for DFAs; a proof that it indeed implements transduction composition (15.9) is given in Appendix A.

In the general case, we consider transducers A and B with labels over $\Sigma^? \times \Gamma^?$ and $\Gamma^? \times \Delta^?$, respectively, where $\Lambda^? = \Lambda \cup \{\epsilon\}$. [3] As shown in (15.10), the composition of A and B should have exactly one path for each pair

---

[3] It is easy to see that any transducer with transition labels in $\Sigma^* \times \Gamma^*$ is equivalent to a transducer with labels in $\Gamma^? \times \Delta^?$.

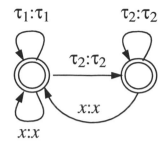

Figure 15.4: Filter Transducer

of paths p in A and p' in B with

$$v = p.\text{lab.out} = p'.\text{lab.in} \qquad . \qquad (15.12)$$

for some string $v \in \Gamma^*$ that we will call the *composition string*. In the ϵ-free case, it is clear that $p = t_1, \ldots, t_m$, $p' = t'_1, \ldots, t'_m$ for some m and $t_i.\text{lab.out} = t'_i.\text{lab.in}$. The pairing of t_i with t'_i is precisely what the ϵ-free composition construction provides. In the general case, however, two paths p and p' satisfying (15.12) need not have the same number of transitions. Furthermore, there may be several ways to align ϵ outputs in A and ϵ inputs in B with staying in the same state in the opposite transducer. This is exemplified by transducers A and B in Figure 15.2(a-b), and the corresponding naïve composition in Figure 15.3. The multiple paths from state $(1, 1)$ to state $(3, 2)$ correspond to different interleavings between taking the transition from 1 to 2 in B and the transitions from 1 to 2 and from 2 to 3 in A. In the weighted case, including all those paths in the composition would in general lead to an incorrect total weight for the transduction of string $abcd$ to string da. Therefore, we need a method for selecting a single composition path for each pair of compatible paths in the composed transducer.

The following construction, justified in Appendix B, achieves the desired result. For label l, define $\pi_1(l) = l.\text{in}$ and $\pi_2(l) = l.\text{out}$. Given a transducer T, compute $\text{Mark}_i(T)$ from T by replacing the label of every transition t such that $\pi_i(t.\text{lab}) = \epsilon$ with the new label l defined by $\pi_{2-i}(l) = \pi_{2-i}(t.\text{lab})$ and $\pi_i(l) = \tau_i$, where τ_i is a new symbol. In words, each ϵ on the ith component of a transition label is replaced by τ_i. Corresponding to ϵ transitions on one side of the composition we need to stay in the same state on the other side. Therefore, we define the operation $\text{Skip}_i(T)$ that for each state q of T adds a new transition $(q, l, 1, q)$ where $\pi_{2-i}(l) = \tau_i$ and $\pi_i(l) = \epsilon$. We also need the auxiliary transducer Filter shown in Figure 15.4, where the transition labeled $x : x$ is shorthand for a set of transitions mapping x to itself (at no cost) for

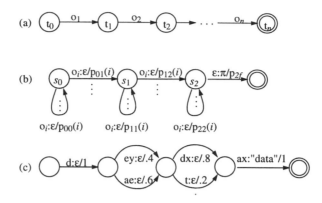

Figure 15.5: Models as Automata

each $x \in \Gamma$. Then for arbitrary transducers A and B, we have

$$[\![A]\!] \circ [\![B]\!] = [\![\text{Skip}_1(\text{Mark}_2(A)) \bowtie \text{Filter} \bowtie \text{Skip}_2(\text{Mark}_1(B))]\!]$$

For example, with respect to Figure 15.2 we have $A' = \text{Skip}_1(\text{Mark}_2(A))$ and $B' = \text{Skip}_2(\text{Mark}_1(B))$. The thick path in Figure 15.3 is the only one allowed by the filter transduction, as desired. In practice, the substitutions and insertions of τ_i symbols performed by Mark_i and Skip_i do not need to be performed explicitly, because the effects of those operations can be computed on the fly by a suitable implementation of composition with filtering.

The filter we described is the simplest to explain. In practice, somewhat more complex filters, which we will describe elsewhere, help reduce the size of the resulting transducer. For example, the filter presented includes in the composition in states (2,1) and (3,1) on Figure 15.3, from which no final state can be reached. Such "dead end" paths can be a source of inefficiency when using the results of composition.

15.3   Speech Recognition

We now describe how to represent a speech recognizer as a composition of transducers. Recall that we model the recognition task as the composition of a language O of acoustic observation sequences, a transduction A from acoustic observation sequences to phone sequences, a transduction D from phone sequences to word sequences and a weighted language M specifying the language model (see Figure 15.1). Each of these can be represented as a finite-state automaton (to some approximation), denoted by the same name as the corresponding transduction in what follows.

The acoustic observation automaton O for a given utterance has the form shown on Figure 15.5a. Each state represents a fixed point in time t_i, and each transition has a label, o_i, drawn from a finite alphabet that quantizes the acoustic signal between adjacent time points and is assigned probability 1. [4]

The transducer A from acoustic observation sequences to phone sequences is built from *phone models*. A phone model is a transducer from sequences of acoustic observation labels to a specific phone that assigns to each acoustic observation sequence the likelihood that the specified phone produced it. Thus, different paths through a phone model correspond to different acoustic realizations of the phone. Figure 15.5b shows a common topology for phone models. A is then defined as the closure of the sum of the phone models.

The transducer D from phone sequences to word sequences is is built similarly to A. A *word model* is a transducer from phone sequences to the specified word that assigns to each phone sequence the likelihood that the specified word produced it. Thus, different paths through a word model correspond to different phonetic realizations of the word. Figure 15.5c shows a typical topology for a word model. D is then defined as the closure of the sum of the word models.

Finally, the acceptor M encodes the language model, for instance an n-gram model. Combining those automata, we obtain $\pi_2(O \bowtie A \bowtie D \bowtie M)$, which assigns a probability to each word sequence. The highest-probability path through that automaton estimates the most likely word sequence for the given utterance.

The finite-state model of speech recognition that we have just described is hardly novel. In fact, it is equivalent to that presented in (Bahl, Jelinek, and Mercer, 1983), in the sense that it generates the same weighted language. However, the transduction cascade approach presented here allows one to view the computations in new ways.

For instance, because composition is associative, the computation of $\text{argmax}_w \pi_2(O \bowtie A \bowtie D \bowtie M)(w)$ can be organized in a variety of ways. In a traditional integrated-search recognizer, a single large transducer is built in advance by $R = A \bowtie D \bowtie M$, and used in recognition to compute $argmax_w \pi_2(O \bowtie R)(w)$ for each observation sequence O (Bahl, Jelinek, and Mercer, 1983). This approach is not practical if the size of R exceeds available memory, as is typically the case for large-vocabulary speech recognition with n-gram language models for $n > 2$. In those cases, pruning may be interleaved with composition to to compute (an approximation of) $((O \bowtie A) \bowtie D) \bowtie M$. Acoustic observations are first transduced into a phone lattice represented as an automaton labeled by phones (phone recognition). The whole lattice typically too big, so the computation includes a pruning mechanism that generates only

---

[4]For more complex acoustic distributions (for instance, continuous densities) we can instead use multiple transitions $(t_{i-1}, d, p(o_i|d), t_i)$ where d is an observation distribution and $p(o_i|d)$ the corresponding observation probability.

those states and transitions that appear in high-probability paths. This lattice is in turn transduced into a word lattice (word recognition), again possibly with pruning, which is then composed with the language model (Ljolje and Riley, 1992; Riley et al., 1995). The best approach depends on the specific task, which determines the size of intermediate results. By having a general package to manipulate weighted automata, we have been able to experiment with various alternatives.

So far, our presentation has used context-independent phone models. In other words, the likelihood assigned by a phone model in A is assumed conditionally independent of neighboring phones. Similarly, the pronunciation of each word in D is assumed independent of neighboring words. Therefore, each of the transducers has a particularly simple form, that of the closure of the sum of (inverse) *substitutions*. That is, each symbol in a string on the output side replaces a language on the input side. This replacement of a symbol from one alphabet (for example, a word) by the automaton that represents its substituted language from a over a finer-grained alphabet (for example, phones) is the usual stage-combination operation for speech recognizers (Bahl, Jelinek, and Mercer, 1983).

However, it has been shown that context-dependent phone models, which model a phone in the context of its adjacent phones, provide substantial improvements in recognition accuracy (Lee, 1990). Further, the pronunciation of a word will be affected by its neighboring words, inducing context dependencies across word boundaries.

We could include context-dependent models, such as triphone models, in our presentation by expanding our 'atomic models' in A to one for every phone in a distinct triphonic context. Each model will have the same form as in Figure 15.5b, but it will be over an enlarged output alphabet and have different likelihoods for the different contexts. We could also try to directly specify D in terms of the new units, but this is problematic. First, even if each word in D had only one phonetic realization, we could not directly substitute its the phones in the realization by their context-dependent models, because the given word may appear in the context of many different words, with different phones abutting the given word. This problem is commonly alleviated by either using left (right) context-independent units at the word starts (ends), which decreases the model accuracy, or by building a fully context-dependent lexicon and using special machinery in the recognizer to insure the correct models are used at word junctures. In either case, we can no longer use compact lexical entries with multiple pronunciations such as that of Figure 15.5c. Those approaches attempt to solve the context-dependency problem by introducing new substitutions, but substitutions are not really appropriate for the task.

In contrast, context dependency can be readily represented by a simple transducer. We leave D as defined before, but interpose a new transducer

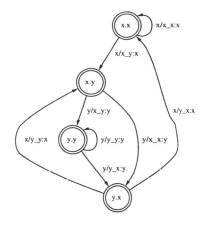

Figure 15.6: Context-Dependency Transducer

C between A and D that convert between context-dependent and context-independent units, that is, we now compute $\text{argmax}_w\, \pi_2(O \bowtie A \bowtie C \bowtie D \bowtie M)(w)$. A possible form for C is shown in Figure 15.6. For simplicity, we show only the portion of the transducer concerning two hypothetical phones x and y. The transducer maps each context-dependent model p/l_r, associated to phone p when preceded by l and followed by r, to an occurrence of p which is guaranteed to be preceded by l and followed by r. To ensure this, each state labeled $p.q$ represents the context information that all incoming transitions correspond to phone p, and all outgoing transitions correspond to phone q. Thus we can represent context-dependency directly as a transducer, without needing specialized context-dependency code in the recognizer. More complex forms of context dependency such as those based on classification trees over a bounded neighborhood of the target phone can too be compiled into appropriate transducers and interposed in the recognition cascade without changing any aspect of the recognition algorithm. Transducer determinization and minimization techniques (Mohri, 1997) can be used to make context-dependency transducers as compact as possible.

15.4 Implementation

The transducer operations described in this paper, together with a variety of support functions, have been implemented in C. Two interfaces are provided: a library of functions operating on an abstract finite-state machine datatype, and a set of composable shell commands for fast prototyping. The modular organization of the library and shell commands follows directly from their foundation in the algebra of rational operations, and allows us to build new application-specific recognizers automatically.

The size of composed automata and the efficiency of composition have been the main issues in developing the implementation. As explained earlier, our main applications involve finding the highest-probability path in composed automata. It is in general not practical to compute the whole composition and then find the highest-probability path, because in the worst case the number of transitions in a composition grows with the product of the numbers of transitions in the composed automata. Instead, we have developed a lazy implementation of composition, in which the states and arcs of the composed automaton are created by pairing states and arcs in the composition arguments only as they are required by some other operation, such as search, on the composed automaton (Riley, Pereira, and Chung, 1995). The use of an abstract datatype for automata facilitates this, since functions operating on automata do not need to distinguish between concrete and lazy automata.

The efficiency of composition depends crucially on the efficiency with which transitions leaving the two components of a state pair are matched to yield transitions in the composed automaton. This task is analogous to doing a relational join, and some of the sorting and indexing techniques used for joins are relevant here, especially for very large alphabets such as the words in large-vocabulary recognition. The interface of the automaton datatype has been carefully designed to allow for efficient transition matching while hiding the details of transition indexing and sorting.

15.5 Applications

We have used our implementation in a variety of speech recognition and language processing tasks, including continuous speech recognition in the 60,000-word ARPA North American Business News (NAB) task (Riley et al., 1995) and the 2,000-word ARPA ATIS task, isolated word recognition for directory lookup tasks, and segmentation of Chinese text into words (Sproat et al., 1994).

The NAB task is by far the largest one we have attempted so far. In our 1994 experiments (Riley et al., 1995), we used a 60,000-word vocabulary, and several very large automata, including a phone-to-syllable transducer with 5×10^5 transitions, a syllable-to-word (dictionary) transducer with 10^5 transitions and a language model (5-gram) with 3.4×10^7 transitions. We are at present experimenting with various improvements in modeling and in the implementation of composition, especially in the filter, that would allow us to use directly the lazy composition of the whole decoding cascade for this application in a standard time-synchronous Viterbi decoder. In our 1994 experiments, however, we had to break the cascade into a succession of stages, each generating a pruned lattice (an acyclic acceptor) through a combination of lazy composition and graph search. In addition, relatively simple models are used first (context-independent phone models, bigram language model) to produce a relatively small pruned word lattice, which is then intersected with the composition of the full models to create a rescored lattice which is then searched for the best path. That is, we use an approximate word lattice to limit the size of the composition with the full language and phonemic models. This multi-pass decoder achieved around 10% word-error rate in the main 1994 NAB test, while requiring around 500 times real-time for recognition.

In our more recent experiments with lazy composition in synchronous Viterbi decoders, we have been able to show that lazy composition is as fast or faster than traditional methods requiring full expansion of the composed automaton in advance, while requiring a small fraction of the space. The ARPA ATIS task, for example, uses a context transducer with 40,386 transitions, a dictionary with 4,816 transitions and a class-based variable-length n-gram language model (Riccardi, Bocchieri, and Pieraccini, 1995) with 359,532 transitions. The composition of these three automata would have around 6×10^6 transitions. However, for a typical sentence only around 5% of those transitions are actually visited (Riley, Pereira, and Chung, 1995).

15.6 Further Work

We have been investigating a variety of improvements, extensions and applications of the present work. With Emerald Chung, we have been refining the connection between a time-synchronous Viterbi decoder and lazy composition to improve time and space efficiency. With Mehryar Mohri, we have been developing improved composition filters, as well as exploring on-the-fly and local determinization techniques for transducers and weighted automata (Mohri, 1997) to decrease the impact of nondeterminism on the size (and thus the time required to create) composed automata. Our work on the implementation has also been influenced by applications to the compilation of weighted phonological and morphological rules and by ongoing research on integrating speech recognition with natural-language analysis and translation. Finally, we are investigating applications to local grammatical analysis, in which transducers have been often used but not with weights.

Appendix A: Correctness of ϵ-free composition

As shown in Section 15.2.4 (15.10), we have

$$(L_A(q) \circ L_B(q'))(r,t) = \sum_{s \in \Gamma^*} \sum_{p \in P_A^{(r,s)}(q)} \sum_{p' \in P_B^{(s,t)}(q')} F(p) \times F(p') \quad (15.13)$$

Clearly, for ϵ-free transducers the variables r, s, t, p and p' in this equation satisfy the constraint $|r| = |s| = |t| = |p| = |p'| = n$ for some n. This allows us to show the correctness of the composition construction for ϵ-free automata by induction on n. Specifically, we shall show that for any $q \in Q_A$ and $q' \in Q_B$

$$L_{A \bowtie B}(q, q') = L_A(q) \circ L_B(q') \quad . \qquad (15.14)$$

For $n = 0$, from (15.13) and the composition construction we obtain

$$
\begin{aligned}
(L_A(q) \circ L_B(q'))(\epsilon, \epsilon) &= F_A(q) \times F_B(q') \\
&= F_{A \bowtie B}(q, q') \\
&= F_{A \bowtie B}(\epsilon, \epsilon)
\end{aligned}
$$

as needed.

Assume now that $L_{A \bowtie B}(m, m')(u, w) = (L_A(m) \circ L_B(m'))(u, w)$ for any $m \in Q_A$, $m' \in Q_B$, $u \in \Sigma^*$ and $w \in \Delta^*$ with $|u| = |w| < n$. Let $r = xu$ and $t = zw$, with $x \in \Sigma$ and $z \in \Delta$. Then by (15.13) and the composition construction we have

$$
\begin{aligned}
&(L_A(p) \circ L_B(q))(xu, zw) \\
&= \sum_{y \in \Gamma} \sum_{v \in \Gamma^*} \sum_{p \in P_A^{(xu, yv)}(q)} \sum_{p' \in P_B^{(yv, zw)}(q')} F(p) \times F(p') \\
&= \sum_{\substack{(q,(x,y),k,m) \in \delta_A \ (q',(y,z),k',m') \in \delta_B}} k \times k' \times \left(\sum_{v \in \Gamma^*} \sum_{l \in P_A^{(u,v)}(m)} \sum_{l' \in P_B^{(v,w)}(m')} F(l) \times F(l') \right) \\
&= \sum_{\substack{((q,q'),(x,z),j,(m,m')) \in \delta_{A \bowtie B}}} j \times \left(\sum_{v \in \Gamma^*} \sum_{l \in P_A^{(u,v)}(m)} \sum_{l' \in P_B^{(v,w)}(m')} F(l) \times F(l') \right) \\
&= \sum_{((q,q'),(x,z),j,(m,m')) \in \delta_{A \bowtie B}} j \times (L_A(m) \circ L_B(m'))(u, w) \\
&= \sum_{((q,q'),(x,z),j,(m,m')) \in \delta_{A \bowtie B}} j \times L_{A \bowtie B}(m, m')(u, w) \\
&= \sum_{((q,q'),(x,z),j,(m,m')) \in \delta_{A \bowtie B}} j \times \left(\sum_{g \in P_{A \bowtie B}^{(u,w)}(m,m')} W_{A \bowtie B}(g) \right) \\
&= \sum_{h \in P_{A \bowtie B}^{(xu,zw)}(q,q')} W_{A \bowtie B}(h) \\
&= L_{A \bowtie B}(q, q')(xu, zw) \quad .
\end{aligned}
$$

This shows (15.14) for ϵ-free transducers, and as a particular case

$$[\![A \bowtie B]\!] = [\![A]\!] \circ [\![B]\!] \quad ,$$

which states that transducer composition correctly implements transduction composition.

Appendix B: General composition construction

For any transition t in A or B, we define

$$\text{Mark}_i(t) = \begin{cases} \tau_i & \text{if } \pi_i(t.\text{lab}) = \epsilon \\ \pi_i(t.\text{lab}) & \text{otherwise} \end{cases},$$

where each τ_i is a new symbol not in Γ. This can be extended to a path $p = t_1, \ldots, t_m$ in the obvious way by $\text{Mark}_i(p) = \text{Mark}_i(t_1) \cdots \text{Mark}_i(t_m)$. If p and p' satisfy (15.12), there will be $m, n \geq k$ such that $p = t_1, \ldots, t_m, p' = t'_1, \ldots, t'_n, v = y_1 \cdots y_k$ and $v = p.\text{lab.out} = p'.\text{lab.in}$. Therefore, we will have $\text{Mark}_2(p) = u_0 y_1 u_1 \cdots u_{k-1} y_k u_k$ where $u_i \in \{\tau_2\}^*$ and $|u_0 \cdots u_k| = m - k$, and $\text{Mark}_1(p') = v_0 y_1 v_1 \cdots v_{k-1} y_k v_k$ where $v_i \in \{\tau_1\}^*$ and $|v_0 \cdots v_k| = n - k$.

We will need the following standard definition of the *shuffle* $s \star s'$ of two languages $L, L' \subseteq \Gamma^*$:

$$L \star L' = \{u_1 v_1 \cdots u_l v_l | u_1 \cdots u_l \in L, v_1 \cdots v_l \in L'\} \quad .$$

Then it is easy to see that (15.12) holds iff

$$J = (\{\text{Mark}_2(p)\} \star \{\tau_1\}^*) \cap (\{\text{Mark}_1(p')\} \star \{\tau_2\}^*) \neq \emptyset \quad . \quad (15.15)$$

Each composition string $v \in J$ has the form

$$v = v_0 y_1 v_1 \cdots v_{k-1} y_k v_k \quad (15.16)$$

for $y_i \in \Gamma$ and $v_i \in \{\tau_1, \tau_2\}^*$. Furthermore, by construction, any string $v'_0 y_1 v'_1 \cdots v'_{k-1} y_k v'_k$, where each v'_i is derived from v_i by commuting τ_1 instances with τ_2 instances, is also in J.

Consider for example the transducers A shown in Figure 15.2a and B shown in Figure 15.2b. For path p from state 0 to state 4 in A and path p' from state 0 to state 3 in B we have the following equalities:

$$\text{Mark}_2(p) = a\tau_2\tau_2 d$$
$$\text{Mark}_1(p') = a\tau_1 d$$
$$(\{\text{Mark}_2(p)\} \star \{\tau_1\}^*) \cap (\{\text{Mark}_1(p')\} \star \{\tau_2\}^*) = \begin{cases} a\tau_1\tau_2\tau_2 d, \\ a\tau_2\tau_1\tau_2 d, \\ a\tau_2\tau_2\tau_1 d \end{cases}$$

Therefore, p and p' satisfy (15.12), allowing $[\![A]\!] \circ [\![B]\!]$ to map $abcd$ to dea. It is also straightforward to see that, given the transducers A' in Figure 15.2c and B' in Figure 15.2d, we have

$$\{\text{Mark}_2(p)\} \star \{\tau_1\}^* = \{p.\text{lab.out} | p \in P_{A'}(0)\}$$
$$\{\text{Mark}_1(p')\} \star \{\tau_2\}^* = \{p'.\text{lab.in} | p' \in P_{B'}(0)\}$$

Since there are no ϵ labels on the output side of A' or the input side of B', we can apply to them the ϵ-free composition construction, with the result shown in Figure 15.3. Each of the paths from the initial state to the final state corresponds to a different composition string in $\{\mathrm{Mark}_2(p)\} \star \{\tau_1\}^* \cap \{\mathrm{Mark}_1(p')\} \star \{\tau_2\}^*$.

The transducer $A' \bowtie B'$ pairs up exactly the strings it should, but it does not correctly implement $[\![A]\!] \circ [\![B]\!]$ in the general weighted case. The construction described so far allows several paths in $A' \bowtie B'$ corresponding to each pair of paths from A and B. Intuitively, this is possible because τ_1 and τ_2 are allowed to commute freely in the composition string. But if one pair of paths p from A and p' from B leads to several paths in $A' \bowtie B'$, the weights from the ϵ-transitions in A and B will appear multiple times in the overall weight for going from $(p.\mathrm{src}, p'.\mathrm{src})$ to $(p.\mathrm{dst}, p'.\mathrm{dst})$ in $A' \bowtie B'$. If the semiring sum operation is not idempotent, that leads to the wrong weights in (15.10).

To achieve the correct path multiplicity, we interpose a transducer Filter between A' and B' in a 3-way composition $\bowtie (A', \mathrm{Filter}, B')$. The Filter transducer is shown in Figure 15.4, where the transition labeled $x : x$ represents a set of transitions mapping x to itself for each $x \in \Gamma$. The effect of Filter is to block any paths in $A' \bowtie B'$ corresponding to a composition string containing the substring $\tau_2\tau_1$. This eliminates all the composition strings (15.16) in (15.15) except for the one with $v_i \in \{\tau_1\}^*\{\tau_2\}^*$, which is guaranteed to exist since J in (15.15) allows all interleavings of τ_1 and τ_2, including the required one in which all τ_2 instances must follow all τ_1 instances. For example, Filter would remove all but the thick-lines path in Figure 15.3, as needed to avoid incorrect path multiplicities.

Acknowledgments

Hiyan Alshawi, Adam Buchsbaum, Emerald Chung, Don Hindle, Andrej Ljolje, Mehryar Mohri, Steven Phillips and Richard Sproat have commented extensively on these ideas, tested many versions of our tools, and contributed a variety of improvements. Our joint work and their own separate contributions in this area will be presented elsewhere. The language model for the ATIS task was kindly supplied by Enrico Bocchieri, Roberto Pieraccini and Giuseppe Riccardi. We would also like to thank Raffaele Giancarlo, Isabelle Guyon, Carsten Lund and Yoram Singer as well as the editors of this volume for many helpful comments. Portions of this paper are adapted from a paper presented at the 1994 ARPA Human Language Technology Workshop (Pereira, Riley, and Sproat, 1994).

References

Bahl, Lalit R., Fred Jelinek, and Robert Mercer. 1983. A maximum likelihood approach to continuous speech recognition. *IEEE Trans. PAMI*, 5(2):179–190, March.

Berstel, Jean and Christophe Reutenauer. 1988. *Rational Series and Their Languages*. Number 12 in EATCS Monographs on Theoretical Computer Science. Springer-Verlag, Berlin, Germany.

Berstel, Jean. 1979. *Transductions and Context-Free Languages*. Number 38 in Leitfäden der angewandten Mathematik and Mechanik LAMM. Teubner Studienbücher, Stuttgart, Germany.

Booth, Taylor R. and Richard A. Thompson. 1973. Applying probability measures to abstract languages. *IEEE Transactions on Computers*, C-22(5):442–450, May.

Eilenberg, Samuel. 1974. *Automata, Languages, and Machines*, volume A. Academic Press, San Diego, California.

Harrison, Michael A. 1978. *Introduction to Formal Language Theory*. Addison-Wesley, Reading, Massachussets.

Kaplan, Ronald M. and Martin Kay. 1994. Regular models of phonological rule systems. *Computational Linguistics*, 3(20):331–378.

Kuich, Werner and Arto Salomaa. 1986. *Semirings, Automata, Languages*. Number 5 in EATCS Monographs on Theoretical Computer Science. Springer-Verlag, Berlin, Germany.

Lang, Bernard. 1989. A generative view of ill-formed input processing. In *ATR Symposium on Basic Research for Telephone Interpretation*, Kyoto, Japan, December.

Lee, Kai-Fu. 1990. Context dependent phonetic hidden Markov models for continuous speech recognition. *IEEE Trans. ASSP*, 38(4):599–609, April.

Ljolje, Andrej and Michael D. Riley. 1992. Optimal speech recognition using phone recognition and lexical access. In *Proceedings of ICSLP*, pages 313–316, Banff, Canada, October.

Mohri, Mehryar. 1997. On the use of sequential transducers in natural language processing. This volume.

Mohri, Mehryar. 1994a. Compact representations by finite-state transducers. In *32nd Annual Meeting of the Association for Computational Linguistics*, San Francisco, California. New Mexico State University, Las Cruces, New Mexico, Morgan Kaufmann.

Mohri, Mehryar. 1994b. Syntactic analysis by local grammars and automata: an efficient algorithm. In *Proceedings of the International Conference on Computational Lexicography (COMPLEX 94)*, Budapest, Hungary. Linguistic Institute, Hungarian Academy of Sciences.

Paz, A. 1971. *Introduction to Probabilistic Automata*. Academic.

Pereira, Fernando C. N., Michael Riley, and Richard W. Sproat. 1994. Weighted rational transductions and their application to human language processing. In *Human Language Technology Workshop*, pages 262–267, San Francisco, California. Morgan Kaufmann.

Riccardi, Giuseppe, Enrico Bocchieri, and Roberto Pieraccini. 1995. Nondeterministic stochastic language models for speech recognition. In *Proceedings IEE International Conference on Acoustics, Speech and Signal Processing*, volume 1, pages 237–240. IEEE.

Riley, Michael, Andrej Ljolje, Donald Hindle, and Fernando C. N. Pereira. 1995. The AT&T 60,000 word speech-to-text system. In J. M. Pardo, E. Enríquez, J. Ortega, J. Ferreiros, J. Macías, and F.J.Valverde, editors, *Eurospeech'95: ESCA 4th European Conference on Speech Communication and Technology*, volume 1, pages 207–210, Madrid, Spain, September. European Speech Communication Association (ESCA).

Riley, Michael, Fernando Pereira, and Emerald Chung. 1995. Lazy transducer composition: a flexible method for on-the-fly expansion of context-dependent grammar network. IEEE Automatic Speech Recognition Workshop, Snowbird, Utah, December.

Roche, Emmanuel. 1993. *Analyse Syntaxique Transformationelle du Français par Transducteurs et Lexique-Grammaire*. Ph.D. thesis, Université Paris 7.

Silberztein, Max. 1993. *Dictionnaires électroniques et analise automatique de textes: le système INTEX*. Masson, Paris, France.

Sproat, Richard, Chilin Shih, Wiliam Gale, and Nancy Chang. 1994. A stochastic finite-state word-segmentation algorithm for Chinese. In *32nd Annual Meeting of the Association for Computational Linguistics*, pages 66–73, San Francisco, California. New Mexico State University, Las Cruces, New Mexico, Morgan Kaufmann.

Teitelbaum, Ray. 1973. Context-free error analysis by evaluation of algebraic power series. In *Proc. Fifth Annual ACM Symposium on Theory of Computing*, pages 196–199, Austin, Texas.

Contributors

Douglas Appelt. Artificial Intelligence Center. SRI International. Menlo Park, California.

John Bear. Artificial Intelligence Center. SRI International. Menlo Park, California.

David Clemenceau. LADL and University of Paris VII. 2, place Jussieu. 75251 Paris Cedex 05, France.

Maurice Gross. Laboratoire d'Automatique Documentaire et Linguistique. Université Paris 7, France.

Jerry R. Hobbs. Artificial Intelligence Center. SRI International. Menlo Park, California.

David Israel. Artificial Intelligence Center. SRI International. Menlo Park, California.

Megumi Kameyama. Artificial Intelligence Center. SRI International. Menlo Park, California.

Lauri Karttunen. Rank Xerox Research Centre, Grenoble Laboratory. 6, chemin de Maupertuis. 38240 Meylan, France.

Kimmo Koskenniemi. Department of General Linguistics. P.O. Box 4. 00014 University of Helsinki. Finland.

Mehryar Mohri. AT&T Research. 600-700 Mountain Avenue, Murray Hill, NJ 07974, USA.

Éric Laporte. University of Reims and Institut Gaspard Monge. Marne-la-Vallée, France.

Fernando C. N. Pereira. AT&T Research. 600-700 Mountain Avenue, Murray Hill, NJ 07974, USA.

Michael D. Riley. AT&T Research. 600-700 Mountain Avenue, Murray Hill, NJ 07974, USA.

Emmanuel Roche. Teragram Corporation. Boston MA, USA.

Yves Schabes. Teragram Corporation. Boston MA, USA.

Max D. Silberztein. LADL, Université Paris 7. 2, place Jussieu, 75005 Paris, France.

Mark Stickel. Artificial Intelligence Center. SRI International. Menlo Park, California.

Pasi Tapanainen. Research Unit for Multilingual Language Technology. Department of General Linguistics. P.O. Box 4. 00014 University of Helsinki. Finland.

Mabry Tyson. Artificial Intelligence Center. SRI International. Menlo Park, California.

Atro Voutilainen. Research Unit for Multilingual Language Technology. Department of General Linguistics. University of Helsinki, FINLAND.

Rebecca N. Wright. AT&T Research. 600-700 Mountain Avenue, Murray Hill, NJ 07974, USA.

Index